A.E. Housman

Illustrations

Contents

For Elizabeth

and

in affectionate memory of my tutor

F. C. Horwood

Sometime Dean and Fellow of St Catherine's College, Oxford.

First published 2018

The Boydell Press, Woodbridge

ISBN 978 1 78327 241 9

The Boydell Press is an imprint of Boydell & Brewer Ltd
PO Box 9, Woodbridge, Suffolk IP12 3DF, UK

and of Boydell & Brewer Inc.
668 Mt Hope Avenue, Rochester, NY 14620–2731, USA

website: www.boydellandbrewer.com

A CIP catalogue record for this book is available
from the British Library

The publisher has no responsibility for the continued existence or accuracy of URLs for
external or third-party internet websites referred to in this book, and does not guarantee
that any content on such websites is, or will remain, accurate or appropriate

This publication is printed on acid-free paper

Typeset by HWA Text and Data Management, London, UK

Printed and bound in Great Britain by
TJ Books Ltd, Padstow, Cornwall

EDGAR VINCENT

A.E. Housman

Hero of the Hidden Life

THE BOYDELL PRESS

Credits

Figures 1, 2, 3, 4, 5, 6, 7, 8, 14, 15 and 16 are reproduced by permission of Gerald Symons, the Housman Society and Edward Pugh; 10, 28, 34, 35, 36 and 42, by permission of the Jackson family; 11, by permission of College Collection Photos, UCL Library Services, Special Collections; 12, 19, 21, 24, 26, 27, 29, 39 and 43, by permission of the National Portrait Gallery, London; 17, by courtesy of the estate of John David Roberts/The National Portrait Gallery, London; 18, by permission of Ralph Hodgson Papers and General Collection Beinecke Rare Books and Manuscript Library, Yale University; 23, by permission of the Estate of Sir William Rothenstein /National Portrait Gallery, London; 25, 37, 38, 41, 44 and 45, by permission of the Master and Fellows of Trinity College, Cambridge; 30, by permission of the Master and Fellows of St John's College, Cambridge; 20 and 31, by permission of E.O. Hoppé Estate collection / Curatorial Assistance, Inc.; 32, by the University of Southampton; 33, by permission of the Estate of Gilbert Spencer/DACS; 40, by courtesy of Punch Ltd.

Cover illustration by Sir John Rothenstein is reproduced by permission of the Master and Fellows of Trinity College, Cambridge.

It has not been possible to trace the current whereabouts or owner of Figure 9, Adalbert Jackson.

The author is particularly grateful for the help and encouragement of Nicolas Bell Librarian of Trinity College Cambridge, Natalie Oleksy-Piekarski of The National Portrait Gallery, Evelena Ruether of Curatorial Assistance Inc, Sarah Watts of the University of Southampton, Anne Marie Menta of The Beinecke Library Yale University, Peter Sisley of the Housman Society and David Butterfield editor of the *Housman Society Journal*.

I am also grateful to publishers, authors, individuals and organizations who have permitted me to quote from copyright works:

Pan Macmillan: *Siegfried Sassoon* by Max Egremont reproduced with permission of Pan Macmillan via PLSclear; Taylor and Francis for *Maynard Keynes An Economist's Biography* first published by Routledge in 1992 and *The Selected Letters of Bertrand Russell* copyright Taylor & Francis and The Bertrand Russell Peace Foundation Ltd; Orion Group *Portrait of a Marriage* by Nigel Nicolson, copyright Nigel Nicolson 1973; Cambridge University Press for *Eye of the Universe An Intellectual Biography* by Henry Sidgwick; Random House for *Hidden Things* by C.P. Cavafy; Mrs Susan Morris for *Still Digging* by Sir Mortimer Wheeler; for annotations by John Carter to *De Amicitia* reproduced by permission of The Provost and Fellows of Eton College; New Directions Publishing Corporation for *Mr Housman at Little Bethel* by Ezra Pound from EZRA POUND'S POETRY AND PROSE CONTRIBUTIONS TO PERIODICALS (Garland Press) copyright 1991 by The Trustees of the Ezra Pound Literary Property Trust. Reprinted by permission of New Directions Publishing Corp; Faber & Faber for verse by Philip Larkin and for *The Strangest Man* by Graham Farmelo; Peters Fraser & Dunlop (www.petersfraserdunlop.com) for Alec Waugh's Introduction to *Author Hunting* by Grant Richards, on behalf of the Estate of Alec Waugh; Curtis Brown for *The Boer War* by Thomas Pakenham; Rosica Colin Ltd for excerpt from Richard Aldington's *A.E. Housman & W.B. Yeats Two Lectures* reproduced by kind permission of the Estate of Richard Aldington c/o Rosica Colin Limited London ; Dundurn Press for *The Creator as Critic and other Writings* by E.M. Forster edited by Jeffrey M. Heath, selection and editorial material copyright Jeffrey M. Heath 2008 for The Creator as a Critic and Other Writings by E.M. Forster by permission of Dundurn Press Limited; Watkins Loomis Agency for *The Letters of Edith Wharton* eds Lewis & Lewis:The Warden & Fellows of Merton College Oxford for quotations from *The Profession of Poetry and other Lectures* by H.W. Garrod; from *Ludwig Wittgenstein: The Duty of Genius* by Ray Monk published by Jonathan Cape. Reproduced by permission of The Random House Group Ltd. ©1990.

In respect of hitherto unpublished letters of A.E Housman: The Society of Authors, the Master & Fellows of Trinity College Cambridge and Kwansei University, Kobe, Japan.

In obtaining many of these permissions help from Rachel Hunt of the Publishers Licensing Society has been invaluable.

The author has done his best to establish the names of copyright holders and to seek their permission. This has not been possible in all cases and the author apologises to anyone who feels overlooked and would be pleased to hear from them.

Acknowledgements

I was prompted to write this book by reading A.D. Nuttal's *Dead from the Waist Down*, essentially about scholars and the hidden life of the mind, and Graham Robb's *Strangers: Homosexual Love in the 19th Century* which deals with the usually hidden emotional life of men who loved other men. I gratefully acknowledge their insights.

For the tradition in which Housman worked and the issues he was confronting, I have relied on C.O. Brink's *English Classical Scholarship: Historical Reflections on Bentley, Porson and Housman;* to understand the ways of individual scholars, *Isaac Casaubon* by Mark Pattison and *The Life of Richard Bentley DD*, Housman's great predecessor at Trinity, by J.H. Monk.

The Classical Papers of A.E. Housman edited by J. Diggle and F.R.D. Goodyear reveal Housman in scholarly action. Sebastiano Timpanaro's *The Genesis of Lachmann's Method,* exemplifies the detective work and mental challenge involved in evaluating the reliability of manuscripts corrupted by ages of copying, emendation and conjectural interpolations, the stuff of Housman's scholarly life. Fifteen essays contained in *A.E. Housman Classical Scholar* edited by David Butterfield and Christopher Stray illuminate Housman's contribution as seen by today's scholars.

I salute the work of P.G. Naiditch who sets a gold standard for accurate and forensic examination of a multiplicity of Housmanian issues, especially in his books *Problems in the Life and Writings of A.E. Housman* and *Additional Problems in the Life and Writings of A.E. Housman*. His authoritative account of *A.E. Housman At University College, London: The Election of 1892* is unlikely to be supplanted; I have relied on its underlying research for my own account of Housman's re-entry to academic life.

I give thanks for Professor Archie Burnett's authoritative edition of Housman's poetry and his monumental two volumes of Housman's letters without which my task would have been immeasurably less productive. All quotations from Housman's poems are taken from Burnett's *The Poems of A.E. Housman* as reprinted in 2004. I follow Burnett's conclusions about the chronology of composition. I place most biographical emphasis on the date of the first draft rather than on final drafts. The chronology of the poetry as published is not the chronology of conception. Poems usually went through many drafts and tinkerings before a final draft was sent to the printers. I make a clear distinction between the volumes published by Housman himself, namely *A Shropshire Lad* (1896) and *Last Poems* (1922), and the two posthumous volumes, *More Poems* and *Additional Poems* resurrected or cobbled together by Laurence Housman from Housman's notebooks. Among the latter are completed poems Housman chose not to publish during his lifetime, probably because they would be too revealing or autobiographical or not up to his own standards.

Pre-eminent among Housman's previous biographers are Norman Page, George Watson and Richard Perceval Graves. To them, as to Henry Maas who produced a short but exemplary study in sixty pages, I am indebted. Carol Efrati's *The Road of Danger, Guilt and Shame* did not profess to be a biography but extended the boundaries of writings on Housman's poetry. She interpreted the whole of Housman's poetry, variant manuscript readings included, as having an underlying homosexual subtext. But none of them attempted to weave Housman's life of scholarship into his life as a poet. Having been at this task for more than a decade I have seen my own thinking mirrored occasionally in the work of others. I have tried to acknowledge all my debts, although ideas, first published by others but similar to one's own, can steal in unnoticed; if any such unconscious thefts have occurred, I ask for understanding.

I wish to thank Andrew Jackson, grandson of Moses Jackson, for being such a helpful link to the Jackson family and their archive of letters and photographs. He and his brothers Martin and Brian have been very generous in allowing me to reproduce passages from letters and photographs in the family's possession. Andrew in particular has allowed me to quote from his book *A Fine View of The Show* and from his articles in the *Housman Society Journal*, 'A pivotal friendship' and 'Moses Jackson's family'. Together they provide much valuable detail of Moses' time in India and Canada and an account of the part played by three of Moses' sons in World War I. He and his brothers gave me access to fifteen hitherto unpublished letters from Housman to his godson Gerald Jackson. They enabled me to sustain and round off my account of Housman's lifelong connection with the Jackson family. Fifty-three Jackson letters are now in the possession of Trinity College Cambridge which has kindly allowed me to quote from them.

Grateful thanks to my friend Richard Freeman, sometime Chief Economist of ICI, who enabled me to examine eighteen unpublished letters from Housman to Herbert Foxwell, a contemporary of Housman's at University College and subsequently at Cambridge (the Foxwell letters are now in the possession of Kwansei University Library in Japan which has kindly allowed me to quote from them); to the late Dr Peter Willey for his help in translating from German; to Jeffrey Dudgeon who led me to the secret diaries of Maynard Keynes; to the late Clive Priestly, formerly of the Cabinet Office, for illuminating discussions and promptings; to Anthony Storey, writer and former Professor of Psychology at Cambridge University, for perceptive and creative insights; to Maryvonne Olivier for commenting on Part XIII: Paris 1932; to members of the Housman Society: Peter Sisley, its former secretary, who enabled me to expand my library of Housman-related books, Jim Page, its former chairman, Max Hunt, its secretary, and Julian Hunt, editor of the *Housman Society Newsletter*; to Sir David Barber and Professor Tony Atkins, neighbours and alumni of Trinity College Cambridge who have been generous with practical assistance; to the ever patient and helpful staff of the London Library, especially Amanda Corp and Guy Penman; and to Michael Parslew for help with Housman's comic verse. I am grateful that Douglas Matthews undertook the index.

I am particularly indebted to five others: Linda Hart, who generously shared with me her encyclopaedic knowledge of Housman, especially her work on Laurence Housman and Sophie Becker, and for reading and commenting in detail on my manuscript; to David Butterfield, fellow of Queen's College Cambridge, Cambridge University lecturer in Latin, joint editor of the Penguin Latin Dictionary and *A.E. Housman: Classical Scholar*, and editor of the *Housman Society Journal*, who kindly made time to read, assess and comment on my manuscript, which has been motivating and illuminating; to Dr James Vincent who read my first draft, scrutinised critically what I had to say about Housman's physical and mental health, and gave me invaluable help: to Michael Knight, psychotherapist, who emphasised the impact of Housman's childhood on his future life and to Megan Milan and Nick Bingham who have been all I could ask for as my editors.

Above all I thank my wife who not only tolerated and supported me while I wrote *Nelson: Love & Fame*, but has remained at her post during my own hidden and at times invisible life among Housman's poems and classical studies. She deserves another medal.

Needless to say, all errors, omissions and faults are entirely my own.

Preface

Housman sought no limelight. He deplored the very idea of biography. Renowned for Latin scholarship and famous for his two little books of poetry *A Shropshire Lad* and *Last Poems,* he was *the* pre-eminent textual scholar in Europe, with whom few dared to cross swords. His two books of poetry have never been out of print following their publication in 1896 and 1922; they made him a celebrity. Had Housman been less reticent, less unwilling to capitalise on celebrity, there might have been no need for this biography. Yet he has remained a truly hidden man, captured in the public mind as prim and grim. It is only now that we can see him plain in all his interesting complexity, thanks to the publication of Archie Burnett's two volumes of Letters in 2007. Burnett's 2,327 letters trebled the number of letters available to biographers, not to mention seventy-one new letters resulting from my own researches and quoted here for the first time.

These letters enable us to see a many-sided man, a master of English prose, a witty and compelling after-dinner speaker, an occasional writer of nonsense verse, a frequenter of the music hall, a lover of foreign travel (he was among the earliest travellers by air), a connoisseur of good food and wine and companionable in small groups he was familiar with. In his dealings with others he was frequently generous to a fault, and always on the lookout for humour and fun. He also reveals himself as a man of ambiguity, paradox, irony and wit, inclined to be secretive and sometimes tricky. As a detached and unsentimental observer of human destiny he was a man who commanded attention; he did not waste words.

The most powerful influences on Housman's life were the death of his mother when he was twelve, traumatic failure in his Oxford finals and the fact that he formed a profound emotional and lifelong attachment to a fellow undergraduate, Moses Jackson. These happenings powered his motivation. A job at the Patent Office paid the rent and ten years of spare-time work in the British Museum produced twenty-five papers for learned journals. With these he created a pathway from the depths of academic failure to a glittering career, first as Professor of Latin at University College, London, and subsequently at Cambridge. He reached the top of his professional tree. That in itself was quite extraordinary.

Here is the first paradox. As Professor of Latin he was renowned for his intellectually brilliant work on the seemingly dry-as-dust reconstruction of ancient texts. The nature of that work and how he mastered it has its own fascinations. As the poet of *A Shropshire Lad* he caught the imagination of an infinitely wider public. He became famous for his poetry in America and Japan. His poems became emblems of nostalgia, parables of the restless impermanence of life and exemplars of life's hard lottery; some of the most remembered and most often quoted poetry in the language.

How could such different work come from the same pen? What caused such a volcanic eruption of poetry in this man's life? The answers to those questions are at the core of this book.

Housman never married but formed a profound emotional attachment to a fellow undergraduate, Moses Jackson. That attachment is usually called 'love', but what it was in Housman's case remains to be defined. Certainly, the emotion was strong enough to last a lifetime. That in itself is very surprising but even more surprising is how it metamorphosed into a connection with the whole Jackson family which is traced in its full extent for the first time in this book. Among his final letters were letters to his godson Gerald Jackson.

Housman's mind was scientific and it was natural for him to seek to answer the question 'Who am I?' His library contained more than fifty volumes classified as Erotica/Sexual studies but he never spoke or wrote about his emotional and sexual needs, central to our behaviour as human beings. Some of the books Housman studied suggested a spectrum of such needs. Might it be possible to demonstrate this spectrum and position Housman on it, by comparison with a set of his contemporaries whose emotional lives were also not straightforward? I have chosen to compare him with T.E. Lawrence (Lawrence of Arabia), Oscar Wilde (poet and playwright), Siegfried Sassoon (poet and war hero), Harold Nicolson (diplomat married to Vita Sackville-West writers, and gardeners both), Maynard Keynes (eminent economist married to Lydia Lopokova, the Russian ballet dancer),

Ludwig Wittgenstein (the celebrated philosopher who for a brief period had rooms above Housman in Trinity College, Cambridge) and Housman's own brother Laurence who shared a home with their sister for the whole of his adult life. I use the lives of these other men to cast light on Housman.

As we come across Housman in his professional life we find him bringing to bear formidable professional learning to identifying problems and formulating solutions, persuading other scholars by the power and eloquence of his writing that his was the voice to listen to, and having the boldness and intellectual domination to counter opposition. These, incidentally, are characteristic of all outstanding individuals. In that sense Housman's scholarly works and how he deals with controversies are relevant and intrinsically interesting and naturally form a major thread of this book. That said, his life of scholarship is examined only insofar as it is directly relevant to his life and behaviour. Housman's professional life produced his monumental five-volume edition of the *Astronomicon* of Marcus Manilius, in itself a life's work, and many other smaller monuments. These works are now silent witnesses to scholarly output and fame.

Nor is the book a deep critique of Housman's poetry. His poems are left to speak directly to the reader as Housman would have wished. My concentration is on where the poetry came from on the genesis of the volcanic eruption in 1895 to 1896. Here was a poetry that was entirely individual, deriving its power from Housman's personal anger and frustrated feelings, its intensity from coping with dangerous personal issues in the era of Oscar Wilde. Housman made his emotional life the basis for his poetry. He sought no other poetic material and never thought of himself as a poet. I seek to isolate and describe the autobiographical elements in his poetry. In this we must note that Housman studiously avoided discussion on the meaning of his poems. He refused to connect them with his own life. He was reticent and resolutely uncommunicative about them.

The architecture of the book needs some explanation. In his letters Housman was not given to expressing opinions on the events and issues of his day or on the social, political and academic controversies of his times. This was essentially part of his time-management; his focus was on scholarship not on correspondence. This allows and obliges a biographer to keep his own focus on the man himself rather than on period context, on his life as he is experiencing it. Thus the architecture of the book arranges the flow of events chronologically not thematically, allowing the reader to see Housman in relation to others in the various phases of his life. Because Housman is allowed to speak for himself through his letters, this portrait is in essence a self-portrait. I hope I have read his words with sympathy and empathy, and with sufficient forensic intent to do him justice.

Housman's homosexuality was undoubtedly a cloud over his life because of the times in which he lived. Its net effect, reinforced by the facts of his own nature, was that he lived his life in an emotional desert. That should not be thought of as overwhelming or immobilising him. His journey through life demonstrated an awesome capacity to follow his own star.

Housman gained my sympathy, respect, admiration and liking. His heroism lay in his unwavering resolve to apply his great intellectual gifts and play to the best of his ability the hand that nature, nurture and circumstances had dealt him, to transmute whatever anger and frustration they caused him into achievement, never betraying the ideal to which he had given his heart, displaying in that a kind of integrity that comes close to what John Keats referred to as 'The holiness of the heart's affections'.

This is the self-portrait of a supremely intelligent and talented man who coped with his own nature and the social and religious intolerance of 1896 to 1936, and made his own way forward with a self-directed impetus that can justly be described as heroic.

From all I did and all I said
let no one try to find out who I was.
An obstacle was there distorting
The actions and the manner of my life.
An obstacle was often there
to stop me when I'd begin to speak.
From my most unnoticed actions,
my most veiled writing—
from these alone will I be understood.
But maybe it isn't worth so much concern,
so much effort to discover who I really am.
Later, in a more perfect society,
someone else made just like me
is certain to appear and act freely.

Hidden Things C.P. Cavafy (1863-1933)

PART I

Childhood

Firstborn

Alfred Edward Housman, the first child of Edward Housman and his wife Sarah Jane Williams, did not make a totally uncomplicated entry to this life. The local doctor, alarmed by unusual pains and no doubt regarding Sarah Jane, then thirty-one, as a rather elderly *prima gravida*, wanted to call in a specialist from Birmingham. Sarah Jane took command and insisted that the Williams' family doctor, who had known her all her life and, as she put it, '*knew me*', should be sent for to take charge of the birth. Some husbands might have played safe and backed the doctor's recommendation. There is no indication that Edward did so. Sarah Jane prevailed, the first indication that she would be the leader in the family, Edward the led; her own doctor was summoned and Alfred was born soon after on 26 March 1859.

Sarah Jane had conceived at the first possible moment. After Alfred's birth, three more children – Robert, Clemence and Katharine (generally known as Kate) – followed at annual intervals, a tribute to their parents' fertility and uninhibited lovemaking. Her fifth child, Basil, was born two years later; her sixth, Laurence, a year after that; her seventh and last child, George (generally known as Herbert), three years later in July 1868. Seven children in nine years proved her Victorian capacity for stoical childbearing and Christian duty.

Loses his mother on his twelfth birthday

About a year after the birth of her final child Sarah Jane was diagnosed with breast cancer and died in 1871 at the shockingly early age of forty-two. Had the adult Housman been asked by a psychologist to which of his parents he had been closer, he would undoubtedly

Figure 1 Housman's father, Edward.
Courtesy Gerald Symons and Edward Pugh.

have replied, 'my mother'. The profound and traumatic effect of her death cannot be overestimated. It was the first great circumstantial shock that shaped his life. He, the eldest of her sons, closest to her in every sense, lost her on his twelfth birthday. Moreover, he had been so distressed at seeing her in the late stages of her illness that he had been persuaded to leave home and go some forty miles south to his godmother's family home, Woodchester House, near Stroud in Gloucestershire. None of the hopeful and optimistic forecasts of the grown-ups were borne out. His mother died during his absence, by the cruellest of ironies, on his own birthday. Even worse, he was left at Woodchester until after the funeral. Physical and psychological separation from his family excluded Housman from his mother's deathbed and from personal experience of his mother's final rites of passage. He, the eldest child, was separated from the rest of his siblings at a critical time in all their lives. However well meant, it was one of his father's typically crass misjudgements. Housman's future life would be deeply affected by such a traumatic loss; by common consent he was a sensitive child closely bonded with his mother. His future psychological weather was likely to include outbursts of anger and bouts of emotional distress or depression.

Figure 2 Housman's mother, Sarah Jane.
Courtesy Gerald Symons and Edward Pugh.

Sarah Jane had been a convinced Christian with High Church leanings. There had been family prayers before breakfast, prayers at bedtime, and a one-mile walk to church twice each Sunday. Her death provided ample grounds, for Housman's childish but logical and decisive mind, to reject the revealed religion she had so liberally fed him. And so he took his first step towards atheism.

Brother Laurence, five at the time of his mother's death, experienced what his brother had been deprived of.

> I was taken into the death-chamber, and there saw my mother lying dead, solemn and beautiful. She was in her forty-second year. At the foot of the bed, on a small table, stood a crucifix in a wooden shrine between lighted candles. I had seen it often before, for during her long illness it had kept her company.

Poor Laurence felt it all and could not contain his feelings. 'I used also to cry in bed at night for my mother to come back to me, and believed that if I prayed faithfully enough she would do so.'[1] On the other hand, Housman left no record of whether or how he mourned his mother. His absence had deprived him of all experience of spontaneous exchanges of grief between father, brothers, and sisters at the actual time of their mother's death and funeral. Whatever emotion he experienced was locked inside. He embraced a mode of dealing with things that would continue throughout his life. Sister Kate remembered that 'It was never Alfred's way to speak of troubles. He was sensitive and easily wounded, but wounds he bore in silence.'[2] Housman, perhaps influenced by his dying mother's uncomplaining belief, could well have thought that stoicism was an appropriate example for an eldest son to set. On the other hand, Laurence, one of the youngest, would always feel free to respond emotionally and histrionically to aspects of his childhood, not least in his 1937 autobiography, *The Unexpected Years*, which gives the only detailed and insightful account of the children's home life and schooldays. Despite their shared upbringing, these two boys showed distinctly different responses to life.

Sarah Jane's death created a vacuum. She had been a powerful, nurturing presence, ruling the house with an easy, self-confident domination. She was to be taken seriously and would certainly have been a model for Housman with her way of expressing clear and decided opinions. She had a certain arrogance and capacity for laying down the law[3] and would have modelled such habits of mind during the hours he spent in her company during her bedridden days. Unfair as it always is for an adult to confide in a child, she may, out of their very propinquity, have made him privy to events in her life which could have been too intimate for him to handle. Laurence remembers a conversation with his brother when Housman said, 'She used to talk to me as if I were a grown up person, and told me many things of her early life.'[4] Laurence's later recollection of hearing his stepmother read from letters his mother had written at the time of her courtship and honeymoon caused him to write that 'from the general tenor of her letters, I gather that my mother's vocabulary was not characteristically mid-Victorian. One specimen of her quality I do remember, too intimate and personal to be recorded here – a little Rabelaisian: our mother was no Puritan.'[5] So there are grounds for believing that Housman's constant nearness to his mother had caused her to make general observations on the relationships between men and women, possibly allied to reflections on her own experience, which disturbed him and conditioned his thinking.

Figure 3 Sophie Becker, German
Governess of Housman's godmother's
daughters, Housman's boyhood friend.
Courtesy Gerald Symons.

The Wises and Sophie Becker

Housman needed a mother and his enforced stay with the Wises at
Woodchester had one very positive outcome: a lifelong loyalty to his
godmother Mrs Wise (an exact contemporary of his mother) and her
daughters Edith, then sixteen, and Wilhelmina, then thirteen. Their
governess was a young German girl, Sophie Becker. At the time of
his mother's death she was twenty-six. Her youthful maturity could
make him feel both secure and allured. He may indeed have fallen in
love with her, as children can at such an impressionable age, when
reactions to dress, perfume and the feel of another person can be
acute. Four years later in 1875, when he was sixteen and she thirty,
they may have collaborated on Housman's translation of Goethe's
Der Fischer. This may have signalled a flow of emotion between the
two, but more of a loving friendship than anything else. Sophie never
married. And probably by the time Housman went up to Oxford
in October 1877, and certainly by the time he met Moses Jackson,

there was probably no question of his forming a sexually romantic attraction for a young woman. Yet that in itself was no reason why his loving friendship could not continue. It would never be Housman's habit to give up those he trusted and with whom he felt safe; he did not wish to lose them and so the Wises and Sophie would remain part of his life. They were not abandoned when he went up to Oxford. In Sophie's case, the absence of a reciprocal sexual feeling across a sexual divide did not automatically lead to alienation or expunge feelings of friendship.

A second mother: The Mater

Two years after the death of his mother, another woman filled the vacuum. His father decided to remarry with his cousin Lucy Agnes Housman. Lucy had originally introduced Edward to Sarah Jane and had been bridesmaid at their wedding so she was well known to Edward. Having had one strong managing wife, Edward may have been attracted to another; and with seven children to bring up, a replacement was necessary. Edward may also have realised that as a member of the rich Vernon family and a relative on her mother's side of John Adams, a local notable, she could add to his family's future financial prospects. She, being fifty, a spinster, definitely on the shelf, past the age of child bearing, but not necessarily past the age of lovemaking, was already well acquainted with Edward. She also had inside information from her dead cousin about his appealing marital behaviour. She may well have thought it was the last offer she was likely to get and probably did not need much persuading, even if she did not go so far as to engineer the marriage herself.

Edward, then only forty, decided that a new home was needed and moved from Perry Hall to the Clock House at Fockbury, just outside Bromsgrove. On 26 June 1873, two years and three months after Sarah Jane's death, Edward married Lucy in London and brought her home to begin married life with the family in their new home. The position of a stepmother in a large family is by definition fraught with obvious problems and dangers, especially in combination with a move away from the reassuring familiarity of 'home'. Suddenly the children's world was changing. Yet Edward and Lucy must have managed her entry into the family with the greatest skill, because on the face of it, the transition could not have been more successful. The eldest and most important member of her new family, Alfred, seems to have

Figure 4 Housman's stepmother, Lucy Agnes.
Courtesy Gerald Symons and Edward Pugh.

transferred his allegiance immediately to Lucy, testament either to an instant likeability in her, or to Housman's pragmatic acceptance of reality. The fragment of a note he wrote to her later that year ended 'I remain my dearest mamma/ Your loving son/ Alfred Housman.' Two years later, in January 1875, he was writing a long letter to her from London where he was staying with her sister. Again he addressed her as 'Dearest Mamma,' ending 'With love to my father & all/ I remain/ Your affectionate son.' By now he had begun to sign himself A.E. Housman but that does not signify any lack of warmth. This letter, albeit a mite precocious, was comprehensive, warm, informative and companionable, well beyond the requirements of a simple duty letter. Housman seems to have been able to suppress entirely any comparison he made between Lucy and Sarah Jane, or any inner conflict in his transfer of allegiance to a new mother, although his calm may have been yet another early example of his capacity to suppress any emotion he did not want to acknowledge.

This new mamma, 'the Mater,' as she was soon to be named by the children, was remembered by Laurence as 'more a Mater than a Mamma, perhaps because of a certain Roman touch in her rule both over herself and others.'[6] Like Sarah Jane she was the authority in the house, referred to again by Laurence as 'my stepmother whose discipline in things domestic and religious was somewhat fixative.' Like Sarah Jane she was a devout Christian, but this time of the Low Church variety. Laurence remembered that the crucifix present during his mother's dying was never seen again and that their Sunday readings were taken from *The Life of Luther*, which for young children must have been a mind-numbing experience. Laurence provided his own insight into the religious life of the home in his characteristic headlong way. In short, he found their prayers 'a stupefying experience … it did more harm than good; and when, in my adolescence religion became more real to me, family prayers were a most painful ordeal, from which I would have gladly escaped if I could because of their unreality.' In later years Laurence found himself rebelling against the religious forms of his childhood. When asked why he had abandoned grace before meals he replied, 'In order to try and cultivate a more thankful spirit than the saying of grace ever produced at home.' He went on 'one found it hard sometimes not to exact vengeance, when our time came for freedom and free speech, for the afflictions of our youth.'[7] There is no record of such reactions in Alfred. By this stage he knew what the limits of his belief were and unlike Laurence, did not feel a need to proclaim them.

Here again was a dominating mother. Lucy had a certain capacity to indoctrinate the children with her own kinks. Laurence recalls that he was always consumed by guilt and excessive modesty as far as his natural functions were concerned. The taboo which blighted his early life was that he must not be observed entering or leaving the WC:

> Those daily dodgings never came to an end; they were as much a part of the domestic round as family prayers, had more influence upon my conduct, and laid a far greater weight upon my conscience. Every day that dawned in that single household, a dozen manoeuvres of modesty had individually to be performed by each in turn behind the backs of half the rest; and when we were well up in our teens, though it terrified us less, the secretive ritual was still in operation, and was expected of us – and others. When I was fourteen, a College friend of my brother's came to stay with us; and though in the main he was approved by our elders, my step mother commented severely upon the fact that, she being somewhere about, he had not observed the proper secrecy of approach: "He ought to have waited. It wasn't modest."[8]

In this environment Housman's fastidiousness was encouraged. Richard Perceval Graves, Housman's most recent biographer, gives an account of Housman's denunciation of the new governess:

> The new governess, Mrs Cooper, had disgusted him by her immoral behaviour, behaviour which she had managed to conceal from his father. Alfred told Lucy plainly that Mrs Cooper was not fit to be looking after his sisters, and then had to explain about her promiscuity which must have embarrassed him considerably. Mrs Cooper was livid with Alfred when she was forced to leave the household, spitting out vicious comments whose gist was that Alfred, though no longer a child, was not yet a mature adult.[9]

What is implied in this account is that what had most embarrassed and affronted Housman had been some attempt on her part to seduce him with suggestive words or actions, which she had expected to be welcomed by a boy of fourteen but were in fact rejected by him. Although to some degree explicable by his family's unhealthy focus on the undesirability of acknowledging bodily functions, the significance of Housman's reaction may have been that he was not open to being seduced by a female.

The boys are circumcised

The family's unhealthy focus was reinforced to an extraordinary degree by another of Edward's crass decisions, this time to have all his boys circumcised, including fourteen-year-old Housman. His sister Kate recorded:

> I do not think it was to fulfil a scriptural rite that he sought, for there was no Abrahamic tradition in our family; but on sanitary mosaic lines, I think he considered it would contribute to their physical salvation – as perhaps it did. He ought to have thought of it in their babyhood. It was severe treatment, mentally and physically, for well-grown boys, and a great mystery at the time to the younger ones who made open complaint, with a mixture of importance and resentment, of the ill treatment which had befallen them while my sister and I were staying at Lyme Regis.[10]

What her father probably had in mind was the common belief that the greatest threat to a boy's health and future had long been identified as masturbation, and it was believed that circumcision was a way of preventing it. A notion also common at the time was that masturbation was linked with homosexuality.

Given Laurence's evidence of the puritanical inhibitions engendered by the Mater, it is not unreasonable to identify her as a likely accessory before the fact if not the instigator and prime mover in this thoughtless episode. Circumcision among Gentiles was indeed becoming routine among the upper professional classes but circumcision at age fourteen, as it would be in the eldest Housman's case, was hardly likely to have been generally advocated. No doubt the Mater was also responsible for the dispatch of the girls to their grandparents' house at Lyme Regis so that they would all be spared any possible immodesty.

The Housman household was not particularly large. There was a gardener, a governess and two or three maids. Even in such a small and necessarily intimate household, the class distinctions the children were brought up with began to offend Laurence.

> We had a married cook, whose husband had work at such a distance that they could see each other but seldom. One day he came, and his wife asked leave to stay out with him for the night. It was refused, and when later it was discovered that she had gone out secretly and spent the night in the barn, her behaviour was considered most indecent.

He tells other stories of their treatment of maids: 'On another occasion, word came that the mother of one of our maids was dying. I heard her in great distress, and with loud weeping asking leave to go home. It was granted; but I was told afterwards, "They make a great fuss, but don't feel about these things as we do."'[11]

Nevertheless, the Mater was remembered affectionately by her stepchildren; she was clearly interested in them and went out of her way to connect with them. Laurence remembered that

> at Fockbury family-reading became an almost daily institution, especially during the winter months, and school holidays. It was, I think, our stepmother's happiest contribution to our early training. She was a good reader, and though not caring greatly for poetry herself, she did her duty nobly, and read to us much of what she believed to be best for us.'[12]

Nor was reading to the family the exclusive domain of their stepmother. Their father read in the evenings and Laurence remembers his rendering of *Pickwick*: 'I have never liked Dickens better, or so well.' His conclusion exemplifies how much togetherness there was in the family; 'those family readings formed so satisfying a bond of common interest between elder and younger, that I can hardly think of family life without it.'[13] Family interest in versifying was encouraged by his mother, and interest in reading encouraged by both father and stepmother.

Housman's talent for comic and nonsense verse flowered. In the memoir he published in 1937, Laurence published a selection of his brother's verse written at various dates between 1887 and 1927. This continuity indicates that the curious vision of the writer of nonsense verse was a distinct part of Housman's make-up. A propensity to mock was a continuous thread in his mental life. It is a fact of life that funny boys and funny men can always command centre stage. Housman would also decide that the children were to put on a play in the evening, would outline the plot and hand out the parts. He likewise masterminded their writing of poetry, infiltrating it with his own lines. He would supervise them as he tested and demonstrated astronomy, positioning them as sundry planets across the lawn. Not surprisingly, he much later commented to Laurence, 'Was there ever such an interesting family as we were?'[14] For Housman, Laurence and Clemence, their joint interests and activities provided an exercise ground in which they all tuned their ears to the sound and feel of words. As a sibling literary collective, Housman, Clemence and Laurence were hardly in the same league as Charlotte, Emily and Anne Bronte, but they were constructed on the same successful model, exercising together a craft in which they would subsequently excel individually. This was evidently an important self-nurturing experience.

Housman could not escape the role of the firstborn. Closest to his mother and sharing some of her dominant attitudes, he became the leader of a group of children in which there was no alternative source of dominance. Closest in age and only a year younger than himself, his brother Robert was sent away to Bath for three years when he was ten and Housman eleven. Thus sibling rivalry with all its adjustments and learning was minimised. Laurence remembered a childish altercation between Alfred and Robert, an indication of what might have been. Alfred turned the other cheek, received another blow for his pains, before turning on Robert and knocking him down. Robert could have proved a serious rival to Housman. Kate said of Robert 'he was a delicate little fellow, full of fun and mischief but troubled by asthma.'[15] Much later Robert was highly popular with Kate's sons; had he not been sent away he might well have proved a real competitor for leadership of the group.

Given that the next two children were girls, his next brother, Basil, about half his age, Laurence and George six and eight years behind, and given his special position as eldest, Housman had no physical or mental challenger in the family. Being bright to the point of precocity, being a naturally dominant personality, having a way with words, Housman was easily the undisputed leader, capable of leading, dominating and manipulating the others to his heart's content. And he always did this in a way that produced no revolution against him which says a lot about his childish persona and his later success in adult life. Writing of his own life when in his sixties, Laurence said that the first ten years of his life were the happiest. 'How we loved; how we hated; how we fought, divided and were reconciled again. How we trained and educated ourselves; and developed a taste in literature and in the writing of it, in which, until years later, our elders had no part, and with which school hours had little to do.'[16]

It also seems clear that as far as the children were concerned, theirs was probably a somewhat incestuous family life. There does not seem to have been a family inclination to encourage the children to make outside friends. They were sufficient in themselves and Kate's account, in *Alfred Edward Housman: Recollections*, shows how physical location encouraged this tendency.

> The house ... was far from the School, town, and our father's office; but it was a good place for children. It had originally been the home farm of the estate, and in addition to its large garden and its orchard we had the range of farm buildings with rick-yards, barns, lofts, and cart sheds. Near us, besides woods and lanes, fields, pools, and brooks, were friendly farms dotted about the neighbourhood, part of our grandmother's property, affording us truly exciting playing places.[17]

As children they had no need to look further afield.

Edward Housman was undoubtedly a loving parent. His particular blend of love and laissez-faire was an undoubted blessing for his children; there was no cruelty, coldness, or emotional absence to leave dark shadows on their psyches – quite the reverse. Laurence remembered him as a pleasant person to deal with, easy and good-natured; and he had a seal-skin waistcoat in winter, against which it was my delight to snuggle. Up to my seventh or eighth year, I never remember his punishing me; and in the ten years after, only lightly or seldom ... when we heard him going downstairs, we would run out and thrust our legs through the bannisters – three or four pairs of them – to have our toes pulled as he passed below.[18]

But Edward became a figure of fun, given to drifting away from the family circle, talking to himself. One day he appeared at breakfast

wearing a strange waistcoat – one half of it blue, the other half brown. There was a family cry: 'Look at Father's waistcoat!' Investigation followed: and it was found that, while too thoughtfully dressing, he had put on two, and having joined the wrong halves had let their remainders slip comfortably out of sight under cover of his coat. The accident was characteristic; it was over some like piece of forgetfulness that the Mater once remarked genially: "Your Mother used to say that a fortnight after her death your Father would be seen ambling down High Street in lavender kid gloves and pepper-and-salt trousers." "Did you?" she asked him. My father considered for a while: "No, I don't think so," he said; but there was doubt in his answer.[19]

Edward liked to be thought of and spoken of as 'the Squire' but none of his children was sufficiently impressed by him to want to use him as a model for their own lives. In Housman's case, closeness to his mother may have intensified alienation from his father. Edward Housman was a keen shot, albeit more of a shooter at targets than a shooter of game birds, which probably more accurately defined his actual middle-class attitudes rather than his gentry aspirations, a good cricketer and an enthusiastic member of the local Volunteers. Housman was not remotely interested in any of these pursuits, nor does he seem to have been drawn into any of his father's abortive ideas for making money, nor enticed by the thought of following his father as a solicitor, or pursuing his role among the local worthies – strange in a firstborn son in whom the urge to emulate can be strong. However, Basil and Herbert inherited their father's love of shooting, both being excellent marksmen and both joining him as members of the local Volunteers; neither seemed to be out of the same mould as their elder brother. Housman preferred to spend his time reading, studying, directing the activities of his younger siblings and walking. Long solitary walks brought him a deep appreciation of nature and the almost tangible pleasure of being alone in nature. Less noticed at that early age was how his walking habit would automatically provide space for his mind to expand and gestate. Less beneficial was the encouragement it brought to the solitary walker to focus on what was going on in his own mind. Kate later observed that 'he took no part in games or athletics; he did not care for them, and they were not pressed on day-boys.'[20] Thus he was not automatically involved in sporting activities. The physical rough and tumble, the joys, disappointments and camaraderie of team games, the experience of being in a group of like-minded individuals, passed him by.

Of great importance for Edward Housman's assessment of his own future was the fact that both his father, the Reverend Thomas Housman, and his father's brother William, had married rich women. Thomas had also become a close friend of John Adams, known as 'The Captain', who bought an indigo factory in Bromsgrove, re-sited it, and built Perry Hall in 1824. John Adams was a man of energy and big personality. Not content with ownership of the indigo factory and Perry Hall, he became Distributor of Stamps, and Captain of the Bromsgrove Trained Band. Nepotism took its favourable course when Edward was articled to his grandfather, admitted a solicitor at age twenty-two and subsequently employed by great uncle Adams as a solicitor at Perry Hall which Adams was then using as his own offices. This was all good news for Edward and his family's future prospects.

When Adams died in 1858, Edward's father Thomas was one of the executors of his will. It was agreed by the trustees that Edward and his wife, who had already been living at Perry Hall for two years, could live in it for life. One would have thought that having Perry Hall as a life tenancy would have been enough for Edward but not so.

Father's sharp practice

Clive Jenkins has summarised succinctly the genesis, essence and outcome of Edward's consequent chicanery.

> In 1870, Edward had been left as trustee of the family properties under his father's will: but they had been left to him, his siblings,

and his mother equally. Edward, however, to raise ready money for himself, abused his position and perverted his legal expertise to take out mortgages on, notably, Perry Hall, Fockbury House, and even his mother's home, Rose Villa in Lyme Regis, as if he were sole owner.[21]

Eventually the family took him to court where judgement was given against him in Chancery *Housman v Housman* (1873–1875). Edward's trickery and manoeuvring continued until the final move in the saga came four years later. In 1879 Joseph Housman, Edward's youngest brother, bought Perry Hall, paid off the existing mortgages and debts, but required Edward to pay the interest on the Perry Hall mortgage in lieu of rent. 'So Joseph had cleared Edward's debts and ensured that he and his family would keep a roof over their heads.'[22]

Squire Edward was now finished. His family's golden prospects were about to vanish from sight. Housman's father had turned out to be a crook.

How and when the children became aware of their father's problems is not entirely clear. Laurence remembered that after their return to Perry Hall in 1878 the family entered a period of 'serious financial strain'. It says a lot for Edward that in his broken down and frequently shambolic state, with his solicitor's practice shrinking, his office staff diminished and his state of personal decay evident, Laurence and Clemence did not desert him. Clemence, in particular, seems to have been angelic in her willingness to salvage something from the wreckage of the wretched Edward's life. In effect, she became his head clerk and

> for two or three years, the expert who worked out all his Income Tax calculations for half the county of Worcestershire. When the main pressure of that work was on, it became the regular thing for the family to go to bed leaving her still at it; and how many hours past midnight she worked nobody knew.[23]

Laurence also says that about two years earlier, when he was eleven, 'the shabbiness of my outfit was already a daily discomfort, for my school-fellows had taken derisive note of it.' His solution was,

> not to pass on word of the public disgrace that had befallen me (for that I was too miserably ashamed) but to put on surreptitiously each day my Sunday-coat and waistcoat – leaving for

school in the morning before the elders were up – and chang-
ing again on my return; till my Sunday-best becoming noticeably
shabby, I was provided with a fresh outfit, and the misappropri-
ated suit was passed into school wear.[24]

Edward, lacking any ingrained sense of honour and reality, probably
held back from confronting the truth until the last possible moment,
but events quickly caught up with him.

Housman himself had fortunately gone up to Oxford on a scholarship
in 1877 and was still there in February 1879 when Joseph Housman (his
uncle Joe) bought their home from under their feet. In April 1881, two
years after Joseph became the owner of Perry Hall and three months
before Housman was due to take his final exams, Edward had a stroke.
But, in an important sense, the worst was yet to come. Edward's mother
Ann had made a new will in January 1879, probably also masterminded
by Joseph. This new will left all her considerable fortune to Joseph and
his two spinster sisters, Mary and Jane. There was to be nothing for
Edward and his seven children. This vast change in the expectations
of Edward's family did not emerge till Edward's mother died in 1882.
At that very moment, there came a single gleam in their financial
darkness. Bequests hitherto held in trust by Edward's mother brought
each Housman child a bequest of £200.

A second blow came seven years later in 1889 when Edward's sister
Jane died and again nothing was left to her brother and his children.
Much later in 1917 there was again nothing for them in sister Mary's
will. Edward who had reaped this whirlwind of maternal and sibling
alienation, lived on until 1894, a broken man. The final metaphorical
nail in his coffin was the sale of Perry Hall in the year after his death,
even though Lucy had expressed a wish to continue to live there. The
sins of the father had been visited on the children in no uncertain
fashion. Even in 1936 Kate would speak ruefully of how the small
bequests they had received on the death of their grandmother was 'a
small portion of the considerable patrimony that was hers.'[25]

Bromsgrove School and Headmaster Millington

The next nurturing system Housman entered was Bromsgrove School
(known then as The Grammar School of King Edward the Sixth). In
September 1870, he was one of twelve scholars on Sir Thomas Cookes'
'New Foundation', to which his four brothers successively were also

elected, no doubt to the great relief of their increasingly financially hard-pressed father. As scholarship boys and day-boys, they were of a somewhat lower status than boarders or day-boys paying full fees. They had to walk to and from school, two miles there and two miles back, in all weathers. They breakfasted at 6 a.m., school began at 7 a.m. and they got home at about 6.30 in the evening.

Kate says Housman was called 'Mouse' by the other boys in his early years, because of his quiet and studious approach to life. He rapidly established himself as a star pupil and a favourite of the headmaster. It is surprising that such a diminutive character, to whom the epithets 'swot' and 'teacher's pet' could have been readily applied, did not attract the attention of bullies. If such was the case, Housman kept the fact to himself. He probably used his quick wit to defuse potentially threatening situations.

By comparison, his younger brother Laurence *was* seriously bullied; keeping his head down would have been an impossible feat for cocky little Laurence, who remembered his school days with a mixture of pleasure and pain. Most of his vitriol was directed at Mr Millington

> my Headmaster, whom I feared more than I have feared any other person before or since. I can only make a guess that his infuriated manner when he caned anyone – a sort of white rage, sometimes hot, sometimes cold – had a terrifying effect on me. There was in it something evil; and when he caned me unjustly, as he did twice, my resentment went deep and has lasted to this day.

He added that 'There must have been in his nature a streak of sadistic cruelty.'[26] The ethos of the school demonstrated the same fixed political and social attitudes as their father. Edward's comfortable circumstances, and his position as a solicitor, brought him feelings of self-importance, self-confidence and the luxury of not having to think too deeply. Laurence remembers him as a 'a hot Tory ... telling us that he was born in the year of "England's great disaster – the passing of the first Reform Bill." His toast when his children had their sip of wine after dinner was "Up with the Tories, and down with the Radicals."' These same social attitudes were demonstrated by Headmaster Millington and Bromsgrove School where 'an atmosphere of upper and under-dog was prevalent'. Laurence particularly remembered the headmaster's class consciousness, his way of referring to the sons of a grocer and farmer as 'Bacon' and 'Cart horse'. These attitudes fundamentally alienated Laurence, who later said:

In many other respects my early life made me what I am now; but in politics, at all events, the child was not the final father of the man; yet only when I was pulled into political agitation thirty years later, did my Conservatism begin to ooze out of me, and continued to ooze till now none of it is left.[27]

Nothing could more clearly illustrate the diametrically different impact of the same nurture on two siblings. Laurence saw the challengeable side of how he had been brought up whereas Housman seems to have imbibed or ignored it. Laurence would become an opinion-former, divergent, contrarian, happy to stand up and be counted and to sound off on his own opinions. Housman would always be reticent about expressing an opinion on things not connected with his scholarly work, although paradoxically he would have no hesitation in making *ex cathedra* pronouncements on gastronomic matters; and in private he was perfectly willing to give clear opinions on the literary merits of writers past and present.

Many years later Laurence asked Alfred, the shining light of Millington's sixth form, what he thought of their late headmaster as a teacher. 'Excellent', Housman replied, 'for those of good ability in subjects he cared about. Over the rest there was silence.'[28] While this was a perceptive remark by Housman on Millington's personality, the fact that he went no farther shows the unbridgeable gap between those who are conformist and reticent by nature, and those like Laurence who are quick to form and express opinion.

Housman became an outstanding classics scholar, self-motivated by his own interest. Millington skilfully nurtured him and became a critically important figure in his development, a driving force, an inspiring teacher, a father figure with whom Housman could readily identify and whose targets he could accept and deliver. The education Housman received at Bromsgrove reflected the fact that he was very good at classics; Greek and Latin were the subjects the headmaster taught, and in those days classics was king of the syllabus. Like many others, then and now, he worked hard at what he liked and what came easiest to him. Thus he was destined to end his school days as the winner of a scholarship to read classics. Bromsgrove School would rightly have rejected any alternative scenario for him though two of his brothers, Herbert and Basil, went on from that same school to read engineering and medicine in Birmingham. Life would tell whether the choice he had made was the right one. The danger for Housman was that he might go on to university with too high an opinion of his own capabilities, unprepared for the transition from being a big fish in a small pond to being a small fish in an infinitely bigger pond. Laurence remarked: 'We lived a small and enclosed family life.' It would be a challenge for them all to make the transition from a self-satisfied Housman-centric world into a wider world.

Insofar as their father had not shaped their lives, the children had been left free to find their own way forward, enabled by their personal aspirations, their own sense of direction and their modest bequests. They were lucky that their father was not in a position to finance their wishes and ambitions or to impose his own on them; they had to look out for themselves. Motivation is a strange and wonderful thing, as are the sources of aspiration and ambition, but the fact is that all Edward's children chose for themselves what they wanted to do and were happy doing it. Our Housman, the eldest son, got an open scholarship to St John's Oxford and in the fullness of time became renowned for his classical scholarship and poetry; Laurence, the nonconformist penultimate child, went to art school in London, subsequently reinventing himself as a playwright, poet and professional campaigner for women's suffrage, peace and wider understanding of gender difference; Clemence, another free spirit, went with Laurence to London and became a novelist, engraver and militant suffragette; Robert went to Mason's and Queen's College, Birmingham, as one of its first students in engineering and became an electrical engineer; Basil won a scholarship to Queen's College, Birmingham, qualified as FRCS in 1891, eventually ending up as a successful Schools Medical Officer; Herbert followed Basil to Queens to study medicine but the love of his life was soldiering and although there was by then no family money to purchase a commission, he enlisted as a private soldier, rose to be a sergeant in the King's Royal Rifles and was killed in the Boer War. The great merit of Edward's laissez-faire attitude to his children's upbringing was that it left each alone to follow their star.

Housman and his six siblings demonstrated how nature and nurture could be so very variable in its outcomes. But that was only the beginning and would not be the final determinant of their stories. Experience teaches that early imprints on the child are never eliminated, but may be overlaid by the effects of the working environment and the habits of mind and behaviours common in it. The Housman children variously pursued careers in academe, industry, the army, the home, medicine, and the arts.

The emotional and psychological weather of their own lives would also have its effects and create other changes. Laurence was already showing the greatest capacity for change and Housman the least. So as time to leave home and school approached, the members of the Housman family were ready to shoot off in very different directions. Time alone would show what if any togetherness survived as the social and psychological distance between them increased.

Genetic inheritance

It can be asked what if anything they took with them as a common genetic inheritance. As a group they would mark a sharp decline in family fecundity. According to Pugh, great-great-grandfather Robert 'The Maltster' fathered seven children; great-grandfather, the Rev. Robert 'The Evangelist', fathered eight children by two wives; grandfather Thomas likewise fathered eight children of whom five survived to maturity.[29] Edward and Sarah Jane's seven was roughly in line but their children were not destined to replicate the procreative urges of their predecessors

Five of the children – Alfred, Laurence, Robert, Herbert, and Clemence – would die unmarried. Clemence would live with her brother Laurence for all her adult life. Basil married but died without issue. Kate alone married and had four children.

There may have been genetic precursors for the Housman unmarried men, in the shape of John, the bachelor son of their great-great-grandfather, and Thomas, their grandfather's eldest son, a black sheep for unspecified reasons, and Joseph, his childless youngest son. On the female side, there were enough spinsters in preceding generations to provide precursors for Clemence. Kate married but does not seem on her own admission to have fallen in love with her husband, although she grew to love him as their life together went on.

It would become clear in their lives that the Housman children were at the lower end of susceptibility to the excitements of the flesh. Neither Housman, Laurence nor Clemence exhibited desire for intimate and lasting connections with other men or women. The law, buttressed by social and religious opinion, placed powerful inhibitions on the expression of anything other than 'normal' desires, but none of that would be sufficient to cause Housman, Laurence or Clemence to take shelter in conventional marriages. The most realistic conclusion

Figure 5 Clemence, Housman's elder sister.
Courtesy Gerald Symons.

Figure 6 Katharine, Housman's younger sister.
Courtesy Gerald Symons.

is that they were endowed with an insufficiency of love or lust for other individuals. In that important way, their actual lives may have been determined by their nature.

But, when all is said and done, Housman, like all human beings, would come to have a distinctive personal essence. The Housman who was about to enter the first stage of his life in the outside world was clever and immature, but self-confident and competitive. His childhood had left him with inner insecurities. Taken together, nature, nurture and circumstances had dealt him an opening hand that would not be easy to play.

PART II

Oxford

The road to academic failure

In October 1877 Housman was going up to Oxford from a small town in Worcestershire on the southern fringes of the Black Country, a provincial boy from a family who would have had difficulty in supporting him without his scholarship. He had come from a relatively obscure school to a monumental and imposing Oxford college. Almost twenty years earlier, his uncle Joseph Brettell Housman (he who would soon buy the Housman family home) had won a scholarship from Bromsgrove School to Oxford's Worcester College, but whereas Housman's was an open scholarship at St John's, his uncle's had been a closed scholarship, that is one restricted to pupils of his own school. After two years of not living up to the description of 'scholar', Joseph suffered the ignominy of being deprived of his scholarship.

Housman was going up to Oxford without the advantage of relatives who had made their mark; he had nobody to lubricate his entrance; nor was he entering a ready-made network of former pupils from his own school, as could be the case with students from big well-known schools, such as Eton, Winchester, Westminster or Shrewsbury. He had first to make friends in his own college, look out for himself and make his own way forward.

He was without sporting prowess which could have provided him with an alternative route to social connections and self-expression. He was without money which would have enabled him, had he had such ambitions, to aim for the upper pinnacles of Oxford's social and political life. Having shone during his school days, his most likely expectation was that he would go on shining.

Only thirteen letters survive to record the events of his life at Oxford. Together they show no lack of willingness on his part to engage with

Figure 7 Housman at eighteen.
Courtesy Gerald Symons and Edward Pugh.

what was around him. But far from recording awestruck impressions of Oxford, its personages and ceremonies, he was generally scornful. When he went with the other St John's freshmen to be matriculated (entered on the university register), a tutor told each one how to write his name in Latin – in his case, Alfredus Edwardus Housman. They then walked down St Giles along Broad Street, past the Sheldonian Theatre and into New College. The scene he painted in a letter to his stepmother was of the Warden of New College, Vice-Chancellor of the university at the time, 'seated in a dim religious light at the top of the hall'. The young gentlemen of St John's filed in as those from a preceding college filed out. They queued to write their Latin names in a big book, then to write them in plain English in a less grand book, then to stand in front of a man at a table to pay their matriculation fee of £2 10s 0d. Next they sat in a row, standing in turn to be presented by the Vice-Chancellor with a copy of the Statutes of the University, bound in violet and accompanied by a note described by Housman as written in 'what passes for Latin at Oxford'. This substandard Latin he translated for his stepmother: 'At Oxford, in the Michaelmas term A.D. 1877, on the 13th day of the month of October: on which day Alfred Edward Housman of the college of St John the Baptist, gentleman's son, appeared in my presence, & was admonished to keep the laws of this University, & was enrolled in the register (*matricula*) of the University.' The Vice-Chancellor then settled his gown round his shoulders, asked for their attention and said in Latin 'Allow me to inform you that you have this day been enrolled in the register of the University, & that you are bound to keep all the statutes contained in this book.' This ceremony led to an unimpressed Housman informing his step mother: 'As to keeping the statutes contained in the violet cover, you may judge what a farce that is, when I tell you that you are forbidden to wear any coat save a black one, or to use fire-arms, or trundle a hoop, among other things.'[1]

He was no more impressed by the energetic bravura of John Ruskin's lectures which he voluntarily attended. 'This afternoon Ruskin gave us a great outburst against modern times.' To make his point Ruskin had illustrated his lecture with a picture by Turner of Leicester, the abbey in the distance, with a sunset over a river. Ruskin had challenged his audience:

> You, if you like, may go to Leicester to see what it is like now. I never shall. But I can make a pretty good guess. Then he caught up a paintbrush. 'These stepping stones of course have been done away with, & are replaced with a be-au-ti-ful iron bridge.' Then he dashed in the iron bridge on the glass of the picture. 'The colour of the stream is supplied on one side by the indigo factory.' Forthwith one side of the stream became indigo. 'On the other by the soap factory.' Soap dashed in. 'They mix in the middle – like curds' he said, working them together with a sort of malicious deliberation. 'This field over which you see the sun setting behind the abbey is now occupied in a proper manner.' Then there went a flame of scarlet across the picture, which developed itself into windows & roofs & red brick, and rushed up into a chimney. 'The atmosphere is supplied – thus!' A puff & cloud of smoke all over Turner's sky: and then the brush thrown down, & Ruskin confronting modern civilisation amidst a tempest of applause.[2]

But Housman, whose eye and ear were so well attuned to catch and brilliantly record the theatricality of Ruskin's performance, had not been persuaded, nor even seriously roused, to engage with any of the ideas behind what Ruskin said. He obviously thought it all a bit of a joke and was revelling in his undoubted capacity to write entertainingly about it. Perhaps more surprisingly, he also wrote at length about current political issues and debates at the Oxford Union Society.

When Housman went up to Oxford, Tories under Disraeli and Liberals under Gladstone were bitterly at odds over Balkans policy. Revolts against the Ottoman Empire had led to the notorious 'Bulgarian atrocities', intervention by the Russians and war between Russia and Turkey. At the Congress of Berlin in mid-1878, Disraeli supported Turkey and issued an ultimatum to the Russians, his policy to use Turkey as a barrier to Russian Mediterranean ambitions. Disraeli claimed 'Peace with Honour'.

This was the setting for the Oxford Union debate of February 1878 which became the subject of a long letter to Housman's father: 'So the motion before the Union was, "That the Eastern policy of Lord Beaconsfield [Disraeli] has been from the first, and remains, utterly unworthy of the confidence of the country."' A few days earlier there had been a Liberal meeting in the Oxford Corn Exchange at which one Thorold Rogers

> who holds, or rather has just vacated, the professorship of political economy, & can therefore perhaps be scarcely held accountable for his actions – he rose from Mr Gladstone's side, and bade the rt hon gentleman be of good cheer, & pay no attention to 'dissipated undergraduates'. Now undergraduate Oxford was rather riled at this, and Professor Thorold Rogers, who goes by the name of the Beaumont Street Gorilla, was considerably groaned for at the anti-Russian demonstration last Saturday.

Housman went on with fluency and skill to paint the scene and the *dramatis personae* of the debate itself:

> Then the speech began. It was not violent, which was a mercy, and not rhetorical, which was a greater mercy still. The man was nothing of the orator, but he was fluent, very cool and impudent. The speech lasted an hour, but the greater part of this time was occupied by the House, & not of the Honourable Member. I should not say that his remarks took more than twenty minutes, but they only cropped up as islets in the oceanic demonstration of opinion.

In the event the motion was lost by a margin of two to one,

> unheard in the transports of enthusiasm, & the general rush
> back to college; for you can only understand the patriotic state of
> excitement in which we were, when you consider that the division
> took place between ten & five minutes to twelve: & if you were
> not back in college at 12 the penalties, I believe, are something
> very fearful indeed.

He had himself attended the anti-Russian demonstration in
a crammed hall at the Corn Exchange, a rowdy and boisterous
meeting echoing with jingoistic songs such as 'Rule Britannia' and
the music hall hit of the year 'We don't want to fight but, by jingo, if
we do, we've got the ships, we've got the men, we've got the money
too.' Some preliminary bouts of fisticuffs took place in the body of
the hall. Cheers drowned out speakers and were accompanied by
the ejection of malcontent Liberals. Housman had been close to the
platform and described the speakers, the first as 'weak', the second
as 'frantic but gentlemanly', the third as 'pointed and clever, but
insufficiently audible'.

He continued:

> These speeches formed the interludes to about a dozen patriotic
> ejections – one being that of an eminent liberal undergraduate
> who speaks much at the Union, & on this occasion attempted
> to scale the platform with an amendment. These ejections were
> vigorously prompted by a man on the platform with a long
> black beard. This I thought bad taste, so as I was close to the
> platform, I caught hold of Sir Drummond Wolff [Conservative
> MP for Christchurch] – selecting his left hand, because he wore
> a large gold ring upon it, & was therefore likely to consider it the
> most valuable part of his frame – and told him that we should
> have scored off Gladstone, if we had abstained from the ejective
> example set by his meeting, and asked him whether he could not
> suppress the man with the black beard. But Sir Drummond Wolff
> was in a helpless state of imbecility, & could do nothing, & as Mr
> Hanbury [another Conservative MP] looked as if he was going to
> faint after his oratorical exertions, and Alfred Austin [editor of
> the *National Review*] was bent on sitting immovable & looking as
> much like Mr Disraeli as he could manage – there was nothing to

be done. But the result was a rather rowdy meeting. The motion – Conservative and Turk – was of course carried with acclamation, & then the meeting fought itself out of doors & culminated in the combustion of an effigy of Mr Gladstone just outside our college.

One is left with a striking impression of a gifted observer, of detached amusement, of vivid word pictures that were the work of an accomplished wordsmith. Housman was not a participant intent on judging the case on its merits. He was intent on exercising his sense of humour and expressing his political prejudices, which he knew would please his dyed-in-the-wool Tory father.

He turned his attentions to the university church of St Mary. Less than impressed by the quality of the argument from the pulpit, he was fascinated by the tricks of the trade employed by the preacher, Canon King of Christ Church Cathedral. 'The exquisitely deprecating way & affected timidity with which he put his strongest points, and the mournful and apologetic modulation of his voice where he was pulling Dean Stanley to pieces, were really almost worthy of Disraeli.' The Bishop of Manchester 'commenced operations by blowing his nose, which is a rhetorical device he has apparently just found out, & which in the first ecstasy of novelty he uses with injudicious profusion.'[3]

This immediate understanding of some of the techniques and mannerisms of public speaking suggests that he would have been at home on the floor of the Union, but there is no evidence that he wished to make a name for himself as a debater. Perhaps, in spite of that inner sense of superiority which gave him the freedom to comment *du haut en bas*, he was still a provincial boy, overawed and inhibited by the Union which he may have seen as a stage for titled undergraduates and extrovert pushy individuals to thrust themselves into the limelight.

A few days later he was writing a light-hearted letter to his godmother, Elizabeth Wise, about *Ye Round Table*, an undergraduate magazine. He sent her some nonsense verses

which will appear in the next number of the "Round Table", composed by several members of the Editorial Staff together; the last verse is mine. I am glad you liked the "Round Table"; the second number will be published next Saturday, & I will send it. I expect it will be considerably better than the first. It is selling here very well & seems likely to become popular.

So here was Housman, in his second term, collaborating with his fellow students at St John's and no doubt impressing them with his capacity as a quick-witted versifier. He was especially proud of his lines, 'For it sank in a flatulent fluid/ and imbibed its auricomous roar/ Till the deadly and dew-spangled Druid/ Had dabbled his tendrils in gore.'[4] The magazine did not become popular and Housman's contributions ended when it folded in June of his first year. Housman contributed to each issue in poetry or prose under his pseudonym 'Tristram'. His verses were clever and perhaps for some, sources of amusement, but not great prompters of instant laughter. Among his prose pieces *Punch and Jouida* exhibits a powerful strain of sensuous fantasy and gives the public hangman a part. Another prose piece was built around a Union debate on capital punishment. Nonsense verse was unlocking his subconscious.

His college friend Alfred Pollard recognised the impact Housman made on fellow students when he recalled 'he was quietly happy and was generally recognized in the College as exceptionally able. When he was in the mood he could recite to very restricted audiences humorous stories of his own making which were made doubly humorous by his prim method of telling them.'[5] His competitive prize-seeking instincts had led him to enter for the Hertford, the university's prize for Latin, and subsequently for the Newdigate poetry prize. In neither case was he winner or runner-up. In previous years the Newdigate had been won by men of the calibre of John Ruskin, Matthew Arnold and Oscar Wilde. Housman was running true to form in entering for these prizes but for the first time was meeting up with real competition, encountering young men more talented than himself. Here were signs that he was not going to set Oxford alight and was accepting the situation with equanimity and realism.

Meanwhile, at home, events had been taking a slow but inexorable course. At the beginning of Housman's second year, his father's chicanery came to its climax. In February 1879 Edward's brother, Joseph Housman, bought Edward's house. It is hard to believe that Housman was not aware of the financial difficulties his family was in. There were no signs, however, that the family's precarious financial position had any effect on Housman's subsequent performance in his Classical Moderations (Mods). He was awarded a First.

Falling in love with textual criticism

Two years' work lay ahead before he would take Greats, his final examinations in the honours school of Literae Humaniores. The syllabus included ancient history, logic and moral and political philosophy. Andrew Gow, a fellow of Trinity College Cambridge who knew Housman for his final twenty-five years, took the view that the tuition at St John's had failed him. His teachers had certainly not inspired him. Three who taught him at St John's were Robert Ewing, tutor in ancient history; Thomas Snow, who in 1908 became the university's Regius Professor of Greek and with whom Housman had a good relationship, and the Rev. Henry Bidder who remembered Housman as 'a man on whom he had done his best to make an impression and failed.'[6] He had tried to teach Housman Greek philosophy, but Housman would not engage seriously with the subject. Housman also found himself out of tune with Benjamin Jowett, then Regius Professor of Greek and Master of Balliol College. Jowett made no secret of the fact that he thought making emendations to classical texts was a futile pursuit. He was fired by a mission to use the Greats course as a means to an end, to send into the world men imbued with the best models and thinking from the ancient world, and thus fitted to be administrators of the British Empire.

Housman wanted to do exactly what Jowett had no time for. The idea of working on versions of Greek and Latin texts in order to produce something closer to the original was the kind of detailed 'scientific' work that appealed deeply to him. Instead of getting down to the Greats syllabus, he began to neglect it and to work instead on the text of the Latin love poet Propertius, who was born and died in the years before the birth of Christ. Ovid found Propertius soft and sensitive, Martial found him humorously eloquent. Quintillian found him polished and tender but Housman had not been seduced by such qualities. What most interested him was that Propertius was 'difficult'. To understand why that was the case we have to appreciate that no classical author had an original manuscript. Classical authors survived from the ancient world only by being copied. It is rare for an author to survive in a copy that does not postdate him by more than five hundred years and often one thousand years. It is through the uncontrollable act of human copying that errors enter the text; the textual critic's job is not simply to choose better readings but first to work out the interrelationship of surviving copies which are now dotted around Europe and sometimes the United States. He then has to assess whether any 'authoritative' manuscript has a viable reading or whether one has to resort to a conjecture, i.e. a guess. In the case of Propertius, the particular problem was that the text had suffered large-scale transpositions, that is movement of parts of the text to different parts of the whole poem.

Housman was excited by such work. It required a combination of logic, learning, instinct for language and poetic meaning, and a grasp of copyists' styles and habitual errors. It was work tailor-made for his fertile, agile, puzzle-solving mind, his deep and reliable memory, his instinct for versifying, his capacity to conjure up solutions. Its task was precise, its process practical, its output finite, its conclusions testable. It was the furthest cry possible from dealing in, or seeking to justify, philosophical opinionation.

When H.A.J. Munro published his *Criticisms and Emendations of Catullus* in 1878, Housman's enthusiasm for textual criticism was intensified and reinforced. He was even moved to write to its author with thoughts of his own. Munro held the Cambridge professorship of Latin between 1867 and 1872 but resigned from it on the grounds that it was hindering his work! Had Housman had the opportunity to go to Cambridge he would have found the Cambridge emphasis on the philological rather than the philosophical much more to his taste.[7] In January 1877 Housman had failed to win a scholarship to Corpus Christi, an Oxford college with a classics tradition. Had he succeeded, his Oxford career could well have been very different in both academic and personal senses. Housman's interest in Propertius was neither trivial nor transient, nor was it a schoolboy enthusiasm. His work on Propertius was his alternative syllabus. In fact, by the time he left Oxford he had enough material on Propertius to seek its publication by Macmillan in 1885. And three years later he would publish a thirty-five page paper, 'Emendationes Propertianae', in the *Journal of Philology*.

This self-directed interest began to take charge in his third year. What he wanted to do was not in line with what he was supposed to do, an attitude that could have only one outcome. Unfortunately, though a very clever young man, Housman was just like his father: incapable of appreciating the likely outcome of his own misguided actions.

The core of the Greats syllabus was ancient history, logic, moral and political philosophy. Housman seems to have been blind to the fact that completing the set syllabus would be the only means to an academic future – at best the prize of a college fellowship at St John's, at worst a teaching post in a good school. It seems obvious that he was misguided in allowing his prejudice against the Greats syllabus, or even misgivings about his likely performance in some parts of it, to govern his actions. There may have been another unhelpful element in his situation. His friend Pollard remembered how in the Lent or Summer term of 1880, after they had taken their college exams or 'collections', the Senior Tutor made an innocent remark of Housman's 'the occasion for informing him before us all that he was *not* a genius'.[8] This sounds like a tutor who has become rather tired of encountering a know-all student, or has been offended by a flippantly dismissive remark in an examination reply. At any rate, he was communicating to Housman that his assessment of his student's quality and prospects was not as high as Housman's own. Housman had little regard for his Senior Tutor and showed no signs of having taken the hint. The college was not providing him with inspiration, and so he was trusting to his own self-direction.

A new element then entered the scene. In their third year Housman and Pollard, who had entered St John's together and had rooms on the same staircase, moved to a different quad in the college. There they encountered Moses Jackson, born in Ramsgate, son of the inspiring founder/principal of Vale College Ramsgate, and the eldest of eleven children. As a seventeen-year-old, Moses' talent for science had propelled him to University College London where he won the Neil Arnott Medal in Experimental Physics and later an open scholarship to St John's.[9] A friendship developed between this 'delightful science scholar', as Pollard called him, and his two contemporaries. At first sight Jackson seemed unlikely as a friend for Housman; he was a sportsman whose afternoons were spent on the athletics field or on the river as an oar in a St John's boat. There was something about him that attracted Housman and led to rambles in the countryside punctuated by alfresco pub lunches.

Housman, Jackson and Pollard

Fourth year students were obliged to live out of college. The trio decided to lodge together and so it was that Housman, Pollard and Jackson took a set of five rooms just across St Giles' Street from St John's. Pollard and Housman were both classics scholars preparing for the same exam and made a natural pair. However, Housman gradually came to spend more and more time in the evenings with Jackson, a naturally gifted scientist who had no need to work excessively hard for his degree. Instead of going off to his own room to study, as Pollard did, Housman preferred to spend time with Jackson. There must have been something about the handsome, athletic young man

Figure 8 Moses Jackson as an undergraduate.
Courtesy Gerald Symons.

and his down-to-earth no-nonsense scientific attitude that evidently made him a pleasure to be with.

Else how can it have been that Housman evidently shared with him his earliest serious poem, *Parta Quies*, first published in the Oxford magazine *Waifs and Strays* in the Hilary Term of 1881? The most significant fact about it is that more than forty years later, Moses Jackson was able to quote the poem virtually word for word in his last letter to Housman (written from his hospital bed in Vancouver in November 1922). Housman replied that

> I was never more astounded at anything than at your reproducing my contribution to *Waifs and Strays*. I remember your reading it at Miss Patchett's, [landlady of the rooms the trio shared] and how nervous I felt. If I had known you would recollect it 42 years afterward, my emotions would have been too much for me.

This is far from an admission that Housman had Moses in mind when he wrote the poem. He could equally probably have been thinking of his mother, by then seven years dead, the poem affirming his lack of belief in her resurrection, his mind making its final conquest over his childhood religious beliefs.

GOODNIGHT; ensured release,
Imperishable peace,
    Have these for yours,
While sea abides, and land,
And earth's foundations stand,
    And heaven endures.

When earth's foundations flee,
Nor sky nor land nor sea
    At all is found,
Content you, let them burn;
It is not your concern;
    Sleep on, sleep sound.

The fact that he had given this poem to Moses to read was at least indicative of Housman's growing trust in him; his reaction to Moses' having remembered it word for word indicated an original emotional connection of such intensity that it could still sound across the years. But there is no evidence that a preoccupation with Jackson caused Housman to neglect his work. There were no signs then or later that Housman's feelings for Moses Jackson were feeding off Propertius' hopeless love for Cynthia, that Housman was using them as surrogates for his own undeclared feelings. He could not have cared less for Propertius as poetry. Housman's work as a textual critic shows that what he was passionately interested in was the state of the text and how it could be restored to its original state; not in its emotional or aesthetic impact. Years later, F.L. Lucas, who attended Housman's lectures at Cambridge, recalled that 'if my memory is correct he once began a course of Lucretius VI by saying he had chosen the Sixth Book because it possessed no literary qualities to distract one from the pure problems of the text'.[10]

David McKie has shown that Housman, unlike Pollard and Jackson, was in college on census day, 4 April 1881, indicating that instead of going home for the Easter vacation, he was doing last minute work on his Greats subjects.[11] If so, it seems psychologically incongruous that Housman should have sent Kate, the day after census day, an extravagantly high-spirited spoof account of his encounter with the census-taker. He said he gave his name in full as 'Albert Matilda Hopkins', described his relation to the head of the house as 'My relations with the President are I regret to say rather strained', and after more in that vein ended, 'he hastily filled up the last column of my census-paper with the words "Imbecile, probably from birth". I went down & corrected it into "Imbecile, probably from being asked a string of impertinent questions."'[12]

This letter can be read at face value as typical Housman nonsense; alternatively, as a subconscious expression of the parallel between the questions of the census-taker and the questions the examiners would soon be posing and Housman's impatience with both. Housman may have been unable to avoid confronting the discrepancy between the demands of Greats and the insufficiencies of his preparations, hence the mixture of anxiety and panic dressed up with bravado. It is very difficult to believe that he was unaware of the perils of his situation, or that he was totally without apprehension, in spite of his resolution. David McKie has offered his own view about what was happening: 'It was perhaps in that last vacation that the path of his counter-trajectory came, by force of his nature, to be set: where excellence could not be attained, its place would better be taken by nothing.'[13]

PART III

The Patent Office

Failure in Greats

When they saw his papers, the examiners – Bywater, Macan, Richards and Bidder – were shocked. Only one of them, Bidder, had actually taught Housman and none of his other college lecturers was an examiner, although they seem to have been informed of Housman's situation before the results were announced. Pollard later recalled that when he went up to Oxford for his viva (oral examination), which customarily takes place between the written examination and the announcement of results, he found his examiners bewildered

> finding themselves compelled ... to refuse even a pass to a man who had obtained a first in Mods ... how it had come to pass that on some of the papers Housman had hardly attempted to offer any answers. What had he been doing? The only explanation I could offer at the time was that I believed he might have occupied himself too much with the text of Propertius, and that remained the only explanation I could offer to myself or to anyone else, until in the emotion caused by his death I realised that for a man who was, if not already a great scholar, at least a great scholar in the making, it was psychologically impossible to make the best of his knowledge on subjects in which he had lost interest.[1]

The fact that the examiners did not wish to viva Housman for a second or third or fourth class degree, shows how awful, empty or insulting his papers must have been. He may have allowed his contempt for some of the questions to shine through or may have deployed his coruscating and sardonic wit in his answers. Canon Nance, a St John's lecturer, said that on the philosophical side 'his performance had been so ludicrously bad as to show that he had not made any effort, and to give the examiners the impression that he was treating that part of the business with contempt.[2] Pollard said nothing about Housman's possible distress at his father's stroke, nothing about bad blood between Housman and his tutors, nothing about Moses Jackson and gave no other reason than his preoccupation with Propertius for Housman's neglect of the syllabus. Housman himself later told Andrew Gow that his examiners 'had no option.'[3]

Yet his resolution had not carried him through the aftermath. When the results of his finals were announced his sense of defeat and humiliation was monumental. His had been an apocalyptic collapse of promise. He was not even able to bring home a disappointing but honourable second, nor a third for which he might have found some excuses, not even a slacker's fourth, but a total failure. In picturesque Oxford slang, the examiners had 'ploughed' him. Kate described how Housman 'returned home a stricken and petrified brother'. Salt in his wounds was added by Pollard who got a first class in classics and would go on to become Keeper of Printed Books at the British Museum, and also by Jackson who got his expected first in science and went on to join the Patent Office in London. Housman's self-belief and self-confidence had been put to the test and had been proved by events to be totally unjustified. No wonder that, according to Kate, he 'was withdrawn from all of us behind a barrier of reserve which he set up as though to shield himself from either pity or blame. He met no word of reproach at home.'[4]

When troubles came they had come not in single spies but in battalions. His father had survived the stroke but his working and earning capacities were now severely curtailed. Housman must have discovered the true state of the family finances. When the £200 legacy from his uncle William came to him soon after his grandmother's death in 1882, he may have been settling his conscience when he handed it over not into his father's unsafe hands, but direct to their family's solicitor to meet future mortgage payments on Perry Hall.

The family was at the nadir of its financial difficulties. Kate recollected their situation: 'The home troubles were calamitous. For years an increasing restriction of means had been closing in on us, with perfectly blank prospects before the four younger brothers still at school.'[5] Sixty years later his sister Kate remained emphatically uncharitable about what she called his blameable failure in the Final Schools at Oxford, for blameable it was that, knowing the severe difficulties besetting his home, making success for him the one bright spot to which his family could turn with confidence, he allowing his intellectual arrogance to lure him into slackness or negligence instead of making assiduous preparation for his Schools.[6]

She could not have declared her lack of empathy and understanding of Housman's situation in a more punishing way, but who could blame her, for evidently Housman neither explained nor apologised and made no attempt to produce an exculpatory rationale for his actions. Kate was in no doubt that failure in finals damaged his life.

Housman the failure crept back to Bromsgrove where Headmaster Millington held out a helping hand. With a combination of thoughtfulness and enlightened self-interest, he engaged him to teach the sixth form, where there was an added embarrassment in the shape of Housman's younger brother Basil, then Head Boy.

Housman had to decide what to do with his life. He was without prospects, with no chance of obtaining any teaching or academic post of quality. No alternative profession, neither the Church, the Bar, nor medicine, seems to have had the slightest appeal for him. There were no signs that he ever gave a moment's thought to the possibility of following his father by being articled to a local solicitor. There was nothing for him in Bromsgrove where he could only be pointed out as the promising boy who had failed his finals. At home he was simply another mouth to feed. Indeed, it would be difficult to overestimate the impact of his catastrophic failure. His thoughts might easily have turned to suicide.

It was a measure of Housman's resilience that he did not remain totally immobilised by his failure. His motivation, although narrowly focussed, was still immensely powerful. He had to decide how to get back on to his own chosen path. Fortunately for him, his scholarship ran until the end of 1882 and so his first step was to undergo the mortification of a return to Oxford to take a lowly pass degree; at least he would have *a* degree. With his mind closed to standard vocations and professions, the only obvious route forward was the open competition for the Civil Service which could at least provide him with a secure and reasonably paid means to an end. The motivation that carried him forward was the motivation he had discovered at Oxford – to be a textual critic. He had work on Propertius almost ready to send to a publisher, and a paper on aspects of Horace ready to send to the *Journal of Philology*. His primary object was a return to the life of the mind, a life of textual scholarship.

The Patent Office via the valley of death and sweat

Towards the end of January 1882 Housman entered for the Preliminary Examination for Clerkships in the Civil Service, passed it in February, and was qualified to go forward to the examination itself in June. This was not a soft option. It was well recognised as a career route for very clever people; passing high in the list conferred its own cachet. Entering the Civil Service was also the route for fulfilling specific ambitions. If you had a father or an uncle who were themselves distinguished grey eminences, and public service was in your family's blood, this was the way to go. If your ambition was to move in ambassadorial circles and be a broker between nations you had the Foreign Office in your sights. If you were interested in the 'condition of the people' you might have craved an appointment in the Home Office. If your ambition was to be a mover and shaker – one of the elite – the Treasury was for you. Housman had none of these ambitions. He needed only a position to keep body and soul together, to make him independent while he worked at his academic last. He joined a long list of people who would use the Civil Service and its frequently not too pressing demands as a base camp from which to scale more important personal peaks. For Housman, it was from the beginning not a career but a second job.

His campaign to rehabilitate himself began before he even sat for the Civil Service. In the second quarter of 1882, his paper 'Horatiana' was published in the *Journal of Philology*. The next year he published in the same journal a short note on two lines from Ovid.

In 'Horatiana' he was confidently entering onto what he saw as the real stage of his life, agreeing on one point with the great Richard Bentley, a few lines later demurring confidently from a Bentley emendation. Then he raised his standard against the whole known world of classical scholarship, suggesting that Horace's Epode IX was written before, not after, the battle of Actium. 'It takes some nerve to say it,' he wrote, but nevertheless 'I think this only wants pointing out to be self- evident.'[7] Housman had announced his arrival on stage *con brio*. He sent a copy to H.A.J. Munro, the former Professor of Latin at Cambridge, whose work on Catullus had so aroused his interest and whom he cited twice in his article. Hoping he had made his mark and perhaps looking for encouragement or enquiries about himself, he was disappointed. Munro replied 'amiably but not enthusiastically'.[8] Perhaps Housman's sense of effortless superiority and confident flowing style was not to Munro's taste. The walls of Jericho were not about to crumble at Housman's trumpet sound. He was now outside the academic system; there could be no quick fix for the situation he had got himself into.

On 28 July the *London Gazette* announced the names of the top eight in the Civil Service open competition. The examination had allowed candidates to focus on their preferred subjects but also obliged them to display a breadth of knowledge in their choice of additional subjects. Top of the list was Robert Chalmers who won the prize of a job at the Treasury, eventually becoming Governor of Ceylon and Master of Peterhouse College Cambridge. His total mark was 2,458 from his seven chosen papers against Housman's 1,560. 'Housman stood ... first in Latin ... third in Greek ... What is surprising is his performance in History... nineteenth.'[9]

He had less success in demonstrating breadth of knowledge in his other three papers. He did better in French than in English History and Moral Sciences. He probably felt obliged to enter himself for Moral Sciences (shades of the Greats syllabus!) because the other alternatives – Mathematics, Natural Sciences, Jurisprudence and Political Economy – were subjects about which he probably knew next to nothing. The exacting nature of the exam was well demonstrated by the fact that fifteen of Housman's fellow competitors scored fewer than one thousand marks.

This open competition was an examination of fearsomely high standards. Many years later, Maynard Keynes, the renowned economist, referred to it as 'the valley of death and sweat'.[10] Maynard Keynes was very bright indeed and set himself a fearsomely demanding work schedule. When he came second in 1906 he scored 3,498, coming first in logic, psychology, English essay, and political science, and pronounced himself 'enraged' by his marks in mathematics and economics. The man who came first, O.E. Niemayer, had a first in Greats and pipped him at the post for the Treasury job; Keynes got into the India Office.[11]

The competition provided a snapshot of Housman's intellectual capacity and general learning, taken at a point when he was undeniably under stress and after less than six months for revision.

It demonstrated his sharply competitive edge against all comers in Latin and Greek. Otherwise there was no evidence of an actual or budding polymath.

Ranked eleventh in the competition, there was no hope of an offer of a position in the Treasury, the Foreign Office, the India Office, or any other prestigious department. Instead he was offered a job in Dublin which he promptly refused. His stepmother applied pressure for him to accept the next job offer. Housman became a Higher Division Clerk in the Patent Office with a six-hour working day and a salary of £100 a year. With annual increments, this would bring his salary up to £400 after eight years. Already working there was Moses Jackson, albeit in a higher paid post, but actually in a career dead end. The fact that the Patent Office was low in the Civil Service pecking order and an unlikely launch pad for a high-flying career did not enter into Housman's calculations. Its silver lining was the six-hour day, by today's standards just about a morning's work. That would give him plenty of time to do what he really wanted to do.

Housman, Moses Jackson and Adalbert Jackson at 82 Talbot Road

On 28 November 1882, when he was twenty-three and a half-years-old, Housman was appointed to the Patent Office. By early December he had taken lodgings in London at 15 Northumberland Road. Within about six months he moved to nearby 82 Talbot Road where Moses Jackson and his brother Adalbert Jackson were already living. The fact that this happened tells us that Moses Jackson had absolutely no inhibitions about inviting Housman to join himself and his younger undergraduate brother, or if the initiative was Housman's, Moses did not fob him off; the conclusion has to be that the move made sound economic sense and was welcomed by all. There could have been an added attraction for Adalbert who was reading classics at University College London.

It might have been expected that Pollard, then working at the British Museum, would seek to renew his friendship with his two Oxford friends, not least with Housman, who would spend so many hours of his time in the British Museum reading room. But Pollard had been deeply upset by his friend's Oxford failure and said later, 'I got it into my head that the sight of me reminded Housman of his troubles and was unwilling to thrust myself on him more than he

Figure 9 Adalbert Jackson, brother of
Moses Jackson.

might welcome.'[12] This was probably the truth of the matter and a sign of Pollard's sensitivity. The possibility that they were both avoiding each other because of Housman's continued connection with Jackson does not hold water and would be disproved by a future joint visit to Pollard's home.

Housman's seeming reluctance to invite Laurence and Clemence to visit when they came to live in London in November 1883 is odd, given Laurence's glowing recollections of their life together as children, but explicable by the fact that Laurence and Clemence were younger siblings, intent on a different life in the world of arts and crafts. They showed no signs of wanting their elder brother to reassume his accustomed family role of leader. Housman himself was finding his feet in London and intent on settling his life into the two-job pattern he was inventing. He was fitting in comfortably with Moses and Adalbert and had no need or incentive to complicate his life by creating a family circle in London. He had little in common with two siblings whose lifestyles and interests were as different as possible from his own; and there was the recent family history that he probably had no wish to talk about in the presence of outsiders.

Building a reputation as a classical scholar

Housman's reader's ticket for the British Museum was issued in early July 1883. He was not letting the grass grow under his feet. Now he could get on with what life had cut him out to do. Talbot Road was to the north of Notting Hill Gate, so it would have made sense for him to go straight to the British Museum reading room after work at the Patent Office in Southampton Buildings, which were situated at the Holborn end of Chancery Lane. One can imagine him leaving the reading room at closing time, with its light and warmth in winter, to make his way home to Bayswater by Underground or by omnibus; on soft spring and summer evenings taking a longer walk home, possibly down to the Embankment and back to Bayswater via St James' Park, Hyde Park and Green Park, his mind quiescent, relaxed by the concentration of his work, half intoxicated by the exercise of his problem-solving skills. For him, his work and such feelings brought fulfilment and pleasure.

Or was he simply creating a desperately needed antidote to life at the Patent Office? One might argue that the intensity of his work was a sublimation of deepening feelings for Moses Jackson but his will to publish demonstrated a powerful thread of self-justification, a sort of 'I'll show you' reaction. There was an unspoken, 'I may have failed Greats and cut myself off from a college Fellowship but look at me now, publishing in the learned journals.' Housman was revealing himself as single-minded, competitive, confident and entirely self-directed. The audience he found in the readers of learned journals was entirely fitted to his kind of cleverness.

Wordsworth wrote in his *Prelude* of 1805 that 'The mind of man is framed like the breath and harmony of music/ There is a dark invisible workmanship that shapes discordant elements and makes them move in one society'. There is something magical about the finest scholarship. Even the dark invisible workmanship of the computer with its effortless gathering, sorting and organising of data cannot compete with the magus figure of the actual scholar, who can magically take the next purely intuitive steps beyond the reach of artificial intelligence. Housman delighted in using himself as such an instrument.

His form of classical scholarship was about deciding what classical authors had actually written millennia ago. Original manuscripts did not exist. All that existed were copies of the original made in various places and frequently separated by hundreds of years. Thus textual criticism was analogous to solving a crime without a body. The one lying on the scholar's desk was not the original body but one of multiple representations of the body, serially mutilated over many centuries by copyists.

To reconstitute the original body required encyclopaedic knowledge of Greek and Latin authors and their habitual use of words and phrases; encyclopaedic knowledge of ancient styles and methods of writing; encyclopaedic knowledge of what previous scholars from the early humanists to contemporary scholars had changed, corrected or conjectured; which amounted to the scholar needing to carry a variorum edition of the work in his head.

Thus armed, the scholar could set about correcting errors, conjecturing how blank spaces ought to be filled, sorting out ambiguous, muddled or obscure passages or repositioning them. He had to be able to detect and pounce on misplaced words and untrue line order. And he needed a grasp of how the elements of grammar, metre, syntax and stylistic devices were employed by individual writers. An acute feeling for words and sensitive antennae for poetic meanings were valuable extras possessed by Housman.

When the scholar was dealing with several alternative manuscripts, they were frequently contradictory witnesses. So he had to decide which were the most reliable of the manuscripts. This was work requiring the combined talents of a detective and a forensic scientist, and requiring a vast knowledge of ancient literature, and the utmost sensitivity to groups of words with poetic purpose. It was work with many brain-teasing elements.

The business of restoration by amendment and conjecture was also extraordinarily creative, requiring the scholar to enter the mind and feelings of the writer and the historical and social context of the writings. Reputation as a scholar was something else. His base of professional knowledge would have to be recognised by others as extraordinary, his talent for solving puzzles had to be conspicuous, and the scholar himself had to possess a persona with the capacity to persuade others that what he said or wrote was right and that he was a man of authority entitled to respect.

It was not quite as simple as all that either. Although the work was essentially analytical and rational it was not entirely so. For example, the words of Propertius, Housman's undergraduate target, were created in the first two decades of Augustus' rule (27 BC–14 AD) but were not committed to paper for another one thousand years; the surviving manuscripts, at least eight in number, were separated by three hundred years. To decide the right order of the verses, and what were their proper constituents in terms of words and expressions, provided the starting point for an academic game based on opinion and judgement. This was a game for any number of players and the best argument won, but who was to judge which was the best argument? Not unlike legal argument it was a game very well suited to the fit, energetic and self-confident, and those with histrionic capacities to persuade or intimidate. Time alone would show how Housman would establish his reputation, what controversies he would be involved in and how he would go about gaining the respect of his peers.

T.C. Snow, who taught Housman for Classical Mods at St Johns, asked him a rather lateral question: 'what profession he would follow, if perfect texts of all the classics were suddenly discovered?'[13] Snow could not remember how Housman answered. But whatever Housman said, his life showed that he would have been eminently fitted to be a second Sherlock Holmes, down to 'Elementary my dear Watson' – a put-down whose spirit he would frequently express in his classical papers.

To put Housman in perspective as a scholar it is instructive to look at him in the light of some of his English predecessors: Richard Bentley (1662–1742), a previous Master of Trinity College, Cambridge, called 'the Newton of European philological and literary studies'; Richard Porson (1758–1808), also a fellow of Trinity; and Mark Pattison (1813–1884), Rector of Lincoln College, Oxford, biographer of the great seventeenth-century scholar Isaac Casaubon and often said to be the model for George Eliot's Mr Casaubon in her novel *Middlemarch*. They were all called scholars but were totally dissimilar in their personal characteristics and attitudes. They all appear to have been cast from totally different moulds. So was Housman.

Throughout his long years as Master of Trinity, where reform was needed, Richard Bentley can come across as a power-crazed chief executive of today, displaying a vast capacity to act like a despot, to build and consume magnificently, and to use his secure base to seek further political and ecclesiastical preferment. But what he found himself up against in Trinity has also to be reckoned with. The polemical nature of its fellows brought out the worst in Bentley's stubborn and combative nature, producing decades of open warfare between Master and fellows. Yet the qualities of Bentley's scholarship made him Housman's hero.

By contrast, Porson, whose work ethic and memory were prodigious and whose four editions of Euripides are lucid and powerful, had a career limited by drink. Samuel Taylor Coleridge encountered his former Professor of Greek in Trinity College library when he was returning home from a brief spell in Malta as secretary to Sir Alexander Ball, Governor of Malta, and one of Nelson's band of brothers at the battle of the Nile. Porson did not recognise Coleridge because he was drunk.

Closer to Housman's own time was Mark Pattison, Rector of Lincoln College, Oxford, whose biography of the real Isaac Casaubon provides many insights into how Casaubon's inborn traits had been enhanced and intensified by the nature of his work. Pattison observed of Casaubon:

> The one only motive which can support the daily energy called for in the solitary student's life, is the desire to know ... In some few this appetence is developed into a yearning, an eagerness, a passion, an exigency, an *inquietude poussante*, to use an expression of Leibnitz, which dominates all others, and becomes the rule of life.[14]

This was Housman. The impact on Housman's behaviour of his scholarly work was visible in the transformation that occurred from his earliest letters with their self-indulgent flow and his holiday letters which were in the nature of travelogues, compared with the short letters of his working periods with their absence of commentary on social, economic or philosophical matters, their seemingly narrow vision. Pattison referred to the same phenomenon in Casaubon: 'His shrinking from intrusion and hindrance amounts to an indifference to external events, an indifference which grows upon him.'[15] Housman was so totally preoccupied by his work and by the pressures and deadlines he imposed upon himself that much of his apparent unsociability and silence can be explained by it. Yet here was another paradox; in spite of the intensity of his focus, Housman was not overwhelmed by his passion for scholarship; he remained in charge of his life, setting himself targets he could meet, not spreading himself too thinly and working more efficiently than most.

Pattison the scholar was not himself a model for Housman, indeed he was his opposite; Pattison thrived on self-indulgent study and wide reading and had a penchant for networking across the fashionable scene in London. He became a celebrated nineteenth-century man of letters, essentially a top-class intellectual journalist as the list of his writings demonstrates. Housman simply wrote him off. Of his references to Scaliger's edition of Manilius, Housman wrote, 'Pattison had never read the book ... He was a spectator of all time and all existence, and the contemplation of that repulsive scene is fatal to accurate learning.'[16]

Just as there was nothing of Pattison's self-indulgent lack of focus about Housman, there was nothing of Bentley's megalomania or Porson's drunkenness. Housman was, from the beginning, utterly focussed, unrelenting in his regimen of steady application, fired by a compulsive urge to know, to get to the bottom of things, to decide, to judge. Yet nowhere was there a sense that he was intent on working himself to death like Casaubon. He was a workaholic but one who would very soon adopt a pattern of taking proper holidays and of compartmentalising his life of scholarship, his enjoyment of food and wine, and his enjoyment of the music hall and friends. This was his method of keeping his own life under his own control.

'The great and real troubles of my early manhood'

Given the absence of explanation from Housman himself it would be fruitless to try to pinpoint precisely when he came to the conclusion that he was sexually different, most probably during his adolescence, but possibly later at Oxford when he became aware of how much he was attracted to Moses Jackson. In appearance and behaviour nobody has ever suggested or hinted that there was anything 'camp' or 'effeminate' about Housman, so there was nothing in his behaviour to suggest difference. But in late 1885 or 1886, there was something of a crisis which led to Housman leaving the house he was sharing with Moses and Adalbert and prompting his move to Byron Cottage, 17 North Road, Highgate. At that point Moses Jackson was working for his doctorate in science at University College, London, from where Adalbert graduated at the end of 1884 on the way to becoming a preparatory school master.

Something then happened between Housman and Moses Jackson, described by Archie Burnett (the editor of Housman's letters and poetry) as an 'altercation', by his brother Laurence Housman as 'something which must have been in the nature of a quarrel', by Richard Perceval Graves (his biographer) as 'rejected by Moses'. According to Laurence, Housman absented himself from the house for a week. The cause could hardly have been trivial to have had such an effect. Moses and Housman had been working at the Patent Office for two to three years, time enough for Jackson to become sufficiently discontented with his work and prospects to think of seeking a new life and career abroad – a disclosure that could have caused an emotional reaction in Housman. Or had Housman declared his feelings for Moses deliberately, spontaneously or unintentionally? It does not require much imagination and empathy to see that any attempt by Housman to deliver what had long been inside him, either as a declaration or a reaction, could have been short-circuited by his own embarrassment and so, with what he had to say hardly begun, he hurriedly left the house and did not come back for a week. Or had a tentative and abortive approach by Housman been headed off with kindness and tact by a Moses, sufficiently worldly wise to realise what danger they might both be in?

We shall never know which of these scenarios was closest to the truth and we do not know what if any part Adalbert Jackson played in the scene. Apparently, Moses was as mystified as anybody else. Laurence reported that Moses had sent an anxious letter to Edward Housman saying that he did not know what had become of his son. Where did Housman go? Surely not to pace the streets or to sleep rough for a week or appear at a local hotel without luggage. Laurence was living at the time in London with their sister Clemence; there is not the slightest evidence that Housman ever appeared uninvited on their doorstep. And if his absence was all that significant, how did he avoid Jackson at the Patent Office and not feel obliged to answer questions about where he was living? Although there may be some evidence for an absence, there is none for an altercation or serious rupture or a lengthy absence.

Unfortunately, the only witness of any kind was Laurence who turns out to be a very unreliable witness. In July 1942, six years after Housman's death, he placed with the Trustees of the British Museum a packet of papers which he specified was to remain unopened for twenty-five years. It contained Laurence Housman's manuscript entitled *A.E. Housman's De Amicitia*, his brother's pocket diary for 1888 and fourteen pages he had extracted from diaries for the years 1889–1891. These papers saw the light of day in July 1967 and gave Laurence's evidence for what happened:

> From 1882 till somewhere about 1885 they shared lodgings together with Jackson's younger brother Adalbert, in Talbot Road Bayswater. In 1885 or 1886, they parted company and my brother went to live by himself at Byron Cottage Highgate. After that they met daily

at the Patent Office, and as a rule lunched together, until Jackson in December sailed for India, where he remained as Principal of a Training College at Karachi for the greater part of his life.

The shared lodging in Bayswater ended in an incident of which I do not know the full explanation. Quite suddenly, and without a word of warning, my brother, after something which must have been of the nature of a quarrel, disappeared for a week; and an anxious letter from Jackson came to his father to say that he did not know what had become of him. Whether the worst was feared I do not know. After a week's absence he returned, but only for a short time; probably the strain of such close association with a friend who could not respond with the same warmth of feeling had proved too much for him; and he found it better to part.[17]

The fact that Jackson reported Housman's absence suggests that he himself felt he had nothing to hide and was as mystified as anybody by Housman's disappearance. This supports a conclusion that Housman had said nothing of significance and that Laurence's words were pure supposition.

In a letter of 19 June 1958, when Laurence was over ninety and of even more uncertain memory, he wrote to Maud Hawkins, then working on her biography of Housman:

I still think there was more mutual attraction between these two than you give credit for. But Jackson shied away from the full implication, knowing he could not share it "in kind". But (and this is what I want you to release [realise?], his attraction to the younger brother was reciprocated.[18]

He concluded: 'I doubt whether Moses ever kissed A.E.H.: but I have no doubt that A.J.J. did.' On 21 July 1958 he wrote: 'I have no doubt whatever that A.E.H. was in a closer and warmer physical relationship with A.J.J. than with his brother Moses.'[19] John Carter concluded:

How much credence should be given to the beliefs of one who never knew either of the Jacksons at all well and who, when he made these statements was very old and very vague, readers of De Amicitia must decide for themselves. But so positive an impression from such a source cannot be wholly ignored.[20]

Of course, it can be and should be. Laurence was not remotely objective and unbiased. He had his own axe to grind. He was himself homosexual and an advocate for a more understanding and scientific attitude towards homosexuality. It was utterly preposterous for Laurence, without evidence of any kind, to suggest that Housman had gone further with Adalbert than Moses. Although he had opinions, suppositions and, one may say, fantasies, Laurence provided no facts, had no evidence and no personal knowledge of either of the Jacksons. He showed himself to be remarkably unaware of the continuing good relations between Housman, Jackson and the Jackson family, and perhaps more important, provided no evidence that he had ever seriously discussed the happenings of 1895 to 1896 with his brother. That is not to say that nothing had ever been said by Housman, because Laurence recorded that they spoke about two portraits hung over his fireplace.

> The youthful one, I learned later, was of Adalbert [the A.J.J. of poem XLII in *More Poems*]. I asked Alfred, when I was staying with him two years before his death, whose was the other. In a strangely moved voice he answered, 'That was my friend Jackson, the man who had more influence on my life than anybody else.' Only those who knew how impenetrable was my brother's reticence over personal matters, will understand how astonished I was that he should have told me that. Why did he tell me anything more than the name, unless he wished me to know?[21]

However, a more reasonable way to judge the episode of 1895 to 1896 is to consider the implications of Housman's much later self-identification with T.E. Lawrence, also quoted by Laurence.

> There was my craving to be liked – so strong and nervous that never could I open myself friendly to another. The terror of failure in an effort so important made me shrink from trying; besides, there was the standard; for intimacy seemed shameful unless the other could make the perfect reply, in the same language, after the same method, for the same reasons.[22]

Housman annotated that passage in Lawrence's *Seven Pillars of Wisdom* with 'This is me.'

Housman was in the grip of something he shrank from admitting and could not pursue further. Whatever the nature and genesis of the event, Housman's declaration could not have been of an open and frank, let alone passionate or suggestive, nature, because Moses himself was puzzled as to what Housman's departure was all about. Significantly, he did not warn off Adalbert, who continued to have a friendly relationship with Housman. Nor did Moses cease to have a friendly relationship with Housman at the Patent Office, after Housman moved to Byron Cottage.

However, Moses then put himself on a different track and moved house in the same year to Bloomfield Street. There he fell in love with the daughter of his landlord, a young widow, Rosa Chambers. The best interpretation of what happened next is the obvious one. Moses had met an attractive and desirable woman in a situation where propinquity encouraged romantic feelings. Wanting to marry, he first needed a better income and better career prospects. He realised that the Patent Office was a dead end (which it was for him as a technical expert). So, like many young men of his time, he sought fame and fortune in the British Empire. He secured and took up an appointment as Principal of Sind College, Karachi, in 1887. There is no evidence to support the alternative interpretation that Moses married the first woman he met and left the country in order to keep himself apart from Housman and avoid temptation.

But Housman, tortured by his emotional longing, intensified his idealisation of Moses. His brief diary entries demonstrate the pain he felt.[23] His meticulous recording of Moses Jackson's voyage in the steamships *Bokhara* and *Mongolia*, reinforced by his lunches with Adalbert, represented a poignant imaginative stalking of Moses through the Mediterranean, the Suez Canal and the Red Sea, through the Gulf of Aden, and then north-east across the Arabian Sea to Karachi. When their colleague Nightingale received the first letter from across the sea, Housman's careful noting of its salutation – 'very truly' – suggests a pang of jealousy. His own letter from Moses did not arrive till some four months later, to be received with a mixture of relief, sadness and maybe a little pique. He did not reply to it for a month, but then Housman never replied quickly to letters.

Diary 1888

MONDAY.	JAN:	4.	*Bokhara* arrives at Gibraltar.
SUNDAY	„	8.	*Bokhara* leaves Naples 4 p.m.
THURSDAY	„	12.	*Bokhara* arrives at Port Said.
FRIDAY	„	13.	*Mongolia* leaves Suez 11. p.m. *Bokhara* an hour later.
TUESDAY	„	17.	Add [Jackson's brother Adalbert] calls at Off: and out to lunch
WEDNESDAY	„	18.	*Mongolia* leaves Aden this evening
WEDNESDAY	„	25.	*Mongolia* arrives at Bombay this morning. (Midnight of the 24th I learn later)
WEDNESDAY	MARCH	28.	Add calls at Off: and out to lunch.
SUNDAY.	July	8.	He wrote this day to Nightingale, having seen his name in the paper as called to the bar. "My dear Nightingale" "yours very truly"
MONDAY	Nov	19.	This afternoon at Off: I receive letter, written on 28th and 31st October
FRIDAY.	December	14.	I posted letter to him.
WEDNESDAY	„	19.	His grandmother died.

For the next six months there was no mention in the diary of further correspondence, and Moses kept quiet about his intentions to marry which had been maturing for some time. Housman's 1889 diary, albeit with a few unnecessary embroideries by Laurence, revealed it. In October 1889 Moses returned on leave, not having told Housman of his intention to marry.

Diary 1889

FRIDAY.	June	28	Posted letter to him.
TUESDAY	July	9.	Nightingale has not heard from him for a long while, but wrote to him about a week ago.

TUESDAY	Oct	22.	He came to the Office: lunch he, I, MCK, [Maycock] Nghtgle. Afterwards he went with MCK into City. He dined at Nightingale's: K [Kingsford]also.
FRIDAY	Oct	25.	Went to see him 6.30 : he had just gone out to Camberwell
SATURDAY	Nov	9.	He started from Newport on a walking tour to Bletchley. I went to Cambridge.
THURSDAY	Nov.	14.	He returned to London
MONDAY	„	18	He came to see me at the office a little after 3.
WEDNESDAY	„	20	He meant to go home today.
MONDAY	Dec :	9	He was married
TUESDAY	„	10	He was to sail.
SUNDAY	„	22	He was near Perim and wrote to Add.

Diary 1890

TUESDAY	Jan	7.	I heard he was married.
THURSDAY	„	9.	I wrote to him (mail tomorrow)
FRIDAY	June	20	Wrote to him by today's mail.
THURSDAY	Oct.	2	His son born
WEDNESDAY	„	29	His son's birth in the paper.
FRIDAY	Nov	7	I write to him by this day's mail

In 1889 Moses had come back on leave to marry Rosa in December of that year. Housman was not invited to the wedding, which has been interpreted as evidence of Moses' rejection of Housman; but there is no evidence that Housman felt rejected or even felt that he ought to have been invited. Moses' wedding may properly have been restricted to family and friends and there is no evidence that anybody else from the Patent Office, for example their boss or any of their colleagues such as Maycock, Nightingale or Kingsford, were invited. Jackson's first son was born in October 1890, ten months after the wedding.

Figure 10 Rosa Jackson, wife of Moses Jackson.
By permission of the Jackson family.

There was one further entry in his diary for 1891 but it related to a subsequent year, 1898. Under Friday 22 May 1891 the entry reads 'Sunday 1898, 10.45.p.m. said goodbye.' In *De Amicitia* Laurence says that this entry refers to Moses Jackson. 'This meeting must have taken place when Jackson was once more home on leave from India.' By then, three of Moses' sons had been born and *A Shropshire Lad* had been published two years previously. Laurence's interpretation of the entry: 'That was the concluding word to the emotional part of his life; after that there is no mention.' One can see how Housman had now to accept the reality of Moses' fruitful life with Rosa and time would show how he reshaped his devotion to encompass these facts of life.

Renewed impetus in scholarship

Housman's period of anguish did not immobilise him. His intellectual activity nourished him and took on a renewed impetus. In 1887 Housman, moving from Latin to Greek texts, had launched himself in the *Classical Review* with a paper on passages in Euripides' *Electra and Euripides.* In December of the next year he published for the first time in the *American Journal of Philology* an article titled 'On certain Corruptions in the Persae of Aeschylus'. Once again, he set himself up against 'most commentators'; championing the work of a relatively obscure German scholar, he delivered penetrating literary common sense and displayed his mastery of word confusions and mistakes committed by scribes in old manuscripts.

Whether or not Moses' departure had spurred him to lose himself in classical studies, the year 1888 was something of an *annus mirabilis.* The *Classical Review* published three of his papers on Greek texts. Housman had begun his text and *apparatus criticus* of Propertius when he was an undergraduate, completed it in December 1885 and submitted it to Macmillan for publication the same month, only to have it rejected. Now, anxious to display his work, he published thirty-five pages of 'Emendationes Propertianae' in the *Journal of Philology.*

> I have some desire to put my corrections on record, as I am for ever seeing them forstalled by other students. ... Mr Konrad Rossberg ... has bereft me of no less than nine. True it is agreeable enough to have one's results confirmed by a scholar who stands next to Mr Baehrens and Mr Palmer at the head of living Propertius critics; but I should like to retain something of my own. ... I have added an examination in detail of the first elegy.[24]

His morality as a scholar

His paper was a tour de force listing 243 separate amendments, including lines which he argues should be moved to another place, a handful of lines that 'have no business here', or 'have no part in this poem', new lines to replace lost lines, and some vitally transforming alterations to punctuation. But he was also scrupulous: 'I hope I have managed to keep my neighbour's goods out of this catalogue, but I dare hardly expect it ... To anyone who will enable me to restore misappropriated discoveries to their rightful owner I shall be honestly indebted.'[25] Both his introduction and conclusion are stamped with Housman's morality. He did not wish to steal other men's work or claim theirs for his own. He wished to give recognition to precursors. And what he began to reveal in this long paper was a truly astonishing grasp of previous authorities, ancient and modern, and his capacity to discriminate.

He developed his moral position and an outline of desiderata for classical scholarship in another paper in the *Journal of Philology* of the same year, titled 'The Agamemnon of Aeschylus':

> Thanks to Wecklein it is at length possible to study Aeschylus in comfort. Next to an accurate collation of the cardinal MSS, a complete register of the conjectures of critics is the student's prime requisite. Nothing short of a complete register will serve: no man can be trusted to sift good from bad; some editors do not know a correction when they see one, others through childish jealousy of this scholar or that ignores his discoveries, the most candid and the soundest judgement is human and errs. The time lost, the tissues wasted, in doing anew the brainwork done before him by others, and all for lack of a book like Wecklein's Appendix, are in our brief irreparable life disheartening to think of.

He goes on:

> In the ensuing pages I have not set down all or nearly all the corrections which I imagine myself to have made in the Agamemnon. I know how easily one is satisfied with one's own conjectures. I have arraigned the MSS only where their delinquencies can be made as clear as daylight, and I have proposed only corrections which I think may possibly convince others as well as myself.[26]

This paper also underlined his grasp of palaeography, of scribal errors and confusions:

> errors of the ear to which copyists are subject. ... The confusion of an aspirate with its tenuis [voiceless stop] is among the commonest of errors of the ear to which copyists are subject. ... Another of their favourite tricks is to reverse the order of two consecutive letters. ... the more unfamiliar a word is to a copyist the more likely he is to corrupt it.[27]

In a later paper for the *Classical Review* of 1889, 'Notes on The Latin Poets', he says that 'One of the absurdities by which the overworked brain of the copyist avenges itself on the author copied is that inversion of two syllables which transforms d-*er-it* into d-*it-er*'[28]; he provides a handful of examples.

Copyists could spend long hours in cold rooms. Monasteries and libraries were not well lit, not required by law to keep work rooms at comfortable ambient temperatures, and copyists could suffer from failing hearing, poor sight or imperfect brain/hand coordination. Incorrect copying, writing over manuscripts, wilfully readjusting the text of a predecessor's script, inserting the wrong word in gaps in the text or where manuscripts were illegible, were all occupational hazards. Copyists' errors are still alive and well. Common experience with proof readers and in word processing reveal that individuals can have inbuilt error habits. These may stem from ignorance of the subject matter and language, failure in their personal methodology or from inbuilt dyslexic tendencies. Housman, still only thirty, was already showing mastery of all these issues, including the differences between ancient scripts and the habits of various scribes. He was already demonstrating a seemingly complete grasp of classical dictionaries and the incidence of words in ancient texts. This grasp of words, grammar and metre was accompanied by an understanding of human situations and motivations, a feeling for what the poet was about, parallels in other poets, and an acute ear for metre and its music. He revealed yet again the breadth of his knowledge of other authorities and handed out compliments such as 'this easy and graceful emendation of Bamberger's... Lighted by this and Mr Margoliouth's beautiful restoration. ... Hermann with high probability writes....'[29]

True to his own values he published a further note on Propertius in the same year, acknowledging that eleven of his emendations had been anticipated by others and giving names and references: 'The three living scholars will, I hope, accept my apologies.' Another six references are mentioned as being 'more or less in common with my own'.[30]

He kept his papers flowing and in 1889 published three further papers in the *Classical Review*. The volume and quality of his work was now clearly making an impact on its editor, John Postgate. There were two outcomes. In October 1889 Postgate proposed Housman's election to the Cambridge Philological Society, where Housman presented 'Emendations in Ovid's Metamorphoses' as his first paper. Then he invited Housman to review T.G. Tucker's *The Supplices of Aeschylus*, published in 1889 by Macmillan. Housman was now respected as an authoritative scholar and admired as a cogent and elegant writer. How would he rise to the challenge? His opening words on Tucker's book were very warm.

> This edition gives proof of many virtues, common sense, alert perception, lucidity of thought, impatience of absurdity, a rational distrust of MS tradition, and a masculine taste in things poetical. The learner who attacks the play with this commentary will find unfailing help by the way and acquire much information before his journey's end. The old miserable experiences of the classical student who wants to understand what he reads, his lonely fights with difficulties whose presence the editor has never apprehended, his fruitless quest of a meaning in notes where the editor has rendered Greek nonsense into English nonsense and gone on his way rejoicing, are not repeated here. Here on the contrary is a commentator who shares the reader's difficulties, rescues him from some of them, warns him of some existing unperceived, and to tell the truth invents a good many where none exists.[31]

That sting in the tail may or not have been justified, but combined with his praise, it was the means by which Housman established his own superiority.

Another review for the *Classical Review* quickly followed, this time an American professor's edition of Euripides' *Iphigenia among the Taurians*. He gave Professor Flagg a generally kind review, albeit with a mildly chauvinistic overtone: 'here and there the taste of an islander is offended by a style which breathes the ampler ether and diviner air of America, but otherwise it is only details that challenge demur'. He is amused by the professor's 'Priestess and victim have been revealed to one another as sister and brother, and forget their peril in transports of emotion; Pylades now interposes to remind them where they stand. Professor Flagg hits off the situation with Columbian vivacity by saying that Pylades "calls time."'[32]

It had become abundantly clear that from the beginning Housman's scholarly writings had their own persuasive and engaging voice. It was the frequently amused voice of the relaxed observer of other men's foibles – at times tongue-in-cheek, at times the flavour of the undergraduate joker or satirist – all expressed in a prose of such undeniable lucidity, economy and fluency that the reader was impelled to follow it to its conclusion. It was scholarship wrapped in a siren's song; polemic of a charming directness.

In the four years between 1887 and 1891 his publications amounted to twenty-five separate papers, more than two hundred printed pages in total. Housman was about to prove that fortune favours the prepared mind and that he made his own good luck.

PART IV

Re-entry to the academic life

The leap that Housman now made from the bondage of the Patent Office seems so extraordinary and reveals so much about how Housman was seen by others that it needs to be laid out in all its glory.

On 15 February 1892 W.P. Ker, who had been appointed Quain Professor of English Language and Literature at University College London in 1889, became the key that unlocked the door of the Patent Office and enabled Housman to escape and re-enter the formal world of classical scholarship. Alfred Godwin, Professor of Greek and Latin, had died earlier in the month, and Ker had been appointed chairman of a committee 'to consider the whole question of the teaching of both Latin and Greek at the college'. A shake–up was intended and Ker was just the man to see it through. Within a week his committee had produced its report. It opted for a professor in each subject. These professorships were advertised in the newspapers on 19 March, applications had to be in by the end of April, appointments were expected to be made by June and the new professors would take up their posts in October 1892.

The status and opportunity provided by the posts had obvious and intrinsic attractions for Housman but appointment would also represent improvement in his personal finances. According to the handout:

> The income of each chair will be derived (1) from a share of the Class fees; (2) a Special Grant of £250 per annum. Of this Grant £150 is guaranteed by the Council for five years only, while £100 may be considered as a permanent endowment. The share of Class fees belonging to the Professor of Latin may be reckoned at £186 per ann., the average of the last three sessions. For the same period the average amount belonging to the Professor of Greek is £188 per ann.

Figure 11 W.P. Ker, Chairman of the University
College London committee charged with
the appointment of new professors of Greek
and Latin in 1892. By permission of College
Collection Photos, UCL Library Services,
Special Collections.

By now Housman was on his maximum of £400 a year at the Patent
Office so a ten per cent increase in pay to £436 a year would be a
significant incentive to add to the other attractions of the post. As to
work load:

> it is estimated that the duties of the Professor will require his
> attendance at the College for some hours of each day on five days
> of the week ... The Professors will have the option of delivering
> special courses of lectures on subjects connected with the study
> of Greek and Latin literature ... will be expected, should it be
> found desirable, to give courses in the evening in order to provide
> instruction for students who by reason of their occupation as
> Schoolmasters, or otherwise, find it impossible to attend ordinary
> College lectures ... The Professors of Latin and Greek, as members
> of the Faculty of Arts and of the Senate of University College, will
> be expected to take an active part in the work of these bodies.[1]

Of course, University College, London, was not as prestigious as an Oxford or Cambridge college, and its 'courses in the evening' give something of the flavour of further education. It would not have a flow of such able students as the classics stream in those ancient universities but Housman was not about to be made a professor at either of those places.

These points had been made by one of the members of Ker's committee, the headmaster of University College School, Henry Eve, who submitted a minority report objecting to the committee's intention to

> withdraw money from other purposes to subsidize the study of Classics at the College. The greater part of the Classical Professors' work is, at present, necessarily 'pass' work: in advanced classical teaching it is scarcely possible to compete with Oxford and Cambridge, with their large body of classical teachers and classical prizes.

He went on: 'Classics, with every chance in their favour, have hitherto proved comparatively unattractive to our *clientele* and can hardly claim exceptional encouragement on other grounds.'[2] Eve was all for lumping Greek and Latin together under a single professor aided by an assistant, as was the case with Chemistry and Physics. Eve's minority report received no support. Ker had won the day.

Although Ker would play a large part in driving the project forward, the key selector was undoubtedly John Percival Postgate, then Professor of Comparative Philology at University College and a fellow of Trinity College, Cambridge, where he was lecturer in classics. Remembered by his son as 'a rather short, dominant man, with prominent blue eyes and a walrus moustache', and described in the *Dictionary of National Biography* as 'a kind of rude natural force to be reckoned with', Postgate would be knocked off his bicycle by a lorry in Cambridge in 1926, and would utter the highly practical last words: 'Take me to Addenbrooks, I have a subscription there.' Now it so happened that Postgate was editor of the *Classical Review* and thus his stock-in-trade was to be deeply conversant with the published work of all the candidates, including Housman. Even more important, Postgate knew Housman personally and had proposed him for membership of the Cambridge Philological Society at which Housman had read his paper 'Emendations in Ovid's Metamorphoses'

Figure 12 John Postgate, Professor of
Comparative Philology at University
College London and member of the
committee that appointed Housman.
© National Portrait Gallery, London.

in October 1889. Two years later he had asked Housman to edit Ovid's
Ibis for his *Corpus Poetarum Latinorum* which provided texts and
critical commentary on the Latin poets. Postgate, an organisation
man if ever there was one, was instrumental in the formation of the
Classical Association of England and Wales, was its joint secretary
and later president. It was part of his make-up to recruit and
influence others. He could attest to Housman's mental capacity. He
had heard him deliver papers to the Cambridge Philological Society
and could speak of his capacity in front of an audience, as well as his
ability to deliver on time. Being six years older and an established
figure, Postgate could also afford to patronise the younger Housman.
So it is highly likely that he gave Housman early warning of the
proposed appointment. By the time the positions were advertised in
the newspapers Housman had already approached several potential
supporters for testimonials; having Postgate behind him could be a
key advantage.

Housman applies for the post of Professor of Latin at University College

The seventeen testimonials assembled by Housman and printed for him by the Cambridge University Press were covered by a single introductory page, both skilful and scrupulous. His curriculum vitae included his scholarship to St John's, his First in Classical Moderations, and without excuse, his failure to obtain honours in the final school of Literae Humaniores, his pass degree, his sixth form teaching at Bromsgrove School, and his Higher Division Clerkship at the Patent Office obtained in open competition. Then came the core of his letter, a simple record of his decade of extraordinary achievement, the titles of eleven of his most important contributions to learned journals over the previous ten years on Latin and Greek subjects. What he promised was modest: 'If I am honoured by your choice I shall give my best endeavours to the fulfilment of my duties and to the maintenance of accurate learning in University College.'[3]

In the matter of testimonials any selector worth his salt has to be skilled in judging their reality, noting what was not said as much as what was said, reading between the lines, and if necessary seeing through them. In Housman's case that would not be a problem. His published material made it self-evident that he could meet the core scholarly requirements of any professorship of Latin anywhere, let alone University College, London. The names of those from whom he sought testimonials was a roll-call of the great and good in the world of classical scholarship, evidence of his conviction that he had earned the right to ask them to speak for him. In the event, their testimony was authentically enthusiastic and provided an unanswerable case for offering Housman the post.

I am reproducing their testimonials, as published by Paul Naiditch, virtually in their entirety because they shed such important light on how his reputation stood and, in particular, on the breadth of the capacities and talents he was perceived to possess.

Henry Nettleship, Corpus Professor of Latin at Oxford wrote:

> He has in my opinion, very remarkable qualifications for the post; I may say, indeed that his peculiar gifts seem to me to deserve, in an especial way, public recognition in England. His love for classical literature is as powerful and dominating as his gifts are

original. He has a remarkable talent for conjectural emendation; a talent of which he has given ample proof in various articles and essays published in the Journal of Philology and elsewhere ... He has given special attention to Propertius; and whatever verdict may ultimately be given to his proposed solutions of problems which have hitherto appeared insoluble, there can be no doubt that he is master of the whole literature of the subject ... Mr Housman's critical articles and essays are always delightful reading. His literary tact, his vein of humour, and lightness of touch never fail to enliven the driest subject, and would, I am sure, prove as attractive in his lectures as they are in his writing ... I think it would be difficult to find a stronger candidate for this post than Mr Housman.

John Mayor, Professor of Latin at Cambridge wrote:

I have read many of Mr A.E. Housman's critical papers, and believe that he has been able, with very slight alteration, to restore sense to passages, even in so familiar an author as Horace, which have hitherto defied the skill of interpreters ... I should expect that Mr Housman would prove a stimulating teacher, whose pupils would learn to examine the grounds on which rational criticism must rest.

Robert Tyrrell, Professor of Greek at Trinity College, Dublin, wrote:

I have never met Mr Housman. Some years ago I was so much struck by the brilliancy of some emendations of his published in one of the learned journals that I introduced myself to him by letter and since that time I have frequently corresponded with him on classical criticism. I have more than once made for myself an opportunity to express in print my admiration for his criticism.

Arthur Palmer, former Professor of Latin at Trinity College, Dublin, wrote:

I have been for some years acquainted with the essays and reviews written by Mr A.E. Housman on Latin and Greek subjects ... and I do not know that there is any scholar living who shews greater brilliancy, learning, and acumen in discussing the most difficult problems in ancient literature ... Mr Housman's position is in the very first rank of scholars and critics.

Lewis Campbell, Professor of Greek at St Andrews, was another judging him exclusively on his published papers.

> They evince great acuteness, ingenuity and originality of mind, together with minute and accurate knowledge, especially of Classical Literature ... his work as a teacher would be recommended by his skill in translation, of which his rendering of Greek Tragic Choruses in Mr Pollard's selection give remarkable proof. Each of them, besides being close and faithful, is in itself a gem of literary art.

This was a group of massively supportive testimonials produced by the leading authorities on classical scholarship in the British Isles, with no evasions, no weasel words, no requirement for reading between the lines. All were demonstrably united in their admiration for Housman's actual achievements and all from foundations well above University College, London, in the academic pecking order.

Next came men who had known him and taught him at Oxford, like Herbert Warren, President of Magdalen College, who referred to him as 'my old friend and sometime pupil'. There was no doubt of the mark Housman had made on him:

> I still cherish a most vivid recollection of the strong impression which he made upon me. He was certainly to me one of the most interesting and attractive pupils I can remember. He had even then, as quite a young student, a combination of force, acumen and taste which I shall never forget, and I have preserved and still possess exercises of his which show these qualities in a marked degree.

Warren made little of his failure at Oxford.

> Mr Housman has, despite great difficulties, won himself a very real position as a scholar, and I believe that he has convincingly shewn that he is a man who, if placed where he could do so, would advance and add to English scholarship, and indeed that it would be a real loss to us if he has not this opportunity.

Robinson Ellis, University Reader in Latin at Oxford, had taught Housman and it has to be said that as an undergraduate Housman had had no great opinion of him. In writing his testimonial Ellis seemed to have forgiven his appearance in Housman's anonymous skit *The Eleventh Eclogue*. Perhaps like many butts of humour he felt flattered to be thus singled out and publicised. Housman had probably also attended Ellis' classes on Propertius in 1879, the year in which Housman began seriously to study the poet, and he may have played some part in arousing Housman's interest. Housman had subsequently sent Ellis a copy of his own work on Propertius before Macmillan rejected it in December 1885. However, Gilbert Murray remembered 'Bobby [Ellis] told me he did not think it was a good edition at all. "But to encourage Housman I wrote him a long letter carefully explaining all my reasons for thinking him wrong." But, said Bobby, gazing at me with pained astonished eyes, "he did not like it at all!"'[4]

In the present situation Ellis' testimonial was important to Housman because Ellis had had a few years as Professor of Latin at University College. Housman may not have known, however, that a testimonial by Ellis could be something of a two-edged sword. Ellis' reputation at the college was not good. He 'was not successful with the larger and less advanced classes there and returned to Oxford'.[5] In the event, Ellis wrote a conspicuously supportive testimonial, linked strongly to what he regarded as the needs for teaching at University College:

> Being always very pronounced in his convictions, he would impress them with more positiveness on his hearers than a professor of perhaps equal knowledge, but less ascertained views; and this is, in its way, an advantage in dealing with a youthful audience such as are most of the students at University College. Mr Housman, besides being decided in his attitude towards difficulties of scholarship, is clear and defined in expressing his own point of view: in a teacher this is generally thought to be, and undoubtedly is, a very important qualification.

In spite of this highly practical evaluation of Housman's likely impact on students, Ellis could not entirely suppress the underlying music of his disapproval for Housman's attitudes.

Housman's former tutor at St John's, Thomas Snow, wrote the shortest of the testimonials. He cannot have remembered Housman with much pleasure, and maybe with a little guilt as a talented pupil of his who had been ploughed in Greats, although J.T. Nance believed Snow was the teacher from whom Housman learned most.[6] He may also have recognised that Housman had made the right choice in neglecting the Greats syllabus to concentrate on Propertius and textual criticism, the rightness of which had become self-evident. Obviously impressed by his former pupil's self-direction, persistence and determination, Snow recognised that

> in the midst of other employments, he has made many remarkable contributions to our knowledge of several authors, both in Greek and in Latin. In all his writings on classical subjects there is a singular union of brilliancy, learning and sound common sense. I am quite sure that, as a professor, he would add a new distinction to the name of University College, not only in England but in the learned world of Europe.

Adding breadth to his application were testimonials from Herbert Millington, his old headmaster, always an unequivocal supporter, and Alfred Pollard, then Assistant in the Department of Printed Books in the British Museum. Housman had mentioned in his letter of application his translations from the Attic tragedies into English verse in Pollard's *Odes from the Greek Dramatists*. He had written to Pollard, explaining that he had influential backing as regards his competence as a Latin scholar, and all he wanted was a few words on his power of expressing himself in English. Pollard fulfilled his remit exactly and wrote:

> Your brilliant emendations in Propertius, Aeschylus and other authors have never been the outcome of mere philological ingenuity: they have always been controlled by a keen appreciation of the poetical requirements of the passages before you. Again, a year ago when I was asking the help of various poets and scholars to do justice in English verse to the beauty of some of the great Choral Odes of Greek tragedy, the three translations you were good enough to send me were singled out, both by reviewers and by many of your fellow-contributors for special praise.[7]

Then there was a broad group of supporters from Cambridge. Henry Jackson, Joint Editor of the Cambridge *Journal of Philology* and as a fellow and praelector in Ancient Philosophy at Trinity College,

Cambridge, would, in the fullness of time, prove like Ker to be a force behind Housman's progression. He wrote of Housman:

> his scholarship is both sound and brilliant. His work is remarkable for tact, judgement and acumen. His exposition is always clear and forcible. I conceive that a scholar such as Mr Housman, at once thoroughly equipped and keenly interested in classical learning, could hardly fail to be a stimulating teacher.

Arthur Verrall, Professor of English at Cambridge, spoke the truth and pointed out the obvious: 'he can scarcely require any other testimony than his own work ... his translation ... equally conspicuous for fidelity and for elegance.'

Finally, to demonstrate the extent of Housman's geographical reach were two foreign testimonials, one from Basil Gildersleeve, Professor of Greek at Johns Hopkins University and editor of the *American Journal of Philology*, and one from Dr Nikolaus Wecklein, a noted German scholar at Munich.

These testimonials are quoted at length so that full justice is done to Housman's ten years of achievement in the academic wilderness. He had secured for himself a credibility among scholars that was frankly unparalleled. He was not regarded as an amateur or dilettante but was regarded as a totally credible part of the academic world and well on the way to fulfilling all the desiderata for a scholar of great reputation.

What distinguished Housman from his eighteen competitor candidates was not only his consistently luminous testimonials but the uniqueness of his candidature. In the words of Ker's report[8] he was 'the most remarkable of all the candidates. He has made for himself a reputation in pure scholarship by his published work, especially by his emendations, this work being the product of his leisure, and unconnected with any professional duties. He is at present a Clerk in the Patent Office.' Housman had made a powerful personal impact on Ker and his committee. He had expressed his views with credibility. The key words in the report say as much: 'The committee were strongly impressed, in their interview with Mr Housman, by his evident interest in teaching, as well as by the good sense and strength of character shown by him on that occasion.' They obviously respected him, liked him and were attracted by the thought of him as a colleague and thus had no difficulty in accepting his frank explanation for his academic failure: 'This failure may be attributed to his exclusive interest in scholarship, and his want of interest in some of the other subjects of the School of Literae Humaniores.' They concluded that 'the election of Housman will bring to the College a scholar of exceptional attainments, and a lecturer who will attract students, and may help to form a brilliant classical school.'

June 1892: Elected Professor of Latin

Thus did Ker and his committee create new impetus for classical studies at University College London when Housman was elected Professor of Latin. On the first day of October 1892 Housman resigned from the Patent Office. His long apprenticeship was over.

A letter from Maycock

The Patent Office does not seem to have provided a farewell occasion for him but his departure produced a most important document and one which he cherished for the rest of his life. It was a letter from J. Maycock, a colleague at the Patent Office, found by Laurence after his brother's death. He recorded that he found Maycock's letter laid alongside Jackson's 'last letter' as if to signify its special importance. Unfortunately, Laurence Housman's characteristic carelessness was extended to this letter; his printed version does not match the autograph letter now in the Seymour Adelman Collection, which is reproduced here:

> I got your testimonials this morning, and shortly afterwards I found that your name was in *The Times* as Professor of Latin to London University. I am as delighted with your success as though I had got something for myself. Now mind, that's saying as much as one can say about anyone else's good fortune. Webb's remark that your success was a score for the Office excited my anger. I told him that it was a score for you, and that it was nothing at all for the infernal Office. It is funny to think how I used to chaff you about your work producing no money, and all the time you were working silently on, with that strength of purpose which I can admire but cannot imitate. I suppose the work will be more congenial to you than any official work could ever be. As a rule English people never allow themselves to say or write what they think about anyone, no matter how much of a pal he may

be. Well, I am going to let myself loose. I like you better than any man I ever knew. There is, as far as I could ever discover, absolutely no flaw in your character as a man, and no one would ever hope for a better friend. I don't say this only on my own account; but I have seen how you can stick to a friend like you have to Jackson. I mean stick to him in the sentimental sense of not forgetting him although he is right out of your reach. I have always, besides liking you so much, had a great respect for your learning. I always do respect a man who can do anything well. Now your work has produced for you substantial honour, I feel proud of your success, and I hope you will be much happier altogether. I know you must naturally feel proud. If you don't you are a duffer. One doesn't get too many moments of elation in this life, so don't check the feeling when you have it. The testimonials are wonderfully good. At one o'clock or thereabouts, Kingsford and I will drink a glass of the Old Falernian to your long life and increasing prosperity. Dear old pal, I'm as pleased as if I had done something good myself.[9]

That was a lovely letter, one to cherish and one of the most important Housman documents, confirming how he came across to those who knew him well, confirming the affection he could engender in others, confirming his modesty, confirming his sterling personal qualities. It deserved to be treasured. And Housman's motive in thus treasuring it may have been as simple as the reaction of a notably reticent man to a letter telling him in no uncertain terms that he was liked and admired.

Laurence Housman may be forgiven for finding the signature undecipherable, but on the Adelman autograph it is perfectly readable as J. Maycock. And the ever-careless Laurence omitted to mention the writing across the top left-hand corner – 'Kitty and George Vize shall know of this. They'll be as pleased as I am' – indicating the existence of an extended group with whom Housman had a good personal connection. Maycock's letter also made two references to testimonials: 'I got your testimonials this morning' and 'The testimonials are wonderfully good.' One presumes Maycock had asked Housman how he had managed to land the job and Housman had sent him the testimonials, to show how his work was judged by distinguished professors and scholars. This might have been rather uncharacteristic of Housman had he not become close to Maycock and his family. He sent their son Henry Vize Maycock a copy of

Robert Louis Stevenson's story for boys, *The Black Arrow* (and would send Maycock himself an inscribed copy of the first edition of *A Shropshire Lad)*. Their relationship was probably close, and probably kept sparking by their shared enjoyment of humorous verse and Maycock's capacity to produce it; verses which appeared in *The Sportsman* of 9 March 1882 have been confidently ascribed to him.[10] *The Blue Fever (with apologies to Mr W.S. Gilbert)* ran as follows:

> If you want a receipt for that popular mystery,
> Known to the world as a Varsity crew,
> Take all the redoubtable athletes in history,
> Tub them and coach them and clothe them in blue.

Introductory Lecture at University College

University College customarily opened its academic year with a professorial lecture to the united faculties of the college. As the most recently appointed professor, Housman was first choice and had to rise to his feet on 3 October 1892.

He began by asking his audience a perennial question, which boiled down to: 'What are we here for?' He set up his straw men: on the one hand, the partisans of science for whom learning was utility; the popular view of science as 'equipping oneself for the business of life' and incidentally encouraging businessmen to put money into scientific education; on the other hand, the partisans of Humane Letters who set out to transform and beautify our inner nature by culture. He demonstrated that none of these positions could hold water. As ever he was totally resistant to general formulations, or special pleading: 'This is too much the language of salesmen crying their own wares', or setting one stream of learning against another. 'There is no rivalry between the studies of Arts and Laws and Science but the rivalry of fellow-soldiers in striving which can most victoriously achieve the common end of all, to set back the frontier of darkness.' He chose to build on the Aristotelian idea that 'all men possess by nature a craving for knowledge', and that the good being aimed for is learning for its own sake. Housman's colleagues were listening to a man with a richly stocked mind, anchored in common sense and reality, a rounded man, a wise man, a man of conviction who could use his words persuasively. His lecture was well lubricated with wit and humour, and demonstrated a determination not to take either himself or his subject too seriously:

And as a man should always magnify his own office, nothing could be more natural or agreeable to me than to embrace this opinion and to deliver here a panegyric of the Humanities and especially of that study on which the Humanities are founded, the study of the dead languages of Greece and Rome. I am deterred from doing so, in the first place because it is possible that a partisan harangue of that sort might not be relished by the united Faculties of Arts, Laws and Science; and secondly because to tell the truth I do not much believe in these supposed effects of classical studies. I do not believe that the proportion of the human race whose inner nature the study of the classics will specially beautify and transform is large; and I am quite sure that the proportion of the human race on whom the classics will confer that benefit can attain the desired end without that minute and accurate study of the classical tongues which affords Latin Professors their only excuse for existing.[11]

As a newcomer he had positioned himself perfectly but much later he would describe his lecture as 'rhetorical and not wholly sincere'. Quite why he should take that view remains obscure. Ker thought the lecture was 'very clever'. Perhaps it depended too much on a stereotypical view of things. Rhetorical it was, and had to be, in order to make an impact, but it is difficult to see where it was not genuine, honest or free from pretence. He was speaking out of his own feelings and out of his own convictions, not setting up any kind of academic imagery or smokescreen, which could have been insincere. He was also communicating his own motivation. The word 'happiness' was used several times, most powerfully when he said 'Our true occupation is to manufacture from the raw material of life the fabric of happiness.' What Housman did made him happy. There was, too, an autobiographical connection which may have been conscious or unconscious. 'Other desires become the occasion of pain through dearth of the material to gratify them, but not the desire of knowledge: the sum of things to be known is inexhaustible, and however long we read we shall never come to the end of our story-book.' Housman was demonstrating to his new colleagues that he was a force to be reckoned with, and was simultaneously renewing his vows to scholarship, his version of 'Till death do us part'.

Housman now had responsibilities for assisting in the governance of the College. He would not become a member of the Council, the supreme authority, until 1897. But by his recent election he automatically became a member of the Senate which was responsible for the academic business of the College through the committees it created, and he was naturally a member of the Faculty of Arts. This administrative burden was not excessive. But unlike some of his colleagues, Housman was a regular attender at Senate meetings. These took up a late afternoon of his time for about five to eight times a year in his early years. Showing no signs of hesitancy in coming forward, Housman was immediately appointed to a committee for selecting a new Professor of History, and a committee considering retiring allowances for professors. On both of these committees he served with Professor Herbert Foxwell, an economist with whom he maintained a friendship for the rest of his life.

Although not the convener, he wrote the report of the committee which selected a replacement for Professor Wyse, Professor of Greek, appointed at the same time as Housman. Contrary to the hopes of Ker, Wyse did not last long at University College and found the attractions of a fellowship at Trinity College, Cambridge, impossible to resist. His replacement was Arthur Platt, a man with whom Housman was *sympathique*. They came to like and admire each other greatly.

Moses Jackson had in effect vanished from Housman's life but Housman was showing no inclination to let him go. Jackson again returned on leave in 1894 and sought election to a fellowship at University College. Housman's submission to the Fellowship Committee was pithily eloquent and hard to resist:

> I believe that if he had been caught young and kept away from chemicals and electric batteries and such things, he might have been made into a classical scholar. Even now in spite of his education, his knowledge of Liddell and Scott's Greek Lexicon has often filled me with admiring envy. He also, when his blood is up, employs the English language with a vigour and elegance which is much beyond the generality either of classical scholars or of men of science.[12]

Jackson was elected. By this time, Jackson and Housman had built bridges which must have stemmed essentially from Housman's capacity to accept the unchangeable. On that same leave Alfred Pollard and his wife invited them both for dinner and an overnight stay. Pollard later reported that 'When I retired to rest, I found an apple-pie bed awaiting me and I think the Professor of Latin was a fellow-victim, though I am not quite sure that he wasn't an aggressor. Anyhow we became very youthful and light-hearted.'[13]

Possessed by the muse: The poetic eruption of 1894–95

Nothing in Housman's juvenilia had suggested precocious poetic talent, neither the poems which gained him prizes at Bromsgrove School, nor his entry for the Newdigate Prize at Oxford. They produced occasional glimpses of his sense of the transitory nature of life. His nonsense verse was streaked with cynicism, barbed wit and *schadenfreude*. But in 1886, the year in which he moved to the solitude of Byron Cottage, he began ten poems. For three years he produced nothing new. Then, in 1890, he began four more; in 1891, six; in 1892, three; in 1893, thirteen; then in 1894 his accelerating poetic urge produced sixteen poems; and in 1895 he began seventy-five new poems. Housman referred to the process of his poetry-making as a 'secretion' but this pattern of production seems more like the subterranean grumble of an awakening volcano, that finally produced an eruption of poetic emotion. Over the whole period 1886 to 1895 he produced a grand total of 127 (some finished, many unfinished), out of which he selected a mere 63 for publication.

Housman's poetic impulse of 1886 to 1895 was so fertile that it produced enough poems for him to publish *A Shropshire Lad* in 1896 and about half the poems he later included in *Last Poems* in 1922. After his death, almost two-thirds of the poems Laurence resurrected from Housman's notebooks and published in *More Poems* in 1936, and two-thirds of the poems Laurence published in 1937 as *Additional Poems,* dated from this period. Of Housman's total output of 197 poems, almost two-thirds had been conceived in those early years, mainly between 1894 and 1895. Most of his drafts would be worked up over a number of years so the sequence of his first drafts is the true way of tracking the sequence of his emerging poetic thought and feeling.

Genesis of Housman's poetry

What was the genesis of Housman's poetry? To say he was suddenly possessed by his muse is metaphorically correct but not biographically accurate. He was primarily reacting to a crisis in his emotional life, responding to his discovery of himself as sexually different and recognising his deep attachment to Moses Jackson. At the time, he did not intellectualize. There was no thinking about past or present poetic models.

The undeniable fact is that poetry came into his head as he walked over Hampstead Heath. In that he was no different from many other walkers, be they poets, writers, quantum physicists or philosophers. Coleridge, Wordsworth, Tennyson, Paul Dirac the scientist, and Kierkegaard the philosopher, were men whose creative life came into action with the tread of their feet. Their ideas sprang from nowhere, like hidden flowers coming to light, startled deer running, trout rising, grouse suddenly whirring into the air on a high moor. Coleridge said that 'At certain times, uncalled and sudden, subject to no bidding of my own or others, these Thoughts would come upon me, like a Storm, & fill the Place with something more than Nature.'[14] During his walks Housman's mind emptied itself of scholarly preoccupations, and left itself open to being invaded. Sometimes, no doubt, unbidden ideas related to his academic life also came to him, perhaps in the form of a phrase he could use to take an academic competitor to task.

Certainly, there was no point of contact between his life as a professor of Latin and his poetry. His personal emotional reaction to the tones of Horace's ode *Diffugere Nives* (the snows are fled) was real but did not prompt him to find an outlet in translating Latin or Greek poetry as an indirect way of expressing what was going on inside him. Propertius' love for Cynthia did not provide him with parallels for his attachment to Moses Jackson. He was not sparked off to translate *The Iliad* like Alexander Pope, or use the friendship of Achilles and Patroclus to illustrate his own life.

From the beginning, he was his own man. In spite of the impressions they had made on him he did not feel impelled to follow the musicality of Tennyson, the erotic sensuality of Swinburne or the elegiac mood of Matthew Arnold. He had absorbed much poetry but none of it turned out to have imprinted on him a poetic model. He had nothing in common with any of the poetic currents swirling past him – not with Thomas Hardy whose scope, reach and poetic ambition far outreached his own; not with Rudyard Kipling, whose earthy soldiers portrayed in *Barrack Room Ballads* had nothing in common with his own symbolic soldier lads; not, of course, with religious poets like Gerard Manley Hopkins, or Francis Thompson who published *The Hound of Heaven* in 1893; not at all with another set of poets headed by Ernest

Dowson, sometimes labelled as 'Decadents', generally Francophiles, whose poetry had received nourishment from Baudelaire's *Les Fleurs du Mal*, and more recently from Rimbaud and Mallarmé; and not at all with the towering figure of his time, Oscar Wilde, aesthete, wit, playwright, poseur, brilliant at conversation and self-promotion, but also inhabiting a different poetic planet from Housman.

Housman's poetry harked back much farther to the simplicities of thought and expression of the old English ballads and to strains from medieval *pastourelles.* He was in effect transplanting his economical and precise prose style into verse. What was in his mind and what appeared on the page was unobscured by poetic ornament or poetic theory. He was one of the least self-conscious poets one might find. Although a contemporary of T.S. Eliot and James Joyce and a contemporary of 'Decadents' like Wilde and Symons, and although the social, economic and political context of their lives was the context of his own, Housman had none of their theories, probably because he never had to make his way in the world of letters. The only time he would write or speak about poetry as such would be in his 'The Name and Nature of Poetry' lecture in 1933. His own process of poetic creation happened naturally and unconsciously, not by intention.

From the beginning, he comes over as a 'one-off' like William Blake. Buffon's declaration that *'le style, c'est l'homme lui-meme'* is clearly relevant to Housman. Congruent with this were his seeming fixations with suicide, execution and the finality of life's end. Housman's poetry was essentially personal and narcissistic; he was never on the lookout for new material.

Almost forty years later, in February 1933, Housman would tell a French researcher, Maurice Pollet: 'I did not begin to write poetry in earnest until the really emotional part of my life was over; and my poetry, so far as I could make out, sprang chiefly from physical conditions, such as a relaxed sore throat during my most prolific period, the first five months of 1895.'[15] In 1933, he enlarged on the experience in his later lecture 'The Name and Nature of Poetry' when he said that 'The experience, though pleasurable, was generally agitating and exhausting.' How anybody like Housman, with an analytical scientific mind, could think that his poetry 'sprang chiefly from physical conditions, such as a relaxed sore throat' is very puzzling, though they were undoubtedly coincidental.

There had been a multitude of significant life events to disturb his emotional equilibrium and it is worth considering them in turn.

The emotional context for his poetry had five dimensions: several bereavements, radical changes in his own life, the imprisonment of Oscar Wilde, a bitter controversy with John Postgate and literary rivalry with his brother Laurence.

We have seen that in December 1889 Moses Jackson, the man to whom he had formed such a powerful attachment, had married; this loss one can properly assume to be the equivalent of a bereavement. Three years later, in November 1892, Moses' brother Adalbert died. Housman, in a short space of time, lost the two men with whom he had the closest affectional bonds. Moses had never been out of Housman's poetry and within a year of Adalbert's death he too became the subject of a poem titled *A.J.J.* – 'When he's returned I'll tell him—oh, / Dear Fellow, I forgot.' This was properly judged by its author to be unworthy of a place in *A Shropshire Lad* or *Last Poems* and remained a work in progress, until revised by Laurence for *More Poems*. Two years later, in 1894, came the death and funeral of Housman's father, a sombre event but not one that inspired him to poetry. Whatever the weight of each in his catalogue of losses, they added a powerful and mournful cross-current in his mental life.

In 1892 there had come another major change, this time in his own life. As he said, he was 'picked out of the gutter' and appointed Professor of Latin at University College, London, when he was only thirty-two. Although supremely confident in his own abilities and ambition, there was an undeniable risk for him. Added to natural apprehensions about a new job were the feelings of vulnerability to public exposure that can lurk in the mind of a man who believes he has a secret to hide. Then came the trial of Oscar Wilde in May 1895 to reinforce that sense of vulnerability.

The trial of Oscar Wilde

The trial of Oscar Wilde was a cause célèbre. Wilde had rushed into a libel action against the Marquess of Queensberry who had described him as 'a posing sodomite' because of Wilde's association with Queensberry's son Lord Alfred Douglas. Enough was said at the hearing for Wilde himself to be arrested, charged and sentenced under the Labouchere Amendment of 1886. Because sodomy was difficult to prove, this amendment had widened the grounds on which individuals could be prosecuted so as to catch other sexual behaviour between men:

Figure 13 Oscar Wilde, poet and
playwright. By Albert Ellis 1854–1930

Any male person who, in public or private commits or is a party
to the commission of, or procures the commission by any male
person, of any act of gross indecency, with another male person,
shall be guilty of a misdemeanour, and being convicted thereof
shall be liable at the discretion of the Court to be imprisoned for
any term not exceeding two years, with or without hard labour.

Wilde was found guilty and given the maximum sentence.

Housman's intense reaction to the fact that a man was being
judicially incarcerated for loving other men was expressed in a poem
that remained unpublished until 1937 when Laurence published it in
Additional Poems.

O who is that young sinner with the handcuffs on his wrists?
And what has he been after that they groan and shake their fists?
And wherefore is he wearing such a conscience-stricken air?
Oh they're taking him to prison for the colour of his hair.

'Tis a shame to human nature, such a head of hair as his;
In the good old time 'twas hanging for the colour that it is;
Though hanging isn't bad enough and flaying would be fair
For the nameless and abominable colour of his hair.

Oh a deal of pains he's taken and a pretty price he's paid
To hide his poll or dye it of a mentionable shade;
But they've pulled the beggar's hat off for the world to see and
    stare,
And they're haling him to justice for the colour of his hair.

Now 'tis oakum for his fingers and treadmill for his feet
And the quarry-gang on Portland in the cold and in the heat,
And between his spells of labour in his time he had to spare
He can curse the God that made him for the colour of his hair.

This poem demonstrates how threatened and vulnerable Housman felt. Yet there is no evidence that Housman identified with Wilde either as a man or as a writer; Wilde's flamboyant and extrovert behaviour and mannered flowery poetry were the antithesis of Housman. He did not at any time send Wilde a copy of this poem. Common sense told him that his newly minted career would end if he came to Wilde's defence. But he did make a gesture. In 1928 he told Seymour Adelman, an American bibliophile, 'A Shropshire Lad was published while Mr Wilde was in prison, and when he came out I sent him a copy. Robbie Ross [Wilde's friend and literary executor] told me that when he visited his friend in jail he had learnt some of the poems by heart and recited them to him.'[16] There is no record of any subsequent contact between Wilde and Housman but Wilde did write to Laurence Housman, who wrote of it in 1923 in his book *Echo de Paris*.

Upon his release from prison I had sent him my recently published book *All-Fellows: Legends of Lower Redemption* hoping that its title and contents would say something on my behalf, which, in his particular case, I very much wished to convey. A fortnight later a courteous and appreciative letter reached me from the south of France, telling me incidentally by the same post had come a copy of *A Shropshire Lad,* sent with the good wishes of the author, whom he had never met. 'Thus you and your brother,' he wrote, 'have given me a few moments of that rare thing called happiness.'[17]

Laurence and Housman had both reached out in their separate ways. Laurence also met Wilde on two occasions, once in London when Wilde was at the height of his fame and subsequently in Paris in 1899. There is no record of his brother having ever met Wilde and there is no evidence that the brothers communicated about him to each other. But Housman's decision, albeit carefully timed, must have been difficult. Although Wilde earned the applause of the public gallery with his bravura defence of 'the love that dare not speak its name', there had been no rush of individuals to support him in public; all there had been was a rush by frightened men for the boat train to cross the Channel.

Housman included in *A Shropshire Lad* two other poems, drafted at the same time in 1895, and printed on adjacent pages. The first, XLIV, was inspired by a newspaper cutting about a young ensign, Harry Maclean, who had shot himself. His suicide note revealed he feared that he was irretrievably homosexual. This too had left its mark on Housman and needs to be quoted in full:

> SHOT? so quick, so clean an ending?
>   Oh that was right, lad, that was brave:
> Yours was not an ill for mending,
>   'Twas best to take it to the grave.
>
> Oh you had forethought, you could reason,
>   And saw your road and where it led,
> And early wise and brave in season
>   Put the pistol to your head.
>
> Oh soon, and better so than later
>   After long disgrace and scorn,
> You shot dead the household traitor,
>   The soul that should not have been born.
>
> Right you guessed the rising morrow
>   And scorned to tread the mire you must:
> Dust's your wages, son of sorrow,
>   But men may come to worse than dust
>
> Souls undone, undoing others,—
>   Long time since the tale began.

You would not live to wrong your brothers:
Oh lad, you died as fits a man.

Now to your grave shall friend and stranger
With ruth and some with envy come:
Undishonoured, clear of danger,
Clean of guilt, pass hence and home.

Turn safe to rest, no dreams, no waking;
And here, man, here's the wreath I've made:
'Tis not a gift that's worth the taking,
But wear it and it will not fade.

Housman's final stanza expressed a heartfelt and touching solidarity with the young ensign. Any reader who knew the background facts would accept at face value the poem's moral position, the overriding attitude of the time, to be summed up as 'better dead than *that*'. Less careful or aware readers could innocently substitute any normal transgression that sprang to mind and still the poem would make sense. Yet the heavy irony and sardonic tone of the moral pose is unmistakeable.

A second poem in the same vein, XLV, was printed on the next page.

If it chance your eye offend you,
Pluck it out, lad, and be sound:
'Twill hurt, but here are salves to friend you,
And many a balsam grows on ground.

And if your hand or foot offend you,
Cut it off, lad, and be whole;
But play the man, stand up and end you,
When your sickness is your soul.

This poem has the sound and feel of Housman speaking for himself and there is an obvious link between these three poems; each is driven by similar gusts of emotion, anger and protest.

On only one occasion in *A Shropshire Lad* does Housman convey a sense of his own feelings, his own personal conflict of fear and desire. This occurs in poem XXX, also completed in the shadow of the Oscar Wilde affair:

OTHERS, I am not the first,
Have willed more mischief than they durst:
If in the breathless night I too
Shiver now, 'tis nothing new.

More than I, if truth were told,
Have stood and sweated hot and cold,
And through their reins in ice and fire
Fear contended with desire.

Agued once like me were they,
But I like them shall win my way
Lastly to the bed of mould
Where there's neither heat nor cold.

But from my grave across my brow
Plays no wind of healing now,
And fire and ice within me fight
Beneath the suffocating night.

These three poems are witnesses to the profound emotional stress the Oscar Wilde affair caused in Housman.

A disturbing academic controversy

Almost coincidental with the trial of Oscar Wilde were the effects on Housman of a bitter academic controversy. In late 1894 John Postgate produced an edition of Propertius. Housman's name appeared in the edition's *apparatus criticus* 160 times and Postgate accepted more than sixty of Housman's previous conjectures, transpositions and changes in punctuation and incorporated them in his text. Postgate was, in effect, sitting at Housman's feet. Housman then published three separate massive articles titled 'The Manuscripts of Propertius' I, II, and III, in the *Journal of Philology*. In none of these did Housman make any reference to Postgate. Then Postgate published an eighty-two page pamphlet *On certain manuscripts of Propertius*. He was careful to give Housman his due, referring to Housman's 'brilliant triad of articles' and taking care to represent his position properly. When Housman replied in early 1895 in *The Manuscripts of Propertius IV* he sounded like a belligerent and outraged aggressor.

One cannot deny that Housman's papers were a pyrotechnic display of vast learning and organisation of material. To make connections between nine manuscripts, which varied between five and eight hundred-years-old, and were in some cases incomplete – with the aim of producing an archetype or original, which in this case had vanished a thousand years earlier – was a mammoth task. It called for a strategic assessment of the various manuscripts in terms of their general reliability and completeness, and whether they were in any way related to one another. In a sea of possibilities and interrelated decisions, the mental energy required to sustain patterns of enquiry and drive forward sustainable arguments was simply immense.

But in spite of his superb mental equipment, in spite of his use of forensic words like 'testimony', 'witness' and 'clue', in spite of his use of judgemental words like 'correctness' and 'integrity', in spite of his weaving facts, judgements and intuitions into an apparently seamless whole, neither Housman nor anyone else could prove the case with certainty one way or the other.

This fact ought to have induced a little humility, but humility had never been Housman's stock-in-trade. Even so, his display of aggression and anger was surprising. Up to this point, his classical papers had not exhibited any especially violent invective. Certainly, there had been plenty of hard words on scholars in general, frank disagreements with individual scholars, and rather self-conscious displays of his own verbal cleverness. But he was also ready to hand out compliments. As we have seen, he was also master of the affable opening followed by the sharp put-down.

But on this occasion, Postgate's pamphlet ignited Housman. 'My name is scattered through the treatise, and I hasten to acknowledge the invariable benignity with which Dr Postgate reproves me, sometimes for doing what I have not done, and sometimes for doing what it was my bounden duty to do.' Then he went for the jugular. 'All the tools he employs are two-edged, though to be sure both edges are quite blunt.' His attack became personal. 'I declare, Dr Postgate's entire observations on DV [manuscripts] remind me of nothing so much as the famous soliloquies, described by Coleridge as "the motive-hunting of a motiveless malignity," in which Iago tries to explain to himself why he hates Othello.' He aimed what he intended to be his knock-out blow:

This ends what I have to say on Dr Postgate's spirited attempt to re-establish chaos among Propertius' MSS. If it were not for the humour of the situation I might well resent the tone of placid assurance in which I, who think before I write and blot before I print, am continually admonished by the author of this pamphlet.

Housman had lost touch with reality, had forgotten that Postgate had fully recognised his contribution to Propertian scholarship and had played a major part in the advancement of Housman's career. Of course, Housman could not be expected to hold back his criticism of Postgate's work on scholarly grounds but his attack had been personal and totally disproportionate. It was as though he had no understanding of what he said and even less of how it might be received. Something seems temporarily to have disturbed the balance of his mind. Housman was neither a heavy drinker nor a drug taker. But his bout of poetic madness at that time may have lessened his self-control and allowed the resentments and anger he was feeling about life to enter his academic work. Or it may have been an all too human reaction to the fact that he who had worked on Propertius for years, and perhaps felt he had proprietary rights, was having to submit to the humiliating patronage of a scholar who he believed to be greatly his inferior.

Postgate was driven to answer in kind. In his *On The Manuscripts of Propertius* published in April 1895, his opening attack could not have been more scathing or personal. 'Mr Housman's style of controversy is now familiar to the public, nor needs it characterizing by me; and the present specimen seems fully to sustain its author's reputation.' He attacked Housman's characteristic modes of argument with such phrases as: 'A controversialist who sets up dummy hypotheses ... Mr Housman's favourite paralogism ... his ebullition of fallacy.' His closing words amounted to saying that Mr Housman hands it out but can't take it himself. With this the controversy came to a sudden full stop.

Housman had been behaving like the bully in the academic playground. Challenged and dealt with in his own coin he backed off. After *A Shropshire Lad* had been published, Housman produced a notably mellow review of Postgate's *Propertius* in the *Classical Review*. For once Housman had been shocked or had shocked himself. Sir Sydney Cockerell (Director of the Fitzwilliam Museum in Cambridge) recalled in a letter he wrote to the *Times Literary Supplement* in November 1936 after Housman's death:

On November 10, 1911, I had a talk with Housman about 'A Shropshire Lad', and next day made the following note in my copy of the book: 'He told me last night that he wrote some of these poems in 1894, but the majority of them in the first five months of 1895 at a time of ill health, and partly perhaps as a reaction from a learned controversy in which he was then engaged. They came to him willy-nilly, and since then he had written a small number of poems under similar emotional conditions, but not enough to make another volume.[18]

Sibling rivalry with Laurence

By comparison with Postgate, an outbreak of sibling rivalry, albeit well controlled, might seem small beer, yet it must have added to the sum total of pressures on Housman. Just as his own poetic pace was accelerating, he was asked by Laurence in December 1894 to comment on *his* first collection of poems, *Green Arras*. Laurence was reverting to childhood habit and seeking his senior brother's opinion and approval. It must have been disconcerting for Housman to find his younger brother at the point of publication. A frisson of sibling rivalry was to be expected. Housman, with years of versifying behind him, most likely thought of himself as *the* most likely member of the family to publish poetry. He could be amusingly dismissive of many of Laurence's efforts.

> I would die many deaths rather than use such words as 'a-croon' or 'a-saw' ... What makes many of your poems more obscure than they need be is that you do not put yourself in the reader's place ... you had in your head some meaning of which you did not suffer a single drop to escape into what you wrote: you treat us as Nebuchadnezzar did the Chaldeans, and expect us to find out the dream as well as the interpretation ... The last stanza of this poem is one of your triumphs of obscurity.[19]

He did not seek comments from Laurence on his own poems, or give him any advance notice that he was himself assembling a volume of poetry. Housman's preference was for secrecy. He beat his brother to publication. *A Shropshire Lad* was published in early 1896, *Green Arras* followed in September. Housman arranged for his publisher to send a copy to Laurence. Laurence recorded that 'like a bolt from the

Figure 14 Laurence Housman aged 20.
Courtesy of Gerald Symons

blue out came A Shropshire Lad and straightway as an author with any individuality worth mentioning, I was wiped out. I became the brother of the "Shropshire Lad" and for the next five years I laboured under the shadow of that bright cloud.'[20]

Distress and depression

Death and loss, feelings of vulnerability in his new occupation, fears of the possible personal consequences for himself in the legal and social environment of the Oscar Wilde trial, a seriously disturbing academic controversy and sibling rivalry had provided a range of potent emotional stimuli for poetic creation. But Housman's period of ill health, identified in his reply to Pollet and amplified by Cockrell's recollection, could be evidence of a more deeply over-wrought and depressed condition than he cared to admit or could even recognise. Kate and Laurence had both previously recognised symptoms of depression in their adolescent brother. His relaxed sore throat may have been symptomatic of a deeper malaise that went undiagnosed. Some disturbance of his mind could account for both the hangman and suicide themes in his poetry. For today's reader the worst thought is that such an upright and talented man could have been driven by his emotional burden to contemplate suicide.

His Cambridge medical friend Dr Percy Withers would later recollect having conversations with him when he was trying to persuade Housman to write more poetry:

> And then he told me what A Shropshire Lad had cost him. He reverted to the topic more than once in later years, and on the second telling, and the third, it was the same – a staccato and troubled utterance, a voice striving ineffectually for composure, a tormented countenance, and all the evidences of an intolerable memory lived over again ... He told me he could never face such self-immolation again, and as he said it a shudder passed over him.[21]

Whatever the genesis of Housman's poetry and the pains of its making, this notable scholar, who had served no evident apprenticeship in the business of poetry, was nevertheless able to produce poems with a totally original poetic voice and a complete certainty of expression. It was also self-evident that this hitherto unknown and undeclared poet had a burning wish to publish and was willing to pay for publication. He had things to say, even though he censored some. Subsequently he refused to discuss the meaning of his poems. Besides his abiding dislike of poetic theorising, there was his abiding dislike of talking about himself. There may also have been a dread of where conversations might go should he allow them to start.

Poetry and autobiography

If the trial of Oscar Wilde provided propulsion for some of Housman's most pointed poems, his inner emotional life and personal predicament provided the stuff of most of the rest. The core of his poems is clearly *me* – my attitudes, my predicament, my philosophy of life. W.H. Auden wrote: 'For a poet like myself an autobiography is redundant, since anything of any importance that happens to one is immediately incorporated however obscurely in a poem.'[22] In that sense a core of Housman's poetry stands out as distinctly autobiographical. But the whole corpus of his poetry is made up of variations on a theme. They all derive inspiration from himself but are less directly autobiographical and more symbolic of his philosophy and experience. Housman had literally nothing to write about other than himself and he experienced himself simply and directly. As we have seen, some of the poems were written very clearly in the voice of the poet. In these poems he confronted his own predicament with sadness, regret, resignation, courage, logic or anger. One of his earliest poems, first drafted in 1886, became poem XL in *A Shropshire Lad*. It was full of regret.

> INTO my heart an air that kills
>   From yon far country blows:
> What are those blue remembered hills,
>   What spires, what farms are those?
>
> That is the land of lost content,
>   I see it shining plain,
> The happy highways where I went
>   And cannot come again.

These are some of the most magical lines Housman ever wrote. The intensity of his nostalgia would be seized on by future readers in need of consolation; they would find, in Housman's image of those blue remembered hills and that land of lost content, a consolatory power. What is for some a clearly autobiographical statement about his own loss has universal application.

Also begun in that year, 1886, was a further autobiographical statement. It would not be finished for another four or five years and was published as poem XLVI in *A Shropshire Lad*. It was a burial hymn for his own sterile self and for others like him.

> BRING, in this timeless grave to throw,
> No cypress, sombre on the snow;
> Snap not from the bitter yew
> His leaves that live December through;
> Break no rosemary, bright with rime
> And sparkling to the cruel clime;
> Nor plod the winter land to look
> For willows in the icy brook
> To cast them leafless round him: bring
> No spray that ever buds in spring.

But if the Christmas field has kept
Awns the last gleaner overstept,
Or shrivelled flax, whose flower is blue
A single season, never two;
Or if one haulm whose year is o'er
Shivers on the upland frore
—Oh, bring from hill and stream and plain
Whatever will not flower again,
To give him comfort: he and those
Shall bide eternal bedfellows
Where low upon the couch he lies
Whence he shall never arise.

The final draft of this poem coincided with the birth of Moses and Rosa's first child. In it Housman acknowledged the impossibility of his own fruition.

Two other poems, begun in 1891 or 1892, were coincidental with that famous diary entry, 'said goodbye'. In them he speaks unmistakeably as himself and directly to Moses from whom he had to part. The first is poem XXXIII in *A Shropshire Lad*.

IF truth in hearts that perish
    Could move the powers on high,
I think the love I bear you
    Should make you not to die.

Sure, sure, if stedfast meaning,
    If single thought could save,
The world might end tomorrow,
    You should not see the grave.

This long and sure-set liking,
    This boundless will to please,
—Oh, you should live for ever
    If there were help in these.

But now, since all is idle,
    To this lost heart be kind,
Ere to a town you journey
    Where friends are ill to find.

And also from A Shropshire Lad, poem XXXII.

> FROM far, from eve and morning
>   And yon twelve-winded sky,
> The stuff of life to knit me
>   Blew hither: here am I.
>
> Now—for a breath I tarry
>   Nor yet disperse apart—
> Take my hand quick and tell me,
>   What have you in your heart.
>
> Speak now, and I will answer;
>   How shall I help you, say;
> Ere to the wind's twelve quarters
>   I take my endless way.

It was not until late 1894 or early 1895 that Housman began to draft what would turn out to be his *Epithalamium* or marriage song for Moses and Rosa. He held it back for more than twenty-five years until he published it in *Last Poems* in 1922. Then he could send the poem direct to the dying Moses and his family, a declaration of his feelings towards them. It is a relatively long poem of forty-four lines of which I reproduce only the first stanza:

> HE is here, Urania's son,
> Hymen come from Helicon;
> God that glads the lover's heart,
> He is here to join and part.
> So the groomsman quits your side
> And the bridegroom seeks the bride
> Friend and comrade yield you o'er
> To her that hardly loves you more.

It must have been the autobiographical core of these poems that had caused Housman the greatest distress: remembrance of the emotions that prompted them, reliving the experience as he composed them, his overwhelming regret at his 'loss' of Moses, his own constancy and his own barren future.

Poems about love and lovers and soldiers

In most of Housman's poems autobiography is more distant and generalised. About a third of the poems in *A Shropshire Lad* involve love and lovers: detached cynical observations of love's unfairness; the sense of give your love but don't expect love in return; the dangers of parting with your heart; the pains of unrequited love; the endless rue of loving; darker laments on lovers' suicide, the passing of fancy, love's fulfilment robbed by death, winners and losers in the game of love; lovers' interchangeability, love's impermanence; warring of fear and desire in love, unconditional love, roads taking you away from love, better late than never. In all of this there is a notable absence of rapture, an absence of the erotic, no dwelling on a lover's charms, no expression of the experience of loving. There are no happy endings. Love is a road of peril and disillusionment.

These poems seem to be a mirror held up to Housman's own actual and psychological journey though they may easily be read as the universal experience of love, whether we choose to identify the lovers as man and woman or man and man or specifically Housman and Moses. Thomas Hardy's favourite poem, according to his second wife Florence, was XXVII, a poem dealing with love's impermanence and the mutability of both friendship and love. It is one of Housman's masterpieces.

> 'Is my team ploughing,
>   That I was used to drive
> And hear the harness jingle
>   When I was man alive?'
>
> Ay, the horses trample,
>   The harness jingles now;
> No change though you lie under
>   The land you used to plough.
>
> 'Is football playing
>   Along the river shore,
> With lads to chase the leather,
>   Now I stand up no more?'
>
> Ay, the ball is flying,
>   The lads play heart and soul;

The goal stands up, the keeper
   Stands up to keep the goal.

'Is my girl happy,
   That I thought hard to leave,
And has she tired of weeping
   As she lies down at eve?'

Ay, she lies down lightly,
   She lies not down to weep:
Your girl is well contented.
   Be still, my lad, and sleep.

'Is my friend hearty,
   Now I am thin and pine,
And has he found to sleep in
   A better bed than mine?'

Yes, lad, I lie easy,
   I lie as lads would choose;
I cheer a dead man's sweetheart,
   Never ask me whose.

What laid so many of his lads underground was war. Although the century from 1815 to 1914 produced no general war in Europe (apart from the Crimean War which remained geographically confined), the ever bellicose British fought six Ashanti wars, five Basuto wars, three Afghan wars, three Burmese wars, two Matabele wars, two Sikh wars, two Sudanese wars and two Boer wars. This amounted to 230 colonial wars, punitive expeditions, and insurrections; soldiers and foreign wars were an ever-present backdrop to most of Housman's life.

For Housman, soldiers were a special form of lad, inevitably doomed by their calling. They took him nearest to social comment, especially his ironic reference to the Queen who is *saved* by men whose tombstones are in Asia or by the Nile. Yet Housman's soldiers display no sharply observed insight into the life of real soldiers. They are not invested with life but are used as symbols of himself, and his yearnings for closeness and comradeship. He idealises his lovely fated lads, 'Dear to friends and food for powder'. Perhaps he thought

that among those who become soldiers were many like himself, men
he might love and be a close comrade of and with whom he would
share an inescapable destiny. Indeed the idea of the military as a
haven for rejected lovers is expressed in *The New Mistress*: 'Oh sick
I am to see you, will you never let me be? /You may be good for
something but you are not good for me.' Rejection meets with the
rejected one's response: 'I will go where I am wanted for a soldier of
the Queen.'

Unreal though Housman's soldiers may be, they had a mighty
resonance for Winston Churchill, participant in a cavalry charge at
Omdurman and in the Boer War as a newspaper correspondent, and
destined to be First Lord of Admiralty in the Great War. In her book
The Perfect Summer: Dancing into Shadow in 1911, Juliet Nicolson
tells how at the time of international crisis, Churchill, then Home
Secretary, was staying with friends at Mells in Somerset. He wrote to
the Foreign Secretary Sir Edward Grey: 'I could not think of anything
else but the peril of war ... There was only one field of interest fiercely
illuminated in my mind. Sitting on a hilltop in the smiling country
which stretches around Mells, the lines I have copied [the first two
stanzas of XXXV] kept running through my mind.'[23]

> ON the idle hill of summer,
>   Sleepy with the flow of streams,
> Far I hear the steady drummer
>   Drumming like a noise in dreams.
>
> Far and near and low and louder
>   On the roads of earth go by,
> Dear to friends and food for powder,
>   Soldiers marching, all to die.

One can ask why so many men who went to war carried *A Shropshire
Lad* in their knapsack. It might have been the transforming nostalgia
of blue remembered hills and coloured counties, and Shropshire
names and places. But for men in war, death is ever present and ever
possible, coming when it is both expected and unexpected. Like Julius
Caesar's 'Of all the wonders that I yet have heard, / It seems to me most
strange that men should fear; / Seeing that death, a necessary end, /
Will come when it will come.' Housman writes in the same vein and
invites us all to be heroes by requiring us to face the inevitability of

death, making it a matter not of if, but when, a truth beyond question. As he himself bravely played the hand that fate, divinity or chance had dealt him, he challenged us in turn to show fortitude. As he says in a couplet in *A Shropshire Lad:*

> Courage, lad, 'tis not for long:
> Stand, quit you like a stone, be strong.

Poet of the countryside

It has been often noted that Housman's vision of Shropshire is not essentially real or actual. Housman wrote to Houston Martin in April 1934: 'I am Worcestershire by birth: Shropshire was our western horizon, which made me feel romantic about it. I do not know the county well, except in parts, and some of my topographical details are wrong and imaginary.' The Shropshire in *A Shropshire Lad* is not to be taken too seriously. It has been rightly said that you might as well use *A Shropshire Lad* as a guide to Shropshire as use Rossetti's 'blessed damozel' as a guide to heaven. *A Shropshire Lad* supplanted Housman's own intended title, *Poems by Terence Hearsay*, at the suggestion of Alfred Pollard who also arranged for the poems to be published at Housman's expense by his own publisher Kegan Paul.

In reality, the poems have no distinctly designed Shropshire inspiration at all. Words and phrases can indeed conjure up a feel of England in the minds of many, through its phrases 'coloured counties ... blue remembered hills ... when smoke stood up from Ludlow ... In summertime on Bredon ... high the vanes of Shrewsbury gleam ... On Wenlock Edge the wood's in trouble ... As through the wild green hills of Wyre ... Clunton and Clunbury/Clungord and Clun.' Housman may be a kind of cataloguer of Shropshire but hardly a poet of Shropshire and though we know he was a keen observer of nature, a keen walker and a keen gardener, he displays no real intimate connection with nature that he wishes to share with us. For him the countryside provides little by way of poetic inspiration, except that poem II in *A Shropshire Lad*, 'Loveliest of trees, the cherry now/ Is hung with bloom along the bough', is properly regarded by many as one of his most beautiful poems and its point – how few years will remain to him to enjoy it – is well made. But it is an isolated case. His appreciation and enjoyment of nature and the inspiration he derives from it lacks, for example, the intensity and amplitude of the countryside of Wordsworth's *Prelude* and the heartfulness and magical expression of Coleridge's version of *Kennst du das Land* from Goethe's *Wilhelm Meister* expressed in Mignon's song.

> Know'st thou the land where the pale citrons grow,
> The golden fruits in darkest foliage glow?
> Soft blows the wind that breathes from that blue sky!
> Still stands the myrtle and the laurel high!
> Know'st thou it well, that land, beloved friend?
> Thither with thee, O, thither would I wend!

Philosophy of life

Most poems in *A Shropshire Lad* reflected, in one way or another, Housman's philosophy of life. He rejected the word pessimist and denied he had ever had 'a crisis of pessimism'. 'In the first place, I am not a pessimist but a pejorist (as George Eliot said she was not an optimist but a meliorist); and that philosophy is founded on my observation of the world, not on anything so trivial and irrelevant as personal misfortune.'[24] He was defining himself as a man who did not have a tendency to look at the worst aspect of things or expect bad results but as one who believed that the world was becoming worse. That is as may be, but for Housman it is indisputable that death is the *summum bonum* or chief good of life. In John Bayley's words, 'Death is the good shepherd.'[25] Housman felt no compulsion to *believe*. In spite of his childhood conditioning he had reached a hard analytical view that life was short, death an end without afterlife. When the prime mover is brought on stage in his poetry it is a case of 'whatever brute and blackguard made the world.'

Unlike many other Victorians, he did not agonize over belief and unbelief. In the brief interval between life and death there were intellectual and masculine virtues to rely on and some pleasures to be enjoyed.

He would tell Pollet that he was a Cyrenaic – a philosopher of the hedonistic school of Aristippus – yet there was precious little serious hedonism either in his life or poetry. He had few aesthetic enthusiasms with the exception of church and cathedral architecture and flowers. Percy Withers tells how he played Vaughan Williams' settings of Housman's poems with disastrous results, and of

Housman's lukewarm appreciation of Beethoven and how Housman turned down reading matter offered by Withers:

> exceedingly fine and detailed illustrations in Yashiro's book on Botticelli ... Instead he turned to my half-dozen volumes of Max Beerbohm's Caricatures and spent the entire afternoon with them in an easy chair by the window... I heard his repeated chuckles, and from time to time a burst of outright laughter. I believe he went through each volume twice, and many times I saw him return to a volume he had laid on one side, pick out the page he wanted and chortle anew at the caricature it presented. He seemed – he was – thoroughly enjoying himself, and the spirit of cheerfulness was sustained at a higher level and for a longer period than at any time within my knowledge.[26]

Housman probably got a similar level of enjoyment from the music hall which he frequented when opportunity allowed. These were revealing anecdotes, displaying Housman's perennial love of fun but also the paucity of Housman's aesthetic life, his almost philistine attitude to cultural artefacts. Beyond the dining table and travel his hedonism was non-existent.

In his Oxford days his enthusiasm for Matthew Arnold had led him to pronounce that Arnold's *Empedocles on Etna* contained 'all the law and all the prophets'.[27] Empedocles was a Sicilian philosopher, poet and historian who flourished in 444 BC, and may have ended his life by throwing himself into the crater of Etna. There had been much to attract Housman in Arnold's economical directness, in his thought that man had only his own mind to guide him. For example, 'Man gets no other light/ Search he a thousand years'; in Arnold's view of the emergence of gods, 'Do we at will invent/ Stern powers who make their care/ To embitter human life, malignant deities'; his view on transitory life, 'Year posting after year,/ Sense after sense decay'; and his conclusion: 'I say: Fear not! Life still/ Leaves human effort scope/ But, since life teems with ill, / Nurse no extravagant hope.'[28]

This probably best represents Housman's philosophical position but intensified by his sense of himself as an outsider. Arnold, not unlike Housman as a man of subversive opinion, was much occupied with the philosophical issues of his day. His poem *Dover Beach* reflected the tide of unbelief that had swirled through society after the publication of Darwin's *On the Origin of Species* in 1859. Housman had been by no means alone in his retreat from revealed religion but wrote nothing about it as magically suggestive as Arnold's

> But now I only hear
> Its melancholy, long, withdrawing roar,
> Retreating to the breath
> Of the night wind down the vast edges drear
> And naked shingles of the world.

There is only a single poem in *A Shropshire Lad* – poem XLII, *The Merry Guide* – that expresses happiness and pleasure in the process of life. Of its fifteen stanzas, I select four below:

> ONCE in the wind of morning
>   I ranged the thymy wold;
> The world-wide air was azure
>   And all the brooks ran gold.

> With the great gale we journey
>   That breathes from gardens thinned,
> Borne in the drift of blossoms
>   Whose petals throng the wind;

> Buoyed on the heaven-heard whisper
>   Of dancing leaflets whirled
> From all the woods that autumn
>   Bereaves in all the world.

> And midst the fluttering legion
>   Of all that ever died
> I follow, and before us
>   Goes the delightful guide.

This is the acceptable face of death: journey to a not too over-emphasised terminus through a picturesque landscape with a heavenly travelling companion who does not pester Housman with any conversation. In one other poem, XLIX, Housman flirts with the idea that unbridled hedonism can make the journey easier and make death seem slower to arrive by not dwelling on it; this poem expresses some disillusion with his own chosen diversion, intellectual activity:

> THINK no more, lad; laugh, be jolly:
>   Why should men make haste to die?
> Empty heads and tongues a-talking
> Make the rough road easy walking,
> And the feather pate of folly
>   Bears the falling sky.
>
> Oh, 'tis jesting, dancing, drinking
>   Spins the heavy world around.
> If young hearts were not so clever,
> Oh, they would be young for ever:
> Think no more; 'tis only thinking
>   Lays lads underground.

For Housman death never conveys fear or terror, unlike Phillip Larkin in his *Aubade:*

> That this is what we fear — no sight, no sound,
> No touch or taste or smell, nothing to think with,
> Nothing to love or link with,
> The anaesthetic from which none come round.

One particular form of death, hanging, oppressed his mind, maybe the result of an inexplicable childhood feeling perhaps emanating from some graphic illustration, or later guilt about his sexuality. Where he got it from we shall never know but his poetry demonstrates a terrible fear of being hanged, being taken to the place of execution, his hands pinioned, the hood put over his head, the heavy rope placed round his neck and the drop of the trap on the stroke of the clock. Did he wake with nightmares that he had been tried and sentenced or was this more evidence of a suicidal frame of mind?

Housman, the comic versifier

Seemingly tangential to *A Shropshire Lad* was Housman's comic verse, which emerged when he was very young: 'I wrote verse at eight or earlier.'[29] He had a natural talent for comic versification and produced nonsense verse on emergent occasions throughout his life. As a smart and witty schoolboy, he would dramatise the games played by himself and his sister Clemence, and his thank-you letters in verse to the Wises were another of his stocks-in-trade. He had a natural talent for writing skits, catchy verse and comic scenes which enlivened his life at Oxford and University College, all characterised by felicitous word play and quick inventive wit. Wit abounded in his speeches, in his debating and in his letters. Appreciation of jokes and humour was part of his make-up. His letters are full of tongue-in-cheek statements and ironic phrases. Humour was a constant in his life, frequently impish, irreverent and subversive. Laughter could provide an escape from the grinding exactness of his daily work, enabling a release of stored up nervous energy. In nonsense verse, logic and rationality can be distorted for the mystification of others and at its heart can be amorality and lack of good feelings.

His brother Laurence spoke of his 'gift of happy and musical laughter'.[30] Housman was always open to incongruity, both as a perceiver of the comic in life and as a person who enjoyed its recognition in the words of others. These underpinned his love of laughter and his readiness to laugh.

A Shropshire Lad: Critical reception and aftermath

Publication of classical papers in learned journals was one thing, casting his poetic bread on the waters was quite another. Housman had done a brave thing and had paid his publisher for doing so. He expressed no anxiety about the outcome. In the event he found he had a public success on his hands.

Reviewers generally recognised his poetic voice as individual, fresh and different.[31] One wrote that 'It calls and we are obliged to listen.' Another spoke of 'its lovely verbal austerity'. William Archer, a notable critic, wrote what time has proven to be true: 'You may read it in half-an-hour but there are things in it you will scarce forget in a lifetime. It tingles with an original, fascinating, melancholy vitality.' These comments alone would have been enough to fill the cup of any poet producing his first volume. Housman himself preferred the review in *New Age* by Hubert Bland, the socialist journalist and co-founder of the Fabian Society: 'essentially and distinctively new poetry ... swift unfaltering touch of a master's hand ... elemental emotions, of heart thoughts ... It is not the highest poetry but comes astonishingly near the highest.'

Figure 15 Housman in 1896.
By permission of the Housman Society

The overwhelming majority of reviewers ranged from the welcoming to the enthusiastic. A few deplored the subject matter and its monotony. A reviewer in Boston wrote that 'most of the heroes of Mr Housman's verse are either lying in their graves ... or else on the verge of suicide or on the gallows.' Norman Gale in *Academy* of 8 October 1898 encapsulated what many may feel about the rather uneven attraction of the collection when read at one sitting: 'Where his feeling is not strong enough to inspire him, he lapses into mere rhymed prose. Where his feeling is acute, he pierces to the quick. And he seems quite ignorant when he is inspired or uninspired.' At least seventeen reviews of *A Shropshire Lad* were published in its year of publication and in 1898. When a fresh edition was brought out, it was welcomed in *The Athenaeum* of October 1898 with the words 'republication must be one of the chief events of the present season'.

Housman had been careful enough to obtain copies of all the reviews of his poetry. After the turbulent experience of writing lines that had come from the depths of his being, and which he had subsequently scanned with a self-censoring eye, he could not help but feel relieved and pleased by them – an undoubted boost to his self-esteem. And he was thrilled with the finished book, telling Laurence 'The binding seems to me so extraordinarily beautiful that I cannot bear to lose sight of it by opening the book: when I take it down with the intention of reading it, the cover detains me in a stupor of admiration till it is time to go to bed.'[32] Kate had reacted 'that she likes the verse better than the sentiments. The sentiments, she then goes on to say, appear to be taken from the book of *Ecclesiastes*. To prefer my versification to the sentiments of the Holy Ghost is decidedly flattering, but strikes me as a trifle impious.'[33] He heard from P.G.L. Webb whose role as an Administrative Principal drafted into the Trade Marks Branch at the Patent Office resulted in a letter of protest by Housman and three other colleagues. They had objected that this Webb, senior to any of them, but with less experience of their work, was being foisted on them. Webb, unlike Housman, was evidently focussed on his career, eventually becoming Assistant Comptroller of the Patent Office. However, he also translated Heine and had produced poetry of his own, hence Housman's rather relaxed reply to Webb's letter of congratulation:

> Yes, I am a great admirer of Heine; he is about the only German I can read with comfort ... The reviews are good, or at any rate well-meaning: only I wish they would not call me a *singer*. One fellow actually says *minstrel* ... Don't look forward to my next book of poems; because most likely I shall never write one. Like Ennius, I only compose poetry when I am out of sorts. This year I have not made a line yet.

He picked up another of Webb's comments in his PS: 'None of my friends have been hanged *yet*: such is the supineness of the police.'[34]

When he received Laurence's *Green Arras* in September 1896 he didn't waste any time on the poems: 'I think I have seen all but one or two before.' He commented mainly on the illustrations, drew Laurence's attention to five further misprints 'besides those given in the Errata' and ended with

> I think you will probably be able to congratulate yourself on having brought out this autumn at the Bodley Head a much better book than Davidson, if the whole of his *New Ballads* are at all like those he has been publishing in the magazines. Not that this is a very lofty compliment.[35]

Housman was now feeling more relaxed about his competitor brother and in an October letter he actually praised one of his poems: 'I was a good deal struck by *Gammer Garu*, which I don't remember noticing much in manuscript. The last stanza is really quite beautiful.' He even went as far as to take him into his confidence: 'A new firm of publishers has written to me proposing to publish "the successor" of A.S.L. But as they don't also offer to write it, I have had to put them off.'[36] A couple of months later he mentioned he had been reading Laurence's *All-Fellows* (the book Laurence had sent to Oscar Wilde): 'I have been reading your latest work – probably by this time it is not your latest work, but I can't read as fast as you write. What I chiefly admire in your stories, here as on previous occasions, is the ingenuity of the plan.'[37] On Christmas Eve he was again writing to Laurence: 'I am extremely anxious that you should spend a happy Christmas; and as I have it in my power – here goes.' He recounted how the previous evening he had been sitting next to 'Rendall, Principal of University College Liverpool and Professor of Greek there, a very nice fellow and a great student of Marcus Aurelius and modern poetry'. Rendall had been interested to hear 'that you were my brother', how he had read *Green Arras* and had continued: 'I think it the best volume by him that I have seen: *The Shropshire Lad* had a pretty cover.' This prompted Housman's aside: 'what a thing is fraternal affection, that it will stand these tests!', and his PS that 'After all, it was I who designed that pretty cover; and he did not say that the cover of *Green Arras* was pretty (Nor is it)', and his PPS: 'I was just licking the envelope, when I thought of the following venomed dart: I had far, far rather that people should attribute my verses to you than yours to me.'[38]

By 1 May 1897 Laurence had brought out another book, *Gods and their Makers*. It had been noticed in *The Pall Mall Gazette* and an acquaintance of Housman's had sent him a copy 'and wants to know if this be I.'[39] In his next letter apropos lines Laurence had quoted to him about the sea, he was sparked off to write:

> I have somewhere a poem which directs attention to one of its most striking characteristics, which hardly any of the poets have observed. They call it salt and blue and deep and dark and so on; but they never make such profoundly true reflexions as the following: 'O billows bounding far, / How wet, how wet ye are!'

Ten verses later, he ends with 'Farewell thou humid main', ending his letter 'Farewell, thou irreligious writer.'[40]

Housman was still on a high following reviewer reaction to his poetry. He was still in a communicative mood in late June when he wrote to his stepmother about a visit to Bromsgrove. It was here that he had witnessed bonfires for Queen Victoria's Golden Jubilee in 1887 and in 1894, and had begun his poem (titled *1887*) that begins: 'From Clee to heaven the beacon burns'. He had placed this poem first in *A Shropshire Lad*. He was now witnessing bonfires for Queen Victoria's Diamond Jubilee. 'It was a fine night and at midnight the sky in the north had enough light for me to see the time by my watch.' Although he had previously seen both the Millingtons and Kidds in Bromsgrove, this had been a solitary walk; his only conversation was with the policeman guarding the bonfire who told him that the crowd was 'not near so large as in 1887'.[41]

It was jubilee time for Housman too. In the short space of five years he had translated himself from clerk at the Patent Office to professor at University College; had kept up the flow of his scholarly papers; and out of his emotional turmoil had published a book of poems that had been received with acclamation and would never be out of print.

PART V

Pastures new

1897: The call of the Continent

A Shropshire Lad and those poems he kept back had been a volcanic and distressing catharsis. Relaxation and pastures new were now the order of the day and so in the summer of 1897 he toured the Continent for a month, first to Paris for a week, then Rome for three or four days, Naples for ten; then homeward bound – a further four to five days in Rome and one in Paris.

Just after he returned to Highgate in late September, he wrote a letter to his stepmother with his observations on Paris, Naples, Pompeii, Vesuvius, Capri and Ischia, He had turned out to be an assiduous and committed tourist, writing about places so as to give the reader a very good sense of them in a colourful and literate guidebook sort of way. He had obviously been very taken by the beautiful buildings in Paris, the wildness and picturesqueness of the Bois de Boulogne, and, like most other visitors to Paris, had concluded 'They make a deal more of their river than we do of ours: it is all edged with handsome quays and crossed with handsome bridges.' In Naples, where the Scirocco was blowing out of Africa, he reproduced the colours and feel of the landscape, and the active presence and sounds of the volcano:

> Here you begin to hear an angry sound such as water will sometimes make in pipes, as if the mountain were gargling, or were trying to talk but had stones in its mouth; which indeed it has. This is the lava boiling inside. The volcano was unusually quiet, so that I was able to go quite to the edge of the crater, which is often impossible. This is a great pit, sending out so much smoke that you can hardly catch a glimpse of the other brim; the sides are ashes with smears of sulphur and of an orange coloured stuff

which I believe is arsenic; in the centre there starts up at intervals a tall fountain of red hot stones, which then fall rattling back again into the funnel with a noise like a wave going down the beach.

A visit to the islands of Capri and Ischia produced visual sensations:

Autumn is not the time for flowers in Italy any more than in England, but in one wood I found cyclamen blooming almost as thick as wood anemones in April. The chief ornament of gardens at this season is the oleander, which grows about the size of a lilac and is covered with trusses of rose-coloured flowers like carnations. The plumbago also grows and blooms very well, and so does the purple convolvulous.[1]

Although these aural and ocular sensations and the lovely names of flowers could go into a letter to his stepmother and though he was showing a heightened awareness of this profusion of flowers, he did not write poems about the beauty of the Amalfi coast, nor about the isles of Capri and Ischia, nor did he make poetry out of Vesuvius and the force of nature that had destroyed Pompeii.

A month or so later and still in a relaxed mood he was able to greet the forthcoming publication of his brother's book of devotional poems *Spikenard* with the rather deprecatory announcement to his stepmother that he might himself produce a hymn book for the use of the Salvation Army, and effortlessly rattled off:

Hallelujah! was the only observation
That escaped Lieutenant-Colonel Mary-Jane
When she tumbled off the platform in the station
And was cut in little pieces by the train;
Mary-Jane, the train is through ye,
Hallelujah! Hallelujah!
We will gather up the fragments that remain.[2]

In this he was revealing his capacity to compartmentalise disparate streams of mental activity. On the one hand, he was writing a highly technical and complex paper on the Greek poet Bacchylides for the *Classical Review*, at the same time, keeping a promise he had made to his godmother Elizabeth Wise, he sent her his ballad *Lucinda* in eighteen verses, and 'if it will deter Edie and Minnie from climbing ladders or using the moon for culinary purposes, it will not have been written in vain.'[3] His ability to move from the sublime to the ridiculous was extraordinary.

Housman's impact on University College

Housman's many and various talents gradually became obvious. In July 1896, as Dean of the Faculty of Arts and Laws, he delivered a lengthy address at the Prize Giving. It contained a remarkable reaching out to the students:

> In addition to this report of matters strictly academical and educational, mention may appropriately be made of a body whose possible influence on the well-being of the College, and especially on its unity and cohesion, is of the greatest moment. The Student's Union Society has in the present term exhibited its vigour and vitality by holding, in conjunction with the Old Student's Society, what is described by all who had the good fortune to be present as a highly successful Soiree. The Students, who are after all, the final cause of this College and of all that it contains, have at least one sphere in which they can do more for the College than all the rest of us. The very number and variety of the studies to which the College opens its doors constitute to some extent a danger. There are so many centrifugal forces: they require to be counteracted by some equally powerful centripetal force. This the Students themselves can best supply; and the activity and success of the Union affords a welcome proof that they are supplying it.[4]

This went down very well with the students. A notably tongue-in-cheek account of the day noted that, 'Professor Housman, looking quite academic and not at all the poet, read an interesting report in which he made pleasant remarks about the Union and the Soiree with which the session closed.'

Support for Moses Jackson

Housman remained committed to helping Moses Jackson. Indeed, he became rather over-committed. When Henry Eve resigned as headmaster of University College School in 1898, Housman, convener of the selection committee, proposed Jackson, who by then had returned to India. The committee was unanimous in deciding to offer the post to another candidate, who accepted only to withdraw. Reconvening the committee, Housman evidently pushed Jackson through against the opposition of others, who subsequently proposed an amendment at the Senate which led to the selection of another candidate. As a sop to Housman, the Senate resolved that if this candidate in turn declined the headship, Jackson should be approached. This may have dented Housman's reputation among his peers but does not seem to have left any seriously bad feelings. On that same leave in 1897 to 1898, Moses had also applied for the Quain Chair of Physics. Despite Housman's support, Jackson's application was unsuccessful. Moses clearly had no inhibitions about renewing a common place of work with Housman and Housman was fighting Jackson's corner with as much persuasion as he could muster.

Helping to manage a crisis

In 1899 Housman was elected to the Council which for the next three years had to guide the College through a crisis in its affairs which led to the departure of its secretary, James Horsburgh. Housman now displayed his capacity for leadership and was not at all backward in taking charge. The College was in a deep financial hole. R.W. Chambers described the situation: 'It had been the tradition of University College to do without any Academic Head. Under the rule of Deans, honorary officials who served for terms of two or three terms only, and were helped only by a secretary more and more incapacitated by his increasing ill-health, the College got deeper and deeper into debt.'[5] F.W. Oliver, at the time Quain Professor of Botany, remembered that in this crisis:

> Housman had the full confidence and moral support of the general body of Professors of whom he was in effect the spokesman and leader... The plan devised for our salvation included the replacement of the then Secretary by the appointment of Gregory Foster (then quite a young man) ,... There was also an offer on the part of the Professors to forgo a substantial percentage of their stipend, an offer however which the Council did not find it necessary to accept... In due course the financial stringency abated through the generosity

of an 'anonymous donor'... The critical day (circa midsummer 1900) on which these measures were adopted by the Council is still fresh in my mind, and how the President, Lord Reay (in the absence of the Secretary whose delinquencies we had been considering), detained Housman at the end of the meeting to draft the minutes, and how I discharged the humbler office of telegraphing on Housman's behalf to his friends who were awaiting him at Henley (it was regatta week) that he would be joining them at a later hour than arranged, but that they should 'keep supper for him.'[6]

Although never motivated to seek administrative power in the College, Housman revealed in these happenings that he had the capacity to direct and manage, and to carry others with him, qualities essential to the exercise of administrative power. However, his only desire was to be a professor of Latin. Thus, early in his career he demonstrated both self-direction and self-limitation.

30 October 1901: Brother Herbert killed in the Boer War

In the same year that Housman was elected to the Council the Boer War had begun. Newspaper headlines were full of the siege and relief of Ladysmith, Kimberly and Mafeking, the awful battle of Spion Kop, the uproar caused by British concentration camps and Boer guerrilla warfare. Not a word to anyone on these subjects has survived in his correspondence, nor have any accounts of his views appeared in the reminiscences of others.

Yet while he seems to have avoided thinking about the war or volunteering his opinions on it, he had sharp experience of its cost. His youngest brother Herbert was killed in action on 30 October 1901 at Brakenlaagte. In November of the previous year, Lord Kitchener had been promoted to replace Lord Roberts as Commander-in-Chief in South Africa. He continued the methods the British had adopted to cope with their mobile guerrilla enemy – burning Boer crops and farms, and eventually establishing concentration camps – while his own mobile columns swept the veldt hunting down the Boers, now deprived of fodder, food and home comforts. Yet the war still went on. Kitchener, almost at the end of his tether, wrote to the Secretary for War in London in a mood akin to despair to tell him what had happened:

Figure 16 Housman's youngest brother,
Sergeant Herbert Housman killed in
1901 in the Boer War. By permission of
the Housman Society.

The Boers observe the movements of a column from a long way off, only showing very few men, then having chosen some advantage, in this case it was the weather, then charge in with great boldness, and the result is a serious casualty list. Benson's was one of the very best columns and had an excellent and efficient intelligence ... my last telegram from him on the 29th was to the effect that the country was clear ... if a column like Benson's operating 20 miles outside our lines is not safe it is a very serious matter and will require a large addition to our forces to carry on the war ... what makes me most anxious is, if they can act in this way with Benson's columns, how far easier it would be for them to catch some of my less efficient columns.[7]

Serving in Benson's column was Herbert Housman, a thirty-three-year-old sergeant. Such was his passion for soldiering that ten years earlier he had given up a career in medicine to join the King's Royal Rifles, not as an officer but as a simple soldier. Sergeant Herbert Housman, Lieutenant-Colonel Benson and eighty others paid the personal price of war.

Kitchener went on to achieve his greatest ambition, to become Commander-in-Chief in India, becoming the face that lured millions of men into the army in the First World War with his piercing gaze and slogan, 'Kitchener needs You'. As a non-commissioned officer, Herbert Housman was by definition unimportant in Kitchener's great scheme of things, but a very important cog in a crack unit, a fact fully recognised in the letters received by the family from his company commander, the lieutenant commanding his section, the corporal of his section, and a fellow sergeant. Herbert had been killed charging with his mounted section to save the guns in a rearguard action. Although these letters conjured up distressing images for the family, their phrasing was revealing. His section corporal wrote:

> He was in the front of his section as we were charging to save the guns, and he shouted "Come on No 4 Section!" and was shot dead immediately – death being instantaneous the bullet entering his right breast and entering his heart ... He was loved by all his men ... Personally he was the best friend I ever had and a true chum and he was always to the fore when there was any fighting to do. It grieves me to have to tell you that after being killed at 3 p.m. 30th Oct he lay on the open veldt all night in the pouring rain until 4 p.m. the 31st with only his under-clothing – the Boers to their lasting disgrace having stripped him of everything.

After recounting more graphic details of their frantic and bloody rearguard action against 4,000 Boers, Corporal Hobden went on: 'I have searched his kit and all I can find is the photos which I enclose, his watch and field glasses being taken by the Boers.' Herbert's lieutenant wrote: 'He was hit through the heart and killed instantaneously which after all is the best death a soldier can die.' His company commander wrote in a very touching way:

> I am writing to you about your poor dear son ... I can't tell you how I feel for you ... I am so very sorry I have not written before, but I was wounded myself and had to communicate with our column before I could find out your address ... His last resting place was on Bakenlaagte Hill and I feel sure it will be well cared for.

The Company Sergeant also wrote to Kate. Like all the others he recounted the key facts of Herbert's quick death, his lying in the rain and the stripping of the bodies of the dead of clothes and personal possessions. But he added one other: 'He was buried almost where he fell the following morning with the rest of our unfortunate comrades, wrapped in a military blanket.'[8]

One might have thought that such letters, so indicative of the mutual care, comradeship, and family feeling that exists in regiments, or the fact that Herbert's corporal had described him feelingly as 'the best friend I ever had and a true chum' would have prompted poetic emotion in Housman. But Herbert's unlucky death seems to have struck no poetic spark, prompted no threnody for young men cut down in their prime and provoked no denunciation of a war that was becoming unpopular with sections of the opposition, press and the general public.

There is, however, a dead soldier wrapped in a blanket in Housman's *Illic Jacet*, [Over there he lies] with its opening lines 'Oh hard is the bed they have made him,/And common the blanket and cheap', but it dates from a first draft of 1895, before the Boer War began. Subsequently it was published in *The Academy* in February 1900, again before Herbert's death, and finally in *Last Poems*. Herbert himself may have provided the inspiration for the line when he wrote to the Mater in January about a hunting expedition in Upper Burma. 'We slept on the cold, cold, oh very cold ground with only a blanket to cover us,'[9] possibly quite enough to leave a rhythmic trace in Housman's subconscious, to be reproduced in his subsequent *Illic Jacet*.

However his poem *Astronomy,* begun in 1895 and first published in 1904 in *Wayfarers Love: Contributions from Living Poets,* may well speak to Herbert's disappointed hopes in his chosen profession:

> The Wain upon the northern steep
>   Descends and lifts away.
> Oh I will sit me down and weep
>   For bones in Africa.
>
> For pay and medals, name and rank,
>   Things that he has not found...

And there is the poem Kate always believed was about Herbert, though it was never in any way so acknowledged by Housman himself. Published by Laurence in *More Poems*, its first two stanzas fit with what we know of Herbert's single-minded devotion to the army and his ambitions to make his own way through the ranks to a place he was fitted for by education and upbringing:

FAREWELL to a name and number
   Resigned again
To darkness and silence and slumber
   In blood and pain.

So time coils round in a ring
   And home comes he
A soldier cheap to the King
   And dear to me;

Everything we know about Herbert was that he was an intelligent man, articulate, literate, self-confident, happy in his skin, sufficiently extrovert to mix well with his fellow soldiers and earn their respect and affection, yet sufficiently confident to mix with people of some social consequence in the regions where he served. For his twenty-fourth birthday Housman had sent him a copy of Rudyard Kipling's *Barrack Room Ballads*. These earned Herbert's commendation in a letter to the Mater: 'The book that Alfred sent me has been the delight of myself and my comrades ever since I got it ... There never was a man, and I think will never be again, who understands Tommy Atkins in the rough, as he does.'[10]

Laurence's literary spoof

Meanwhile, brother Laurence was about to step into the limelight. We shall never know what combination of the tendency to secrecy engendered by his stepmother, or what trace of genetic inheritance from his trickster father, or what measure of sibling competition with his brother, what attention-seeking and innate desire to shock, or more simply, what desire for money, drove Lawrence to publish in late 1900 his anonymous and sensational literary spoof, *An Englishwoman's Love-Letters*. It has been called 'the last great literary sensation of the Victorian era.'[11] Laurence hatched the idea in concert with his agent J.B. Pinker: 'My agent Pinker, hit on the ingenious device of planting the rather obvious fake on the most respectable and staid of publishers, Mr John Murray whose reputation seemed to guarantee authenticity.'[12] The book was made up of sixty letters written by a girl to a man she was about to marry. He suddenly broke off the engagement and refused to see her again. (Not revealed to the reader but implied was the fact that they shared the same father.)

Murray, not party to the spoof, quickly appreciated its unique selling points. His marketing of it was astute. The critics were taken in and the book was propelled forward on a wave of approval for its undoubted literary quality. The erotic charge in the woman's letters was pushing against the frontiers of what at the time was judged fit to print. Laurence's suggestive design for the book helped.

> The need to untie the lingerie-like silk ribbons to allow access to the letters solicited a feeling of stolen intimacy which the letters themselves did nothing to dispel: a typical illustration can be found in Letter LXXVIII, 'take me in your arms! I ache and ache not to belong to you. I do: I must. It is only our senses that divide us; and mine are all famished servants waiting for their master.'[13]

A guessing game began in which the names of Edith Wharton, Elizabeth von Arnim and Oscar Wilde all featured as the book's author. It became an overnight best-seller, went quickly into nine impressions and made Laurence £2,000 in its first year alone. Murray promoted the book to the top of his list and printed 'Mr Murray regrets the inevitable delay which purchasers are experiencing in obtaining copies of this book. He is doing all he can to expedite the work. So immediate and unprecedented a success holds him excused.'[14] Such hyping told Laurence that he had struck gold: 'I went home feeling my fortune was made, and bought myself an overcoat such as I had never been able to afford before, and two beautiful Persian rugs.'[15] Of course, there had to be a reaction when it dawned on the press and critics that they had been taken in and were dealing with a work of fiction. A boom in writings designed to ridicule the book followed. Laurence did not admit his authorship until late 1902 and thereafter realised that, as a serious writer, his adventure had been a step backwards from which his career might never recover.

As he said in his autobiography, 'Love Letters was still remembered against me.'[16] Alfred Sutro recorded an occasion when he was dining at Laurence's flat, brother Alfred being the only other guest. When Sutro referred to the rumour that Laurence had written the Letters and added that it was preposterous to think that he could have produced such tawdry stuff,[17] Laurence merely laughed, but Sutro noted that Alfred's chuckle was grim. Laurence had known that the book would have no appeal for Alfred who had passed his copy on to their younger brother Herbert, just leaving for the war in South Africa, with the remark that after that, the Boers would have no terrors for him.

Laurence's willingness actively to deceive and produce a book with steamy love at its centre was one thing, and strange though that was, it could be regarded as part of his protean and excitable nature. His deception of Murray, even though Murray seems to have behaved like a man more than willing to have the wool pulled over his eyes, was something else. It was reminiscent of his father's carelessness about the outcome of his actions when he attempted to take his relatives for a ride, and of his elder brother's carelessness for consequences at Oxford.

Recollections and reflections of Housman at University College

At University College, the Dean of the Faculty was revealing himself as a man of parts. What were they making of this dual personality? What was its impact on them? A female undergraduate of the period, G.H. Savory, later recalled him vividly:

I attended his Latin lectures at University College, from 1900 to 1903. I was one of the comparatively few women undergraduates of those days, and I remember him as a tall, slender, serious-faced man, who never seemed to see his class. There was an occasional flash of humour, sometimes so dry that we might easily miss it; there was never a moment wasted or misspent; and we had great satisfaction in listening to his calm, judicial pronouncements on the interpretation of the Latin texts we read – Livy, Ovid, Plautus, Lucretius, Cicero, Horace.

A favourite phrase of his was 'really and truly'. He said it hundreds of times. We mocked it once in the college magazine. 'So-and-so would translate the passage thus', he would say, 'And so-and-so in this way, but' — the habitual pause — 'really and truly'. And we would wait breathlessly for the real thing to come. I kept my lecture notes for years; they were so convincing.

He gave additional voluntary lectures, reading aloud without textual criticism various translations which he thought we should enjoy. When he read Catullus, it was with an obvious pleasure in the love lyrics of Lesbia; but with unmoved dignity he would sometimes say: 'the next song is too sensuous to read here. I shall omit it.'

Of course we all knew that he was the author of *A Shropshire Lad*, which had appeared not long before. One of us parodied his poem, 'When I was one and twenty.' 'When I was one and twenty, I heard the Housman say, 'Give nouns and verbs and pronouns, In such and such a way.' The parody had some vogue, but no one dared to show it to Housman.[18]

One parody of 'The lads in their hundreds to Ludlow come in for the fair,' was published in the college magazine, *The Parallelogram*. Gerald Gould, one of Housman's students, happened to be its editor and called it *Ballad of the B.A. Classes (with apologies)* spoken by Professor Housman himself. Here are the first and last of its four stanzas:

> The lads in their hundreds come up—(it's a twopenny fare
> If you travel by tube, which myself I do not ever do)—
> The lads for the Inter., the lads for the final, are there,
> And there, with the rest, are the lads who will never get through.
>
> My students may come to my lectures or not as they please;
> But I know, if they don't, the result that is safe to ensue;
> They will carry back bright to the Office the requisite fees—
> The lads who go up and come down and can never get through.[19]

Housman appeared in a poem titled *The Emendation* on the subject of a neat textual emendation of the student's own:

> Where were Scaliger, Porson and Bentley?
> And Housman—ah! Where wandered he?
> (Yet with him I should wish to deal gently,
> That he may deal gently with me.)
> Has he e'er in his books or his lectures
> Once chanced on a comment so fine?
> But I'm ready to praise his conjectures
> If he will do justice to mine.[20]

And there was a limerick printed in the magazine of March 1907:

> There was a Professor of Latin
> Who honoured the Chair which he sat in,
> In preparing a text

He was never perplexed
When to strike this word out and put that in.[21]

Mortimer Wheeler, one of his pupils who became a celebrated archaeologist, produced caricatures of Housman and remembered him in a sharply observed description:

Housman I knew then as the austere and aloof Professor of Latin. He had very little liaison with his students, who came and went at their own individual discretion. He had, if I remember rightly, something of a special dislike for female students, but his tongue could on occasion be as biting to all of us as his published prefaces. In spite of this we all liked him in a kind of way, and felt a certain awe of him as a man of mystery and of manifest ability. The Shropshire Lad never emerged: but when he interpreted a page of a Latin text, his precise and incisive translations, free from all ambiguity and humbug, are remembered still. No one, I think, knew him, and I doubt very much if he knew very much about himself. Somewhere, however, I have a copy of the Shropshire Lad which, greatly daring, I asked him to sign on my last day. He did so with his usual matter of coarseness [sic] but with a slight unwonted tinkle [sic] in his eye.[22]

Richard Aldington, poet, novelist and critic, biographer of D.H. Lawrence and T.E. Lawrence, spoke at length of his own mistaken assessment of Housman in a New York lecture of about 1938. He had spent a year at University College with high expectations of sitting at Housman's feet but found himself gravely disappointed, his expectations dashed:

It would hardly have been possible to make a greater miscalculation True, I saw Housman stalking across the quadrangle or through the long drab corridors of University College; but that was all. His lectures were delivered to senior students taking honours – heights to which I could not aspire. And, so far as I know, he never addressed a word privately or publicly to any of the other students. He would walk past us, staring straight in front of him, with a forbidding expression on his face which left us silent and awed. It was as if he were enclosed in an invisible envelope of frigidity ... This was the more remarkable since the relations between the students and the other professors at London University were friendly and cordial ... We had a Literary Society of about two hundred students, and professors would attend and take part in the discussion about any paper that was read... During the eighteen years Housman was at the University he read only eight papers; and not one while I was there ... we got an impression of Housman as a morose, gloomy, high-hatting kind of man, who looked upon us with contempt as ignorant youths, as indeed we were, but it was after all his business to make us less so. The unfavourable impression he made on me was a lasting one; I thought he was an unpleasant character, a regular old curmudgeon. In later years I more than once stayed in Cambridge as the guest of one or other of the Fellows; but when asked if I cared to meet Housman I invariably replied: 'Certainly not. I saw more than enough of him at London.' Whereupon they would laugh, and tell me I was wrong, but I didn't believe them. He went on 'Well, I was wrong.' Though he had his full share of acrimony which seems inseparable from great classical learning, the real reason for his extraordinary behaviour was that he was hopelessly and helplessly shy and sensitive, as well as proud and exacting.[23]

There were women students at University College but Housman evidently saw no need to encourage them. He probably qualified as a misogynist of the first order. Percy Withers, a friend of his later Cambridge days, later summed him up like this:

He was an avowed misogynist, uneasy and self-conscious in the company of unfamiliar women, courteous always, but strained in courtesy, and frank and emphatic in his denunciation of the sex generally. 'Where would you expect her to be?' he was once asked at table when savagely inveighing against a hostess who, after presiding at a dinner-party of men, joined them later in the drawing room. 'In the pantry!' he snapped. Indeed no subject was more certain of rousing him to willing and decisive speech.[24]

Even so, there is no evidence that Housman actively persecuted female students. Rather, he made no allowances for them nor tailored his behaviour to meet their supposed needs. He did not identify them as a group or seek to ingratiate himself with them as a group, although he ought to have remembered their names. He seems to have been as cool and distant with them as he was with any male student.

Professor Oliver remembered a move in the Professors' Dining Club to admit women. 'This was killed by Housman's invective,' but then he went on to say:

> I think he was right. If women had been admitted they would have come rather in the spirit of conducting a 'children's hour'. It is proper that men should dine together, and that women should partake of their poached eggs and coffee in their own way; whilst there are occasions (apart from the domestic circle) when both may sit together at a common table. Had women accepted admission to the Club, a good thing would have been destroyed for something different – something unpredictable, from which, like marriage, there could be no honourable release.[25]

Although many may have shared or gone along with his attitudes, Housman showed himself to be narrow-minded and prejudiced. His general intolerance of women was as irrational and prejudiced as the intolerance shown to Oscar Wilde by late Victorian society.

Jeannie Fletcher

What light does this shed on the case of Jeannie Fletcher who was removed from his classes which she attended several times a week? It seems that her parents entertained Housman to Sunday supper from time to time in the 1890s, very understandably since her father Dr George Fletcher was himself an Old Bromsgrovian, and his father, also a doctor, had been a Housman family doctor. Richard Perceval Graves' idea that Housman passed their door on Sundays and knocked on it because he had few friends in Highgate and longed for company and had a special need for Jeannie's company is bizarre on every count. It is not impossible that Housman was attracted to her and was trying to find out whether he could form a relationship with a woman, as many homosexuals do.

More likely, the young woman herself suggested that her parents should invite him, or, even more likely, her father hearing that Housman was teaching her, took the not unnatural initiative of inviting Housman through his daughter and after a first meeting made a welcoming offer of future Sundays. But this all stopped at the end of Jeannie's first year when she was taken away from University College, not because her parents feared dishonourable intentions but because, as Paul Naiditch has shown,[26] they knew that Housman's maternal grandmother had been deranged and his father had died an alcoholic. Being protective of their daughter, they did not wish her to form an attachment to a man with such a genetic background. The episode at least demonstrates that Housman was not entirely averse to social connection with women, liked Jeannie enough to accept invitations, and she found him sufficiently good value to welcome further visits. There is no evidence that Housman remarked on her disappearance from his classes, or thereafter communicated with her. Most likely it simply did not matter to him; he might well have felt relieved.

Housman's time at University College gives the lie to his unsociability. He had reached out verbally to the students in his speech as Dean and thereafter, in twenty-first century parlance, 'walked the talk', and in spite of what Aldington said of him, became fully involved in the College Debating Society, the Literary Society and the Arts Society.

The students soon began to appreciate Housman's style. The minutes of the debating Society's first debate on extending the franchise to women saw him taking the chair where he presumably used his casting vote against the motion. At a debate on democratic government, again in the chair, he summed up in favour of democracy on the grounds that it was difficult to betray a government you had yourself chosen. As a guest at the annual dinner of the Society, he was reported to have made a most delightful speech, full of wit and wisdom, and as little didactic as the speech of a professor could be expected to be. Housman was an extremely effective speaker but his social contribution to the College was not only as a sparkling solo performer. Together with W.P. Ker and Arthur Platt, he was one of a triumvirate of witty men of learning who provided vintage years for the lucky students and gave them an education in how to argue and score points with wit and grace.

In his time Housman gave at least five or six lectures to the Literary Society, on Matthew Arnold, the 'Spasmodics', Erasmus Darwin, Robert Burns, Tennyson and perhaps Swinburne. R.W. Chambers, who was an undergraduate at the time, reflected in his book *Man's Unconquerable Mind* that 'his affability to students was astonishing – I mean that, however severe his criticism of our work might be, he was willing to meet us in the College Literary Society and at Arts Dinners, and to break a lance with any Professor, any junior teacher, or any student who was reckless enough to challenge him.' He went on:

> In these debates Housman, like his colleague Ker, had the power which belongs to the great, as it belonged to Dr Johnson: if his pistol missed fire he knocked you down with the butt end. He would make a retort which, from anybody else, would not have been altogether conclusive, but the effect of which as uttered by Housman was devastating.[27]

Chambers instanced the occasion of the discussion following Housman's paper on Tennyson:

> Platt who was in the chair, followed his practice of dropping on any member of the audience to speak, and called on me. I excused myself on the ground that Housman had uttered not merely his own but God's opinion on Tennyson, and that though I was willing to debate with Housman, I could not debate with one who had come armed with God's judgement. So I sat down, quoting Job's excuse for his silence, 'Wherefore I abhor myself and repent in dust and ashes.' I felt somewhat complacently that I had escaped rather well. When Housman rose to reply he said that he could attach no importance to what Mr Chambers said since he had been credibly informed that Mr Chambers read the *Church Times*. I felt, and everyone in the room felt, that I had been entirely flattened out. To lay an adversary low by a reply which would have been ineffective in the mouth of a smaller man, is the mark of the great debater.[28]

Chambers also illustrated Ker's witty ability to avoid confrontation when, after a Housman lecture on Robert Burns, full of jibes at Scots and Scotsmen, he simply said 'Forgiveness is the last refuge of malignity. I will not forgive Professor Housman.'[29]

By the time of the 1907 Arts Dinner – an enthusiastic, joyful and noisy affair – Housman's reputation was secure. An account of the dinner placed him at the centre of the College's life:

> The chairman, Professor Housman. This most brilliant gem in the Faculty's crown – if I may so metamorphically designate the staff – is nothing if not versatile, and were he not so distinguished in other ways, he would still be entitled to fame as an after-dinner speaker.[30]

Housman's time at University College was one of fulfilment, happiness and success across the board. He made good, close and lasting friends among his peers and in spite of that personal distance which he characteristically put between himself and his students his was a distinctly positive presence in the life of the college. He was able to display every facet of his talent, character and behaviour without allowing any intimacy to undermine the walls of his private inner and emotional life or diminish his authority, or put himself in a false position, or make himself vulnerable. So it was not entirely surprising that R.W. Chambers remarked 'Yet beneath all lay Housman's impenetrable reserve. There was something ironical in his sitting amid an enthusiastic crowd of students, all singing that he was "a jolly good fellow"'[31]

Paradoxically, he generated affection. The fun his students made of him was based on their liking him because he was truly on their side; and on their respect, approaching awe for him, as a teacher. It needed only his histrionic gifts, his capacity for public speaking and debating, to put them at his feet. He published verse serious and light in College publications including his translation of Horace's celebrated ode, *Diffugere Nives* and perhaps more risky to his professorial image, had it ever been leaked, his authorship of comic verses *The Parallelogram, (1904) The Amphisbaena (1906) and The Crocodile (1911).*

University College had become his new family to which he gave and from which he received in like quantities. He had resumed his role as the elder son.

1903: *Volume I of Manilius dedicated to Moses Jackson*

Meanwhile, his life of scholarship and lecturing had continued in full flood. His flow of classical papers had continued. To these was added an even more significant achievement, the first volume of his edition of Manilius, *M.Manilii astronomicon,* published by Grant Richards in 1903. This first volume was remarkable, not least for the arrogant pronouncement on its title page: *Editorum in usum edidit* (for the use of editors), Housman's way of putting lesser scholars in their place. Naiditch concludes 'In short *editorum in usum* is a phrase meant to be identified by the reader with elementary instruction, and as such is a calculated insult.'[32]

This first volume contained a vast data bank of prefatory material laid before the reader in all its organised density, identifying and comparing manuscripts, making judgements on the work of previous editors frequently in strikingly emotive language, making detailed observations on corruptions of many kinds, continually providing explanations and conjectures of his own and others. This was direct evidence of Housman's amazing capacity in a pre-computer age, to organise, arrange, check, make intelligible and present, in his statuesquely handsome handwriting, a mountain of interrelated data. Even more striking is the paradox that the same mind could produce the spare beauties of *A Shropshire Lad*, that such an organised and orderly mind could also be a conduit for poetry – as striking a paradox as the *merde*-minded Mozart being a conduit for heavenly music. More remarkable was the fact that Housman dedicated this first volume not to an inspiring teacher or forerunner, for example his hero Bentley who had begun work on his edition of Manilius more than two hundred years earlier, or H.A.J. Munro who had sharpened his youthful appetite for textual criticism and who Housman referred to as 'the foremost English Latinist of the century'. Nor did he invoke an anonymous muse.

The dedication there, on his first page, was deeply personal. This first volume of his life's work was dedicated to *Sodali Meo* (my mate, my comrade) *M.J. Jackson*. This was an act of startling self-revelation, yet naively provocative, since it was accompanied by the qualification *Harum litterarum contempori* (who pays no heed to these writings). This dedication, like his effort to obtain advancement for Jackson, was startling evidence of the continuing depth of his feelings.

The twenty-eight lines of Latin dedication reflect in various translations how he and Moses had watched the stars appear while they roamed a silent countryside, how the fate of Manilius' verses had barely preserved their author's name. Housman was not in the court of appealing to stars or gods – 'I couldn't bear to beg eternal gods or stars' – and so he addressed Moses directly:

> But touched by love of virtue that will quickly pass,
> I searched for someone with determination;
> A man, I chose a man, a brave and fleeting friend
> Who in my book should want this dedication.
> O you who thrive or fall, I'd say, within these pages,
> Though with a name that merits living on:
> I send this gift conveyed from western shores to you
> Who followed stars ascending at the dawn.

Come now, accept; that day we join the dead is coming,
Which gives the dirt our bones as they decay
With spirits destined not to live eternally
And bonds between dear friends that fade away.

The sentiments of this dedication contain the essence of Housman: acceptance of the finite nature of human life, calm recognition that all we love and cherish will die and fade, explicitly including the bonds of friendship between himself and Moses. In August 1903 he was clearly intent on keeping that friendship alive and told his publisher Grant Richards that he wanted one of the morocco bound copies before he went on holiday 'in order to send it to India to the friend to whom the book is dedicated.'[33]

This dedication in Latin to a man totally unknown in the world of classical scholarship appears to have gone unnoticed; perhaps readers were simply baffled, and of course the publication of Housman's classical work was reviewed nothing like as widely as *A Shropshire Lad*. In the *Athenaeum* review he was praised as one of the most skilful Latin scholars of the day whose brilliant and uncompromising expositions of textual matters were a pleasure to read although the reviewer remarked 'a little modesty would improve his case.'[34]

Housman's slashing invective

This brief notice in the *Classical Review* also referred to 'the slashing style which we all know and few applaud'. This was not surprising, for the preface to *Manilius* was permeated with Housman's censures on critics in general and individuals in particular. Denigration of other scholars was a thread running through his classical papers, book reviews, notebooks and marginal comments.

His earliest reviews had been confident, showing his mastery of the sting in the tail, used to keep other scholars in their place. Where American scholars were concerned, he had a good line in chauvinistic amusement. None of this could be described as 'slashing'.

Following his election to the Latin Chair at University College in 1892 he produced three massive and masterly papers on Propertius, each notably devoid of attacks on fellow scholars. It was only when the *Transactions of the Cambridge Philological Society* subsequently published Dr Postgate's pamphlet of eighty-two pages on 'certain manuscripts of Propertius' that Housman's tone changed. Their bruising encounter has already been described; it witnessed Housman's descent to what can only be called a compound of low personal abuse spiced with powerful doses of self-righteous pomposity.

However, when he came to review Postgate's *Sexti Properti Carmina* in 1895 he was considerably more restrained. His judgements were still blunt but this time he employed the opposite of the sting in the tail – the patronising pat on the head: 'Many alterations are to my thinking unsuccessful, and import a good deal which is wrong and a great deal which is doubtful; but the general result is a text which I should call not only nearer but much nearer to the truth than any which has gone before it.'[35]

Nevertheless, the strain of personalised attack was still alive and well, and it is instructive to fast forward six years. In 1901 he would write, 'For scholars to argue against me as Mr Heitland argues is just the way to foster in me that arrogant temper to which I owe my deplorable reputation.'[36] Heitland had made the mistake of correcting Housman: 'Thus Mr Heitland, who shrinks from the conjectural emendation of Lucan, proceeds to the conjectural emendation of me; though I have not been dead nearly so long, nor do nine centuries of transcription intervene between my autograph and last December's *Classical Review.*' In another paper of the same year, *The New Fragment of Juvenal*, he referred to eight critics who had written about Juvenal in learned journals in Berlin, France, Belgium, Germany and Italy. 'None of these writings makes any contribution to the explanation or emendation of the fragment.'[37]

In 1902 in his *Remarks on the Culex* he referred to the editions of Baehrens in 1880 and Leo in 1891 as 'patterns of insobriety ... Witness one piece of precipitate blundering which I select from many others.'[38]

He employed his verbal rapier in his review of H.E. Butler's work on Propertius:

> These are the words of a dying soldier whose last thought is of his sister, and Mr Butler thus translates them: 'nor let her ever know that whatever bones she may find on the Tuscan hills are mine.' Certainly the discovery that her brother had 1000 skulls, 2000 femora and 26,000 vertebrae, would be at once a painful shock to her affections and an overwhelming addition to her knowledge of anatomy.[39]

His capacity to slash, to wield his pen like a sabre, to mow down an antagonist was best shown in his reaction to S.G. Owen's work on Ovid:

> His first edition of the *Tristia* had value, which it still retains, as furnishing full collations of the principal manuscripts; but its reader was repeatedly jolted out of his chair by collision with obstacles in the text. Picking himself up from the hearthrug, and feeling his neck to make sure it was not broken, he would find that what he had encountered was either a lection which no other editor had ever admitted or a conjecture which no other editor could easily have made.[40]

Owen was clearly one of Housman's *bêtes noires*. Later in 1918 in his paper *Juvenal and Two of his Editors* he would give him another broadside:

> The causes which render me unintelligible to Mr Owen and Mr Owen unintelligible to me are probably many and various, but perhaps it is not difficult to distinguish and isolate one. I am accustomed to reach conclusions by reasoning and to commend them by argument. How Mr Owen reaches conclusions I have no means of knowing except by observing how he commends them; and I observe that argument is not his favourite method. His favourite method is simple affirmation which he applies to the settlement of disputed questions with the utmost freedom and confidence. For this confidence I see so little ground that I infer it has some ground which I cannot see; and the less evidence of reason I find in Mr Owen's writing the more I am forced to the hypothesis that he has access to a higher and purer source of illumination.[41]

If we were to speculate on where this undoubted strain of anger came from, it is much more likely that its genesis lay in the blows life had dealt him, in the death of his mother and his impossible attachment to Moses Jackson, rather than with abstract notions of honesty and truth. The causal relationship between unhappiness and anger is well established in psychological theory.

There was an additional source of unhappiness, revealed in verses from *A Shropshire Lad* XLI, *In my own shire, if I was sad.* In the country Housman had been able to find solace in nature and its seasons, 'homely comforters', which he felt to be in sympathy with himself and his own mood. By comparison: 'here in London streets I ken / No such helpmates, only men; / And these are not in plight to bear, / If they would another's care. / They have enough as 'tis.' The next six lines, seen by Paul Naiditch as 'arguably autobiographical,' point us to a more general source of Housman's invective and unhappiness, his sense of alienation from other men. He sees them as 'Too unhappy to be kind,' as he was himself:

> I see
> In many an eye that measures me
> The mortal sickness of a mind
> Too unhappy to be kind.
> Undone with misery, all they can
> Is to hate their fellow man.[42]

PART VI

Who am I?

Morality and sexual difference then and now

It is most likely that Housman had concluded by the late 1880s that he was different, most likely homosexual. There was no suggestion that Edward or Lucy were ever aware of this fact or that any behaviour of Housman's prompted enquiry. No additional shadows were placed over his life by parental rejection, though for Housman the potential must always have been there.

Writing today about Housman's sexual orientation may seem to be superfluous but it is relevant to examine how he handled his situation then and throughout his life. In particular, the moral and social significance of sexual relationships in British society seems to have been totally recalibrated. Commonplaces of British society today are that unmarried young people live together careless of reactions from parents or society; couples frequently have children before they marry; birth control makes the procreation of children a matter of choice; divorce will be the fate of about half the population of marrieds. Civil partnerships and marriage for same sex couples have been introduced; after a debate in the British House of Commons on gay marriage, the Prime Minister David Cameron was reported at the time as saying in a broadcast:

> There will be young boys in schools today who are gay, who are worried about being bullied, who are worried about what society thinks of them, who can see that the highest Parliament in the land has said that their love is worth the same as anyone else's love and that we believe in equality ... And I think that they'll stand that bit taller today and I'm proud of the fact that has happened.

Sexual activity seems to have been deprived of its social and religious significances. It has become clear that enjoyment of any particular variety of sexual pleasure is not restricted to a particular part of the gender spectrum. Our vocabulary and usage seems not to have caught up with these facts, and not with the reality of a spectrum that ranges from platonic friendships based on pleasurable traits and companionship, through all kinds of physical alliances prompted by the giving and receiving of bodily pleasure, to rounder and more complex attachments where sexual compatibility and unconditional devotion co-exist. Any equation of the words 'sex' and 'love' is today misguided in the extreme.

In Housman's time it was all simpler and fundamentalist. He came from a home suffused with religious observance, High Church in the time of his mother, Low Church in the time of his stepmother, but both governed by the Old Testament strictures of Leviticus, which regarded sexual transactions between men as an 'abomination' punishable by death.

The social fact of Housman's time was that the Labouchere Amendment of 1886 (when Housman was twenty-six) had widened the grounds on which individuals might be prosecuted, so that any sort of sexual transaction between men was publicly categorised as 'unmentionable' and 'unnatural' vice; those involved were a separate population, labelled indiscriminately as 'sodomites', 'mollies', 'margeries' and 'poufs'. And so it was that in 1895 Wilde – unwisely – decided to sue Queensberry for criminal libel and lost the case. Queensberry was acquitted but sufficient had been revealed of Wilde's connections with pimps and rent boys for Queensberry's lawyers to forward the trial papers to the Director of Public Prosecutions, whereupon Wilde was promptly arrested and charged with 'gross indecency'. At his first trial, the jury failed to reach a verdict. He was tried again, convicted and sentenced to two years' hard labour.

Housman's reading and research on sexual difference

In the setting of his time Housman dealt with his own sense of difference in the only way he knew – by making it an intellectual issue and by researching it. Housman's library included 'a group of works concerned with sexual matters 51 titles or 94 volumes.'[1] Insofar as a third of the books could be classed as serious research on the nature and origin of sexual difference, their existence in his library substantiates the view that he was searching for the truth about himself. On the other hand, a number of volumes on flagellation, sadism, masochism and fetishes, sundry erotica and legal cases may suggest interest in alternative means for sexual release.

One specially significant book in his library was a French translation of Albert Moll's *Die contrare Sexualempfindung* (1891) with its preface by Dr Richard von Krafft-Ebing, *Les Perversions de l'instinct génital. Étude sur l'inversion sexuelle basée sur les documents officiels* (Perversions of the sexual instinct. Study of Inversion based on official documents).

Moll's book was based on hundreds of interviews with Berlin 'uranists' [homosexuals] and on the testimony of the sympathetic head of the Pederasty Division of the German police. Moll concluded that homosexuality was not 'picked up' like a vice or a habit but appeared in early childhood and was probably congenital. Moll countered the idea that homosexuality was 'unnatural' with his own argument: 'Man generally performs the sexual act with women, not with the conscious aim of producing children, but to satisfy an irresistible urge.'[2] Thus, a homosexual who had sex with another homosexual was performing a natural act.

Graham Robb observes in his *Strangers: Homosexual Love in the Nineteenth Century*:

> Over half a century before the Kinsey Report, Moll replaced the quasi-ethnic division of humanity into hetero- and homo-sexual with the notion of a sexual continuum when he said: 'One can easily see that sexual inversion is not isolated from normal sexual life by an unbridgeable gulf. In bisexuality, as in all other domains, one finds intermediate cases ranging from a mere trace of homosexual love to the most pronounced uranism.'[3]

Moll's was an acute insight but one whose time had not yet come.

Also in Housman's library was a series of volumes issued by the German Scientific and Humanitarian Committee founded by Dr Magnus Hirschfeld. He had been deeply shocked in 1895 by just such an event as had inspired Housman to write his poem *Shot? so quick so clean an ending?* Hirschfeld 'was shaken by a suicide letter from one of his patients: a young homosexual lieutenant who killed himself on the eve of his wedding. His dying wish was that Dr Hirschfeld (who was also homosexual) would help to improve the lot of people like himself.'[4] His committee was formed in May 1897 and subsequently produced a *Yearbook of Sexual Intermediacy* (Jahrbuch für sexuelle Zwischenstufen unter besonderer Berüchsichtigung der Homosexualität). Housman's library contained an almost complete collection of the *Yearbook* for the years 1899 to 1923.

In characteristic scholarly fashion Housman had set about informing himself, but on this occasion without leaving any note of his reaction to what he read. His reading would have told him that there were others like him, and that people like himself did not fit any particular stereotype.

There is no evidence that his needs were so pressing that he sought risky solace with others, or actively sought to identify people like himself. The distance he put naturally and instinctively between himself and others deepened his own isolation; he was neither an uninhibited talker, nor a self-obsessed exhibitionist nor an obviously beautiful young man. Silence and isolation were thrust upon him essentially by his own nature, but he would have been inhuman had he not felt pain, shock and fear which served to reinforce the private and repressed person he was. He may also have realised that his brother Laurence was sexually different. It may have occurred to him to think that there was a family disposition.

Searching for reflections of Housman

Housman's almost total silence on the subject produces a seeming impasse for the biographer, encouraging speculation and guess work. But the fact is that other men who had found themselves sexually different were not a homogenous group; for them the words sex and love had demonstrably different meanings.

The behaviour and life trajectories of some of Housman's older and younger contemporaries may be used to provide a kind of mirror to help us position Housman along Moll's continuum. Biographical information about Oscar Wilde, Maynard Keynes, Siegfried Sassoon, Harold Nicolson, T.E. Lawrence and Laurence Housman demonstrates that the only trait they had obviously in common was that they were all achievers, and in their different ways made a positive contribution to society.

Oscar Wilde (1854–1900), celebrated wit, playwright and novelist, was in every way the complete antithesis of Housman. He began as a married man in 1884. Within two years he had become the father

Figure 17 Distinguished economist John Maynard
Keynes and his wife, ballet dancer Lydia Lopokova,
by William Roberts 1932. By courtesy of the estate of
John David Roberts.

of two sons, Cyril and Vyvyan. Thereafter he was overwhelmed
by his feelings for men. Wilde was a highly talented exhibitionist,
a posturing aesthete who lived flamboyantly, dangerously and
promiscuously. Loving an audience, he was intent on living his life
in public. He embraced his public crucifixion at the Old Bailey, in
Graham Robb's phrase 'providing the hammer and nails himself'. His
intention was 'to oblige a hypocritical age to take him as he was'.
And so, with a memorable choice of words, he stood in the dock
and spoke up for 'the love that dare not speak its name' and was sent
down for two years.[5]

Maynard Keynes (1883–1946), one of the most influential
economists of the twentieth century, came from a family possessed
with a will to achieve. Maynard revealed himself as a man of protean
ability – intellectual, financial and artistic – allied with extraordinary
mental energy and a singular capacity to impress others; he
demonstrated a facility to network and to move himself in any social
direction he wished. Following the First World War he became the
chief Treasury representative at the Versailles Peace Conference; after

the Second World War, he was leader of the British delegation at the Bretton Woods Conference of 1944, which set up the International Monetary Fund, the IMF.

Keynes kept a meticulously arranged diary of his sex life, each sexual act with men clearly categorised as a C, A or W, for which his diary provided no key, but which calls for no great imagination to interpret. In 1921, he fell in love with Lydia Lopokova then dancing with Diaghilev's ballet in London; he married her in 1925. With Keynes' active support, she continued her career as a ballet dancer and subsequently as an actress. Although they produced no children, theirs was a mutually supportive marriage. Keynes wrote to Vanessa Bell, with whom he maintained an uninhibited and intimate correspondence: 'I still love Lydia very much. We had a good deal of *eclairissement* on Sunday, which was very painful for a moment, but seems to have made no real difference to us at all. Indeed we are extremely happy.' This sounds as though they had spoken frankly to each other about their sexual needs and that what they had confessed did not matter to them at all. Lydia and Maynard lived happily together until Keynes' death in 1946.[6]

It is surprising that Siegfried Sassoon (1886–1967) and Housman never met. During the First World War, Sassoon had a copy of *A Shropshire Lad* in his knapsack, and it was in his list of books to take when he was drafted to Egypt in 1917; there is no record of his ever having commented on it. By the time he left school Sassoon knew that he was different. According to his biographer Max Egremont, 'Siegfried Sassoon knew what set him apart: his Jewishness, his delicacy and his homosexuality.' Sassoon did not react by becoming a loner; he did not cast himself as an outsider; he positively identified with all that was manly and excelled at fox hunting and cricket. When war came in 1914 he took a commission in the Royal Welsh Fusiliers and became a fine and courageous leader who was awarded the Military Cross for gallantry in action. When a wounded Sassoon was invalided back to England, he was not afraid to publish his famous *Statement* (essentially a refusal to perform any further military duties because of the government's policy, as he saw it, of prolonging the war). Hauled up to account for himself, he was sent to Craiglockhart War Hospital by a medical board in lieu of court-martial, which would have led to his dismissal from the army or worse. Vivian de Sola Pinto, a fellow poet and Sassoon's second-in-command in 1917, described him to his sister: 'the noble head, mane of dark hair, piercing black

Figure 18 Siegfried Sassoon, poet
and war hero, at Flixecourt, 1916.
By permission from Ralph Hodgson
Papers, General Collection, Beinecke
Rare Book and Manuscript Library,
Yale University.

eyes and strongly sculpted features'. Sassoon had been profoundly
impressed by Edward Carpenter's book *The Intermediate Sex* and
wrote to Carpenter in July 1911 of its 'opening a new life to me, after a
time of great perplexity and unhappiness'. He wrote 'What ideas I had
about homosexuality were absolutely unprejudiced, and I was in such
a groove that I couldn't allow myself to be what I wished to be, and
the intense attraction felt for my own sex was almost a subconscious
thing, and my antipathy for women a mystery to me.'

Because of his sociable chameleon-like character and because he
was open-handed with money, Sassoon was able to move easily in
society and in literary and homosexual circles. It is noteworthy that
when he passed through Cambridge in 1915 he met Sydney Cockerell,
Director of the Fitzwilliam Museum, fellow of Jesus College and a
friend of Housman. There is no record of Sassoon's having met
Housman, or of seeking him out. In 1927 Sassoon met Stephen
Tennant, a famously narcissistic and effeminate twenty-one-year-

old given to parties, dressing up, making-up and interior decoration. After a night together in the open air at Stonehenge, Sassoon noted in his diary: 'He now seems to me the most enchanting creature I have ever met.' To chattering Bloomsbury and the sharp-tongued Sitwells, it was a case of 'the craggy war hero and the precious shrieking aesthete.' Max Egremont described Sassoon as 'attractive, poetically handsome, gentle and sympathetic in manner yet with a strongly masculine presence.'

In 1933 Sassoon met Hester Gatty and exclaimed to his diary, 'O Hester, you must redeem my life for me.' Their first son, George, was born in 1936 when Sassoon was fifty. Sassoon was very attached to him – 'the best thing that life can give.' But by 1938, Hester had decided she could not risk another child, 'a matter of sadness and later of brooding for Sassoon.' Their marriage began to go downhill, essentially because of sexual incompatibility and conflict over George. They were legally separated in December 1950.[7]

Harold Nicolson (1886–1968), diplomat, politician and socialite, was married to Vita Sackville-West by whom he had two sons. He was involved with other men while Vita had a passionate affair with Violet Trefusis, both women having other lesbian entanglements. Yet Harold and Vita lived happily ever after. Nigel Nicolson, their son, had access to his mother's most intimate diaries. He wrote in his foreword to his *Portrait of a Marriage* published in 1973:

> It is the story of two people who married for love and whose love deepened with every passing year, although each was constantly and by mutual consent unfaithful to the other. Both loved people of their own sex, but not exclusively. Their marriage not only survived infidelity, sexual incompatibility and long absences, but became stronger and finer as a result. Each came to give the other full liberty without enquiry or reproach. Honour was rooted in dishonour. Their marriage succeeded because each found permanent and undiluted happiness only in the company of the other. If their marriage is seen as a harbour, their love affairs were mere ports–of–call. It was to the harbour that each returned; it was there that both were based.[8]

Laurence Housman was not quite the exact opposite of his elder brother but he was not remotely intent on conforming. Laurence, a prolific writer and playwright with a passion for causes, wanted to

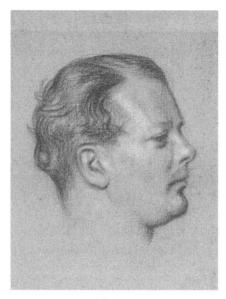

Figure 19: Harold Nicolson, diplomat, writer, garden designer, by Sir William Rothenstein 1925. © National Portrait Gallery, London.

Figure 20 Vita Sackville-West writer, gardener and creator of Sissinghurst. © E.O. Hoppé Estate Collection / Curatorial Assistance, Inc.

change the world, whether he was campaigning for female suffrage, opposing stage censorship, campaigning against war or against the death penalty. He was also homosexual, but he did not campaign openly against the laws on homosexual acts. Personal contact with Edward Carpenter came from sharing a platform at a Trafalgar Square meeting of the Men's League for Women's Suffrage. Subsequently, in 1913, when Magnus Hirschfeld spoke at the Fourteenth International Medical Congress in London, Carpenter involved Laurence Housman in a meeting set up so that Hirschfeld might 'speak with men interested in reforming the laws on homosexuality'. The eventual outcome was the emergence of a new group, the British Society for the Study of Sex Psychology, of which Carpenter and Laurence Housman were co-founders. According to Shelia Rowbotham, 'Housman, [Laurence] signalled its remit; "We are a note of interrogation."'[9]

In his autobiography, *The Unexpected Years*, Laurence spoke of his income: 'Since the War I have had an income amply sufficient for a bachelor, sharing house with a relation who is also self-supporting.' He went on:

> my small income has not prevented me from living a happy life. It is true that such an income made it impossible for me to marry, had I wished it, in 'the class' to which I was supposed to belong; I could not, until I was well over forty, have run the risk of a family. But as the not impossible She never came within the horizon of my waking dreams, that deprivation was more theoretical than real.[10]

So Laurence used lack of money as his excuse for not doing the conventional thing; living with his sister was his convenient cover.

Such glimpses into the lives of others produces what we ought to expect, a banal and totally predictable conclusion, that Oscar Wilde, Maynard Keynes, Siegfried Sassoon, Harold Nicolson and Laurence Housman were different from each other in every imaginable way. What each seems to have needed by way of physical pleasure or sexual satisfaction was very different, both in kind and intensity; what they in the narrative of their lives would describe as 'love' was very different and had different levels of intensity, different mental pictures and emotional longings. A multiplication of cases would merely extend the proof for Moll's contention and produce additional points on the spectrum of difference, serving only to reveal the great

Figure 21 T.E. Lawrence (Lawrence of Arabia) by Augustus John 1919. © National Portrait Gallery, London.

variety of feelings that the hearts and minds of men and women may encompass. Their various personalities can never be homogenized or categorised by a single label. Their feelings and behaviour do not fit into the simple words 'Sex' or 'Love'.

Of all Housman's contemporaries, it was in a younger contemporary, T.E. Lawrence (1888–1935), that Housman recognised himself. 'Lawrence of Arabia' was and remains, an enigmatic character. He went down from Jesus College Oxford in 1910, just before Housman became Professor of Latin at Cambridge. From a young age, he single-mindedly pursued his interests – twelfth-century castles in England, Wales and France, the Crusades and Crusader castles – his travels involving 'extraordinary feats of climbing and walking in France and Syria under conditions of personal privation'. After graduating, he spent three years with the British Museum's archaeological explorations at Carchemish on the Upper Euphrates. During his subsequent, almost personal war in the desert, he led the Arab revolt against the Turks. He carried with him not *A Shropshire Lad* but a copy of Malory's *Morte D'Arthur*, medieval romance being a powerful shaper of his idealistic, romantic attitudes. A philosophical action man, charismatic leader, manager of events and men, Lawrence was notable for his self-direction, ferocious energy and fascination with detail. His writings, sometimes over-complex and confusing but frequently full of insight, portray a man at war with himself. Housman never met him but reacted very powerfully to a passage in *Seven Pillars of Wisdom*, seeing himself as if in a mirror. Lawrence wrote:

> I was very conscious of the bundled powers and entities within me; it was their character which hid. There was my craving to be liked – so strong and nervous that never could I open myself friendly to another. The terror of failure in an effort so important made me shrink from trying; besides, there was the standard; for intimacy seemed shameful unless the other could make the perfect reply, in the same language, after the same method, for the same reasons.

Against this passage Housman scrawled 'This is me.' His annotation may or may not have also covered Lawrence's next paragraph, 'There was a craving to be famous; and a horror of being known to like being known. Contempt for my passion for distinction made me refuse every offered honour. I cherished my independence almost as did a Beduin.'[11]

About this the poet Stephen Spender wrote in April 1940:

> Housman once compared himself with T.E. Lawrence. One of the qualities he must have shared with that other great scholar – although he did not indulge it to the same extent – is surely a shrinking from publicity with an almost violently censured tendency towards exhibitionism.... Both writers evidently want the mystery to remain a mystery. At the same time they cannot help throwing out hints.[12]

Lawrence has been memorably described as having a capacity for 'backing into the limelight'. In a moment of self-searching Lawrence had asked himself 'I began to wonder if all established reputations were founded, like mine, on fraud', and:

> It irritated me, this silly confusion of shyness, which was conduct, with modesty, which was a point of view. I was not modest, but ashamed of my awkwardness, of my physical envelope, and of

my solitary unlikeness which made me no companion, but an acquaintance, complete, angular, uncomfortable as a crystal.[13]

Lawrence sheered away from physical intimacy in any form. 'To put my hand on a living thing was defilement; and it made me tremble if they touched me or took too quick an interest in me.'[14]

John Mack, Lawrence's pre-eminent biographer, could find no evidence in any form that Lawrence

ever as an adult entered voluntarily into a sexual relationship for the purpose of achieving intimacy or pleasure. This applies equally to heterosexual and homosexual relationships. There are a few passages in his letters and notes which indicate a longing for sexual experience, but no evidence that he could act on these longings and much evidence that he could not.[15]

According to Mack:

The clearest statement of Lawrence's sexual puritanism, inhibition and conflict appears in a letter to Mrs Shaw [wife of George Bernard Shaw] in 1925: 'I'm too shy to go looking for dirt. I'm afraid of seeming a novice in it, when I found it.' And to Mrs Shaw he also confessed 'I hate and detest this animal side'.[16]

Lawrence had an almost religious sense of bodily integrity. Traumatised by an assault on him by Turks at Dera, always ashamed of his illegitimacy, fearful of his feelings for his mother and as a child frequently whipped by her, he was a mass of psychological complexities. Certainly, in his later years he was given to flagellation administered by a fellow member of the Tank Corps. These sessions, staged by means of an elaborate set of fictions and rituals, were regarded by Mack as characteristic of Lawrence's inventiveness and creativity.[17]

Thus Housman seems to be positioned on a continuum somewhere near T.E. Lawrence but infinitely distant from Oscar Wilde, Maynard Keynes or Siegfried Sassoon, all of whom experienced periods of obsessive physical need which *had* to be satisfied. Housman seems to have had no obvious desire for fleshly satisfactions; any drives in that direction seem to have been effectively suppressed or to have been non-existent. Housman's form of devotion to somebody he considered well-nigh indispensable was close to that of Harold Nicolson and Vita

Sackville-West. He felt a profound attachment to one other person, whom he could keep in his mind and heart despite time, distance and absence. These feelings could survive and did survive until they were gradually transmuted into a loyal and supportive friendship, even though their object was thousands of miles away. Housman seems to have been so psychologically structured that he could begin with an idealised love in his mind, romanticise it and allow it to develop.

Venetian connections

In the autumn of 1900 Housman made his second expedition to the Continent, again recorded for his stepmother, this time in a trio of letters which reflected precisely his modus operandi as a classical scholar. Encyclopaedic in their profusion of detail, they were larded with decided opinions, precise observations and comparisons. As the train carried him through northern France, through Artois, Picardy and Champagne, he registered the fleeting sight of cathedrals at Laon and Rheims, passed at daybreak into Switzerland, steamed along the length of Lake Lucerne, penetrated the St Gotthard tunnel, descended to Lugano and across the Lombardy plain, where he observed that Lombardy poplars were not actually very common in Lombardy. But there was no mention of other passengers, no human behaviour or incidents to relate. He seems to have gone on his way, wrapped in his solitary observing self, except when required to present passport or ticket. And so to Venice, where he and his luggage were decanted into one of those strange, quasi-mythical, misshapen yet beautiful things, a gondola. Housman records it only as a gondola, which took him via the Grand Canal and lesser canals to his hotel. His letters suggest that in today's parlance he was 'underwhelmed', unreceptive to the special magic of this unique place, rising like a decoration from the water, seemingly unaware of its pathfinding constitutional and political history. We might have expected him to recall what Wordsworth had said in his *On the Extinction of the Venetian Republic*: Once did She hold the gorgeous East in fee;/ And was the safeguard of the west : the worth/ Of Venice did not fall below her birth, / Venice the eldest Child of Liberty. Nor did Venice bring to mind any of Browning's many poems with Italian settings. Housman's thing was architecture. His critical eye turned on architectural detail such as the uniformity of the pattern of the palaces, 'part of the surface consisting of very rich arcades and windows, the rest of painfully flat wall, made worse by being painted'. He didn't remember the city as an entity or describe it in broad brush strokes. On the works of art he came across he had decided opinions: 'that lurid and theatrical Tintoret ... Paul Veronese, whom one soon sees enough of ... surprisingly few Titians, though two of them are very fine and famous'. His descriptions demonstrated an acute sense of colour; he frequently climbed the Campanile, the great bell tower, in the Piazza San Marco, from where he could exercise his sense of colour in word pictures, describing how 'the lagoon lies all round dotted with the stakes which mark out the navigable channels, and the water declares its depth or shallowness by its colour: as the sun goes down it turns partly a golden green and partly a pale vermillion'. He responded enthusiastically, albeit with characteristic caveats, to the wondrous Byzantine Basilica:

> which I think is the most beautiful, not the grandest building in the world. It might be possible to erect in the Gothic style a more beautiful building, but I doubt if such a one exists. It is not lofty, and not large, except that it is broad for its length; but every square yard of it is worth looking at for an hour together. I used to go there nearly every day; but it would take years to exhaust it. It is all covered with coloured marble and alabaster, except where it has gold mosaics, or richly carved stone capitals to the pillars; and yet it does not look a bit like a piece of patchwork; everything helps towards the general effect. The preciousness of the material and the delicacy of the workmanship makes it look almost more like jewellery than architecture, and one feels as if it ought not to be left out of doors at night.

Andrea, my gondolier

Then out of the blue he mentioned a person who must have made a considerable impression on him to be given such an extensive and detailed entry. He described him as 'my gondolier', very much the possessive, but used even to this day by pompous people of a certain generation to demonstrate their superior status, in the vein of *my* builder, *my* architect, *my* gardener, *my* surgeon. It is not surprising that a particular gondolier should have become something of a fixture, taking Housman to and fro. Housman was an energetic and indefatigable tourist, visiting churches, going out to the Lido several times, and to Mestre on the mainland. His gondolier provided him with information; Housman annotated his copy of *Baedeker's Italy: Handbook for Travellers* 'my gondolier disagrees'. Regular contact naturally encouraged a relationship of sorts. Confronted by a well-dressed but solitary Englishman, this gondolier was on the make and so Housman informed his stepmother:

> My gondolier expressed a wish that he was your son. He wanted me to come to Venice next Christmas, and I explained that at Christmas I went to see you; and then he made his remark. The reason is, that if he were your son he would be well off and would have no family to provide for: so at least he says. At present he has to earn a living for one wife, two sisters, one mother, one mother-in-law, and half an uncle (who was once a champion oarsman and is now paralysed); which is pretty good for a young man of twenty-three who has had one eye kicked out by a horse.[18]

Even given the more relaxed and foreign atmosphere of Venice, one can hardly imagine Housman gathering such personal information by actively questioning the gondolier. But they must have been able to rely on a good smattering of English on Andrea's part and Housman's ability with language. Most likely Housman found himself in the position of a passenger in a London taxi cab, at the mercy of a driver intent on engaging his passenger in conversation, in this case as a means of encouraging him to tip generously, or maybe as a means of sounding him out as to whether there were other services he could provide for his passenger. Housman seems to have taken his histrionic gondolier's words at face value, but we have to remember that Venice was notorious for homosexuality, and gondoliers had a long tradition of supplementing their wages, especially in winter. Among their patrons were Lord Ronald Gower, a younger son of the Duke of Sutherland and an artist who spent much of his life living with a Venetian gondolier; and John Addington Symonds the Victorian poet and critic who 'became intimate comrades with the Swiss peasant Christian Buol and the Venetian gondolier Angelo Fusato.'[19]

Horatio Brown and Walter Ashburner

Two other men figure in Housman's Venetian visits, Horatio Brown and Walter Ashburner. Brown, an expert on Venice, had lived there since 1879. More significantly, he had been a friend and former student of John Addington Symonds whose books *A Problem in Greek Ethics* and *A Problem in Modern Ethics* had been privately printed in 1883 and 1891 but suppressed by his family after his death. Brown's biography (1895) of Symonds and his *Letters and Papers of John Addington Symonds* (1923) were very discreet because of the homosexual content of Symond's private papers. As Symonds' literary executor, Brown effectively suppressed Symonds' *Memoirs* and had them locked in the London Library until 1976. Contemporaries remembered Brown as 'pleasant and sociable ... having artistic tastes which he could afford to indulge', and as 'a fair-haired, breezy out-of-doors person with a crisp Highland-Scottish speech'. Brown and his mother had settled in Venice where they eventually converted a tenement block on the Zattere overlooking the Giudecca. In Venice, Brown 'lived a life of liberal scholarship and sexual liberty that would have been impossible in liberal [sic] England'.[20] Brown never married and 'became devoted to a gondolier, Antonio Salin, whom he installed with his wife and family in the back parts of the house'.

Brown was already known to Ashburner and it is most probable that Housman met Brown through him. Housman had become acquainted with Ashburner at University College where they both served on the Council and the Management Committee. Fortunately, Ashburner did not arouse Housman's general antipathy towards Americans, indeed it was more a matter of like encountering like. Ashburner's obituary describes 'his gracious old-world speech and manners, his urbanity, his precise memory, his versatile interests, his dry wit, and sometimes caustic anecdotes', all traits which would appeal to Housman and make him comfortable in his company. Ashburner's style was a nice mixture of occasional aloofness and general magnanimity, tinged with a certain hesitation, a 'savour of timidity'. Their obvious and shared enjoyment of the pleasures of the table and the classics made them highly compatible. Ashburner's own career was also on a rising trajectory which would culminate in his being made Professor of Jurisprudence at Oxford in 1926. All in all, he was the sort of man Housman could respect and enjoy spending time with and vice versa. Housman thought well enough of him to send him copies of his *Manilius* and *Juvenal* and it is likely that Ashburner sent him copies of his *The Rhodian Sea-Law* which included original Greek texts.

Housman and Brown met in Venice when Housman wrote from the Hotel Europa: 'I shall be pleased to lunch with you and Mrs Brown on Sunday. Apparently I nearly encountered you both yesterday afternoon, for Andrea tells me you were on one side of the Lido while I was on the other.'[21] Obviously he had already met Brown and knew him well enough to introduce the name Andrea without explanation. Later that month he reported back to Ashburner, 'I met Horatio Brown in Venice in September just after he had left you in the Engadine.'[22] About ten months later in July 1902 Ashburner tried to bring the three of them together but Housman declined, being due to dine with Brown himself and 'a literary gent in whom he takes an interest, and might find me monotonous as an ingredient in the bill of fare two evenings in succession.'[23] The next year, 1903, he had dinner with Ashburner at the Café Royal and saw Brown twice in 1904. His next mention of Andrea came in 1908 when he told Walter Ashburner that he expected to be passing through Lausanne and added 'I am afraid I am hardly likely to be in Venice as late as the 18th, unless Brown or Andrea or the weather is quite extraordinarily fascinating, or unless Garda detains me on my way there longer than I expect.'[24] In November he gave Kate a more extensive account not mentioning any companions but only that the Campanile which had collapsed in1902 'has now risen to half its old height and the work is going on briskly.'[25]

In February 1910 he was giving Grant Richards, who had taken over as his publisher in 1897, advice on Venice:

> In Venice I almost always go to the Europa, which has absolutely the best possible situation and is not too large. In dignity, according to my gondolier it ranks next to Danieli's, where the food and drink are better, but which is noisy, and not central enough, and dearer ... the best restaurant to my thinking is the Vapore and my gondolier tells me that all foreigners say the same ... At Milan I always stay at the Cavour ... The Hotel de la Ville, in the centre of the city, is, according to Horatio Brown, the best in Italy, but Ashburner dislikes it: you have met them both, so you can choose which to believe.[26]

It is rare for Housman to mention the names of two people plus his gondolier who in their various ways can be described as friends. For more than a decade there would be silence about both Venice and Andrea until he wrote to Ashburner on 1 June 1926.

I am glad to hear there is a chance of your coming to England this year and hope I may see you. Next week I shall be nearer to you than I have been for a long time, as I shall be in Venice from the 7th to the 10th. to see my gondolier who is dying, or thinks so. I don't know if I shall catch Horatio.[27]

The next day he told Kate, 'I am going abroad on Saturday for a fortnight or three weeks: first on a short visit to Venice, where my poor gondolier says he is dying and wants to see me again, and then to Paris.'[28] He reported back to Kate on 23 June 'after three days' beautiful weather in Venice ... My gondolier was looking pretty well, as warmth suits him, but he is quite unable to row and gets out of breath if he goes up many stairs.' Housman obviously was concerned enough to find out about the prognosis. 'He is being sent by the municipal authorities for another three months' treatment in hospital, as they still find bacilli in his blood, and I suppose he will go steadily down-hill.' On this occasion, he did experience Venice whole:

I was surprised to find what pleasure it gave me to be in Venice again. It was like coming home, when sounds and smells which one had forgotten steal upon one's senses: and certainly there is no place like it in the world: everything there is better in reality than in memory. I first saw it on a romantic evening after sunset in 1900, and I left it on a sunshiny morning, and I shall not go there again.[29]

He never did, which suggests that he had not experienced Venice as a notorious place of forbidden pleasures and had not developed a taste for pursuing such pleasures. The irregularity of the meetings between Housman, Ashburner and Brown is far from suggesting intense relationships between them or that they came together with purpose as a coterie of like-minded individuals bent on mutual pleasure. And what he wrote to Percy Withers the next month revealed the true genesis of his relationship with Andrea. Writing to say how grieved he was that Withers was unwell, he revealed what he himself was suffering from: 'I suffer on both sides of my nature, the altruistic and the egotistic... My gondolier, who had summoned me to his death bed was quite revived by the summer weather: pray follow his example.'[30] Housman had obviously adopted Andrea and in turn had been taken for a ride by him. Andrea did not die till December 1930. Housman's last mention of him was to Kate. Writing to her about her husband Edward's illness he added: 'My poor gondolier is dead, after a bad pulmonary attack of about three weeks. Now there is nobody in the world who respects me as much as Noble [the Housman's family dog] did.'[31] Housman had been carried away by his own altruism and he seems to have adopted Andrea, but in remembering him, he thought of a faithful dog. For all the years he knew him, Housman had been contributing to the gondolier's family budget. Percy Withers recorded:

> Housman told me when he died and told me with considerable acerbity, how the relatives were pestering him to continue his gratuities and copiously lying. The pleas were at first fawning, then suddenly passed to anger and vituperation. He too was angry, and I think very sore that a benefaction that had proved so useful to the recipient, so pleasant to himself to make, should end in mendacity and squabbling.[32]

Enter Grant Richards

In 1898 Housman was introduced to Grant Richards, a twenty-four-year-old who on the last day of December 1896 had set up as a publisher in Henrietta Street. Richards already knew and admired the writings of Laurence Housman and Clemence Housman, whose novel, *The Were-Wolf,* he had come across in 1895. So when he encountered *A Shropshire Lad* in its first edition published at Housman's expense by Kegan Paul in February 1896, he was already familiar with the name Housman. Richards had been greatly influenced by the editor of *The Academy* and Richard Le Gallienne, both of whom had written eloquently about *A Shropshire Lad.*

Richards would be closely associated with Housman professionally and personally for more than sixty years. His three autobiographical books, *Author Hunting, Memories of Years Spent Mainly in Publishing, Memories of a Misspent Youth,* give a good idea of the persona of Grant Richards, or at least how he thought of himself. His father was a fellow of Trinity College, Oxford, had gained a first, and had been *proxime accessit* for the Hertford Prize. (His uncle Herbert, a fellow of Wadham College, Oxford, had been one of the examiners who had failed Housman.) Having neither the desire nor the capability to follow in his father's footsteps and having a passion for books, Grant Richards began his working life in 1880 as a sixteen-year-old with

Figure 22 Grant Richards, publisher,
uncatalogued pastel by William
Rothenstein from *Memories of a
Misspent Youth* (1932) by Grant
Richards.

Hamilton Adams & Co., booksellers in Paternoster Row. Luckily, he
had an uncle, Grant Allen, whose favourite he was. Allen knew that
the best way to deal with young people is to find out what they want
to do and encourage them to do it. This kindly and perceptive uncle
used his influence to get Grant a better job with W.T. Stead, editor
of the *Review of Reviews*, who promptly blooded the young man
by setting him the task of creating a guide to the Christmas books
sent in by publishers for review. There was no doubt of Richards'
motivation; everything about books appealed to him. His presence
and self-presentation matched his motivation. An 1893 pastel by
William Rothenstein shows him adopting the pose of a self-confident,
rather superior young man, head held high, stylishly dressed in a
high-collared shirt, loosely tied cravat, his monocle adding a certain
hauteur. Certainly, he was a suave and elegant young man, at home
in salons or drawing rooms and able to command attention because
his manners and charm equalled his physical presence. He moved

easily in literary circles and became confident of his ability to identify likely winners in the contemporary literary stakes. On a first exciting visit to Paris in 1892, Richards met William Rothenstein the artist. Paris and Rothenstein made such an impression on the young Grant Richards that he returned to Paris in the spring of 1893 to enjoy further enchantments, his eye for the girls taking him 'perilously near to falling in love with a young lady of the Casino de Paris'.[33] William Rothenstein was brought into even sharper focus: 'Trust Rothenstein to know if anyone interesting was in Paris!' and 'Will was always at the beginning of reputations'[34] neatly encapsulating key similarities between the two twenty-one-year-olds. By the time his father and two uncles put up fourteen hundred pounds to enable him to set himself up as a publisher in Henrietta Street his relationship with Rothenstein had developed to the point where Rothenstein had done his portrait in pastel and Richards had introduced Rothenstein to John Lane, the publisher who commissioned the series of drawings that became *Oxford Portraits*.

By February 1898 Richards had Housman in his sights. He made an almost immediate offer to publish a second edition of *A Shropshire Lad*, but nothing came of it because the first edition had not yet sold out. Nothing deterred Richards, who tried the backdoor. On 21 February Housman wrote to Richards, 'My brother Laurence has sent me a proposal from you to take over the remaining copies of *A Shropshire Lad* and publish a second at your own risk'. Housman was undoubtedly flattered by Richards' proposition: 'I suppose no author is averse to see his works in a second edition, or slow to take advantage of an infatuated publisher; and it is impossible not to be touched by the engaging form your infatuation takes'. But being the sort of man he was, he did not simply accept Richards' offer but responded with conditions of his own. He wanted the form and price of the book to be unchanged and he wanted to avoid upsetting Kegan Paul 'because their manager has been nice to me and takes a sentimental interest in the book, like you'.[35] Housman had the perverse satisfaction of turning down Richards' offer of a royalty: 'I prefer that it should go to reduce the price at which the book is sold'.[36] But price was something Richards had control of and the second edition was sold at three shillings and sixpence (compared with two shillings and sixpence for the first edition).

John Lane of The Bodley Head also wanted to take on the book. In the small incestuous world of publishing, John Lane, Richard Le

Gallienne, Grant Richards and William Rothenstein were all well known to each other. According to Housman, Lane had originally written to him in October 1896 'proposing to publish "the successor of A.S.L." but as they don't offer also to write it, I have had to put them off'. Housman's reply was elegant but rather detached:

> It never occurred to me that anyone else in the wide world would want to produce a second edition of a book whose first edition, I believe, is not yet sold out: but apparently I overestimate the prudence of publishers ... As to another volume, I have no reason to suppose that I shall ever write one.[37]

These were definitely not the words of a man who wanted to make money out of his writing, definitely not the words of a man who wanted to create a literary reputation for himself, or even establish himself as part of the literary scene. As for changing any text for the new edition, he likened himself to Shelley who did not alter, unlike Wordsworth and his 'perpetual tinkering'. But there was in fact a streak of Wordsworth in Housman for he added a proviso that 'after the book is set up I should like to have the sheets to correct, as I don't trust printers or proof readers in matters of punctuation'.[38] In fact Housman sent a copy of the first edition to Richards with forty alterations in punctuation alone, not all of which he could classify as misprints. The second edition of five hundred copies appeared on 14 September 1898 and by the end of the year Housman was corresponding with Richards on the subject of a further 'pocket edition'.

This was the beginning of a professional relationship and friendship that would last till the day Housman died, a tribute to Housman's loyalty but also to less tangible elements summed up by Alec Waugh in an introduction he wrote for Martin Secker's 1960 reprint of *Author Hunting*.[39]

> I first met Grant Richards in the spring of 1917 when I was nearly nineteen and he was in his middle forties. He had just accepted my first novel and I called on him in his offices, across the way from Ciro's. I knew more or less what to expect. My father knew him well:
>
> 'Grant Richards,' he said, 'is the best dressed publisher in London and he wears an eyeglass.' He was certainly an impressive person. He was not the first 'man of the world' that I had met,

and today, forty years later I have not met anyone who fits that role more effectively. He looked and behaved as the young Arnold Bennett from the Potteries dreamed of looking and behaving. He was supremely knowledgeable about food and wine, clothes and travel, about the practical ordering of existence. He had in a high degree what the Edwardians called 'style.' It was a sense of assurance, of self-confidence that he diffused. He was never in a hurry, he was never flustered, his voice was warm, his manner suave ... His monocle heightened this atmosphere of well-being. It was not attached to a cord; [though in the Rothenstein portrait it was] it had no frame; it stayed in place. Only a very composed man can wear a monocle.

The American author Theodore Dreiser, author of *Sister Carrie*, who spent a lot of time with Richards when he was writing *A Traveller at Forty*, was equally impressed, admiring Richards' *joie de vivre*, his capabilities as an opener of doors, who knew people everywhere they went in Paris, Italy and Holland. He also identified his Achilles heel – his attitude: 'One more day of delight, let the future take care of itself ... He had a delicious vivacity which acted on me like wine. With that kind of nature he inevitably took more out of the business than it could afford.'[40]

Vivid pen-portraits by Waugh and Dreiser tell us why Housman found Richards so congenial – a good-looking and self-confident young man, who demonstrated charm, tact and *savoir faire* in the office, at the lunch table and in his personal relations.

Enter William Rothenstein

We have seen that William Rothenstein, an indefatigably sociable, likeable, articulate and intelligent young man, had met Richards some years earlier and, like Richards, had also known Laurence before he became Housman's publisher. He had lived a colourful life in Paris, studying at Julian's Academie de Peinture in the Rue du Faubourg St Denis. His life in Paris in the 1890s had been nourished by *fin de siècle* and bohemian influences. He consorted with all those we now associate with Montmartre, including Toulouse-Lautrec and Aristide Bruant, as immortalised in Toulouse-Lautrec's poster and as Rothenstein described him, 'a swaggering, massive figure, a broad brimmed hat, blue black hair, piercing, sombre eyes, and a cloak and top boots.'[41]

Figure 23 Alice Rothenstein, wife of Sir
William Rothenstein (with Eric Gill), by
William Rothenstein circa 1913. © Estate of
Sir William Rothenstein/National Portrait
Gallery, London.

Other characters immortalised by Toulouse-Lautrec were individuals
whose descriptions by Rothenstein make them into living presences:

> the strange forbidding figure of Valentin, hollow eyed, hollow
> cheeked, with his flat-brimmed, tall hat and his emaciated frame
> clad in an ungainly frock coat and tight, wrinkled trousers ... La
> Goulue, an arresting blonde, short and plump, with a handsome
> insolent face. She wore her yellow hair piled on top of her head,
> with a low thick fringe and curling love locks, and a black ribbon
> tied round a full strong throat ... Jeanne Avril ... a wild Botticelli-
> like creature, perverse but intelligent, whose madness for dancing
> induced her to join this strange company.[42]

He summed up Toulouse-Lautrec: 'There was nothing romantic
about Lautrec. He was a frank, indeed a brutal cynic ... Lautrec
explored a society which even a physician hesitates to enter ... no
artist has ever shown so brutally, so remorselessly, as Lautrec, the
crude ugliness of the brothel.'[43] Back in England in 1893, Rothenstein

Figure 24 William Rothenstein featured in 'The Selection Jury of The New English Art Club 1909' by William Orpen. © National Portrait Gallery, London.

collaborated with Arthur Symons, one of the English 'decadents'. He organised a reading tour for the poet Verlaine. He introduced him to John Lane who Rothenstein had persuaded to commission a series of Oxford portraits painted by himself. There seemed to be nobody this extrovert and charming Rothenstein did not know, or get to know, as one contact led to another.

In his autobiography of 1931, Rothenstein recollected the emergence of Housman:

> In 1896 A.E. Housman's Shropshire Lad was published. It had an immediate success – perhaps success is not the right word, for rarely has a work of genius been at once accepted at its true value. But people who had sneered at minor poetry were silenced. Here was fine poetry, and a poet taking his place quietly as an immortal, as a great fiddler goes to his seat in the orchestra. There was no legend about Housman. No one seemed to know anything about him, save that he was Laurence Housman's brother.[44]

Here in 1896 was a man Rothenstein did not know. In fashionable circles, Laurence Housman was clearly the pre-eminent brother.

Rothenstein married in 1900. From her first letter to Housman in 1906 when Housman was sitting for her husband, Alice Rothenstein was forever inviting him to parties. It was characteristic of Housman that he was more often chosen as a friend than he was the chooser; but having once decided to accept a proffered friendship he did not renege on it.

The Rothensteins were social entrepreneurs like today's networkers. Laurence Housman had his own close and friendly relationship with them. In June 1902 Laurence Housman, then living in Battersea Park, was wanting to take over the lease of the Rothensteins' house and asked whether Clemence might come and look it over. Eventually he got the house. But this relationship with the Rothensteins seemed to exist in a separate universe; it was never referred to by the brothers. Rothenstein was not a fair weather friend; he had not avoided Wilde on his release from prison.

> When Oscar Wilde came out of prison, he went straight over to France. Most of his old friends and acquaintances had shown him the cold shoulder; but for my part I remembered his kindness and encouragement, and how often I had been his guest in happier days. I knew he would feel the need of friendship, and wrote offering to come over if he cared to see any of his old friends.[45]

Wilde replied warmly and met him on the quay at Dieppe the next day. Rothenstein summed him up thus:

> Men said that Wilde posed up to the last; I prefer to say that even prison, with its attendant pain and humiliation, failed to break Wilde's spirit; that he was *himself* to the end. He was never a great poet, and suffering couldn't make him one; but in his strikingly intelligent outlook on life and literature, his unfailing sympathy with all conditions of men and his deliciously humorous acceptance of any situation in which he found himself he showed his genius.[46]

Rothenstein had the idea of introducing Housman to George Calderon (son of the Spanish painter Philip Calderon) and described their encounter vividly:

> Scholar, writer, athlete, politician, reformer, anti-suffragist, dramatist, above all else Calderon loved discussion, deeming the

spoken word greater than the written one. With his friends, and since I was so near a neighbour, with me perhaps most of all, he daily practiced dialectic. Calderon sometimes annoyed people who did not understand his character, by waving, so to say, a red flag in their eyes; he annoyed Conrad; and he failed to arouse any response in A.E. Housman. I remember how Calderon, after meeting Housman at our house, remarked, as I accompanied him downstairs: 'Well William, so far from believing that man wrote *The Shropshire Lad*, I shouldn't even have thought him capable of reading it!'

Rothenstein went on:

It is true Housman neither looked nor talked like a poet. He prided himself on this, I think; he was grim and dry and seemed to disdain the artist in himself, to be contemptuous of temperament. But Housman and W.H. Hudson had an attractive quality in common; they were the only two men I knew whose opinion on any subject could never be gauged beforehand. Housman had few friends; but to those he admitted to intimacy he was very faithful. Those he entertained usually at the Café Royal; the food and wine were carefully chosen; for Housman had a superfine palate. After dinner came a box at the play. Housman had formerly lived at Highgate, from whence he travelled daily by train to Andrew Gower Street. But the story goes that one day someone jumped into the carriage in which he was, and tried to get into conversation with him; upon which he moved to Pinner.[47]

Notwithstanding this personal connection, Housman had a very poor opinion of Rothenstein's work which Rothenstein himself acknowledged:

Housman sat to me more than once, never failing to tell me how repellent he appeared to himself in my drawings. One day finding ourselves in the neighbourhood of Pinner [Housman moved to Yarborough Villas, Pinner, in November 1905] my wife and I called on him, to his housekeeper's alarm; such a thing had never happened before, but Housman made us welcome nevertheless.[48]

Rothenstein was an attractive man, interested in 'reading' people, in stimulating thought across a wide canvas, a man of liberal opinions and adventurous conversation. It has often been said that Housman had no small talk but the fact is that for most of the time he had no large talk either. He was not an interesting person to talk with in a social setting. He had no wish to dominate and project himself on groups of strangers. Unlike Rothenstein, he had no interest in self-promotion or in drawing attention to himself. He preferred to be in the background and so he inspired minimal copy for the writers of memoirs and reminiscences.

However, Housman responded positively on 17 October 1906 to a first invitation to supper from Alice Rothenstein. He reciprocated in early 1907 by asking Rothenstein to join himself and others for dinner at the Café Royal and the music hall. But Alice Rothenstein had other plans, so Rothenstein had to cry off, and Housman wrote: 'I am sorry you cannot come; but I will make an effort on some future day, when perhaps we may contrive to defeat the counterplots of Mrs Rothenstein.'[49] Three days later, when Alice Rothenstein had issued a swift invitation to supper to put things right between them, it was a case of 'I shall be very pleased to come to supper on Wednesday. I am suffering much more from sorrow than anger.'[50] Their relationship deepened. Housman returned a W.H. Hudson book Rothenstein had lent him which Housman now characterised as 'a weighty indictment of the nature of things'. Housman was prompted to enclose a copy of his own poems but wearing his quality control inspector hat pronounced it 'practically free from misprints, except one in the last piece, which I have corrected.' He drew Alice Rothenstein into his letter in a friendly way: 'The copy now in your possession I beg you to throw in the fire, before Mrs Rothenstein has had her spring cleaning and put Brunswick black on the grate,'[51] and adding an invitation to Rothenstein to dine at the Café Royal. The Rothensteins did not drop Housman once the painter had achieved his objective of a portrait and Housman himself was keeping the door wide open and may not have been totally candid in his reactions to Rothenstein's work, for he invited Laurence and Clemence to come over to see the portrait Rothenstein had given him as a present. Between that letter in early 1907 and March 1910, when he wrote again to William Rothenstein, Housman wrote twelve letters of increasing sociability to Alice Rothenstein in connection with invitations from her. William Rothenstein sent Housman copies of poems by Frances Cornford (granddaughter of Charles Darwin) to which Housman replied in his rather formalistic sort of way: 'I am much obliged to you for sending me Mrs Cornford's poems. I do not call them exactly good except in phrases here and there ... and the triolet about the unhappy lady in gloves [To a Fat Lady seen from the Train] has moved me to the imitation on the opposite page.' It was very unusual for Housman to direct humorous verse to other than intimates so the fact that he did so on this occasion shows how close he felt they had all become:

> Oh why do you walk through the fields in boots,
> Missing so much and so much?
> O fat white woman who nobody shoots,
> Why do you walk through the field in boots,
> When the grass is soft as the breast of coots
> And shivering sweet to the touch?
> O why etc.[52]

A year or so before the Great War the Rothensteins moved to Oakridge in Gloucestershire and Housman could walk over to them from Woodchester. Rothenstein was getting to know Housman better.

> I said earlier that one might never forsee Housman's views, on men and their works, on politics and on life. He was the only conservative poet I knew, one who had no patience with idealism, vague or otherwise. I delighted in his grim, dry comments; and as I had no claim to precise knowledge or scholarship, he was an indulgent listener. Max [Beerbohm] once wrote in a book Housman gave me:

> How compare either of these grim two?
> Each has an equal knack,
> Hardy supplies the pill that's blue,
> Housman the draught that's black.[53]

The unlikely fact is that on the face of it, the two seemed to have little in common: Rothenstein the extrovert, Housman the introvert; Rothenstein the liberal idealist, Housman the dyed-in-the-wool conservative; Rothenstein the man who wanted to collect people, Housman the man who avoided connecting with people, let alone collecting them; Housman the reticent and Rothenstein never short of a view. Yet they enjoyed each other's company, although Rothenstein may have been doing most of the talking and Housman most of the listening. They were both captivated by France, and

Housman perhaps envied the bohemian life Rothenstein had led in Paris and may have liked to hear about it. He welcomed Rothenstein's companionable presence just as one must assume he came to enjoy the presence of Alice Rothenstein. And, in a year or so, Housman would be able to provide him with an entrée into the exclusive world of Trinity College, Cambridge.

PART VII

Paradoxical Housman

The return of Housman's muse

It is now time to return to the main thread of the narrative and observe what was happening to the poetic thread in Housman's life. In 1900 Housman's muse returned.

Five years had elapsed since he had sent *A Shropshire Lad* for publication. Between 1900 and 1905 he experienced a new surge of poetic activity that produced twenty-six poems. Between 1917 and 1922 he wrote another eighteen. In 1922 he had a total of forty-four new poems. He would eventually include only seventeen of them in *Last Poems*.

Four of them were soldier poems, *Grenadier, Lancer, The Deserter*, and *Astronomy* reflecting the impact of the Boer war on his choice of subject matter in the years 1899 to 1902. *Astronomy* was evidently biographical and related to his brother Herbert killed in that war: factually, he was not in a poetic drought, whatever he might say to other people.

Housman and his stepmother

Long letters he sent to his stepmother reflect his wish to entertain her. The effort he put into them showed his need for a continuing mother figure, even a stepmother. In September 1904 he wrote vividly about his visit to Constantinople, about Turkish graveyards and tombstones, which made 'the downs look as if they were sprinkled with large hailstones or coarse grained salt'. His sunsets were atmospheric:

> The sky would be orange and the hillside of the city would be dark with a few lights coming out, and the Golden Horn would reflect the blue or grey of the upper sky: and as there was a new moon,

the crescent used to come and hang itself appropriately over the mosque of Muhammad the Conqueror.

He went on at length about animals he saw, white oxen, black buffaloes and sheep,

> with the whitest and prettiest wool I have ever seen, but above all dogs which were all over the place and were extremely meek and inoffensive. Turkey is a country where dogs and women are kept in their proper place, and consequently are quite unlike the pampered and obstreperous animals we know under those names in England.

But he reserved his encomiums for the handsome people:

> The population is very mixed and largely descended from kidnapped Christians. Pure Turks are rather rare, Greeks and Armenians common ... I have come across the handsomest faces I ever saw ... some of the Greeks make you rub your eyes, the features and complexions are more like pictures than realities: though the women unfortunately bleach themselves by keeping out of the sun. The Turks when they are good looking, I like even better; there is an aquiline type like the English aristocracy very much improved; if I could send you the photograph of a young man who rowed me to the Sweet Waters of Asia, and asked you to guess his name, you would instantly reply 'Aubrey de Vere Plantagenet.'[1]

Love for the music hall

The music hall was at the height of its vibrancy in the late Victorian and Edwardian periods. Nothing is known about Housman's introduction to it but one can see how its sentimentality, the catchiness and patter of many of its songs, the *double entendres*, appealed to this writer of comic and nonsense verse. Being part of an audience that was uninhibited in its pursuit of enjoyment appealed also to a young man whose family and school life had been so sheltered and inhibited. Here was a scene where it was legitimate for him to show frank enjoyment and join in pantomime-like audience responses. His pleasure in being quick on the uptake was exercised both in his work and his play.

Yeats thought of the music halls as a

reaction from the super-refinement of much recent life and poetry. The cultivated man has begun a somewhat hectic search for the common pleasures of common men and for the rough accidents of life. The typical young poet of our day is an aesthete with a surfeit, searching sadly for his lost Philistinism, his heart full of an unsatisfied longing for the commonplace. He is an Alastor tired of his woods and longing for beer and skittles.[2]

According to Matthew Sturgis, Arthur Symons had a more basic motivation:

> He found in the music halls a safety valve for the pressure-cooker of repressed Victorian sexuality. It was, he considered, the one place where there was a perfectly frank, healthy and delightful display of the beauty and strength of the human form. At a time when public prudency had all but banished Terpsichore from the legitimate stage, the music halls were a haven for the ballet, and dance had always been a sexual solvent.[3]

For Housman, the music hall was not a solitary occupation where he sought to enjoy secret pleasures. He issued invitations to friends to accompany him and dine before the show at fashionable restaurants. In September 1901 when he invited Walter Ashburner to have dinner with him at Kettners at seven o'clock, he explained the early hour:

> In order that you may not be lured into any horrors for which you are unprepared, I should explain that, as I do not belong to any club, after dinner we adjourn to a box in the adjacent *Palace* (the most proper of all the music-halls, not meet to be called a music-hall), and that when the *Palace* closes there is no refuge but Bow St. Police station; which is the reason why I put the hour so early.[4]

Two years later when he wrote to Gilbert Murray, who was clearly wanting to be taken to a music hall, Housman wrote: 'I am bound to say however that on the last three occasions of going to a Music Hall I found the entertainment of the most harrowing dullness: I don't know whether it is that the Halls are deteriorating or that I am improving.'[5] He had still not managed to pin Murray down to dates by October 1904 but instead Murray had evidently given him tickets for a performance of his own translation of Euripides' *Hippolytus* at the

Court Theatre. He had gone with 'a good deal of apprehension, as I find it generally a trial to hear actors and actresses reciting verse. But though I can't say that witnessing the play gave me as much pleasure as reading it, it did give me pleasure and indeed excitement.' He was not enthusiastic about the acting: 'The most effective and unexpected thing to me was the statue of Cypris standing quiet there all the time.'[6]

On 14 January 1907 it had been William Rothenstein's turn, so Housman issued his standard invitation: 'Will you dine with me at the Café Royal on Friday February 1st at 7.30? The form which these orgies take is that after dinner we go to a music hall and when the music-hall closes, as I have no club, we are thrown on the streets and the pothouses: so you know what to expect.'[7]

Rejection of academic recognition

Amid all the stir caused by the publication of *A Shropshire Lad* and the academic mark he had made with the publication of *Manilius I*, Housman seemed to be turning his back on the fruits of his labour – more academic recognition. Having worked so hard to ascend to the heights, it seemed as though the opinions of others no longer mattered to him. He was to be the sole judge of his own work. As long as his work met his own criteria for success that was enough for him.

And so he resisted the attempts of his most long-standing and enthusiastic sponsor, R.Y. Tyrrell, Regius Professor of Greek at Trinity College, Dublin, to interest him in an honorary doctorate. In 1905 he also refused an Honorary Degree of Doctor of Laws from Glasgow University. Housman may have shared Casaubon's view that honorary degrees were lavished on rank or political partisanship and were not a proper distinction of learning.[8] He chose instead to give an explanation that was as opaque as it was definite:

> For reasons which it would be tedious and perhaps difficult to enumerate, though they seem to me sufficient and decisive, I long ago resolved to decline all such honours, if they should ever be offered me.

He wrapped up his refusal with emollient expressions such as, 'flattering offer ... high appreciation of the kindness ... this valued distinction ... my great regret.'[9]

The fact is he did not need or want recognition.

Dislike of writing to order

In 1903 brother Laurence was co-editor with Somerset Maugham of *The Venture: An Annual of Art and Literature.* Laurence wanted an article on Coventry Patmore, and his brother, as usual, shrank from writing to order: 'To write a paper on Patmore would be an awful job, especially in the holidays, so I send you two poems, of which you can print whichever you think the least imperfect.' He couldn't resist a cruel dig at Meredith, a contemporary novelist and poet: 'I hope you won't succeed in getting anything from Meredith, as I am a respectable character and do not care to be seen in the company of galvanised corpses. By this time he stinketh: for he hath been dead twenty years.'[10]

Housman could be a man of violent antipathies. In this case he may have been prompted by Meredith's description of *A Shropshire Lad* as 'an orgy of naturalism.'[11]

On the centenary of the death of Nelson and the Battle of Trafalgar, J.L. Garvin, editor of *The Outlook,* asked him to compose a poem about the battle. Housman declined: 'I am afraid too that I admire Napoleon more even than Nelson.'[12]

He also turned down flat Laurence's suggestion that he contribute to his friend Edith Nesbit's magazine *The Neolith*: 'I suppose she already knows that I am morose and unamiable and will not experience any sudden or agonizing shock.'[13] To this, for some unknown reason, he appended a verse:

> Now all day the horned herds
> Dance to the piping of the birds;
> Now the bumble-bee is rife,
> And other forms of insect life;
> The skylark in the sky so blue
> Now makes noise enough for two,
> And lovers on the grass so green
> —Muse, oh Muse, eschew th'obscene

And to the Editor of *Country Life:* 'I am obliged by your proposal, but several causes, of which barrenness is the chief, prevent me from contributing verses to periodical publications.'[14] Mr Thompson, who was running a Bazaar somewhere in London University, got a more amiable response:

> I expect to suffer from the Bazaar, especially in purse; but my reputation, such as it is, I will preserve intact, and not injure it by writing verse to order. I have never done so for anyone, even when offered bribes, literature not being my trade. I shall certainly not molest my poor brother, who ought not to suffer for mere consanguinity, which is no crime.[15]

Housman was not one of those prepared to do anything to see their name in print; he was no rent-a-versifier or rent-a-pen.

Richards in crisis

By November 1904 Richards' publishing venture was in crisis. He had good literary instincts, plenty of push and good connections in the literary scene but these were counterbalanced by a marked tendency for self-indulgence and a lack of business strategy. He preferred to fly by the seat of his pants; budgets and business plans were not for him; he equated success with audacity.

In 1905 Richards was declared bankrupt. By now Richards had published a fifth edition of *A Shropshire Lad* but Housman had become aware of slow progress on his *Juvenal*, to be published by Richards but printed at Housman's expense. By 17 November Housman was complaining of the delay, but once the truth of Richards' situation became known, Housman took a totally supportive yet business-like and matter-of-fact attitude.

> Almost immediately after I wrote to you last week, I heard, and was very sorry to hear, that there is a crisis in your affairs. I hope that this will come out straight, and in the meantime I do not want to worry you with correspondence: I only write just to let you know, as is proper, that I propose to find someone else to undertake the publishing of the *Juvenal*, though I shall not find anyone who will do it for nothing, as you were good enough to say you would.

Just to underline his equanimity and support he added, 'I don't know if you would have the leisure or inclination to come and dine with me somewhere next week, but I should be very pleased if you would: say Friday Dec 2nd. Perhaps I could get my brother to come.'[16] They all dined together at the Café Royal, probably proceeded to a music hall, and ended up at the Criterion Bar. Richards later recollected 'I had never before, and have never since, seen him in a bar.'[17] Housman chastised Richards for organising a return dinner at the Carlton where he had the chef Jacques Kraemer produce a highly original dinner of hedgehog accompanied by whisky, followed by snails with white wine. In the interim, between Richards being declared bankrupt and setting himself up again under his wife's name in Regent Street, he continued to act to all intents and purposes as Housman's publisher. Housman had kept the copyright of *A Shropshire Lad* and had been advised to take possession of remaining copies of *Manilius*, and fell back on his original intention of paying for the printing of *Juvenal* himself. And so, in spite of the alarums and excursions around him, Housman does not seem to have fretted unduly. By June *Juvenal* was printed and Housman had the printers send the copies he did not retain for himself to Richards for distribution. His own equanimity, compounded now with some equivocation, was evident in a card he sent to Richards which was not quite an outright invitation:

> As I hear you want to see me soon, it occurs to me to send you the enclosed, in case you may be willing and able to use it. If you go, I shall be there about 9 o'clock, just drunk enough to be pleasant, but not so incapable as a publisher would like an author to be. If you don't go, you will probably escape a very tiresome entertainment.[18]

Housman would appear to have had enough of Richards and his way of going about things. Just over a week later Housman was laying down the law about how his *Juvenal* should be publicised:

> Your flamboyant production is not on any account to be printed. The following might serve:
>   'A critical edition of Juvenal by Mr A.E. Housman, intended to make good some of the principal defects in existing editions, and especially to supply a better knowledge of the manuscripts, will be published by...'

He added: '(No nonsense about Shropshire Lads).'[19]

Letters in June and early July displayed Housman in much the same mood. 'I suppose the delay is more annoying to you than to me, so I will not declaim about it,'[20] and his rather curt, 'Many thanks. I don't think any advertisement is required: books of this sort are best advertised by reviews and the lists of 'books received' in the learned journals.'[21] Housman displayed no interest in how beneficial it might be to enlarge his reputation or cross-sell his academic publications as 'by the author of A Shropshire Lad' and vice versa. Housman might well have been right, since his books were aimed at distinctly different audiences. He seemed to believe that his reputation as a scholar would be depreciated by notoriety as a poet.

Many successful artists and writers have an entrepreneurial streak; they know how to present themselves; they know who they should know; they have an instinct for sensing a good opportunity; they know that within reason, all publicity is good publicity. Housman did not have the slightest trace of such instincts. He was more concerned to preserve his reputation as a scholar than become famous as a poet or author. He wanted to keep scholar and poet in separate boxes.

Enter Witter Bynner

In 1903, Witter Bynner, nascent American poet and playwright, appeared on the scene for the first time. Following classical studies at Harvard, he had begun as an office boy with *McClure's Magazine*, where Viola Roseboro, its chief reader, introduced him to *A Shropshire Lad*, thus enabling the magic of Housman's poetry to make such an impact on the young American that it was to be the foundation of a lifelong devotion to Housman and his works.

Bynner quickly assumed the role of a one-man promoter of Housman on the continent of North America: 'For years the little Lane edition [given to him by Richard Le Gallienne, then in America] went everywhere with me in my pocket and was read aloud not only to friends but later, when I took up the lecture platform, to audiences all over the United States.'[22] Bynner was soon made poetry editor of *McClure's* and over a period of a few years published a steady stream of his favourite Housman poems. *McClure's* was, in Grant Richards' words, 'huge and important', and though coincidental, it was not surprising that by 1908 there were five American editions of *A Shropshire Lad*.

Bynner's first letter to Housman in the Spring of 1903 was accompanied by two stanzas of Bynner's own composition, gently evoking the bitter sweet of Housman's poetry. Housman's reply signalled that he was touched.

A further letter to Housman in June completely won him over. 'No normal author can resist a well phrased letter containing compliments that are well made.' In this respect Housman was entirely normal. 'You seem to admire my poems even more than I admire them myself, which is very noble of you ... However, it is not for me to find fault with you; and naturally there is pleasure in receiving such ardent letters as yours.' Surprisingly he went on to answer questions Bynner had put to him:

> I wrote the book when I was 35, and I expect to write another when I am 70, by which time your enthusiasm will have had time to cool. My trade is that of professor of Latin in this college; I suppose that my classical training has been of some use to me in furnishing good models, and making me fastidious, and telling me what to leave out. My chief object in publishing my verses was to give pleasure to a few young men here and there, and I am glad if they have given pleasure to you.[23]

This was the first and only time Housman wrote of the audience he was writing for and Bynner was not slow in moving the conversation forward. He asked Housman to let *McClure's* publish his next volume only to be brought up short by Housman. 'There is no 'next book of verses' in existence, nor do I know that there ever will be; but if there ever is, I will bear in mind what you say.'[24] When Bynner sent him a draft in payment for *McClure's* publication of his work, Housman, never greedy for royalties, was impressed by Bynner's honesty of purpose, for he replied in the closing weeks of 1903: 'I have never taken money for any of my verses, and accordingly I return you, with many thanks, the draft which you have kindly sent me.' He replied to Bynner's request for a copy of *The Olive*: '

> I have no copy of the piece called *The Olive* which is not particularly good: it was published on the conclusion of peace in 1902, in *The Outlook*. I enclose however a poem [*Astronomy*] which I have contributed to a collection which the Duchess of Sutherland is bringing out for charitable purposes; only, as the book is not yet published, you must not go printing it in America.[25]

Bynner was determined to stay in contact and offered to send Housman books from the *McClure's* list. Housman chose Tolstoy's

Ivan Ilyitch, Lowes Dickinson's *Letters from a Chinese Official* and Edwin Markham's poem *The Man with the Hoe*. In just over three weeks Housman had his books and wrote warmly to say so: 'Your office seems to be the spot on earth where I am most esteemed.'[26] He received further books from Bynner the following year including Willa Cather's *Troll Garden*. Housman went so far as to send him his new Pinner address.

2 May 1905: Brother Robert Housman dies

On 2 May 1905 Robert Holden Housman, born seventeen months after Housman, died; he had been standing waist deep in the river Avon at Bath taking scenic photographs, developed a fever and died three days later. Like his elder brother, he never married; unlike him, he became a keen shot and photographer like their father. But both of them inherited Edward's kindliness towards children, especially Robert who was Kate's favourite brother, always ready to play games with her children and involve them in his exploits. There is no mention of his death in any letter of Housman's, and no record of him in any published family letter, which is rather surprising given that the Mater was still alive. The most likely explanation is that Laurence may have destroyed letters of purely family interest when it came to sorting through his brother's remains.

Anthologists, composers, illustrators and American publishers

In 1905, when Richards proposed a new edition of *A Shropshire Lad*, Housman sent him a copy of the first edition with his injunction: 'Here is a copy of the first edition; but if you are going to publish a new one, let me see the final proofs. There is no other way to ensure accuracy.'[27]

Reverberations from Richards' bankruptcy continued. He was attacked in *The Athenaeum* by E.V. Lucas, one of his authors who complained that a recent anthology published by Richards was derivative in 'idea, format, illustration and binding' of his own anthology, and claimed that Richards still owed him royalties. Richards took the line that Lucas' case was based on "'misapprehension, or on ignorance of all the facts', almost to portraying himself as an innocent victim:

> If I sold matches in the street I should certainly please some people, but under the most favourable circumstances I could not hope to earn enough ... to wipe out the bankruptcy proceedings ... By and by I hope my creditors may realise that in being connected with the starting of a new publishing house I am selling what talents I have for their advantage.[28]

Housman's reaction was: 'I have been reading *The Athenaeum*: you seem to me to have the advantage in argument and especially in temper',[29] a loyal reply certainly, but warning bells ought to have been ringing for Housman. By then he and Richards were on intimate terms, Housman being totally open with Richards about the machinations of John Lane who was intent on publishing *A Shropshire Lad* in America. In the course of this Housman discovered that Richards had made arrangements with another American publisher, Mitchell Kennerly. Housman gently chastised him (Richards' wife actually since the firm now bore her name).

> It may interest my publisher to learn she has broken all the traditions of the trade by making arrangements with another publisher in New York without giving John Lane Company the opportunity of taking [distributing] the new edition: that company is reluctantly, in self-defence, compelled to issue an edition of its own. There is etiquette, I daresay, even in Pandemonium.[30]

However, the pandemonium caused by Richards' business method did not halt a deepening relationship based on their mutual interests in food, wine and Paris. Five months later, when asked for permission for *A Shropshire Lad* to be included in the series *The Smaller Classics*, he was still managing, albeit precariously, to mix business with pleasure: 'I have refused and have told them how atrociously you behaved in ever including the book in the series, and how glad I am to have the chance of stopping the scandal.' He added, 'I suppose you won't be in Paris between next Tuesday and Saturday. I shall be at the *Normandy*.'[31]

Housman had also to deal with composers wanting to set his poems to their music. 'Mr Balfour Gardiner may publish *The Recruit* with music if he wants to. I always give my consent to all composers, in the hope of being immortal somehow.'[32] This hope was not something he ever mentioned again; he was totally uninterested in what composers did; although he virtually never refused permission, he gave it without enthusiasm. However, reproducing his words was another matter. In November he wrote in no uncertain terms to Grant Richards, 'Permission must not be given to Mr Williams to print the poems in his programme.'[33] However, dealing face to face with a pleading Ralph Vaughan Williams, Housman proved to be a soft touch and did a U-turn, informing Richards:

> As to Mr Vaughan Williams, about whom your secretary wrote ... I said he might print the verses he wanted on his programmes [six poems making up *On Wenlock Edge* a song cycle for tenor voice, piano and string quartet.] I mention this lest his action should come to your ears and cause you to set the police after him.[34]

Later, in 1920, when he was returning proposed illustrations for *A Shropshire Lad*, by Lovat Fraser, he let Richards know how offended he had been by Vaughan Williams:

> The trouble with book-illustrators, as with composers who set poems to music, is not merely that they are completely wrapped up in their own art and their precious selves, and regard the author merely as a peg to hang things on, but that they seem to have less than the ordinary human allowance of sense and feeling.
>   This reminds me. I am told that composers in some cases have mutilated my poems----that Vaughan Williams cut two verses out of *"Is my team ploughing* (I wonder how he would like me to cut two bars out of his music), and that a lady whose name I forget has set one verse of *The New Mistress*, omitting the other. So I am afraid I must ask you, when giving consent to composers, to exact the condition that these pranks are not to be played.[35]

Housman had been deeply upset by what Vaughan Williams had done. He had mutilated *"Is my team ploughing* by leaving out stanzas three and four, and Housman's footballers, and his goalkeeper. Vaughan Williams' bold justification was: 'The composer has a perfect right artistically to set any portion of a poem he chooses provided he does not actually alter the sense,' and added cheekily and arrogantly 'I feel that a poet should be grateful to anyone who fails to perpetuate such lines as: 'The goal stands up, the keeper/ Stands up to keep the goal.'[36] Vaughan Williams had missed Housman's poetic point; he had proved Housman's case against composers and illustrators in general. He had offended not only the censor and copy-editor in Housman's make-up, but much more dangerously, Housman the straight dealer. Housman would never forget what Vaughan Williams had done.

12 November 1907: The Mater dies, Housman moves to Pinner

In June 1905 Housman was involved in the final stages of publication of his *Juvenal* and in October he faced the upheaval of moving. His landlady Mrs Hunter left Byron Cottage where Housman had lived for almost twenty years. Housman did not like losing people he had become attached to and so moved with her.

However, he could not prevent time's erosion of his past and on 12 November 1907, the Mater died. Housman seems to have left no personal testimonial of the part she had played in his life and the life of the family. Yet the record shows that there was something in his attention and connection with her that went well beyond the efforts of a dutiful stepson, especially one who was separated by distance, had a time-consuming occupation, and for whom the temptation to forget was considerable. When he formed enduring bonds with women such as Mrs Wise, Sophie Becker, the Mater or even his landlady, he was revealing an overriding need for a replacement mother.

Connections with other classicists

Following the publication of *A Shropshire Lad*, his work on classical subjects had continued apace. In addition to publishing his *Juvenal* and *Manilius I*, and continuing work on the second volume of Manilius, his classical papers continued at a rate of between two and six a year. In the year of the Mater's death he produced five papers – a total of eighty-four pages. He was in regular contact with other scholars. There was Robinson Ellis, under whom he had studied at Oxford and whom he had made fun of in *The Eleventh Eclogue*; Housman was now thoughtfully offering him sight of a Manilius manuscript from Goettingen which would be in University College for a month or so; he heard from J.D. Duff a fellow of Trinity College, Cambridge, who frequently sought his opinion on meanings and constructions and with whom he conducted a totally business-like academic correspondence. He wrote to Henry Jackson, Editor of the *Journal of Philology* and his main contact at Cambridge, in mock punctilious fashion, 'I hope I am doing correctly and acceptably in directing to you as 'Dr.' I have been told by some authority that it is the higher title [than Professor]. I may be in Cambridge this day week, and if so I will come and look you up.'[37] And when in 1908 Henry Jackson was appointed to the Order of Merit, he received a notably warm letter from Housman who wrote:

> My dear Jackson, No doubt you are snowed up with congratulations: do not take any notice of this. There is something to be said for a Liberal government after all. If you experienced a sudden access of salubrity about 1.45 today, that was caused by Rothenstein and me drinking your health.[38]

When Gilbert Murray, Professor of Greek at Glasgow University, became Regius Professor of Greek at Oxford in 1908 he earned a warm and elegant letter from Housman:

> I congratulate you on having survived a Scotch professorship long enough to obtain what I hope will be consolation even for that. I think you are now well on your way to take that place in the public eye which used to be occupied by Jowett and then by Jebb; and as you are a much better scholar than the one and a much better man of letters than the other, the public will be the gainer without knowing it, and good judges (by which I mean myself) will be less at variance with the public.[39]

Somewhat earlier in 1908, Housman had told Richards that Ingram Bywater was resigning the Greek chair at Oxford and that Richards' uncle, Herbert Richards, one of the examiners who had failed him in Greats, should be his successor. He added: 'It is a Regius professorship, and the King generally asks the advice of one or two persons whom he supposes to be good judges. He has not applied to me: possibly because we have not been introduced.'[40]

Laurence's theatrical contretemps and mistaken identities

Contact with brother Laurence continued to be regular and Housman also heard indirectly of his doings when he visited the Mater, while she was alive and living at Hereford. There he heard of the collapse of Laurence's collaboration with Harley Granville Barker on the libretto for Liza Lehman's light opera based on *The Vicar of Wakefield*. Barker was the first to pull out and a sorry tale of clashing theatrical egos culminated in Laurence ordering 'his name to be removed from all playbills, posters and advertisements'. On the night of the premiere at the Prince of Wales' Theatre, Laurence records that Mr Curzon, the lessee and prospective husband of the show's leading lady, 'came and ordered me out of the theatre, threatening me with personal violence if I had not gone before the end of Act I'.[41] Housman's reaction to news of these volatile theatrics was lukewarm: 'Your bad behaviour in the theatre I first heard of from your letters which were read to me at Hereford; I had seen nothing in the papers.'[42] He added a seemingly friendly invitation: 'Rothenstein has made me a present of one of his three portraits of me, Perhaps when the weather is warmer and the spring more advanced you and Clemence will come out here and look at it', as if to say it is not just you who is famous enough to be painted.

He was irked by cases of mistaken identity: 'So overpowering is your celebrity that I have just received an official letter from my own college addressed to "Professor L. Housman". Eighteen months later he wrote to Laurence that

> I was at Cambridge a week or two ago, and met a lady who asked if I were the author of *Gods and their Makers*. Always honest, I owned that I was not: I said I was his brother. "Oh well", said she "that's the next best thing". It appears that the work is a household word with them: they have a dog or a cat called after one of your divinities.

Yet he was always ready if asked to produce critiques of Laurence's poetry, not easy for him since poetically the two were miles apart. When Laurence asked him to look through his proposed *Selected Poems*, Housman protested apropos something Laurence had said: 'Did I ever say anything abusive about *Spikenard*? I think on the whole it is about the cleverest of your poetry books.'[43] Nonetheless, Laurence said in his *Memoir* that his brother had described it as 'nonsense verse'.[44] Housman was above all a man who cared about words and he rightly found much of Laurence's work 'obscure and untidy', with some lack of integration between his 'lively fancy' and the actual words of his poems. He could not stand lapses in Laurence's rhyming: 'you have a way of treating words like "Messiah" and "royal" as if they were a syllable shorter than they are.'[45] In June 1908 he wrote to Laurence to say how much he had enjoyed parts of his play *The Chinese Lantern*, then playing at the Haymarket Theatre, apart from

> a good deal of your wet wit. And then there is the infernal music. Theatres are beginning to exhibit notices asking ladies to remove their hats; my patronage shall be bestowed on the theatre which goes a step further and requests the orchestra to be silent. The sleep-walking scene ought to have been good; but it left me faint and weak from the effort of straining to hear the human voice through the uproar of pussy's bowels.[46]

Rothenstein had been at the play with Housman and 'asked me to express to you his great pleasure and admiration.'

When he looked over Laurence's *Selected Poems* published in 1908, his eagle eye had noticed 'The misprint on p.101 is eloquent of the printer's cockney pronunciation.' He tried to hide the ambiguity of his reactions: 'I suppose if I say anything in praise of the cover and get-up you will detect insinuations as to the contents, so I had better not.'[47]

This ambivalence towards Laurence and all his activities (at that time, the campaign for votes for women) may have found oblique expression in letting off steam to Mrs Thicknesse, a literary lady whose husband Ralph had produced in 1909 *The Rights and Wrongs of Women: A Digest with Practical Illustrations and Notes on the Law in France.*

> My blood boils. This is not due to the recent commencement of summer, but to the Wrongs of Women, with which I have been making myself acquainted. 'She cannot serve on any jury'; and yet she bravely lives on. 'She cannot serve in the army or navy'– oh cruel, cruel – 'except' – this adds insult to injury – 'as a nurse.' They do not even employ a Running Woman instead of a Running Man for practising marksmanship. I have been making marginal additions. 'She cannot be ordained a Priest or Deacon': add nor become a Freemason. 'She cannot be a member of the Royal Society'; add nor of the Amateur Boxing Association. In short your unhappy sex seems to have nothing to look forward to, excepting contracting a valid marriage as soon as they are 12 years old; and that must soon pall.'

Laurence described Lily Thicknesse as 'a friend whose suffrage sympathies he [A.E.H.] did not share.'[48] She took this rather blimpish and old-fogeyish but elegantly expressed outburst in good part.

It was unsurprising that when Laurence organised a declaration by authors in favour of votes for women, Housman refused point blank to sign. 'I would rather not sign your memorial; chiefly because I don't think that writers as a class are particularly qualified to give advice on the question.' A more important reason was that Housman was careful to avoid being lumped with those he disliked. He seems to have believed in the idea that 'birds of a feather flock together' and there were those with whom he did not wish to be identified, hence his subsidiary objection 'moreover it is certain to be signed by Galsworthy and Hewlett and everyone I cannot abide'. He knew also that Clemence was facing prison at that time for withholding payment of her rates in protest against taxation without representation for women, so he ended his letter 'Love to Clemence: I hope she has read, or will read *Ann Veronica* (the prison scenes).'[49] No hand wringing from Housman; Clemence had got herself into this and would have to take the consequences.

Being introduced by Richards to William Hyde, a potential illustrator of *A Shropshire Lad*, Housman would have preferred the illustrations to be black and white but he approved three out of four, though Richards earned a tart reproof: 'I suppose it was you who sent him on a wild goose chase to Hughley [the church that featured in *Hughley Steeple* has no steeple].'

He sent Richards a letter of protest about the use of his poems in anthologies:

Pray who gave Mr E. Thomas leave to print two of my inspired lays in his and your *Pocket Book of Poems and Songs*? I didn't though he thanks me in the preface. Just the same thing happened in the case of Lucas' *Open Road*, issued by the same nefarious publisher. You must not treat my immortal works as quarries to be used at will by the various hacks whom you may employ to compile anthologies. It is a matter which affects my moral reputation: for six years back I have been refusing to allow the inclusion of my verses in the books of a number of anthologists who, unlike Mr Thomas, wrote to ask my permission; and I have excused myself by saying that I had an inflexible rule which I could not transgress in one case rather than another. Now these gentlemen, from Quiller-Couch downward, will think I am a liar. Mr Thomas thanks me for 'a poem', and prints two: which is the one he doesn't thank me for?

My temper, as you are well aware, is perfectly angelic, so I remain yours sincerely[50]

In allowing Housman's words to be reproduced in anthologies Richards had committed a hanging offence. Richards made an inadequate response and so Housman had to put his objection in words of one syllable:

What you have got in your head is the fact that I allow composers to set my words to music without any restriction. I never hear the music, so I do not suffer; but that is a very different thing from being included in an anthology with W.E. Henley or Walter de la Mare. I did not remonstrate about the *Open Road*: I was speechless with surprise and indignation.[51]

Yet all the time, bonds between them continued to be formed. Housman asked Richards to obtain photographs of the first 107 pages of a manuscript of Manilius in the Biblioteca Nacional at Madrid: 'I am prepared to go to £20 though it ought to be less, and in Rome at any rate would be very much less, probably about £5.'[52]

Housman's relationship with Alice Rothenstein was blossoming. He was even making excuses:

I hope that my conversation through the telephone yesterday did not sound brusque. I am very little accustomed to using that instrument ... Please tell Rothenstein that all my Jewish students are absenting themselves from my lectures from Wednesday to Friday this week on the plea that these are Jewish holidays. I have been looking up the Old Testament, but I can find no mention there of either the Derby or the Oaks.[53]

The next day he replied to her invitation that he walk over to their house to see them and if necessary meet them on the Heath. His correspondence had certainly taken on a relaxed and convivial tone, perhaps because he had been able to tell Richards that the end was in sight for his second volume of Manilius.

Housman was now treating Richards as an old friend so that when he sent Housman a copy of the *Essais* of Montaigne he had published in his *Elizabethan Classics* series with spine decorations by Laurence Housman, he opened up:

> I have received your noble present of Montaigne, and I only wish the rest of my library were fit to keep it company. I have never read him yet in Florio's translation: as a boy I used to study Cotton's, which is good, but less good I suppose. Thank you also for the guide to Paris. The question whether I ever go to Vienna depends on the question whether you produce a similar guide to it.[54]

Intriguingly, in October 1910 he sent a list of fifteen volumes to a person identified in Burnett only as an 'Unknown Correspondent', asking for certain books to be sent to him. His list included a copy of *Man and Woman* by H. Havelock Ellis published in 1894; its subtitle was *Study of Secondary and Tertiary Sexual Characteristics.*[55] Although there is no record of Housman's having a copy of his previous book, *Sexual Inversion*, which Ellis published in 1897 with J.A. Symonds, his action indicates he had not ceased his research.

Meanwhile, close on a hundred miles to the east in Cambridge another life-changing event was in the making.

PART VIII

Cambridge:
The glittering prize

Elected Professor of Latin at Cambridge and fellow of Trinity College

The notice of a vacancy at Cambridge was published over the name of the Vice-Chancellor, R.F. Scott, in the *Cambridge University Reporter* on 12 December 1910:

> The Professorship of Latin is vacant by the death of Professor J.E.B. Mayor.
>
> The Professorship is governed by the provisions of Statute B, Chapter XI, and by the Ordinances already made or hereafter to be made by the University.
>
> The Electors will meet for the purpose of electing a Professor on Wednesday 18 January 1911, at the University Offices at 2.30 PM.
>
> Candidates are requested to send in their names to the Vice-Chancellor on or before, Monday 9 January 1911.[1]

How different the process was from that of University College! This time no testimonials were called for; the University archive contains no list of applicants, no arguments between the electors on the merits of the various candidates, no final report. There is nothing other than a bald statement:

> At a meeting of the Electors for the Latin Professorship held at the University Offices.
>
> It was agreed to elect Alfred Edward Housman, Professor of Latin, University College, London, to the Professorship.

Figure 25 Housman by Henry Lamb
1909. By permission of the Master and
Fellows of Trinity College, Cambridge.

The statement was signed by each of the eleven Electors of whom the most eminent were the Vice-Chancellor R.F. Scott, the Regius Professor of Greek Henry Jackson, the Public Orator J.E. Sandys, the Professor of Sanskrit E.J. Rapson and The Professor of Latin in the University of Oxford Robinson Ellis.[2]

What is immediately noticeable is that two of the electors, Jackson and Ellis, had supported Housman at the University College election and that he has another Cambridge supporter, Arthur Verrall, a senior fellow of Trinity.

It is a reasonable assumption that on this occasion Henry Jackson was the kingmaker, just as W.P. Ker and John Postgate had been the joint kingmakers at University College, London, and that Jackson and Verrall were chiefly instrumental in getting Housman elected as a fellow of Trinity. Henry Jackson was a leader, a forward looking man, gregarious and persuasive and had a powerful presence. R. St John Parry, his successor as Vice-Master at Trinity, wrote of him:

> No account of Jackson's place in the College would be nearly complete which did not emphasise the unique position which

Figure 26 Henry Jackson, Fellow of Trinity College, editor of *Journal of Philology* 1879–1921, Regius Professor of Greek, Vice-Master of Trinity College 1914, by Charles Wellington Furse 1889. © National Portrait Gallery, London.

he occupied in its social life. His rooms in Nevile's Court were a centre of unceasing hospitality. The oak was never sported except when he was out. His habit of sitting up very late made him accessible at all hours of the evening and far into the early hours of the morning and there were few evenings throughout those more than thirty years when he was alone ... he had to move the venue by borrowing another set and then to two of the large lecture rooms in the Great Court, thrown into one and furnished for the occasion with card table, smoking apparatus and a piano.[3] Jackson was also a reformer, advocating the removal of religious tests, the abolition of Greek as a requirement to enter the university, and the foundation of colleges for women.

On 18 January 1911 the *Reporter* published Housman's election, announced that he had been admitted as Professor of Latin; on 2 February that he had been made a fellow of Trinity and given an MA *honoris causa* (as a mark of esteem), presumably to remedy the

Figure 27 Arthur Platt, Fellow of Trinity
College 1884, Professor of Greek at University
College London 1894–1925 and one of
Housman's closest friends.
© National Portrait Gallery, London.

existing deficiency in his academic standing – at that time he had only a pass degree from Oxford. Also published was the date of his Inaugural Lecture, 5 pm in the Senate House on 9 May.

Housman was elected to the biggest and richest college in Cambridge. Founded and endowed by Henry VIII, it is the only college whose master is appointed by the Crown rather than by the fellows. On his election to a fellowship at Trinity, Housman wrote charmingly to the Master and the College Council:

> I accept their offer of a fellowship with great gratitude and a high sense of the honour done me. Macaulay used to rank a Fellow of Trinity somewhere in the neighbourhood of the Pope and the Holy Roman Emperor: I forget the exact order of the three, but I know that the King of Rome was lower down, and His most Christian Majesty of France quite out of sight. Platt [a fellow of Trinity since 1884] will no longer be able to despise me.[4]

Figure 28 The Jackson Family circa 1907. From L to R: Gerald, Moses, Rupert, Rose, Hector, Oscar. By permission of the Jackson family.

Moses Jackson moves to Canada: Housman's generosity

Also reaching a major turning point in his own life was Moses Jackson. Appointed Principal of the newly established Dayaram Jethmal Sind Science College in Karachi in 1887, he modernised and expanded it. His lack of ostentation, identification with his students and devotion to discipline made a profound impact as alumni testify. However, his time at Sind came to an end on a matter of principle; the board of directors failed to support him in the case of two students he believed had cheated in exams. A former student, Dr Mohanal Sonpar, recorded: 'When disagreement occurred between the Board of the College and himself, he did not care to bow to the Board, but bent his knee before the altar of his principles. He quietly resigned the post and severed connection with the institution which he had reared with his own hands.'[5]

From Sind, Moses moved 450 miles east to Baroda where the forward looking Maharaja invited him to become acting principal of the College of Science and director of science studies for the State of Baroda. He was also asked to oversee the education of the Maharaja's daughter, his sons being destined for education in England and America.

Within a year Moses had drawn up a proposal for full university status for the college separate from the University of Bombay, of which it was then a Faculty. Although supported by the Maharaja, the Baroda Education Commission rejected his proposal and after more than twenty years, India ceased to hold attractions for Moses. His ambitions frustrated and having to endure separation from his wife and children, he retired from the Indian Civil Service. In April 1910, he sailed back to England where Rosa had been living in Godalming in order to provide a stable home background for her sons.[6]

Moses, now aged 52, set about finding a new position in England. Housman's support continued unwavering. On 6 February 1911, coincidentally with his own imminent move to take up the Latin Chair at Cambridge, he was writing a letter supporting Moses' application for the post of Director of Education at Bradford:

> It is more than thirty years since Dr M. J. Jackson and I were undergraduates together and during the whole of that time I have held his character and intellect in the highest admiration; indeed there is no one to whose example I owe so much.[7]

The passage of twenty years had had an impact on Housman, transmuting the disturbing pain of their parting into something deep and continuing, an attachment he would never revoke, whether we care to translate his Latin dedication *Sodali Meo* as my comrade, my friend, my chum, or my soul mate.

Lines of communication between Housman and the Jackson family in Godalming were open. Eldest son Rupert was reading medicine at Cambridge, second son Hector was in his final year at Charterhouse, third son Oscar was at Oundle school near Peterborough, and ten-year-old Gerald, Housman's godson, was still at Branksome Preparatory School in Godalming, not far from the family home in Peperharow Road. In December 1908 Housman had sent Rosa Jackson a copy of the latest edition of his poems adding 'I was grateful to have your information about Mo. How did Rupert fare at Cambridge? A merry Christmas to you all.'[8]

By then Moses must have realised, as have many expatriates since, that long absence from England effectively ruled him out from the kind of post he would be happy with. How on earth could a recital of his achievements and experiences in Sind and Baroda be expected to impress education committee members in Bradford or mean anything to them? And so rather than face a life of retirement he looked for a way to apply his still considerable energies and to provide future opportunities for his sons. Once again, he decided to emigrate. In January 1911 Housman visited Godalming to say goodbye to Moses who was now bound for Canada where he would remain for the rest of his life. Housman was fully aware of all that was happening and on 12 June 1911, while he was still awaiting his own move to Cambridge, he wrote a letter, still in the possession of the Jackson family:

> My Dear Mo,
>
> I hear from Godalming that you have fixed on an estate of 160 acres, but I do not know precisely, nor what the main crops are to be. I got your long and instructive letter while I was at Cambridge, where the term is now over so that I am back here [Pinner] till October. I had no official duties to perform, but I gave them an inaugural lecture, which they wanted me to print, but I did not. Pollard came to hear it. Everyone is very amiable, but dinners, calls, garden parties, the climate and the hot weather made me rather tired.
>
> It never rains but it pours, so they have made me an honorary fellow of St John's. I went there for a dinner about six weeks ago, and met, of the undergraduates of our time, Roberts and Mitcheson. Watson had married a wife, and therefore he could not come. She is, or was, a Miss Gamlyn (I think), cousin of a man who is secretary of some Society or Association at Oxford.
>
> I do not want to make investments on my own account in the wild-cat colony you now inhabit, where you have to put Angleterre on your letters to get them to England; but if you happen to want extra capital you might just as well have it from me and prevent it from eating its head off in a current account at a bank.
>
> I am going to Godalming for the coronation. Rupert came to breakfast with me once at Cambridge. When he accepted my invitation to "brekker," I formed the gloomiest anticipations, and expected to find him deeply sunk into undergraduatism; but he is really quite simple and unspoilt.[9]

Although the chief importance of this letter is by far Housman's offer of financial help, he was also recording, in a throwaway sort of way, that he was breaking his rule about accepting honorary marks of academic distinction; he obviously felt that the offer of an honorary fellowship at St John's was one he could not refuse.

Housman's generous but tactful offer cemented his relationship with the Jackson family. Moses wrote to his eldest son Rupert, then at Cambridge, 'You will often see Housman at Cambridge and Ward in London.'[10] (A.E.N. Ward was a London solicitor and a friend of both Housman and Jackson and appears to have acted as Moses' and Housman's solicitor, although there is no correspondence to support either of these family views.)

On the Coronation Day of George V on 24 June 1911, Housman avoided celebrations in Cambridge and went instead to Godalming where he enjoyed 'a very wet day there, but a fine bonfire in the evening'.[11] Housman's intention was evidently threefold: to find out how things were going in British Columbia and where the family were to settle, to renew contact with Rosa, and make enquiries about family plans for his godson Gerald. When the purchase of their new home, a farm called Applegarth near Aldergrove in the Fraser Valley about 50 miles inland from Vancouver, was in its final stages, Moses summoned his family to join him. They arrived at Quebec on 14 September 1911 and after a further week they reached their new home.

Housman moves to Trinity: Farewell to University College, London

The same month that the Jackson family moved to their new life in Canada, Housman began his own new life in Cambridge. At the relatively late age of fifty-two and after nineteen years at University College, he was moving into Trinity College, Cambridge. His entry was not entirely without friction. In May 1911 Bertrand Russell, also a fellow of Trinity, wrote to Lady Ottoline Morrell that he had been visited by the Senior Tutor to be informed that the Council of Trinity would like his rooms:

> for A.E. Housman (the Shropshire Lad) but wished I would say I should not mind moving. However I should mind, so I said so and the Council will discuss the whole matter again. There is something curiously petty about life in a community. We all enjoy small advantages which others covet, and there is a tendency to petty spite, just because it is often people's duty to be unpleasant. I think all forms of communism develop the competitive instinct in bad ways. This is a paradox but true.[12]

Figure 29 Bertrand Russell, philosopher, mathematician, political activist, patron of Ludwig Wittgenstein and contemporary Fellow of Trinity. This portrait of 3rd Earl Russell by Roger Fry about 1923. © National Portrait Gallery, London.

And so Housman found himself forty steps up in Whewell's Court in a notably gloomy and unimpressive set of rooms situated in a detached and isolated part of the college, requiring him to cross a main road to enter the Great Gate of the college. Neither his rooms nor their remote location fazed him nor encouraged him to make them more agreeable and comfortable. Notwithstanding the success of *A Shropshire Lad*, it is also notable that neither Lady Ottoline Morrell nor Bertrand Russell seems to have marked out Housman for literary lionisation.

Another slant on the society he was now entering is given in A.C. Benson's diary entry for 19 July 1911. Benson, whose father had been Archbishop of Canterbury, was President of Magdalene College, Cambridge, and would in 1915 become its Master. Before he left Eton, where he was a housemaster, Benson began his diaries which eventually ran to something like four million words. On one point Benson's feelings were crystal clear:

The mistake I made in coming up to Cambridge was to feel that people here lived in an intellectual atmosphere. They do not – they live in affairs and gossip. They hate their work, I often think, and have few other interests.[13]

Cambridge was described as a refuge by Housman and he would remain there for the rest of his life, institutionalised as if he were in a monastery or regiment. At Bromsgrove Housman had been a big fish in a small pond, at Oxford he had been a small fish in a big pond, at University College he had been a big fish in a relatively small pond. Would he take the opportunity offered by Cambridge to set his sights on becoming a big fish in a big pond? Would he capitalise on his reputation as a poet and seek to make an impression on the university, apart from being its Professor of Latin?

William Tuckwell, a fellow of New College, Oxford, writing in the late nineteenth century, observed that dons fell into four categories: cosmopolitan, ornamental, mere and learned.[14] Those in academic careers today certainly divide between those with wider worldly ambitions in the media or politics; those who chase status and recognition in the hierarchy of their profession and take their ultimate reward in honours and decorations; those who are entirely consumed by their work and form part of an intellectual aristocracy, and those described as *mere* who simply do the job and occasionally make the top position in the college as a compromise candidate. It would not be long before Housman's intentions became clear.

The gulf between University College and Trinity College, Cambridge, was immense. Cambridge was ancient, full of tradition, hierarchy and authority. It provided a challenging social and intellectual arena. Housman had been happy, appreciated and seemingly fulfilled at University College: it had provided him with a perfect platform for his work of scholarship. With its metropolitan setting, its dispersed faculty and students, it was not claustrophobic and fitted his needs for personal yet secluded space. Cambridge provided his competitive self with knowledge that he had reached the top of his professional ladder so there were no deep regrets about leaving University College. Cambridge provided an altogether higher quality of students, though his role would never require him to mingle closely with them. Trinity College provided him with a home, albeit an institutionalised home, which University College with its commuting students and lonely digs did not.

His farewells provided a setting for vintage Housman. At a Complimentary Dinner at the Professors' Dining Club (of which he had been Treasurer), he formulated precisely what Cambridge might expect of him:

> Cambridge has seen many strange sights. It has seen Wordsworth drunk and Porson sober. It is now destined to see a better scholar than Wordsworth and a better poet than Porson betwixt and between.[15]

According to Chambers:

> He professed by a polite fiction, that he was leaving us because of the rule then just introduced, of superannuation at sixty-five. This of course would not have been binding upon appointments, like his, already made. But he asserted that he had been kept awake at nights, pondering what he should do between the age of sixty-five, when he would be morally, though not legally compelled to retire, and the age of seventy when he would become eligible for the old age pension. 'I have now found a refuge. Death, raving madness, or detected crime are the only enemies I have now to fear.'[16]

On the same occasion, he said that University College had 'picked him out of the gutter, if I may so describe His Majesty's Patent Office'. Arthur Platt later told Henry Jackson that in planning his own speech he had considered likening Housman to Attila the Hun or to Bentley bullying the fellows of Trinity.

The dinner given for him by the students was touching:

> We, his old students of the past nineteen years, gave him a silver loving-cup with the inscription round it, *Malt does more than Milton can to justify God's ways to man.* It was then that he described his predecessor at Cambridge, J.E.B. Mayor, as a man who drank like a fish – 'If drinking nothing but water might be so described. When they see me coming to Cambridge with this cup', he said, 'they will understand that things are going to be changed.'[17]

Thus they did him proud; a true measure of his standing with them and their affection for him.

Housman arrived in Cambridge as a still rising and productive scholar, even though he was now more than fifty-two years old. Between 1893 and 1910, the year before he took the Latin Chair at Cambridge, he had published a further seventy-four papers, never less than one a year and on average four a year. He had completed his first volume of Manilius' *Astronomicon* in 1903. In that same year, he had been asked by John Postgate to edit Juvenal for his *Corpus Poetarum Latinorum* which Housman completed in two years and published in 1905. Housman's capacity for work was prodigious. He was a scholar at the height of his powers and he now carried all the celebrity that went with being the poet of *A Shropshire Lad*.

University College had been an altogether more domestic and less hallowed environment, its common room not to be compared with the polished and glistening surroundings of the Trinity College Combination Room and the ranks of college servants. Nowhere in his letters was there any sense of uncertainty. Housman's inherent sense of entitlement and indestructible self-confidence made him sure of himself. And here in Cambridge his introverted nature proved to be a great advantage. His lack of chatter and easy bonhomie, his tendency to grow on small groups, the clarity and acuity of his opinions were profound advantages; they made you feel you had to listen to him and take note of what he said.

He was aware, however, that there would be a price to pay. He wrote to Alice Rothenstein, whom he expected to see from time to time at Cambridge with her husband, 'To have less work and more pay is always agreeable, and that will be the case with me. The drawback is that I shall be obliged to be less unsociable.'[18] He wrote to Mildred Platt, wife of his friend Platt:

> Yours was the first letter so I will answer it first and thank you for your congratulations, which show a very Christian and forgiving spirit, considering my remissness in attending your at homes. The prospect of exchanging you for Mrs Frazer is one of the clouds on my horizon; but please do not repeat this remark at all to your Cambridge aquaintances.[19]

To Lady Ramsay, wife of the professor of Chemistry at University College, he wrote 'Joy does predominate over sorrow, as I am fond of money and of leisure, but as I am also fond of solitude, and shall not have it at Cambridge, there is some sorrow mingled with joy apart from leaving friends and the College.'[20] To Edmund Gosse he wrote, 'In most respects, though not quite in all, I think the change is a matter for congratulation. If the exhalations of the Granta give me a relaxed sore throat, more poems may be expected.'[21] To Laurence, 'Although you are very conceited and Clemence, I fear, very rowdy, I thank you both for your congratulations. It is not by any means certain that I could have secured the Oxford chair by waiting for it: and on the whole I think I prefer Cambridge.'[22] To Walter Ashburner he made a shrewd observation. 'I attribute my election to the fact that I was personally unknown to the majority of the electors and the other candidates were not.'[23]

By 11 June he was already feeling oppressed, writing to Laurence:

> Although I had very few duties during the Cambridge term I was much occupied with social duties, which are a great deal worse, and either from the climate or the heat was generally tired when I was not occupied, so that I have not thanked you for the proofs of your play.'[24]

Housman was not an extrovert. He was not gregarious. He was not energised by contacts with others. He liked to have plenty of time to himself, to recharge his batteries.

The Cambridge Inaugural Lecture

Housman gave his Inaugural Lecture at the Senate House on 9 May 1911 to 'a crowded and curious audience,'[25] some no doubt drawn to hear how this hybrid poet/scholar who had landed in their midst would introduce himself, more or less disposed to welcome him according to their estimate of *A Shropshire Lad*, or in the case of those in the know, to welcome the apotheosis of a pre-eminent scholar and long-time member of the Cambridge Philological Society. No doubt, given his audience of academics, there would also have been bitchy asides about his provenance, and gossip about his failure in Greats.

Housman's strategy soon became clear; he had first of all to make them sit up and listen; then he had to get the audience on his side and leave them with a clear message.

His audience was immediately forced to open its ears by quite unexpected statements on how he intended to use the occasion, and his perspective on his own subject:

An inaugural address is a fitting occasion for taking stock of our vanities, or at least for looking the worst of them in the face and forming resolutions for their amendment. I propose today to consider two current errors, as it seems to me, of some magnitude and of opposite nature. The study of Latin is a science conversant with literature: there are therefore two ways in which it ought not to be pursued as if it were a science conversant with the operations of nature or with the properties of number and space, nor yet as if it were itself a branch of literature, and no science at all.

Having first startled his audience into attention, he set about getting them on his side, paying gracious and warm tributes to Benjamin Hall Kennedy in whose honour the Chair of Latin had been founded and who, as chief editor of *Sabrinae Corolla*, a collection of translated Greek and Latin verse, had been instrumental in awakening the young Housman's liking for the classics; then to his predecessor, Hugh Munro, the first holder of the Chair in 1869. On the completeness of his edition of Lucretius he was fulsome: 'None of our great original critics, neither Bentley not Markland, Porson nor Elmsley, has left behind him a work making any pretence to such completeness.' Housman had not known Munro personally, as some in his audience had, 'but I did in those days molest him with letters, and I still preserved his patient and amiable replies to the young man who never even in the dreams of youth imagined that he was one day to be the successor of his illustrious correspondent.' He was equally generous to his immediate predecessor, John Mayor, 'whose inclinations were exactly in harmony with his talents.' Then he used the examples of Kennedy, Munro and Mayor to exemplify traditional differences between Cambridge and Oxford scholarship: 'Cambridge scholarship simply meant scholarship with no nonsense about it; Oxford scholarship embodied one of those erroneous tendencies against which I take up my parable today.'

Now he could take aim at his main targets, Latin professors who posed as literary critics and literary critics per se. 'Scholarship, in short, is not literary criticism; and of the duties of a Latin Chair literary criticism forms no part.' He nailed his own colours to the mast: 'If, in spite of the doctrine of probabilities, the twentieth century is also to behold a Latin scholar who is a literary critic, all I know is that I am not he.'

In his view, a scholar should appreciate literature but had no right to presume that his own aesthetic perceptions are superior to those of anyone whom he addresses. He spoke contemptuously of how easily audiences could be led: 'Present to them the literary opinions which they already hold, couched in the dialect which they believe to be good English, and sprinkled over with epithets like *delicate, sympathetic*, and *vital*, and you will easily persuade the great majority that they are listening to literary criticism.' However, other disciplines could be different. 'The botanist and the astronomer have for their provinces two worlds of beauty and magnificence not inferior in their way to literature; but no one expects a botanist to throw up his hands and say "how beautiful", nor the astronomer to fall down flat and say "how magnificent". He had made his point, but perhaps his *reductio ad absurdum* was not entirely convincing when he said that scholars should write about literature in the language of the third book of Newton's *Principia*: 'Let S represent the sun, T the earth, P the moon, CADB the moon's orbit.'

He was on strong ground in distinguishing different purposes:

> The aim of science is the delivery of truth, while the aim of literature is the production of pleasure; the two aims are not merely distinct but often incompatible, so that large departments of literature are also departments of lying. Not only so, but man is generally more of a pleasure seeker than a truth seeker and the literary spirit, if once admitted to communication with the scientific, will ever tend to encroach upon its domain.

He took as his text a line from Shelley's lyric, *A Lament*. The line, 'Fresh Spring, and Summer, and Winter hoar', was deficient on two grounds: Autumn was missing and from a metrical point of view the line was also missing a syllable. Swinburne had championed the usual text on grounds of its 'divine and sovereign sweetness'. But Housman alleged that Shelley had actually written 'Fresh Spring and Autumn, Summer and Winter hoar'. Thus, the result of a misprint had been exalted. Housman continued: 'What value shall we attach to similar judgements pronounced by men who are not themselves men of letters, but merely scholars with a literary taint, on disputed passages in books written hundreds and thousands of years ago by an alien race amidst an alien culture?'

Housman then directed his fire on German scholars.

> But if in England the scholar's besetting sin is the literary attitude ... the German fault is to pretend it is mathematics ... blind followers of rules will be blind followers of masters ... this

nonsense of orthodoxy and this propensity to servitude ... believes that the fashion of the present, unlike all fashions heretofore, will endure perpetually.

In today's terms he was saying that one size does not and cannot fit all.

Having applied a powerful and rational corrective to what he saw as the vanities of English and German scholars, he went on to ask how we are to avoid them and had to admit 'that I do not altogether know, and that perhaps after all we cannot'. Self-examination was difficult but we had to bear in mind the difficulty of self-examination and the ease of self-deception. Returning to his idea of servility to fashion, he counselled that we should think more of the great among the dead who had proven themselves by enduring.

As with all speeches there were the words; quoting them does a kind of literal justice to their thrust and meaning; the music he created was a different matter, a matter of emphasis or tone, of voice and of facial expressions, at times signalling irony. A lecture is an amalgam of what is said and the way of saying it; he portrayed a man not overcome by the conceit of his position, able to connect with his audience, willing to be critical of his profession, not portraying himself as a new broom; formidably equipped, yet humble in his search for answers to the problems he had identified.

It was worth noting the music he created around the word Germany and German scholars. The year of his Inaugural, 1911, was coincidentally a year in which tensions between the great powers of Europe were making themselves widely felt. Neither here nor elsewhere in his correspondence did Housman make any reference to the gathering crisis, but the music of his statements about German scholarship were couched in strikingly disapproving terms of the Germany that was emerging.

> For the past hundred years the study of the classics had its centre in Germany. That Europe looks thither no longer is one of the many fruits of the diplomacy of Bismarck. On the battlefield of Sedan you may set up the gravestone not of one empire but two; for where the military predominance of France fell down and perished, there also the intellectual predominance of Germany received a wound of which it bled slowly to death... not in classical studies alone ... 'German capabilities', said Prince Bulow four years ago 'have taken refuge in our industry and our army'.

Housman went on:

> Students of Greek and Latin are by far more numerous in
> Germany than in any other country, and their studies are also
> far more completely and efficiently organised; but the students
> themselves are not pre-eminent, as once they were, in the power
> or the will to perform intellectual operations.

Instead,

> Blind followers of rules will be blind followers of masters: a pupil
> who has got out of the habit of thinking will take his teacher's
> word for gospel, and will be delighted with the state of things
> in which intellectual scrutiny not only ceases to be a duty but
> becomes an act of insubordination.

Combination of the five greatest universities of Germany in producing
a *thesaurus linguae Latinae* demonstrated 'the disadvantage of
employing slave labour.' The reading of a particular word by the
German scholar Buecheler 'was enough for the chain gangs working
at the dictionary in the ergastulum [workhouse for debtors or slaves]
at Munich.' In the same passage Housman spoke of 'the mental
habits of the slave.' Those trenchant and insightful words seem to
be remarkably prescient about the outcome of German militaristic
attitudes at the beginning of the First World War, and the psychology
underpinning Hitler's management of the German people in his mad
quest to enslave Europe.

Among his listeners, it was not only the content of his lecture
that met with approval. Henry Jackson writing to Arthur Platt put it
succinctly:

> Housman's discourse was excellent. He smote with all his might
> two tendencies of modern scholarship – on the one hand aesthetic
> criticism; on the other hand, the slavish mechanical methods of
> the Germans. The V.C. [Vice-Chancellor] was absent, and asked
> .... to speak at the end. I fear that ... was shocked that Housman
> washed his hands of aesthetic criticism: he hoped that what
> Housman had said was all ironical. So in effect his neat speech
> was at once stupid and rude. For myself I rejoiced exceedingly in
> the texts of Housman's preachment. And the manner was perfect.
> He trounced Swinburne most effectively in respect of a reading in

Shelley. His denunciation of the 'slave labour' of the big German-Latin Dictionary rejoiced me especially. And personally, I was much pleased with what he said about Munro and Mayor. He was kind, just and truthful.[26]

J.M. Image, also a fellow of Trinity, echoed Jackson in being enthusiastic about Housman's actual on-stage performance. 'Brilliant is the only epithet – flashing and scintillating with dry humour (admirably enhanced by his solemnity of face) and "delicious irony".'[27] He responded with even more feeling to Housman's words: 'His enthusiasm for Munro and for the Cambridge School of scholarship warmed my heart. His eulogies on Cambridge lips would have sounded fulsome. Coming from a Member of the rival University they sounded true and generous.'[28] Sydney Cockerell, Director of the Fitzwilliam Museum, wrote of it as a 'brilliant performance'.[29] A highlight for Housman was seeing his old friend Pollard who recorded how he was 'richly rewarded by the cry of pleasure with which I was greeted when he caught sight of me after it. I think that somehow my presence seemed to him a recognition that he had reached his haven at last.'[30]

F.M. Cornford, a fellow of Trinity and husband of Frances Cornford the novelist, wrote to congratulate Housman whose reply demonstrated an accomplished speaker, consciously aware of his audience's reactions, so that his changes of pace, emphasis and tone of voice gave him a sense of holding his audience: 'I caught sight of your face at one point of the lecture and was gratified by the expression it wore.'[31] From across the Atlantic came a letter from Witter Bynner, to which Housman replied: 'It is true that I am now Professor of Latin here, and I thank you for your congratulations. Of course it is nonsense when they talk about my "steadily refusing to write any more poetry": poetry does not even steadily refuse to be written by me; but there is not yet enough to make even a small book.'[32] This was an understandable distortion of the facts; the truth was that since 1900 he had begun twenty-six new poems as described earlier.

Housman had demonstrated by his track record and now by this lecture that he was a potentially formidable leader or competitor in the Cambridge scene. Would he wish to be diverted from his scholarly preoccupations to ascend the greasy pole of college politics and work towards the mastership? Or would he wish to put himself in the running for Vice-Chancellor one day? Or would he prefer to create a reputation in the salons of London and the greater world of politics, as part of the establishment of the great and the good, confidante of politicians and prime ministers?

To the outside world he appeared clad in the mantle of his Cambridge professorship with his home in Trinity College, Cambridge, and with the halo of *A Shropshire Lad* round his head. The outside world crowded round him, proffering further honours. Yet he went on his seemingly perverse way, refusing nomination as a fellow of the British Academy in 1911. 'The honour is one which I should not find congenial nor feel to be appropriate.'[33] And in 1913 he turned down the offer of an honorary fellowship of the Royal Society of Literature, with a seat on its academic committee, this time for the understandable reasons that 'both favours, however gratifying and honourable, are remote from my tastes and pursuits.'[34] Housman was not to be persuaded even by A.C. Benson:

> Your suasions fall upon the deaf ears of an egoistic hedonist. I suffer a good deal from life, and do not want to suffer more; and to join the Academic Committee or any similar body would be an addition to my discomforts. Not overwhelming, but still appreciable. To analyse my feelings, which may be morbid, would only be a matter of curiosity; what concerns me is the feelings themselves, and there they are ... For any practical purpose it would find me quite useless, and it can very well dispense with any lustre which might be shed upon it by my exiguous (though eximious) output.[35]

Benson was just the man to enjoy Housman's distinction between 'exiguous' and 'eximious'. Housman had a clear and restrictive image of himself as a scholar. Events may have shown him to be an excellent performer on the podium and to have leadership and managerial capacity but he did not hanker after the life of a committee man or a chairman just as he did not hanker after being recognised as a great poet.

He had all the essential capabilities of a great achiever but clearly had no wish to deploy them outside his profession as a Latinist. His life of the mind as a scholar was intense and focussed; when he went for his walks he was in automatic pilot mode, perceiving chatter as intrusion; he simply allowed his mind to lie fallow in a combination of physical activity and creative idleness. Among scholars there seems to have been a spectrum, at one end extrovert scholars suffering from logorrhea; at the other, reticent, focussed, almost autistic scholars. In our own time Maurice Bowra and Isaiah Berlin were both full of talk; far away from them at the other end of the spectrum was the Nobel Prize winner Paul Dirac, a quantum physicist. Dirac was a man of inhuman reticence, causing his Cambridge colleagues to invent

> a new unit, for the smallest imaginable number of words that someone with the power of speech could utter in company – an average of one word an hour, 'a Dirac'. On the rare occasions when he was provoked into saying more than yes or no, he said precisely what he thought, apparently with no understanding of other people's feelings or the conventions of polite conversations.[36]

References to Housman's reticence frequently came from men who admired verbal pyrotechnics and who might themselves be characterised as talkers or chatterers.

Manilius II nears completion: Paris calls

On 15 August 1911, still writing from Pinner, Housman gave Richards the good news that the second book of Manilius was nearly finished, that he intended going off to Paris in early September, and expected to make a permanent move to Cambridge about the twenty-fourth of that month. In these mundane practical matters, Housman's precise, ordered, and disciplined way of working was evident. In the midst of issues crowding in on him consequent on his move to Cambridge, he could focus; making sure that Richards knew precisely what his movements would be, zooming in on the detailed business of printing *Manilius II* as though he had nothing else to think about:

He gave detailed instructions on how capital J was to be printed as capital I, lower case j as i, and lower case v as u, adding his practical advice: 'The compositor's simplest way to avoid error will be to put lids on the receptacles containing the types of the forbidden forms, so that his hand cannot get into them; but no doubt he is too proud to take advice from me.' Housman was just getting into his stride:

> On former occasions the proofs have come to me full of the usual blunders, – numerals wrong, letters upside down, stops missing, and so on. I have then, at the cost of much labour, removed all these errors. Then, when the last proof has left my hands, the

corrector for the press has been turned on to it, and has found nothing to correct; whereupon, for fear his employers should think he is not earning his pay, he has set to work meddling with what I have written, – altering my English spelling into Webster's American spelling, my use of capitals into his own misuse of capitals, my scientific punctuation into the punctuation he learnt from his grandmother. What ought to be done is the reverse of this. The errors which are introduced by the printer should be removed by the press corrector, who will do it more easily and more rapidly, though not more efficiently than I; then and not till then the proofs should come to me, and after that no corrections should be made except by me.[37]

On this occasion Richards decided to change the printer, somewhat against Housman's wishes: 'I am a conservative, and do not like changing anything without due reason, not even a printer, – nay, not even a publisher,'[38] a reasonable enough sentiment but perhaps he carried resistance to change too far and on this occasion, Richards' decision proved a good move. It produced praise from Housman: 'I have been very agreeably surprised by the accuracy of Messrs MacLehose's printing.'

It must have been somewhat galling for Housman to find in 1911 that H.W. Garrod, a fellow of Merton College, Oxford, had produced a translation and commentary on Manilius, but nevertheless he gave it a gracious welcome:

> I have no wish to prevent other scholars from editing Manilius, but rather the reverse; and I think the world is probably wide enough for both our books, as each contains a good deal which the other does not. I congratulate you on your addition to our knowledge of the cod. Venetus.[39]

This was not to be the whole story; Housman refused to review it, and nineteen years later attacked it in the preface of the final volume of his own Manilius.

Housman, heavily preoccupied with his second volume of his great work, was adjusting to his new home, to the ways of his college and Cambridge, preparing lectures, having new contacts thrust upon him, picking up old relationships, coping with his publisher and dealing with his own celebrity as lyric poet and Cambridge professor;

not surprisingly, he impeded as much as possible the growth of a celebrity myth; he did not allow Grant Richards to set up a newspaper interview with him.

At the end of December 1911, he gave Kate something of a review of his first term:

> I am staying here through the vacation as I am seeing a book through the press and I found I could not do much at it during the term. Being conscientious, I took a great deal of time to prepare my lectures; and being a newcomer, I was much asked out to dinner. People here are very hospitable and friendly. The attendance at my lectures was from 20 to 30 (which, though not large, is from 20 to 30 times greater than the attendance at my predecessor's), several of whom were lecturers themselves. I believe the lectures are considered good (as indeed they are).[40]

In early November he had been invited to spend the weekend with Wilfred Scawen Blunt, a well-born land owner, poet, horse breeder and Arabist married to Lady Anne Noel, granddaughter of Lord Byron. Blunt was addicted to love affairs and mistresses. An anti-imperialist, he advocated revolution in Egypt and independence for the Irish, the latter earning him a spell in an Irish prison. Housman's fellow guest was Wilfred Meynell, editor, journalist, biographer and husband of Alice Meynell the poet. For Housman this was loquacious, unbridled and opinionated company. Blunt was not set alight by Housman. Some disappointment can be read between the lines of his diary entry:

> Housman's appearance is one of depression and indifference. He does not smoke, drinks little and would, I think be quite silent if he were allowed to be.[41]

Housman subsequently told Andrew Gow, a young fellow of Trinity, that 'the description was perfectly accurate (except that so far as he could remember there was little to drink).' Blunt also recollected Housman as 'a typical Cambridge don, prim in his manner and rather shy ... talking fairly well, but not brilliantly or with any originality, depressed in tone, and difficult to arouse with any strong expression of opinion... Nevertheless I like him.'[42] Perhaps this was because Blunt and he found they had something in common. 'We sat up again till twelve at night telling ghost stories.' On 3 December 1911 Blunt wrote to Sidney Cockerell, Director of the Fitzwilliam Museum and a fellow of Jesus who had been Blunt's secretary and protégé. 'We all liked Housman when he was here a week ago, though anything less like a Shropshire Lad it would be impossible to conceive.'[43] Housman was not a person who took others by storm or who espoused causes and probably could not take the eccentric Blunt too seriously.

Re-enter Herbert Foxwell

On 29th November 1911 Housman reached out to a friend he had made at University College. Herbert Foxwell had been elected Professor of Political Economy in 1881. Housman served with him on three Senate committees. Foxwell, a rising star in the world of economics, also lectured on banking and currency at the London School of Economics and in 1907 was appointed a Professor of Political Economy in the University of London. Also a fellow and lecturer at St John's College, Cambridge, he actually lived in Cambridge at 1 Harvey Road. It was therefore natural that Housman should write to 'My dear Foxwell', asking him to be his guest at a Trinity Feast on 11 December.[44] Foxwell was an inveterate hoarder of letters and papers and kept eighteen of Housman's letters, from his first on 29 November 1911 to his last on 12 December 1933, all intact in their envelopes and addressed in Housman's elegantly statuesque handwriting. For the next twenty-two years Housman and Foxwell kept their friendship alive by eating and talking together once or twice a year. Foxwell, a keen theatre goer and a charming man, had a very energetic love life in London, specialising in actresses he picked up at the stage door. His passion for hoarding overcame discretion; his correspondence contained many letters from his conquests, a half-dozen of whom became regular correspondents, one writing him close on two hundred letters. At least one of his correspondents produced an illegitimate son, and at least one was sent to Belgium for an abortion. Foxwell received many pleading or threatening letters and bought silence with gifts of money or clothes. Shortly before his marriage in 1898, his fiancée received an anonymous letter concerning his amorous activities; her response was to send the letter to Foxwell saying she did not believe the accusations.[45]

The significance of the Foxwell letters lies not so much in their content as in the seeming incongruity of a long-standing friendship

Figure 30 Herbert Foxwell, Fellow and Lecturer
in Economics at St John's College Cambridge.
As Professor of Economics at University College
London a contemporary of Housman. Their
friendship continued when Housman went to
Cambridge where Foxwell had always lived. By
permission of the Master and Fellows of St John's
College, Cambridge.

between these two men which led them to dining and talking together
on twenty-two occasions. It is hard to believe that Housman was
attracted by Foxwell's academic work on banking, bimetallism, imperial
preference and tariff reform, or by his interest in Karl Marx. Most
likely it was Foxwell's sparkling and extrovert personality and their
mutual enjoyment of witty repartee that cemented their friendship,
clearly one of opposites, not unlike Housman's with Grant Richards
and William Rothenstein. Spice may have been added by sharing
racy stories, very much part of Housman's repertoire – and given the
breadth of Foxwell's worldly experience, probably part of his too.

In October 1912 Housman received a letter from Edward Marsh,
then editor of *Georgian Poetry.* Marsh met Housman at a supper given
by the great networker Edmund Gosse, man of letters, minor poet
and sometime Clark Lecturer at Trinity College. Marsh wanted to

include a Housman poem in his anthology *Georgian Poetry*. Knowing Marsh to be a friend of Gosse and son of the Master of Downing College, Cambridge, Housman handled him carefully. Although he was prepared to sugar the pill it still had to be delivered.

> If you want to get poetry out of me, you must be either a relative or a duchess. As a brother and a snob I am accessible from two quarters, but from no others. Besides I do not really belong to your 'new era' and none even of my few unpublished poems have been written within the last two years.

But he still tried to be helpful and recommended G.K. Chesterton's *Ballad of the White Horse*, 'absurd in its plan and its conception and often cheap and brassy in its ornament, but it contains quite a lot of really magnificent verses, which impressed me more than anything I have read for a long time ... However literary criticism is not what you were asking for.'[46] Even though he was ruling out his poetry as not fitting Marsh's anthology, he was at the same time demonstrating a lack of interest in using his contact with Marsh to further his own reputation as a poet. He preferred to keep himself locked away in his scholar's cell.

In the final days of 1911 he had been much occupied with eleven diagrams to be included in the text of Manilius which would provide certain challenges for the printers. On this occasion he had a novel complaint. 'The only fault I find with it is that the artist has imitated too closely my own imperfect draughtsmanship.'[47] Housman saw no obvious paradox in describing a printer's error as 'a perfectly atrocious action, and I cannot imagine how such a thing could come to pass', in the same breath saying 'I want to have pp.1–16 again, as I overlooked some things which were wrong.'[48] By the beginning of February, the book, its index and also corrigenda had been completed and by 11 February, he enclosed his last corrections. All was in motion except that a coalminers' strike was due to begin on 1 March 1912, and as Housman put it, 'the destruction of the national wealth is a question of days'. This brief allusion to what was happening in the outside world occurred only because it might impinge on the production of his precious book. As time went by, he became very anxious.

> Two months ago I sent you a list of the persons and newspapers to which I wished copies of the Manilius to be sent. Probably you

Figure 31 Housman circa 1912.
© E.O. Hoppé Estate Collection /
Curatorial Assistance, Inc.

have lost it, in which case let me know at once and I will draw up a new one: don't keep the poor wretches waiting another couple of months.

He went on: 'Whether I can lunch with a person who is so far from being what he should be is a question which I will consider between now and my next visit to London.'[49]

At last he began to receive feedback on his second volume of Manilius. First in the field seems to have been his friend John Mackail, by then reaching the end of his tenure as Professor of Poetry at Oxford. Housman replied 'You well describe as extraordinary the pleasure with which you are kind enough to say you read my commentary. I don't believe any one in Cambridge will read it, whether with pleasure or agony: the Latinists here are very well disposed towards me but terribly afraid of Manilius.'[50] Housman went on to comment on more than twenty-five of Mackail's points, expansively where necessary but without the slightest tinge of aggression or personal parade, which indicated that he was prepared to treat Mackail with the greatest respect; not surprising, because Mackail had been garlanded with scholarships and prizes as an undergraduate and made a fellow of Balliol before he branched out into the education department of the Privy Council.

Housman's friendly combat with Richards continued and on 2 July he wrote saying he would be in London for a few days 'so that if you are there, and still cherish your benevolent intention of asking me to lunch, you will have your chance'. But he couldn't resist a sting in the tail: 'I see that you are coming out as a novelist: *Huitres* or *Crevettes roses* or some such title'.[51] Richards' first novel was actually called *Caviare*; Housman took it with him on his continental trip to Venice and Paris and announced that he had read it 'with great interest all through, though the Monte Carlo parts perhaps are not equal to the Parisian and American. These last seem to me particularly good. I have just seen a favourable review in the *Telegraph*. I hope you will not now take to writing poetry or editing Manilius'.[52]

Housman's stay in London had included a night with George Vize, a former heavy-weight boxer, 'one of the best known all-round athletes of his time', and his wife Kitty, friends of John Maycock, Housman's colleague at the Patent Office. Housman was not totally committed to keeping himself to himself and to his work.

He wrote to Mildred Platt on 10 October 1912 to take her up on a previous offer of hospitality. 'I shall be coming to town on the 17th to attend a meeting at University College, so I give you notice, as you kindly told me to do, in order that you may ask me to dinner if you feel inclined.' On Boxing Day 1912 he was thanking her for 'your kind and beautiful present of the Dogana [the Venetian counting house] in its sumptuous frame ... I am very grateful and hope that heaven will reward you with a happy new year.' Two years previously she had given him sloe gin. Housman the bachelor had probably aroused Mildred Platt's maternal instincts and he had got into an easy relationship with her, allowing himself to say how he needed:

> something to divert my mind from the horrors of my situation, for Trinity College is a besieged city. A week ago there came a telegram to say that one of the junior Fellows, Pearse, whom Platt will know by name, had left his home, mad and armed, and would probably make his way here. All entrances to the College have therefore been closed, except the Great Gate, which is guarded by a double force of Porters. Cambridge was perplexed at first, but has now invented the explanation that it is the Master who has

gone mad, and has made these arrangements in order that he may shoot at the Fellows from the Lodge as they come through the Great Gate. The Provost of King's gives imitations of the Master thus engaged: 'Ah there is dear Dr Jackson!' bang!! ... Whewell's Court is left quite unprotected, and I have to look under the bed every night.

My remembrances therefore to your husband and family; tomorrow I may be no more than a remembrance myself.[53]

The Rothensteins were now living at Oakridge Lynch on the other side of Stroud. Housman proposed that during the summer he would take the opportunity provided by a visit to the Wises to also meet the Rothensteins, taking a train and walking the rest of the way. He wrote again to Alice Rothenstein on 14 February 1913:

Bertrand Russell said to me yesterday "Have you seen anything of the Rothensteins lately," and it went through my heart like a spear of ice that neither had I seen them nor had they heard from me, though you wrote to me at the beginning of the year. But if you ever have to examine for University Scholarships you will find as I do that all one's leisure is fully occupied by wishing that one was dead; and I am only just at the end of this tribulation.

Housman was feeling guilty and regretful that in concentrating on his work he was neglecting his friends. He gave her information that he had not been in Gloucestershire since he last saw them, and how 'You and William ought to be in the country now to observe of this extraordinary spring, or winter as it calls itself', how he had told Bertrand Russell that he remembered when Russell's parents lived on the hill just opposite Woodchester, and enquiring whether she had seen Mrs Cornford's latest book and its portraits in the frontispiece. It was a very relaxed and humane sort of letter.[54] His connection with Edmund Gosse had also become regular and when he wrote to Thomas Hardy on the death of his wife, Emma, in 1912 he mentioned, 'Several times since I was at Dorchester in 1900 I had met Mrs Hardy at the Gosses' when she was visiting London'.[55]

Housman was demonstrating that he was by no means a recluse even though he was a busy self-driven academic who gave most of his attention to his work and preferred not to have it interrupted. Although work was the core of his life, his correspondence with Grant Richards, made necessary by Housman's preoccupation with the accurate printing of his texts, was widened and deepened by the stimulus of shared interests. His correspondence with the Rothensteins was carried along by their dynamism and his own growing liking for them. Family correspondence with brother Laurence and sister Kate was regular. What also became very noticeable was that Housman seems to have replied to virtually every letter addressed to him; few seem to have been consigned to the bin.

Housman's first but oblique reference to the gathering clouds of war over Europe was on 8 March 1913. His focus on work seems to have left no room for expatiating on the ins and outs of the clashing territorial ambitions of the great powers or for forcing his opinions on others. He gives the impression of not being interested in much beyond Cambridge, yet Blunt's description of him as 'informed', the obvious fact that he read newspapers and that in his own Inaugural he had registered in a very thoughtful way the menace of Germany, demonstrates that he was likely to have been totally aware of the significance of current events and not so detached from what was happening at the time that he could not read the runes. He sheltered behind humour. In writing to Lily Thicknesse whom he had now known for at least a decade: 'The chief excitements of the term here have been an agitation, by a highly undistinguished set of persons, to introduce conscription for undergraduates, as a last effort to frighten the Germans; and an exhibition of post-impressionist undergraduate art, which is calculated to frighten the Germans a good deal more.'[56]

For the rest of 1913, his correspondence was devoid of allusions to the threat of war. Instead, it was full of personal connections. In January, having heard that Richards was unwell, he sympathised. 'One of my chief objections to the management of the universe is that we suffer so much more from our gentler and more amiable vices than from our darkest crimes.'[57] In April 1913, knowing that Richards had just been in Paris, Housman wrote saying that he had forgotten to advise him to eat morilles – a type of mushroom – then in season. He wrote telling James G. Frazer, a brother fellow of Trinity, author of *The Golden Bough* and at that time Professor of Anthropology at Liverpool, about the feast of the Nativity of the Virgin in Capri. Three days later, most probably having been pressed for more by Frazer, he wrote a notably tongue-in-cheek and frankly amused and exaggerated account of what he had witnessed of the same ceremony nine years earlier in Naples:

The pious orgy at Naples ... began at 8 in the evening ... with the whole population walking about blowing penny trumpets ... I went to bed at midnight and was lulled to sleep by the barrel-organs which supersede the trumpets about that hour. At four in the morning I was waked by detonations as if the British fleet was bombarding the city, caused, I was afterwards told, by dynamite rockets. The only step possible beyond this is assassination, which accordingly takes place about peep of day. I forget now the number of the slain, but I think the average is eight or ten, and I know that in honour of my presence they murdered a few more than usual. I enclose the extract from the *Standard* about Satan in Scotland.[58]

Housman's irrepressible sense of humour was descending into slapstick.

He had to decline an Alice Rothenstein invitation because he had been asked by Sydney Cockerell to dine in Jesus and meet Thomas Hardy. A month later he was able to offer her the possibility of his going over to the Rothensteins for the day when he was at Woodchester. And then, speaking of his most recent visit to Paris, he mentioned how he occasionally met their friends 'the other day McEvoy the painter'. And so he continued as a correspondent, courteous, frequently amused, urbane yet candid, generous and modest in spirit. Wilfred Meynell, who was Francis Thompson's literary executor, seems to have sent him a copy of *The Collected Poetry of Francis Thompson*, to which Housman responded, 'This is indeed rather overwhelming, but I manage to gasp out my thanks.'[59]

Housman was all the time keeping in touch with Richards, telling him of his travels in Normandy, 'riding about in a motor car which I hired very cheap in Paris',[60] telling him he had read his latest novel, thanking him for a cheque. 'It is rather a weight off my mind, as I thought you might have been betting on horses.'[61]

With William Rothenstein he was equally personal. 'This is to remind you that when you come here on your mission to our dusky brethren you are going to stay with me.' Burnett notes that Rothenstein proposed and co-founded the India Society for the promotion and understanding of Indian art and literature.[62]

Mistaken identity was still occurring but when it ascended to a familial scale he wrote to Laurence without other comment:

An American ecclesiastic was here the other day, who asked to be presented to me, and from whom I gathered that his favourite work would be *A Shropshire Lad* but for the existence of that fascinating story, *The Were Wolf* which, again would be his favourite work, but for the existence of the most brilliant political satire ever written, *King John of Jingalo*.[63]

Two days later, he was writing to his valued American correspondent Witter Bynner sending praise for his latest play *Tiger*. 'I thought the drama very vivid and telling and I can praise it more impartially because I am quite out of sympathy with its propaganda.' Then there came an extraordinary signal of his growing affection for this young American and his mounting trust. 'I remember my promise, and when new poems are published you shall have them. Perhaps you are even entitled to have one which I wrote more than a year ago in an album, so I copy it here.'[64] It was 'The sigh that heaves the grasses', then written in his notebook and destined to be included in *Last Poems*.

In December 1913 the indefatigable Gosse had included him in a dinner party that included Herbert Asquith, the Prime Minister, and Robert Bridges, the Poet Laureate. Gosse evidently believed that Housman was capable of holding his own in such company and of contributing to it. Housman wrote 'I enjoyed your dinner and the august and agreeable society which you had got together. Never before have I seen, and never do I expect to see again, a Prime Minister and a Poet Laureate composing a Missive to a Monarch [probably on the subject of home rule for Ireland].'[65] Housman said not a word of darkening skies over Europe, or the activities of Mrs Pankhurst's suffragettes at home.

Housman opened the fateful New Year of 1914 by giving an unknown correspondent whom he had to address as 'Dear Sir' what amounted to his credo on meaning in poetry:

When the meaning of a poem is obscure, it is due to one of three causes. Either the author, through lack of skill, has failed to express his meaning; or he has concealed it intentionally; or he had no meaning either to conceal or express. In none of these three cases does he like to be asked about it. In the first case he feels humiliated; in the second it makes him feel embarrassed; in the third it makes him feel found out. The real meaning of a poem is what it means to the reader.[66]

Besides acknowledging the indisputable fact that poems have a life of their own by subjective interpretation, he was also rationalising his long-standing dislike of being dragged into conversation about his own poems and what they meant. People could ask many questions about the characters and situations he portrayed in *A Shropshire Lad*. Here was a formula which could help him to avoid unwanted discussion.

In early May 1914, Housman had been in the south of France; he used it as an opportunity to create benchmarks for judging the quality of French cooking and wrote to Richards:

> I took the walk you mapped out from Cassis to La Ciotat on a very beautiful day, and followed your lines I think pretty well... I ate much bouillabaisse, the best at Isnard's, the next best in the suburb of L'Estaque; but in several places it was not so good as at Foyot's in Paris. Brandade [a way of cooking cod] I did not think much of and Aioli at Pascal's was rather nasty, perhaps because lukewarm.

On this occasion, Housman had:

> hired a motor with an amiable meridional chauffeur who knew the country, and went to Aix, Arles, Aigues-Mortes, Montmajour (which is probably what you meant when you wrote Fontveille), Les Baux, St Remy, Beaucaire, Nimes, Pont du Gard, Avignon, Villeneuve les Avignon, Vauclure, Carpentras (where I did not see Dreyfus, nor much else), Vaison, Orange, and I think that is all. Weather good with a few days of mistral; judas trees in very magnificent bloom. I was in Paris with the king, but he did me no harm except once keeping me waiting half-an-hour to cross the street.'[67]

In his next letter Housman wrote to Richards about the new illustrated edition of his poems. 'I observe that the illustrated edition is now bound in black... I daresay black is appropriate to the funereal nature of the contents.'[68] It was also appropriate to coming events.

Within a month A.C. Benson was noting in his diary that the Archduke Franz Ferdinand and his wife had been killed at Sarajevo. Benson did not speculate on the possible consequences of this assassination. Nor did Housman's correspondence mention war in the Balkans, Sarajevo or England's declaration of war on 4 August 1914, consequent on the German invasion of Belgium. Nor were Housman's reactions to any of these momentous events recorded by anyone else. That did not mean they had passed him by.

PART IX

The Great War 1914–1918

Propaganda and poets

Truth is the first casualty of war and it was not surprising that an early step of government was to set up a war propaganda bureau to promote British war aims. Secret conferences were held involving men of letters and poets to see what they could do to underpin the war effort. Housman does not seem to have been recruited; he was not moved to identify himself publicly with pro-war or anti-war groups, or use the war for purposes of self-promotion and self-advancement. It is known that those involved included the Poet Laureate Robert Bridges, Laurence Binyon, G.K. Chesterton, Arthur Conan Doyle, Thomas Hardy, John Masefield, Owen Seaman, H.G. Wells and Rudyard Kipling.

Nor was Housman signatory to *The Writers Manifesto* in support of the war published as a letter to *The Times* by Professor Gilbert Murray on 18 September 1914 and signed by most of the same literary luminaries, Granville Barker, Barrie, Bridges, Chesterton, Conan Doyle, Galsworthy, Hardy, Kipling and Masefield.

Like Housman, neither G.B. Shaw nor W.B. Yeats (both Irishmen) added their names to the manifesto:

> The undersigned writers, comprising among them men and women of the most divergent political and social views, some of them having been for years ardent champions of good will towards Germany, and many of them extreme advocates of peace, are nevertheless agreed that Great Britain could not without dishonour have refused to take part in the present war.

Gilbert Murray had been chasing Housman for a decision; Housman wrote on 14 October 1914: 'I suppose I ought to have written, and I am sorry I gave you the trouble of telegraphing. My chief objection was not to the terms of the manifesto but to signing any manifesto at all.[1]

It was always unlikely that Housman would lend his hand to the simplifications of war propaganda, or deal in the big words – glory, honour and sacrifice – or evoke other big words – patriotism, religion, empire, chivalry or freedom – in the cause of war; his own knowledge and feel for words was too precise and demanding. He was too concerned with meaning; he was not a man to be seized and motivated by irrational emotions.

It hardly needs saying that Housman was not a 'war poet'. The real war poets were soldier poets, men like Wilfred Owen, Siegfried Sassoon, Richard Aldington, Edmund Blunden, Rupert Brooke, Robert Graves, Isaac Rosenberg, Ivor Gurney, Edward Thomas and Julian Grenfell, men who fought in the war, experienced 'the pity of war', endured their share of 'the winter of the world' until at last they came to be counted, either among the survivors or the fallen. Other good witnesses were women like Mary Borden and Vera Brittain who worked in hospitals; they saw close-up the mental and physical results of war. An older generation of poets, men like Thomas Hardy, Rudyard Kipling, Robert Bridges, John Masefield, Walter de la Mare, wrote poems about the war out of their poetic imaginations. Some felt impelled to construct poems around abstract convictions of honour and patriotism. Others spared by age from the odium of not volunteering could give themselves carte blanche to use the war as a surrogate for all kinds of feelings ranging from jingoism to lack of trust in either politicians or God.

Housman poems are occasionally peopled by soldier lads, destined to die for queen and country in far-off places. In real life, they marched with many men in their knapsack, and it is a fact that sales climbed steeply during the war. Housman inspired other soldier poets: for example, Patrick Shaw-Stewart, whose only surviving poem was found inside his copy of A Shropshire Lad, began 'I saw a man this morning/ Who did not wish to die',[2] or J.E. Stewart, whose poem, inspired by Housman, ends 'Yet over the down the white road leading / Calls; and who lags behind? / Stout are our hearts; but O, the bleeding / Of hearts we may not bind.'[3]

Housman was not totally detached, for Laurence records of his brother:

He was equally and spontaneously generous towards the National Exchequer in its time of need. At the beginning of the War he sent the Chancellor a donation of several hundred pounds, and again during the financial crisis in 1931, when the National Government was first formed, came to the rescue as far as his means allowed.[4]

In Cambridge Housman was subject only to the minor irritations of war. References in his letters to the war's impact were generally amusing and detached. For example, writing to Lily Thicknesse in November 1914: 'The thirst for blood is raging among the youth of England. More than half the undergraduates are away, but not mostly at the front, because they all want to be officers. I am going out when they make me a Field Marshal.' He added: 'Meanwhile I have three nephews being inoculated for typhoid and catching pneumonia on Salisbury Plain and performing other acts of war calculated to make the German Emperor realise that he is a very misguided man.'[5]

On 27 November 1914 he thanked Thomas Hardy for a copy of his poems *Satires of Circumstance*, from which he singled out the second stanza of *In Death Divided* as 'quite beautiful'. It was not a poem about comrades in arms. Most likely it caused him to think of himself and Moses, once more so many thousands of miles apart.

> No shade of pinnacle or tree or tower
> While earth endures,
> Will fall on my mound and within the hour
> Steals over to yours;
> One robin never haunts our two green covertures.

Armageddon: Nephew killed in action

Throughout 1914 to 1918, Housman's correspondence evidenced neither morbid interest in a war characterised by mass slaughter, nor an armchair preoccupation with its major events, nor its campaigns and tactics, its political effects and changing public feelings towards it. He could not have failed to read about its daily progress in the newspapers, could not have failed to read the never ending casualty lists or have escaped all participation in debates and arguments about the war in the Trinity Combination Room. Certainly, he was not moved to poetise.

This context of war was terrible. In the spring of 1915 the Germans first used poison gas; a German submarine sank the *Lusitania*. At home, the government fell to be replaced by a national coalition; Asquith remained Prime Minister, and Lloyd George entered onto the stage of history as Minister of Munitions. 1915 was a year of mounting casualties, escalating to 62,000 at Loos in October.

Yet Housman could still write amusedly to Edmund Gosse who had complained that a letter he had sent to Compton Mackenzie in Capri had been held up for a week before being sent on by the censor, who had attached a note to Mackenzie to advise his correspondent to write shortly and clearly. Naturally Gosse had written to *The Times* about that. Housman reflected on the size and scope of the censor's vocabulary: 'If the censor finds your letters long, it is not because they are long by measurement, but that they take a long time to read when most of the words have to be looked out in the dictionary.'[6]

In spite of the war across the Channel and in spite of men dying he was still thirsting for continental travel and clearly wanted Richards to join him in the Easter vacation. 'What are your present ideas about the Riviera? My own notion is to spend about 3 weeks abroad, and it would suit me best if those 3 weeks were either at the beginning or the end of the vacation.' In the first instance, he wanted Richards to come up to Trinity for lunch but had to add 'All our feasts and also our usual guest nights are suppressed, and our meals are somewhat simplified.' That had not totally brought an end to his pleasures: 'I have lately invested in some rather good Corton 1898.' He would try to find 'a kindred spirit', cautioning him in a follow-up note: 'do not be surprised if a sentry tries to keep you out with a bayonet, as this is now a barracks, sparsely inhabited by four Fellows of Trinity.'[7] In early March 1915 he was also pleased to tell Sir James Frazer of *The Golden Bough* fame that he was heading soon for the Riviera which 'Providence for my benefit has cleared of Germans. In its normal state I always refused to visit it.'[8]

Life in Trinity had changed. The university and colleges were denuded of men of military age. Rooms were taken over by young men undergoing officer training. The cloisters of Nevile's Court were used as a hospital for war wounded. College numbers had dropped immediately to a third and from January 1915 onwards the town presented the appearance of a large military camp. Housman had already told Frazer: 'Whewell's Court is now a barracks, and soldiers above my ceiling practise step-dancing with a vigour which ought to be a prophylactic against frost-bite.' He elaborated on the theme for Lily Thicknesse.

On the 16th I shall be beyond the Channel or beneath it: more probably the former, for steamers seem to ram submarines better than submarines torpedo steamers. Hitherto I have always refused to go to the Riviera, but now is my chance, when the worst classes who infest it are away. Here we have 1,000 undergraduates and 20,000 soldiers, 500 of them billeted in the building in which I write these lines and one of them doing a quick-step overhead.[9]

Escape to the Riviera

And so on 16 March, Housman and Richards crossed the Channel from Folkestone to Dieppe in record time, during which Housman displayed neither nervousness nor anxiety about mines or torpedoes. It was still early season on the Riviera but the impact of the war was evident; Richards recorded that when they arrived there, 'Neither at Cannes nor at Nice nor at Monte Carlo was there more than a tiny sprinkling of the habitual visitors.' He had promised Housman:

> good food and good wine, good plumbing, sunshine and walks through unspoilt woods and over apparently untrodden hills. He wanted to see all there was to see. The day should be given over to open air, excursions, exercise; the night – well after dinner, if there should be theatres and if there were casinos open, we would visit them – but casinos and such attractions were to take a very secondary place in our programme.

On one occasion he had steered Housman in the direction of the tables at Monte Carlo but he was definitely not a gambling man and according to Richards, looked on with distaste when Richards himself had a flutter. They had stationed themselves at Nice but on one occasion, having gone to Villefranche by tram and intending to walk round Cape Ferrat by footpath, they were challenged by a sentry. Housman's 'presence of mind, his good humour, his readiness and lack of embarrassment,'[10] and quite probably his willingness and capacity to speak French, impressed the officer they were brought in front of. 'We were immediately released, with the warning that the absence of a sign-board was no excuse and that if we were found wandering in other similarly forbidden zones we were unlikely to be treated so tenderly and were directed to the high road.' Their other excursions along the Riviera produced plenty of walking and the occasional notable lunch like the fresh trout and fresh truffles at the Grand Hotel du Loup. Their visit to Ventimiglia was the cause of Belfort Bax's future fixation with the idea that Housman had been invited by the Mayor and Council of Ventimiglia to visit the town, had been met by a guard of honour with an artillery salute, a banquet, an oration in Latin, a response by Housman in Latin and a splendid send off at the station. The truth was that Richards had himself concocted the story. 'I often fell back on the spinning of fairy-tales to allay his [Bax's] thirst for useless knowledge, and insatiable curiosity.'[11] Richards was hoist with his own petard; the Baxes could not be prevailed upon to stop telling the story which they did on innumerable occasions.

This Riviera trip was a first for Housman but no written account of it, either to Kate or Lily Thicknesse, has survived. Perhaps he was inhibited about expressing enjoyment at holidaying on the Riviera when thousands of his countrymen were being killed a few hundred miles to the north.

Richards chose to remember:

> I found Housman a delightful companion, equable in temper, seldom moody, a good talker, appreciative of attention, polite to those who smoothed his path. And untiring. No one who has made his way with me by wooded, rocky, uneven, tiring paths from Eze to the shore, has done it with more spirit or shown more energy. He liked walking; he was willing to scramble. And he loved the southern countryside with its views, its trees and its flowers.
>
> And best of all, from my point of view, he told me, as we travelled up to London on our return, that he had enjoyed every day of the holiday, and that he had never known a more agreeable and able courier.[12]

The 'kindred spirit' Housman had hoped to invite to meet Richards turned out to have been a mathematician, as Housman later explained:

> The mathematician whom you sat next to at our high table, upon hearing that I had been to the Riviera with you, said that he hoped you had not been running after women the whole time. Whether this was an inference from your conversation or a generalisation from his own experience of travelling-companions I do not know.[13]

Housman followed up with another letter in mid-April:

> You should not let what the mathematician said worry you. When his mind is not occupied by mathematics or pottery it is apt to run on the relations of the sexes, and I seldom sit next him without that topic arising. He possesses all the editions of *Fanny Hill*, a book with which I daresay you have never polluted your mind.[14]

Possibly the mathematician was more curious about Housman than he was about Richards.

On 2 July 1915 Richards had married for the second time and, for whatever reason, preferred not to mention it at the time. When he did tell Housman in October that he had married 'a Hungarian lady, younger than myself by eighteen years', Housman's reaction was warm. 'I congratulate you very heartily and send you every wish for your happiness; and perhaps you will also convey my respects to Mrs Richards and, I am inclined to add, my congratulations too because, whatever your other faults, there can be few ladies who have a more good-tempered husband.'[15] This was a handsome tribute to Richards. Housman and he may from time to time have found each other a trial but their relationship was surviving.

Inevitably, the war came close to home. In October 1915 Housman received news from Kate that her third son, twenty-two-year-old Lieutenant Clement Aubrey Symons, had been killed in France. This again produced no poetic response but in his notably calm way, Housman sent Kate a copy of his *Illic Jacet* ('There he rests'), along with his letter redolent with feeling:

> I have been scanning the casualty lists in these last days, and when I saw your card this morning I feared what the news must be. Well, my dear, it is little I or anyone else can do to comfort you, or think of anything to say that you will not have thought of. But I remember your telling me at the beginning of the war that he had almost a hope and expectation of dying in battle, and we must be glad that it was a victorious battle in which he died. I do not know that I can do better than send you some verses that I wrote many years ago because the essential business of poetry, as it has been said, is to harmonise the sadness of the universe, and it is somehow more sustaining and more healing than prose. Do assure Edward of my feeling for you all, and also, though I do not know her, the poor young girl.[16]

Illic Jacet's four stanzas were unknown to Kate; even though written in December 1895 the poem had not been selected by Housman for *A Shropshire Lad*. It begins:

> O hard is the bed they have made him,
>   And common the blanket and cheap;
> But there he will lie as they laid him:
>   Where else could you trust him to sleep.

And ends

> And low is the roof, but it covers
>   A sleeper content to repose;
> And far from his friends and his lovers
>   He lies with the sweetheart he chose.

This letter to his sister came close to displaying a lack of awareness of what might be in the heart and mind of a mother; she had just lost her son and all her future hopes for him. To make matters worse, Jerry, her youngest son, was also in France; she could lose him too. It seems not to have occurred to Housman that Kate would not necessarily find any relevance in the grand idea that poetry could harmonise the sadness of the universe; or derive comfort from the thought that comrades' arms had lowered her son into his grave; or be reconciled by the idea that this last resting place was a place of content.

Housman's classical work continued uninterrupted. He was now finishing the text and notes for his *Manilius III* before sending them to Richards 'which though it will not sell so well as your novel is really a much more classy work.'[17]

In spite of his steadfast refusal to allow his poems to be reproduced, Housman did allow Walter Raleigh, first Professor of English at Cambridge, (1904–1922) to include poems from *A Shropshire Lad* in one of *The Times' Broadsheets for the Trenches*. Broadsheet No. 38 published six of his poems, *Reveille, The street sounds to the soldiers' tread, On Wenlock Edge the wood's in trouble, On the idle hill of summer, The Isle of Portland* and *"TERENCE, this is stupid stuff.*

In 1916 there was a step-change in Housman's relationship with Richards: 'When you say you *"would* like to" go to France with me, is that a mere sigh or a serious wish? Because I should be both agreeable to it and desirous of it; only I understood that the difficulties now put in the way of getting a passport are almost insuperable.'[18] When Richards suggested that Housman accompany himself and his wife to France, he got the obvious reply: 'Mrs Richards is exceedingly kind, but I should not think of going abroad with the two of you, even if dates suited.'[19]

When the sinking of the SS *Sussex* by a German submarine off the French coast in March 1916 dissuaded the Richards from crossing, Housman was undeterred.

> I argue thus: only a certain number of steamers are destined to sink; one of that number has already sunk without me on board; and that diminishes by one the number of my chances of destruction. But women cannot reason, so I supposed your designs are knocked on the head. I have pretty well made up my mind to go at least as far as Paris.[20]

Richards tried to put him off but Housman was resolutely macho.

> Many thanks for your letter and your wish to preserve my life; but I have just applied for leave to go through Folkestone and Dieppe … After all a quick death is better than a slow journey; and as I am only an author and not a publisher I am comparatively well prepared to meet my God.[21]

In the event, the Folkestone route was closed and Housman had to confess that as 'the voyage by Southampton-Havre, without the solace and protection of your company, is a long and weary subtraction from the short holiday I meant to take, I am not going to France.'[22]

Meanwhile Richards had floated the idea that Housman should join the Richards family for a week or two at their cottage near the Lizard in Cornwall. Housman found the invitation 'very attractive, so far as I can judge at present and I should like to come … I have never been into Cornwall except just across the Tamar.' He added the first and only piece of actual war news that can be found in his correspondence, one assumes because it impinged on his own plans.

> From what I hear, it seems as if the advance on our front were to begin tomorrow. Civilians are not to cross to France for the next three weeks or so, and all vessels crossing for some time back have been filled with big guns, even to the exclusion, except at fixed dates, of officers on leave.[23]

Figure 32 Housman, detail from a 1916
mural by W. Rothenstein now in the Senate
Room of Southampton University. ©
University of Southampton

The Somme offensive began on 1 July 1916.

William Rothenstein, now back in touch, was invited to Trinity. 'We don't dress as you probably remember.'[24] Alice Rothenstein was quick off the mark in inviting him back to Oakridge but Housman had to decline. 'After Cornwall I shall probably be going to my sister in Somerset, and not long after, if possible, to France, so my holidays will be pretty well filled up.' He gave her the good news of William's visit to Cambridge: 'Your William has behaved quite nicely here and I have just sent him off all safe and sound.'[25]

A beach holiday with the Richards

In August he went off to Cornwall for a holiday *en famille* with Richards, his new wife Maria, five children with ages ranging from eight to sixteen, Grant Richards' aunt, a 'not very well bred terrier', a nurse and maids. According to Richards, Housman 'seemed to enjoy all the incidents of what was in many ways a children's holiday', showing signs of impatience only when he 'found himself involved in some infantile larking or boisterous horse-play.'[26] Housman enjoyed their picnics and scrambling, restricting himself to being a spectator when they bathed, occasionally going off on a stroll by himself. He appointed himself to look after the cheap *vin gris*, placing bottles in the sea to keep them cool. He kept a watchful eye on the younger children and talked for hours with Maria Richards about the impact of the war on her country (Hungary), the future of their children, and Grant's future. He had lively conversations with Grant's aunt and with the children about everything that interested them. So Richards painted a picture of a Housman we have not really seen before, an energetic and involved participant, a conversationalist equally at home with Maria, Grant's aunt and the children, all probably occasioned by his having to adapt himself to a large and diverse family group and finding he could interact with them in ways perhaps reminiscent of his leadership of the Housman family group more than forty years previously. Richards summed it up when he wrote:

> To our regret he went away on the day appointed. His plans were never elastic. I know that he enjoyed this unusual holiday, but that it would not have suited him to remain longer away from his usual life and interests, from his books and his own desk, or the attractions of near-solitude, architecture and well-balanced meals.[27]

Later in mid-September Housman read in *The Times* that the Richards' eldest son had been killed by the collapse of a sand cave on the beach at Poldu. His letter of condolence was notably restrained, surprisingly so from someone who had recently spent time in the boy's company. 'I hope you and Mrs Richards are well, and not more overcome by sorrow for his loss than must needs be',[28] typically precise and economical, but in this case perhaps again lacking the dimension of empathy. However, the family holiday had strengthened his bonds with them and within a month he was inviting both the Richards to lunch in Trinity at the start of their countrywide bookselling tour.

Housman was still retaining his links with the young Jacksons, telling Richards, probably in answer to some query from him, 'My young friend who was at Oundle is now lost to my sight in the RAMC [Royal Army Medical Corps] and I have not heard from him for six months.'[29] Housman was referring to Rupert Jackson, Moses' eldest son then viewing at close quarters the slaughter on the Somme. Housman seemed to be living in a self-protective cocoon, not allowing events to penetrate and disturb his equilibrium, demonstrating a detached attitude to what was going on in France, so that when Richards unilaterally doubled the price of *A Shropshire Lad* to meet increased costs of production, Housman did not complain but wrote in rather dubious taste:

> It diminishes my chances of the advertisement to which I am always looking forward: a soldier is to receive a bullet in the breast, and it is to be turned aside from his heart by a copy of *A Shropshire Lad* which he is carrying there. Hitherto it is only the Bible that has performed this trick.[30]

Enter Percy Withers

By March 1916 Trinity had become the headquarters of officer cadet training in Cambridge and so it remained till the end of the war. The fifth battalion of officer cadets was quartered in Trinity where Henry Jackson, the Vice-Master, continued his hospitable habits of music, smoking and cards every night after dinner. Housman nowhere noted that his dining hall was heavily populated by men in uniform, nor that the College housed five to six hundred officer cadets who breakfasted and dined in Hall, their officers dining at High Table, now a medley of khaki, Sam Brownes and academic gowns. Cambridge and Trinity was much more transformed than Housman ever communicated. It was in this scene of warlike preparations that Housman first met Dr Percy Withers, 'transferred to war service in Cambridge in the early summer of 1917'. An admirer of *A Shropshire Lad*, he had written to Housman's publisher for an introduction and would remain Housman's friend for the next twenty years. Housman wrote to Richards on 14 October 1917: 'I have ... called on Mr Withers, who seems an agreeable man.'[31] Housman had arrived quite unexpectedly at his rooms overlooking the Fitzwilliam Museum, then part of the military medical set-up. Withers noticed Housman's

> winning smile... his shy hesitant manner... his erect soldier-like figure, slight and of medium height, his small but shapely head, the cropped, carefully brushed hair, touched with grey, and the blue eyes, once doubtless full of fire, but now rather disappointingly dull – not, I felt, the eyes of a poet.

Figure 33 Percy Withers, a doctor
drafted to Cambridge in mid-1917 to
examine conscripts. Sought an
introduction to Housman and became a
friend. Drawing by Gilbert Spencer. ©
Estate of Gilbert Spencer. All Rights
Reserved, DACS 2017.

At the time, Withers, who was convalescing from months of illness, noticed how Housman 'inquired most feelingly about my health, incited me by questioning to tell the whole story, and listened with so much concern that I quickly forgot the limpness of the hand I had grasped.' They had hit on a topic for conversation which Housman

> could be trusted to embark on spontaneously, and sustain with questioning and sympathetic comment even till it was worn thread-bare. Not illness merely, but physical disabilities and cares generally, light or heavy, real or threatened, won his immediate interest and solicitude, and however diffident the inquiries he made, there was no doubting their absolute sincerity; he genuinely wished to know as one confident of the sympathy he had to give, and desired to give.[32]

Housman did not pass back to Richards any real account of Withers beyond his comment that he seemed an agreeable man, and in the same letter remarked apropos of nothing, 'The young friend who was educated at Oundle has been staying with me, and says it is probably the best equipped school in England for engineering.'[33] Housman adds nothing by way of explanation, but since this letter is dated October 1917, he was most likely again referring to Rupert Jackson.

In March 1917 Housman gave a poem of his own choosing to a young officer cadet, a Lieutenant Lee, temporarily stationed at Trinity, who wanted it for publication in *The Blunderbuss* magazine which he was editing. Housman gave him the following, which would be later published as II in *Last Poems*:

> As I gird on for fighting
>   My sword upon my thigh,
> I think on old ill fortunes
>   Of better men than I.
>
> Think I, the round world over,
>   What golden lads are low
> With hurts not mine to mourn for
>   And shames I shall not know.
>
> What evil luck soever
>   For me remains in store,
> 'Tis sure much finer fellows
>   Have fared much worse before.
>
> So here are things to think on
>   That ought to make me brave,
> As I strap on for fighting
>   My sword that will not save.

Housman can hardly have been unaware of the likely fate of the young officer to whom he gave this poem. It is not entirely fanciful to think that the message of his poem was intended to be comforting in its empathy for those on whom the exigencies of war and ill luck would impose a variety of nameless shames; in its assertion that he should be made brave by the thought that better men than he had had it harder, it was consolatory and sustaining.

Housman had not composed the poem *for* Lieutenant Lee; it had been composed in 1895 and would be redrafted in 1922 for *Last Poems*. Perhaps Housman detected something 'different' in the young man. Giving him the poem was a gesture of solidarity as well as a kindness.

Come August 1917, Housman was longing for France but had to tell Richards:

> The War Office does not view with favour my proposed escape to France so I shall start at the beginning of next month on a tour to Rochester, Canterbury, Chichester, Winchester and Salisbury. When I am turning home I will write to you and if you then wish me to come to Bigfrith I shall be very pleased.[34]

Epitaph on an Army of Mercenaries

By September 1917 Housman had been moved to produce a poem which certainly elevated him to the rank of war poet emeritus, *Epitaph on an Army of Mercenaries*, his one and only Great War poem:

> THESE, in the day when heaven was falling,
>   The hour when earth's foundations fled,
> Followed their mercenary calling
>   And took their wages and are dead.
>
> Their shoulders held the sky suspended;
>   They stood, and earth's foundations stay;
> What God abandoned, these defended,
>   And saved the sum of things for pay.

The poem, signed A.E. Housman, was published in *The Times* of 31 October 1917, under a leading article entitled 'The Anniversary of Ypres'. Kipling thought the poem 'the finest lines of poetry written during the war'. The original British Expeditionary Force of 1914 consisted entirely of regulars, career soldiers in all ranks, neither conscripts nor pressed men but factually mercenaries. They saved the day and paid the price. And thus his poem strikes notes more characteristic of today's professional soldiers, men on whom we rely who are simply doing their job, a true and wonderful epitaph that will be good for all time. And it underlines that God has no place in the story of war or its commemoration. About the same time, Housman received a letter from the editor of *The Yale Review*, asking 'Have you not a war poem which you would care to send me?' Housman replied 'I neither have any poem which I wish to publish nor am likely to write one at any early date.'[35]

Otherwise, with swarms of real soldiers around him, with the daily bloodbath in nearby France and Belgium, in the hour of the soldier he remained poetically unmoved. The soldiers of his poems had been cardboard cut-outs serving his unconscious symbolic purposes. And so the Great War prompted no poetry from Housman, apart from the realistic observation of his 'Epitaph', more evidence, if any is required, that his outpouring of poetry in the 1890s was purely narcissistic and about himself.

Scholarly output unabated: Manilius III published in 1916

Across the years of war, the unwavering constant in his life was his classical scholarship. Between 1914 and 1918 he produced fourteen papers, amounting to one hundred and thirty-nine pages, plus his lectures, plus his work on *Manilius III* published in 1916. All in all, a formidable work load which would have exhausted a lesser man.

Three Jackson sons at the Front

Meanwhile, three sons of Moses and Rosa Jackson, sons who Housman had fervently hoped in his *Epithalamium* would serve 'to stay the rot of time', were on active service in France. Hector and Oscar volunteered for the Canadian Expeditionary Force in Vancouver, Hector in August 1915 and Oscar in May 1916. The eldest son Rupert, who had read medicine at Cambridge followed by clinical training at Guy's Hospital, had volunteered for the Royal Army Medical Corps in 1914 and was commissioned in 1915. At one time, all three brothers were serving relatively close to each other.

Hector left for England in March 1916, running the gauntlet of German submarines about the time the SS *Sussex* was torpedoed in the Channel. Being an energetic and extrovert young man, his military training was combined with a hectic social life in London and Godalming where there were still family contacts. The Battle of the Somme, which had prevented Housman's cross-Channel journey,

Figure 34 Hector Jackson MC Captain Canadian Engineers. By
permission of the Jackson Family.

had begun on 1 July 1916 and by the time Hector reached the front
in late October, the battle still had a month to run. Rupert, who had
been serving with the 91st Field Ambulance Company in the French
sector of the line from the beginning of the battle, had been awarded
the Croix de Guerre.

By December 1916, Hector had moved to the northern end of Vimy
Ridge and reported to his mother on 27 January 1917 that he had
heard from Mr Housman a few days ago, and would 'answer tonight
if possible'.[36]

On Easter Monday, the Canadian blood bath on Vimy Ridge
began. Hector was recommended for a Military Cross (MC) but the
recommendation was turned down. About this time, he found out
that brother Oscar was serving nearby, and that Rupert had been
awarded an MC to add to his Croix de Guerre. Back in England for a
hectic ten days' leave in July 1917, he put the war out of his mind in
the social whirl of London.

At Applegarth, the remaining Jacksons were facing harder times than
they could ever have imagined. Economic recession, the drought of
1914, the cut-off in supply of German potash – an essential ingredient
in fertiliser production – brought a huge rise in farming costs. There

Figure 35 Rupert Jackson M.C.,
Croix de Guerre, Major Royal Army
Medical Corps field ambulance unit. By
permission of the Jackson Family

were no young men available to replace their absent sons and as death began to swallow up their sons' generation, they had only the knock on the door to look forward to. Some of this communicated itself to Hector who wrote to his aunt Margaret: 'Applegarth seems finally going to pot. I wish there was a large volcano started under the whole thing, and nothing short of that will make them leave the rotten old place.'[37]

The Passchendaele blood bath was Hector's next stop. He always cheerfully calculated for his relatives' benefit that the order for danger was infantry first, artillery second, engineers third. Nevertheless he was awarded an MC, or as he put it, 'the Booby Prize at last after four attempts'. The citation read: 'for conspicuous gallantry and devotion to duty in marking out and digging a trench under fire. Having completed the work, he made a reconnaissance, with two sappers, to look for wounded, and finding two brought them five miles to the dressing station'. Over three-quarters of the 20,000 Canadians involved at Passchendaele were killed or wounded, the Allied casualties were 310,000 and the Germans' 260,000. Housman's correspondence passed over in silence these shattering figures.

Figure 36 Oscar Jackson, Canadian
Signals, soon after arriving in France.
By permission of the Jackson family.

Hector's Christmas leave took him to Charterhouse for Founders
Day and to all the people he knew; on 20 December 1917 he wrote to
his mother: 'At 1.30 am having lunch with Mr Ward and on Friday am
going down to Cambridge to see Mr Housman.'[38] On 26 December
1917, on his way back to the front, he wrote again to his mother:
'I saw Mr Housman and stayed a night at Trinity.'[39] On 8 January
1918, he told his mother 'I suppose I better send something along
to our mutual enemy, he was quite jovial when I went down there.'[40]
Andrew Jackson, Gerald's son, comments in a note to me: 'This may
refer to Housman, whom both Rosa and Hector may have regarded
as being a potential rival for Moses' affection.' Hector's rather
flippant/complacent/semi-affectionate way of referring to Housman
suggests that the Jackson family had come to terms with Housman's
long-standing attachment to their father, and his willingness and
evident capacity to support the family financially. But one wonders
how Housman could have become the 'mutual enemy'. Perhaps the
clue was given in Hector's judgement on Applegarth as it now was,
a judgement crystallised by his adult experience of a wider world
more to his taste than the back-of-beyond Applegarth. Perhaps the

truth was that in helping Moses to settle in Canada, Housman may indeed have been enabling Moses to do what *he* wanted but not at all what Rosa wanted. She was naturally loyal to her masterful husband but there is no doubt that in their earliest days in Canada she pined for England and Godalming, and who could blame her, having to adapt to a primitive house without electricity, water from a well, and a five mile walk to the nearest store and post office. She had swapped the middle-class comfort and amenities of Godalming for frontier life.

In 1918 Hector, by now Captain Jackson, was slightly gassed. It was Ward, the London solicitor, who was contacted by the Canadians and he in turn passed the message to Moses and Rosa, so it was Ward and not Housman who had been nominated to the military as the conduit for news of the Jackson boys.

Nine days after Hector left the front the war ended. Back in England he tried to see Alfred Pollard, the university friend of Moses and Housman, 'but he was away'. After the Armistice there was no mention of Hector's having tried to see Housman again.

The previous October Housman had promised to invite Withers to dine with him at Trinity Hall and Withers had sent Housman on his way with a copy of *Georgian Poetry*, 'which he carried off willingly but without enthusiasm'. The book provided Withers with an excuse to call on Housman. And so Withers made his way to Trinity and

> mounted the forty-odd chilling stone steps to his landing, selected the door that looked most promising, and knocked ... The voice bidding me "Come in" came through another door than the one I had knocked on. When I opened it, he was sitting before a table strewn with books bolt upright in a straight-backed chair, holding a book in front of him, but laid it down and sprang to his feet the moment I entered, and gave me the most cordial welcome.

They discussed the purpose of the dumb-bells on the floor. 'He told me he used them for ten minutes every morning after his cold bath, and again at night, whenever he felt drowsiness coming on as he sat besides the fire reading'. Withers noticed 'how incapable he was of initiating small talk, but how readily he gave ear to it, and if the merest tittle-tattle were spiced with a touch of humour or even a touch of venom – at least when its object was approved – how easily, almost as a child, he was amused'. Withers' ostensible object for the visit had been to collect

Georgian Poetry, which he now did. Housman handed it over without comment. 'Have you nothing to say about it?' I asked. "No" he answered and not politely. Then I noticed there was something still to come, and something he enjoyed the thought of imparting. "Yes," he went on "one opinion I have formed: that your friend John Drinkwater is not a poet". Withers says he expressed, 'both wonder and envy that he could give judgement so confidently, and mildly asked how'. Withers recalled that Housman looked as though he was about to explode. 'He bristled; a dark flush came over his face; and for a time that appeared interminably long, he seemed incapable of utterance. Then, growing more calm, and with oracular impressiveness, he said: "You feel poetry in the throat, in the solar plexus, or down the spine. Drinkwater's verse touches neither spine, belly nor throat".'[41]

For most individuals such an encounter would have cut short the relationship but Withers must have felt a need to cling to his growling literary lion and Housman might just have realised that he had behaved badly. This may explain why in January of the New Year of 1918 he undertook to help Withers to meet Jose de Navarro, admitted to Trinity in 1915, destined to take a starred first in the English Tripos of 1920 and to be Trinity's first Catholic fellow. The fact that Navarro was a Catholic accounted for Housman's proviso 'I shall not cross the threshold myself, but I am not going to keep you out of Paradise'.[42]

In the Spring Mary Withers sent him jam:

> Porters so seldom bring one things on Sundays that I am even more overwhelmed than I otherwise should be by your kindness in enriching me with blackberry jelly from your end of the town, where the grocers still have jams. I have been enjoined this evening not to write you a charming letter, so I will put a firm constraint on myself and abstain from doing so; but I am very tempted to be very charming indeed.[43]

He had been touched by her motherly solicitude. Indeed by mid-1918 he was passing on to Richards that Withers had been asking after him, and thanking Alice Rothenstein for messages she had sent him via Withers, describing him as 'our friend Dr Withers'.[44] And in spite of his acid remarks about John Drinkwater, he was able to overcome his dislike of him as a poet and was willing to meet Drinkwater the man. When he learned from Sir Arthur Quiller-Couch, editor of *The Oxford Book of English Verse* and a fellow of Jesus College, that Drinkwater was in Cambridge, he offered him an invitation to come and see him, if he had time. 'I could offer you such tea as the times permit.'[45]

In June Housman relaxed his usual rule of not allowing his poems to be printed in anthologies, giving Richards permission for one of his poems to be produced in a Braille anthology. 'I suppose I must follow the example of the anonymous great poet [very likely Alfred Noyes] and relax the rule, in order that the poem may be read by blind soldiers.'[46] Later in 1919 he would give permission for the whole of *A Shropshire Lad* to be published in Braille. In July 1918 he heard of the success of William Rothenstein's exhibition of drawings of the fighting in Flanders although he had not himself gone to London to see them. He was actively intending to walk over to see Alice Rothenstein when he was next at Woodchester: His opening, 'It is probable, – do not be agitated – that I shall be coming to Woodchester or Amberley at the end of August; and then you may be sure that I shall walk over to see you', was a characteristic example of Housman's self-presentation, having a touch of hyperbolic egocentricity, a kind of stagey and mannered pomposity. In the event he was not able to fulfil his intention since the hotel where he planned to stay was full. 'For me the cloud has a silver lining, as I escape the horrors which now encompass travelling: for you, of course, the gloom is unmitigated.'[47]

So he continued to plough this rather unexpected social furrow, writing in October to the Richards saying he would be coming to see them at Cookham Dean 'when your woodlands ought to be looking very well. I was in Gloucestershire most of September and saw the Rothensteins. From the fragments of your autobiography which I see in the weekly press I gather that you too have had a holiday or holidays.'[48]

An invitation from Richards to lunch with J.C. Squire, poet, literary journalist and editor of the *New Statesman*, had to be called off because a month previously, Richards had gone down with influenza, playing his infinitesimally small part in the greatest global epidemic in world history which killed somewhere between three to six per cent of the world population, and was then in the process of causing a quarter of a million deaths in Britain. Official censorship, preoccupied with public morale, was anxious to suppress the fact that one form of mass death was now competing with another. For Grant Richards, it was a matter of life or death; his influenza had developed into pleurisy and subsequently pneumonia, a sequence ending in death in most cases. Housman seems to have been half-aware of the situation when he wrote to Maria Richards in mid-November:

I am sorry to hear of Grant's relapse. I had gathered from the Times Supplement that he was alright again; and I hope now it will not be long before he is well. I have escaped hitherto and have not heard that Mr Squire has been attacked; and I hope that you will not catch it from the patient.[49]

But there were no references elsewhere in his correspondence, either to members of the college or other family members or specifically Kate, whose husband was a Medical Officer of Health, about the impact of the epidemic on them and those they knew. And when Richards came through his ordeal Housman returned with little ceremony to business as usual. 'Yours is a terrible long illness but I am glad that you seem to be fairly comfortable ... I have sent to your office a list of 8 mistakes in the 8vo edition.'[50]

Housman's war

Too old at fifty-five to serve in the war, he had done his bit by sending the bulk of his savings to the Chancellor of the Exchequer. He had not set himself up to second guess the generals and politicians. He had written kind and comforting letters to those who had suffered the loss of dear ones. He made no comment on the number of Old Bromsgrovians or contemporaries from St John's, Oxford, or, with one exception, members of his own college who had been killed. This does not mean that he was untouched by such a slaughter of the young, merely that he did not make a parade of his feelings. Three sons of Moses Jackson had been in the war; all had survived, two of them decorated. One of his own nephews was killed, the other had survived and earned an MC. Pollard's two sons had both been killed. He had made a single contribution to war poetry in his 'Epitaph' but had not otherwise felt impelled to create poetry out of war. He had said all he had to say about soldiers, death and the carelessness of the creator of life and nature. Fundamentally, he accepted *lacrimae rerum*, of which war was a part. He was not the sort of man to tear his emotions into shreds about things he was powerless to change; but he cannot have avoided thinking that to be without sons in time of war was a blessing in disguise.

The end of the war was ushering in a revolution in the life of England and its social structure, but never a word from Housman on the Armistice or what the future might bring. Nearer to home came

Figure 37 Housman in his cricket
cap. By permission of the Master and
Fellows of Trinity College, Cambridge.

the aftermath of Trinity's own little war. Bertrand Russell, a fellow
of the college since 1895, had delivered to the Cambridge University
Press in 1909 his *Principles of Mathematics*, 'a colossal manuscript
... to be published in three volumes between 1911 and 1913'. The
current entry in the *Oxford Dictionary of National Biography*
pronounces impressively but paradoxically, 'It is indeed unreadable,
but it is nevertheless one of the most impressive intellectual
monuments of the twentieth century'.[51] Then Ludwig Wittgenstein
came to Cambridge to study logic with Russell and his *Tractatus
logico-philosophicus*, 'undermined the entire approach to logic
that had inspired Russell's great contributions to the philosophy of
mathematics'.[52]

At the outbreak of war, Russell's energies had been directed
at denouncing what he regarded as the betrayal of Liberalism by
Asquith's government. By 1916 there was a pressing need for
more men and the government passed the Military Service Bill,
introducing compulsory conscription for all single men between

eighteen and forty-one. Russell threw himself into the fight to defend the rights of conscientious objectors. He was charged with impeding recruiting and discipline on account of a leaflet he had written in support of the No-Conscription Fellowship. Found guilty and fined £100, the college sacked him from his lectureship, even though twenty-two fellows disagreed. Subsequently, in 1918, he wrote an article in *Tribune* in which he alleged that American troops would be employed in Britain to break up strikes. Charged with prejudicing Britain's relations with its ally, he was sentenced to six months in prison.

In 1919 Henry Hollond, a lawyer and fellow of the college since 1909, prepared a letter to the Master, requesting Russell's reinstatement. Hollond canvassed each fellow. Housman's opinion was as usual clear and fair to the man.

> Russell is a great loss to the College, not merely for his eminence and celebrity, but as an agreeable and even charming person to meet; on the question of conscription I agreed with him at the time, though I now see that I was wrong, and I did not feel sure that the action of the Council was wise, though his behaviour was that of a bad citizen. So far therefore I am nearly neutral.

What biased him against Russell and against signing Hollond's letter was a bit of Russell's behaviour he could not stomach:

> what prevents me from signing your letter is Russell's taking his name off the books of the College. After that piece of petulance he ought not even to want to come back. I cannot imagine myself wanting to do so; and my standard of conduct is so very low that I feel I have a right to condemn those who do not come up to it.

Somehow his use of the word petulance is not convincing and his egocentric self-referencing remark which adds up to 'I would not have done it like that myself' sounds petty, disproportionate and Olympian. Housman went on:

> I am writing this, not to argufy, but only in acknowledgement of your civility in writing to me. I hope I shall not be able to discover "conscious effort" in the amiability of yourself and Hardy when I happen to sit next to you in future. I am afraid however that

if Russell did return he would meet with rudeness from some Fellows of the College, as I know he did before he left. This ought not to be, but the world is as God made it.[53]

In the event, Hollond's letter was signed by twenty-eight fellows and supported by another five and so in November 1918 Russell received an invitation from Trinity to be reinstated as a lecturer. He eventually wrote to Trinity in 1920 resigning his lectureship.

Housman's neighbour Wittgenstein

It is worth pausing to notice how similar were Housman and Russell's protégé Ludwig Wittgenstein except that Wittgenstein was in most points of personality a more extreme case. Wittgenstein, scion of an immensely rich Jewish Viennese family, had followed his father's wishes that he equip himself for a career in the family businesses. He studied mechanical engineering at the Technische Hochschule at Charlottenburg in Berlin and went on to Manchester University to pursue studies in the emerging science of aeronautics. Ray Monk, his biographer, highlights the most decisive event of Wittgenstein's life as reading Russell's book *The Principles of Mathematics.* In October 1911, shortly after Housman himself came to Trinity, Wittgenstein had a first meeting with Russell who took only a term to reach the conclusion that Wittgenstein was the man 'to solve the problems I am too old to solve.'[54] Wittgenstein was impelled by his reading of Russell to divert his energies from engineering, just as Housman had been encouraged by reading H.A.J. Munro's *Criticisms and Emendations of Catullus* to focus his energies on editing Propertius at the expense of the Greats syllabus. Housman and Wittgenstein were powered by a similar capacity for self-direction and an innate sense of superiority, though Wittgenstein outshone Housman in his contempt for those who attempted to teach him and from whom he believed he had nothing to learn. When Wittgenstein was viva'd by Russell and Professor G.E. Moore for his doctorate, 'Russell advanced his view that Wittgenstein was inconsistent in claiming to have expressed unassailable truths by means of meaningless propositions.' He was, of course, unable to convince Wittgenstein, who brought the proceedings to an end by clapping each of his examiners on the shoulder and remarking consolingly: 'Don't worry, I know you'll never understand it.'[55]

Figure 38 Ludwig Wittgenstein,
philosopher, wearing his customary
open-necked shirt. By permission
of the Master and Fellows of Trinity
College, Cambridge.

A second similarity was that Wittgenstein was not merely sexually
different but very different. Proposed for membership of the Apostles
by John Maynard Keynes, Wittgenstein accepted but soon resigned.
According to Russell he found it 'a mere waste of time', hardly
surprising given Wittgenstein's rigorous intellectualism. He was not
attracted by its apparent *raison d'être* as a platform for uninhibited
talk of sexual experience.

Wittgenstein had a remarkably different view of the relationship
between sex and love. Monk, having had access to all Wittgenstein's
papers and coded remarks, summed it up thus:

Wittgenstein was uneasy, not about homosexuality, but about
sexuality itself. Love, whether of a man or a woman was something
he treasured. He regarded it as a gift, almost as a divine gift ... he
sharply differentiated love from sex. Sexual arousal both homo-
and heterosexual, troubled him enormously. He seemed to regard

it as incompatible with the sort of person he wanted to be: What the coded remarks also revealed was the extraordinary extent to which Wittgenstein's love life and his sexual life went on only in his imagination ... Wittgenstein's perception of a relationship would often bear no relation at all to the perception of it held by the other person.[56]

Monk, speaking of Wittgenstein's written reflections on his relationships with Keith Kirk, David Pinsent and Marguerite Respinger, concluded:

Wittgenstein's infatuation with Kirk — entirely unspoken, unacknowledged and unreciprocated as it was — exemplified in its purest form a feature that had characterised his earlier loves for Pinsent and Marguerite, namely a certain indifference to the feelings of the other person. That neither Pinsent nor Marguerite — and certainly not Kirk — were in love with him seemed not to affect his love for them. Indeed, it perhaps made his love easier to give, for the relationship could be conducted safely, in the splendid isolation of his own feelings. [57]

This pattern, so well and convincingly documented by Monk, is similar to that hypothesised in this book as possible in the case of the Housman-Jackson relationship.

Wittgenstein's rooms were above Housman's, on staircase K in Whewell's Court, a set which he kept when he was made a fellow in 1930 and later when he became a professor. Neither Wittgenstein nor Housman seems to have been remotely interested in each other, even though Wittgenstein was regarded as a genius by those in the know, and Housman had his own reputation. The only interchange between the two men is recorded by Graves in a story which he says has a better pedigree than most because it came direct to himself from an ex-pupil of Housman's friend Andrew Gow. This implies but does not claim that Andrew Gow was the ultimate source of the story, or had corroborated it. The story was that Wittgenstein, who had no lavatory in his set of rooms, was inflicted by diarrhoea, and sent a message to Housman asking to use his lavatory, his alternative being to descend and cross the court to find one. According to the story, Housman refused to help Wittgenstein in his hour of need, because he, Housman, was 'a philosophical hedonist'.

A second-hand story from a man who merely knew someone who knew Housman is not to be taken seriously. Was it even likely that such a thing could have happened? Could Housman have refused a fellow such a request under such circumstances? If still governed by the Mater's pathological attitude to bodily functions, he might well have been repelled by the thought of somebody else using his lavatory; or maybe it could have been that he disliked Wittgenstein. Joan Thomson, daughter of the Master of Trinity, wrote that Housman was 'apt to take a strong antipathy to a person at first sight, merely if it happened that he disliked the shape of his nose or his complexion. So strong might this antipathy be that Housman would find it almost impossible to look at the person concerned, far less to associate with him.'[58] Housman could well have taken exception to Wittgenstein's sporting an open–necked shirt, in startling contrast to his own rigidly formal dress. Or his aversion to philosophy may have been intensified by what he had heard of Wittgenstein's arcane work. But 'really and truly', as Housman might have said, the story feels more like an academic concoction aimed at satirising the insular nature of both of these formidable fellows.

They were both self-described as seekers after truth but were both determined to rely on their own versions of it, and here there was a difference: Housman's touch was lighter and could not have been more different from Wittgenstein's intense, monologic, passionate, unendingly argumentative style, a man who wearied or alienated many listeners. An otherwise friendly don described him as 'a man who is quite incapable of carrying on a discussion'.[59] Even Russell was exhausted and alienated by Wittgenstein's capacity to argue his case, seemingly forever.

In 1917 Edmund Gosse had sent Housman a copy of his *The Life of Algernon Charles Swinburne* which Housman welcomed: 'It is a great comfort to have it done by some-one who knows chalk from cheese.'[60] Housman, anticipating a second edition, offered eleven specific comments of amplification or matters of fact. Gosse, obviously taken aback by such candour, expressed his dismay, but that got him nowhere. Housman wrote back immediately: 'If you are going to indulge in depression of spirits because I manage to find half a dozen mistakes in 350 pages, you will cut yourself off from my valued corrections in the future.' Gosse must have felt foolish when he read:

> As for my finding little to like, you know perfectly well that you write delightfully and that your taste and knowledge made you just the man for the work; and you do not need to hear it from me, especially when all the world is saying it. For my own part I always feel impertinent and embarrassed when I praise people: this is a defect of character, I know; and I suffer for it, like Cordelia. The chief fault of your book is one which I did not mention, that there is too little of it.

In his critique Housman had made a jocular reference to Swinburne's passion for flagellation.

> I am sending *The Whippingham Papers* by parcel post ... the verse seems to me to be good enough for Swinburne, and in the second poem the stanza is like him. You will see that on p. iii the poet is said to be the author of another work, *The Romance of Chastisement*, which I have not come across: my library is sadly incomplete, and not at all worth leaving to the British Museum when I die.[61]

The following year, Gosse returned to the subject when he circulated privately to Housman and five others, including Max Beerbohm and Walter Raleigh, 'a memoir' relating to Swinburne's addictions to flagellation and alcohol. Housman again aired his colourful knowledge about what he called 'the Menken interlude'. Adah Isaacs Menken, a much-married American circus performer, had been given ten pounds by Dante Gabriel Rossetti to seduce Swinburne. She did her best but in the end returned the money, not having been able to bring Swinburne 'up to scratch'. Included in the memoir was Swinburne's account of how he had been beaten by his tutor at Eton who had allowed him to bathe his face in eau-de-cologne before being birched, using the pleasurable scent to intensify the subsequent pain. Housman's comment on that anecdote was an example of his deadpan humour at its best: 'Etonians tell me that the only person privileged to flog is the headmaster'. His own analysis of Swinburne was precise: 'Sade is the author who most inflamed Swinburne, and though Swinburne's writings are full of sadism properly so called, his own propensities were those of Sacher-Masoch', that is to say Swinburne derived sexual pleasure more from receiving pain (masochism) than from inflicting it (sadism).

Housman was revealing that he had at his disposal a wide range of gossip, anecdote and technical knowledge about flagellation, revealing also his sponge-like mind in action. Yet the overriding sense conveyed is that all this material was very much grist for his humour mill which never stopped grinding. This became even more clear when he addressed the subject of Swinburne and drink, which 'had a great deal to do with his best poetry, though the poetry declined before the drinking stopped', and his personal reflection that the history of the Mohammedan world confirms Horace's 'nulla placer diu nec vivere carmina possunt, quae scribuntur aquae potoribus' (no poems can please long, nor live, which are written by water drinkers).

He had also been intrigued by Gosse's reference to Quagg and Grace-Walkers, 'I gather they occur in some book which appealed to Swinburne's sense of humour, it might be worth looking up. If on the other hand they belong to the "Mysteries of Verbena Lodge", mysteries let them remain.'[62] Verbena Lodge was, according to Gosse's memoir, 'the mysterious house in St John's Wood where two golden-haired and rouge-cheeked ladies received in luxuriously furnished rooms, gentlemen whom they consented to chastise for large sums'. Apparently, Swinburne became a regular visitor in the mid-1860s, but stopped going in 1869.[63]

Housman was well aware that Gosse had a large circle of friends and acquaintances. This letter reveals him as possessing a deal of arcane knowledge of a rather specialised nature expressed with his usual amused observations. Obviously, he felt no need to keep this information to himself.

Housman was getting on very well with Maria Richards who had sent him home from a lunch party clutching a daffodil: 'The daffodil was rather languid when it reached Cambridge, but it is now reviving in water'. He was quick off the mark in planning a visit to Cambridge for them. He suggested a weekend when they could both lunch with him in his rooms on Saturday and Sunday, and Richards could dine at High Table with himself on Saturday night 'if Mrs Richards will not cry her eyes out at being deserted'. He declined the Richards' invitation to Newmarket: 'I do not admire that demoralising animal the horse as much as you do, so I shall let you do your gloating at Newmarket alone.'[64] *En passant*, he mentioned that he was reading Wilfred Blunt's *My Diaries: Being a Personal Narrative of Events 1888–1914* with its comment on meeting Housman, but rather unfortunately indexing Laurence as author of *A Shropshire Lad*.

It was this visit that led Maria Richards to draw the obvious female conclusion that Housman's rooms needed brightening up to say the least. She sent him screens she had made for his reading light and candles. He was touched. 'They beautify my surroundings very much, and I am very grateful to you for your skill and amiability.'[65]

He was surprisingly curt in his twelve word reply to Siegfried Sassoon[66] who asked for a contribution to 'the tribute to Mr Hardy'. Housman contributed a poem written in late 1895, *Oh stay at home my lad and plough*[67] which would be published in *Last Poems*. There seems to have been nothing in this exchange either of Sassoon's reactions to Housman's poetry or vice versa. Perhaps Housman had become aware of Sassoon's public protest as a soldier-hero against continuation of the war in 1917. Invalided home after being wounded at the battle of Arras, Sassoon was surrounded by people like Robbie Ross, Edmund Gosse and Bertrand Russell, who at the suggestion of Ottoline Morrell had sent Sassoon his anti-war book *Justice in Wartime*, 'which made me [Sassoon] feel worse than ever about the senseless slaughter which is going on.'[68] In 1917 Sassoon wrote his famous *Statement* with the help of John Middleton Murry and Bertrand Russell. It would be surprising if Housman had not learned of this from Gosse or Russell. He would not have approved of Sassoon's conduct or have accepted his arguments. True, Sassoon had taken *A Shropshire Lad* to war with him, but had probably seen no reflection of his own war experience in Housman's poems. A Housman poem he would particularly admire was XL in *Last Poems, Tell me not here, it needs no saying*. In 1938 Sassoon described it as a 'perfect poem'. In 1917, it had not been written.

In the same post, 23 May 1919, came a letter from Mackail, pressing him to publish more poetry. Housman replied:

> I cannot help being touched and flattered by your anxiety to make me publish ... But my unwillingness remains ... it is not due to any doubt of the possibility of deluding the public, by printing and binding and so on, into the belief that it is getting its money's worth, but to my own notions of what is proper. However, I shall be contributing a new piece shortly to a MS anthology which is being got up, and in due season I will send you this drop of water to moisten your parched tongue.[69]

The fact was that new draft poems begun between 1900 and 1917 now amounted to thirty.

On 14 July 1919, Henry Jackson, now aged eighty, retired as Vice-Master of Trinity, having spent sixty years of his life in the college. Housman had been entrusted with the drafting of a letter to be signed by the Master and fellows and to accompany the presentation of a copy of Porson's tobacco jar, 'trusting it may often meet your eyes, and bring us before your mind, in moments tranquillised by its contents'.

Housman had the perfect opportunity to deliver what had been requested of him but also something in the nature of a funeral oration while its subject was still living, and a perfect opportunity to express his own deeply felt sense of obligation to Henry Jackson. It deserves to be quoted in full as a wonderfully concise, elegant, and moving *Nunc Dimittis*:

> Our tribute carries with it the personal affection of friends and the gratitude of a community. From the day when first you were elected a Fellow of the College, no measure has been undertaken for the promotion of its welfare or the increase of its efficiency which has not been furthered by or due to your initiative. In Trinity, in Cambridge, in the whole academic world and far beyond it, you have earned a name on the lips of men and a place in their hearts to which few or none in the present or past can make pretension. And this eminence you owe not only or chiefly to the fame of your learning and the influence of your teaching, nor even to that abounding and proverbial hospitality which for many a long year has made your rooms the hearthstone of the Society and a guesthouse in Cambridge for pilgrims from the ends of the earth, but to the broad and true humanity of your nature, endearing you alike to old and young, responsive to all varieties of character or pursuit, and remote from nothing that concerns mankind. This College which you have served and adorned so long, proud as it is of your intellect and attainments, and grateful for your devotion, is happy above all that in possessing you it possesses one of the great English worthies.[70]

This was the work of a master of word portraiture who wanted to describe his subject truthfully as perceived through his own heart and eyes.

Declines to be considered for Public Orator at the University

Housman's commitment to sincerity in important matters was a fundamental part of his make-up. This became clear in the next year when he was invited by Trinity's new Vice-Master and other friends to stand for the position of Public Orator. This he declined to do.

> Not if the stipend were £150,000 instead of £150 would I be Public Orator ... You none of you have any notion what a slow and barren mind I have, nor what a trouble composition is to me (in prose, I mean: poetry is either easy or impossible). When the job is done, it may have a certain amount of form and finish and perhaps a false air of ease; but there is an awful history behind it. The letter to Jackson last year laid waste three whole mornings: the first, I sat staring in front of me and wished for death; the second, I wrote down disjointed phrases and sentences which looked loathsome; the third, after a night in which I suppose my subliminal self had been busy, I had some relief in fitting them together and finding they could be improved into something respectable.

For some writers Housman's words will ring very true. However, his instinct for justice and sincerity for getting the wording right is not invariably a common characteristic of those who have a way with words. Housman realised at once that he was not cut out to be Public Orator. 'I can stand this once in a way; but to be doing it often, and having it always hanging over one, and in connexion with subjects much less congenial than Jackson, I could not bear.' Truth and sincerity, as he saw them, were more important to him than effect or an opportunity to strut the stage.

But Housman was also a good university man and basically humble.

> The University has been very good to me, and has given me a post in which I have duties which are not disagreeable, and opportunities for studies which I enjoy, and in which I can hope to do the University credit; and I should not really be doing it a good turn if I sacrificed that work, as I must, to the performance, even if more efficient than mine would be, of the duties of the Orator.

He finished: 'Do not think this an unkind reply to a kind letter. I have also written to Jackson, as an interview would be useless and distressing to us both.'[71]

In the parlance of today, Housman was 'telling it how it is' in a totally acceptable way and emerging from the episode with the greatest credit

PART X
After the war

Destination Paris, Brive and the Limousin

In July 1919 Housman was thinking of touring again in France with Paris, Brive and the Limousin in his sights. He intended leaving his travels until after the end of August because 'August heat in France might put my health out of order again'. Richards earned further credit from Housman as his 'guardian angel' for taking charge of getting him a visa. Richards was always willing to go the extra mile to be of service to his author. Such care and attention helped to cement their relationship. Housman also made the effort to stay with the Richards for two nights on his way home. Housman was now in a position of being able to smooth the rough edges of travel by using hire cars: 'After my sacrifices for my country during the war I am beginning to spend money on myself instead of saving it up for the Welsh miners,'[1] a reference to the money he had sent to the Chancellor of the Exchequer at the beginning of the war and the Welsh miners who were threatening to strike as a protest against new income tax regulations. He was also revealing himself as willing to fit in with others, go out of his way to see friends and take on more complexity than many others would at the end of a holiday.

During Housman's tour, he kept in touch with Richards, writing to him from Brive, characteristically always planning ahead and never falling into the stereotype of the absent-minded don. When Richards turned up unexpectedly in Paris on business, Housman wrote to him from the Hotel Terminus:

> This is a great pleasure, apart from its unexpectedness. It will be no good looking for me here this evening, and I am also engaged tomorrow evening and Monday evening; otherwise I have no tie.

Usually I leave the hotel not long after 9, and tomorrow I will look
you up at the *Normandy* soon after that time, unless I hear from
you to the contrary.[2]

It is surprising to find that Housman was so fully occupied, but it is
more surprising to find that he did not seek to involve Richards in his
plans or give any indication of what they were. Housman was showing
his enigmatic side; the content of his communications seemed always
to be governed by the principle of 'need to know'.

On his return, Housman spent time with the Richards at Bigfrith
and arrived back in Trinity hoping that 'neither you nor Mrs Richards
are suffering much from the cold you caught from me, which lies heavy
on my conscience, as I do not like to return evil for so much kindness'.[3]

As an inevitable outcome of his growing celebrity, letters from
strangers continued to find him. J.C. Squire informed him that he had
founded and was editing the *London Mercury*, and said flattering things
about Housman's poetry, but was really looking for an unpublished
poem. Housman replied: 'I am sensible of the compliments you pay
me, but all the same I am keeping my few poems in the desk for the
present, and I don't think I am likely to publish anything in periodicals
unless I should happen to be inspired by current events'.[4] Here was
the first public indication that his muse was awakening and his first
mention of the possibility of being inspired by current events, on past
form very unlikely.

A Mrs Trotter asked for permission to reprint 'Epitaph on an
Army of Mercenaries' in her anthology *Valour and Vision: Poems
of the War 1914-1918*. For some unknown reason he allowed its
inclusion, perhaps feeling he could not refuse in the case of such an
appropriately named volume. He even corrected her copy, giving her
its history: 'The poem appeared in *The Times* of October 31, 1917, the
third anniversary of the battle of Ypres'.[5]

He found time to react to Richards' request for advice on whether
he should secure the English language rights of Marcel Proust's work,
A La Recherche du Temps Perdu. Housman replied:

I have read enough to form the opinion that an English translation
would not sell and, apart from that, could not be really satisfactory,
as the merit of the French is in great part a matter of diction and
vocabulary ... The 2nd section of the book, in which I am now
rather stuck, is not at all the equal to the first'.[6]

According to Richards, 'Housman was an admirer – even for some time at least, a great admirer of Marcel Proust's work.' However the thrust of Housman's reply suggests that he was joining the ranks of the many who had begun *A La Recherche du Temps Perdu*, but was not likely to join the much smaller number who had finished it.

Housman also heard from Thomas Hardy who had liked the poem Housman had sent to Sassoon. Housman replied sweetly:

> As you deny us the light of your countenance, your handwriting is more welcome than ever; and it is kind of you to let me know that you liked my poem. It is one which has not been published, as I thought was only proper. I was glad to hear a good account of you not long ago from S. Cockerell. Your College, [Magdalene] as perhaps you know, is lamenting not only your absence but that of its Master [A.C. Benson], who has been kept away more than two years by obstinate depression of spirits, and is a great loss to Cambridge.[7]

M.R. James, Provost of Kings and Vice-Chancellor of the university, posed classical questions which Housman was not able to answer. In return, he thanked James for providing him with the Latin word for 'rifle'. The Latin for 'gunpowder' he already knew from Newton's *Principia*, and now what he chiefly wanted to know was the Latin for a 'tank' – all somewhat reminiscent of the games the French have to play when they feel obliged to translate English technological words into French rather than simply importing the English word. Although it might seem to be an even more pointless operation with a dead language there is frequent need in classical education to translate into Latin or Greek, prose and verse of modern English writers. And, of course it is part of the art of the University Orator to be able to speak about modern things in Latin.

Insofar as James' letter had a military context, Housman was prompted to sound off about the recently formed Rifle Brigade having lost its original designation, 95th Regiment of Foot. 'I suppose that traitor Haldane took it away, to enfeeble the spirit of the British Army.'[8] For once Housman was wrong. The Rifle Brigade had been formed in 1916. Haldane had ceased being Secretary for War in 1912, had been recalled in 1914, only to be forced out in 1915 'by public suspicions over his liking for Germany and German philosophy'. The patriotic Housman shared the public's Germanophobia to some extent – witness his disparaging references to Germans in his Inaugural Lecture – but he could also empathise with individuals caught by conflicting loyalties like Oppenheim, the German born Professor of International Law at Cambridge, who had married an English woman, taken British citizenship in 1900 and supported the British war effort. Housman had no difficulty in empathising with a man who had been obliged to choose between the country of his birth and the country he had adopted; he wrote to Oppenheim's wife Elizabeth, 'I am afraid this is one of the calamities which we owe to the war, which from the very first was a great grief and shock to your husband, as I could easily see when he spoke to me about it.'[9]

In spite of the harsh words in his Inaugural he also wanted to be fair to German scholarship. Writing to John Phillimore about an address Phillimore had given to the Classical Association, Housman said:

> Your strictures on German scholarship have something of the intemperate zeal of the convert ... I should say that for the last hundred years individual German scholars have been the superiors in genius as well as learning of all scholars outside Germany except Madvig and Cobet; and that the herd or group vices of the German school which you particularly reprehend took their rise from Sedan and may be expected to decline after this second and greater Jena.[10]

Housman was essentially open-minded, but in the aftermath of the war, prejudice against all things German was the order of the day. Housman had formed the impression that a book he had just received from Richards, Andre Simon's *Wine and Spirits: The Connoisseur's Textbook*, was also tainted with prejudice: 'mortal passions have invaded the sacred precincts of the cellar to such an extent that he knows of no German or Hungarian wine and does know of stuff from Australia and California'[11]

Manilius IV: Being difficult

Housman's chief preoccupation was with the progress of *Manilius IV*, which had now been with the publisher for three months; he was wondering when the printers were going to start on it. His insouciant approach to costs and pricing continued: 'I had thought of 6/- net as the price ... Of course the increase in the cost of production is greater than that, but I have always sold at less than cost price, so it does not make the difference between profit and loss.'[12]

Such an Alice in Wonderland approach to product pricing illustrated his totally non-commercial attitudes. Richards got nowhere when he suggested that the selling prices of his earlier works should be increased by a shilling or so in order that they would all cost the same, which earned him a decided negative: 'No, Manilius I, II, III and Juvenal should be sold at the old price.'[13] When he heard in December that they were reprinting the 1908 illustrated edition, originally designed as a gift book for the Christmas season, Housman threw a tantrum. 'I suppose I ought to congratulate you on having at last sold off your pet edition. So far as I remember, the text was correct.'[14] This was followed in Richards' own words by 'quite a bitter letter', from Housman which ran:

> This is molestation and persecution. You sent me the proofs to correct when the edition was preparing, and when you do that there are practically no errors. I am too full at this moment of more interesting work to waste my time trying to find mistakes where none are likely to be. Besides I have a copy of the edition, probably more than one. If you do not like illustrations, why did you print this edition? It was all your doing, none of mine; and I thought the public quite right in not buying it.[15]

Housman had indeed gone off the deep end and was behaving contrarily. It was his custom always to require proofs of any new edition but here he was saying that it was enough that he had signed off the proofs of the previous edition. A peace-maker was needed and appeared in the form of Maria Richards who sent Housman a gift of walnuts and scented apples. This earned a sweet-tempered reply including a conciliatory gesture intended for Richards himself. 'Tell Grant that I am eating and drinking a great deal, as there are so many feasts of one sort and another.'[16]

At about the same time he received from Laurence a copy of his latest book *The Wheel: A Dramatic Trilogy*. Housman produced a stock comment: 'You do not need to be told that there is a good deal to be admired in it; and there are passages such as the last four lines which I like very much.' Having heard from Kate that Laurence was off to America he could sign off on a hopeful note: 'I wish you a pleasant and prosperous tour. If they pay you in dollars you ought to come back rich.'[17]

Contact with Percy Withers was resumed in January 1920: 'I was in the Cotswolds for a fortnight at midsummer, but no nearer to you than Stroud. September I spent in France, partly in Paris but mostly at Brive in the Limousin.' Withers must have asked him about new poems because Housman said 'Last year I think I wrote two poems which is more than the average, but not much towards a new volume.'[18] As we know, this studied vagueness had no basis in fact; tucked away in his bottom drawer were thirty new poems.

Alice Rothenstein sent him a celestial globe, a thoughtful and very appropriate gesture that greatly pleased him. 'I am very grateful for it, and I am now completely equipped for dealing with the 5th book of Manilius, for which I required it. I am now just finishing the 4th.' He added 'If you are going to settle at another spot, I hope you will let me know where it is, and I will try not to miss you if I find myself near it.'[19]

A couple of months later William Rothenstein asked Housman to provide a written piece to accompany his drawing of Hardy in his *Twenty-Four Portraits* and got a dusty answer:

> I am sorry if it upsets your arrangements, but I am not going to write literary criticism for you or anyone else; and moreover I should feel awkward and embarrassed in writing about Hardy under his nose. I do not mean that it would violate any principles or general notions which I may happen to have, but it would distress my sensations, which I believe are in some respects morbid.[20]

It sounds as though he was saying that he didn't like the idea of seeming to write a literary obituary or judgement on Hardy before he was dead, or was just trying to find a way to avoid the hated literary criticism. It did not prevent him from sympathising with the Rothensteins on leaving Oakridge in Gloucestershire for Campden Hill in London and expressing hopes of seeing William in Cambridge.

A letter to Kate mainly about her researches into King Edward's School Bath ended 'I have written a poem suited to your infant mind, on the paper enclosed.'[21]

> Amelia mixed the mustard,
> She mixed it good and thick;
> She put it in the custard

And made her mother sick;
And showing satisfaction
By many a loud huzza
"Observe" said she "the action
Of mustard on mamma."

Rent-a-pen

By now it was evident that Housman was admired as a superb
wordsmith and speaker. Having been considered a likely candidate
for the oratorship and having been asked by the Master and fellows
to compose the presentation address for Henry Jackson, it was now
being suggested that he should write something about James Frazer
of *The Golden Bough* fame. Housman explained to Cornford, another
fellow of Trinity, that 'After declining to stand for the Oratorship I
suppose I shall make myself unpopular if I refuse the next request
which is made me, so I will try to write something for Frazer. But oh,
why was I born? This is a rhetorical question, and does not expect
an answer.'[22] So, in spite of his reluctance he went ahead to do Frazer
justice. He was writing of a man who had had an annual lecture in
Social Anthropology founded in his name by four universities –
Oxford, Cambridge, Glasgow and Liverpool. Writing of Frazer's
magnum opus, Housman apostrophised Frazer's spreading influence:

> *The Golden Bough*, compared by Virgil to the mistletoe but
> now revealing some affinity to the banyan, has not only waxed
> a great tree but has spread to a spacious and hospitable forest,
> whose king receives homage in many tongues from a multitude
> resorting thither for its fruit or timber or refreshing shade. There
> they find learning mated with literature, labour disguised in
> ease, and a museum of dark and uncouth superstitions invested
> with the charm of a truly sympathetic magic.[23]

No wonder Housman was recognised and sought out as a master of
words.

The next day he heard from Percy Withers, who had bought himself
a first edition of *A Shropshire Lad* which Housman now signed for
him. 'I have decorated your infatuated purchase with my signature
and the shortest of my unpublished poems, *The sigh that heaves the
grasses* [which would be published as XXVII in *Last Poems*].' Housman

admitted to having used it before 'for Meynell in a book belonging to one of his daughters'. He did not spare Withers from his usual contempt for bibliophiles. 'I should have thought though, that this would detract from the value of the book for a true bibliophile; but no doubt this is already a spoilt copy, the leaves having been cut'. The Withers had moved house to Souldurn Court to the north of Bicester in Oxfordshire, so he passed on information about the Rothensteins' move back to London, 'owing he says to the ambitions of his children'. Withers had mentioned his current ailments which prompted a medical review by Housman.

> Sciatica is one of the few ailments I sympathise with, as I used to have it myself, no doubt in a mild form, twenty years ago, till I learnt to change my things when I got into a sweat. Cancer is worse they say, and being shot through the palm of the hand makes one scream louder.[24]

This was another early sign of a Housman whose reticence would not apply to health as a topic of conversation.

Housman had been down in Berkshire for a long weekend to see the Richards again and one can reasonably assume that he had taken the opportunity to monitor the progress of Manilius. But even ten days later, when sending off the final manuscript of the index, he was finding more new errors in page proofs which had previously been correct. There were typos like Vrigo for Virgo, which must have caused Housman considerable amusement, being the replacement of a word meaning the embodiment of female virginity by one meaning burning sexual desire. 'As for preventing letters at the beginning and end of lines from getting out of their place, it seems a hopeless business: as fast as they are put straight in one place they fly crooked in another place'.[25] Whatever the trials of these final stages, *Manilius IV* was finally off his hands on 1 July. His struggles in these final stages had been enlivened by reading Richards' *Double Life*: 'Your rather immoral but very readable novel ... I did not think the Monte Carlo part so good as the rest, but your knowledge of the turf and everything connected with it fills me with admiration and horror'. Switching to his normal copy-editor mode, he identified a handful of inconsistencies, illogicalities and confusions in the novel. But all of that was by way of prelude to a startling announcement: 'I may attempt Paris by the aeroplane route in September, so any information about it which you may possess or acquire would be welcome; also about passports'.[26]

1920: Housman takes to the air

Within a few weeks, Richards, who embraced with enthusiasm his role as Housman's honorary travel agent, had showered Housman with leaflets. Housman had decided to travel by Air Express, his decision 'confirmed by the crash they had yesterday, which will make them more careful in the immediate future'.

Whether or not Housman's sangfroid was justifiable is a moot point. Commercial flying across the Channel had started only in 1919. The planes were converted wartime Handley Page biplanes, the pilots men who had flown in the Royal Flying Corps. Crashes and forced landings were relatively frequent so flying was rightly regarded as both adventurous and exclusive.

Meanwhile, his life continued to produce its usual tapestry of events and experiences. Kate's second son Denis had been made Doctor of Public Health giving Housman an opportunity to play the court jester with his title's acronym 'DPH, Devastator of Public Health or Dispenser of Pharmaceutical Horrors'.[27]

He tried to create a policy for dealing with composers who wanted to set his words to music and editors who wanted to include his poems in anthologies. He wrote to Richards:

> if you would answer such letters for me it would save some little trouble. But I seem to remember that on one occasion in the past you mixed up my benevolence to composers with my hard-heartedness to anthologists, so that a poem of mine was published in one collection on your permission when I refused mine to the editors of others, who had applied to me.[28]

However, he seemed reluctant to play the ogre when Constable published one of his poems without permission. 'Revenge is a valuable passion, and the only sure pillar upon which justice rests, so I do not want to hinder your pursuit of Constable if it can be conducted without making me seem to be the pursuer.'[29]

On the eve of his flight to France Housman arranged dinner at the Café Royal with Richards and his son, whose birthday it was, mentioning that they could talk about the publication date for *Manilius IV* when they met. And then, as if an afterthought, he wrote words Richards had been hoping to hear or read for the past twenty-two years: 'Suppose I produced a new volume of poetry, in what part of the year ought it to be published, and how long would it take after the MS left my hands?'[30]

In his book *Author Hunting by an Old Literary Sportsman*, Grant Richards tells how he was constantly questioned about a successor volume to *A Shropshire Lad*: 'There was seldom even a day that one person or another – sometimes a bookseller's 'collector', sometimes someone whom I met at a party – did not ask me when it would have a successor. American publishers, as I have written, would often open their conversations with such an enquiry.'[31]

While in Paris, Housman kept in touch with Richards and tried to arrange to meet him. Housman had other people to meet, for he mentioned that 'At 2.30 a newly engaged couple are going to make a short call on me here, but otherwise I am not engaged in the afternoon.' As to a dinner date, 'I could dine with you if you are willing to dine early and lightly; that is to say I shall dine lightly; but there is no reason why you should.' By way of further explanation all he said was 'I should have to leave you soon after 8.30, but the nearer I was to a station on the Vincennes-Maillot line of the Metropolitain, the longer I could sit at table.'[32] He gave no further information about these late night rendezvouz. In the event it all came to nothing because Housman decided to return home with an unexplained stomach upset.

Back in Cambridge and full of enthusiasm for air travel, he wrote to Laurence: 'I have just flown to Paris and back and I am never going by any other route, until they build the Channel Tunnel, which I will give a trial, if it is much cheaper.'[33] He adopted an even more triumphant air with Kate:

Well I flew there and back all right, and am never going by any other route in future ... Surrey from overhead is delightful ... It was rather windy and the machine sometimes imitated a ship at sea (though that is due to differing densities of atmosphere and not to wind) but not in a very life-like manner. Members of your unhappy sex were sick however. The noise is great and I alighted rather deaf, not having stuffed my ears with the cotton wool provided. Nor did I put on the life-belt which they oblige one to take ... You are in the air 2 ½ hours; from Leicester Square to your hotel in Paris you take little more than 4; though on the return journey we were 2 hours late in starting because the machine required repairs, having been damaged on the previous day by a passenger who butted his head through the window to be sick.

My chief trouble is that what I now want is no longer a motor and chauffeur but an aeroplane and a tame pilot, which I suppose is more expensive.[34]

Housman was less happy about returning to work on the address to Frazer. What he had written was not entirely pleasing to himself: 'I despair of making it better by keeping it longer. It seems to me not only too ornate, as some of Frazer's own writing is, but also stilted which Frazer's writing is not.'[35]

Exercised as he was by the Frazer address, Housman rejected out of hand a request from the editor of the *John Keats Memorial Volume.*

Certainly I have all the will in the world to honour Keats whom I admire in the strict sense of the word, more than any other poet; but unfortunately I am not able to write poetry (nor even prose that is worth writing) at will; and it would be no good my making you any promise. If anything should come into my head, I would send it to you; but it is very unlikely.[36]

Richards again in financial difficulties

Then it was back to more serious business. Richards was once again in financial difficulties and Housman immediately answered his call for help and in mid-1920 sent him £500, a remarkably generous response: 'not more I am afraid for I have other friends who are in difficulties. But I hope this will be some good. I am not losing any interest, as I always keep in my current account enough money to flee the country with.'[37]

Richards had drawn to his attention the words of the editor of the *Nottinghamshire Journal and Express:*

Mr Housman has just published, with his friend Grant Richards, another book of his edition of Manilius. The Professor is less known than the poet of 'The Shropshire Lad' and still less known is the Mr Housman the gourmet, to whom I believe such a skilled epicure as Mr Grant Richards gives first place.

Housman was delighted: 'undeserved renown is what I chiefly prize. I am much more celebrated in Cambridge for having flown to France and back last September than for anything else I have done.'[38]

Christmas 1920 approached and Housman expressed delight to Mildred Platt for her invitation to dine and stay the night but excluded New Year's Eve.

> I and other choice spirits here always see the New Year in on oysters and stout to do what we can for the cause of human progress and the improvement of the world. I congratulate you on having managed to live with Platt so long. This is a compliment of the season.[39]

The Platts valued Housman and felt an affinity with him. His relationships with the Withers and the Rothensteins also generated cheerful and empathetic New Year messages to them, with promises to visit the Rothensteins in their new house and wishing them a happy new year, 'not even excluding the ambitious children who have uprooted you from Oakridge'.[40] He himself was content to be staying in college over Christmas. To the Withers he sent cheerful greetings with regrets that Trinity's new and much superior Combination Room would not be ready for his spring visit because of a builders strike: 'I am here for Christmas as usual, my own family having an aversion for Christmas gatherings and Trinity College very much the reverse.'[41]

On 5 January 1921 he seemed to be making a U-turn when he told Richards, 'My "new book" does not exist, and possibly never may... What I asked you was a question inspired by an unusually bright and sanguine mood, which has not at present been justified.'[42]

It was not impossible for the reticent Housman to be sociable on the spur of the moment and act spontaneously, aided no doubt by his chauffeur-driven hire car. In June he reached out to Percy Withers at short notice:

> Next Tuesday I am motoring to Stroud; and as you lie on my way I was wondering if I might drop in on you for lunch and renew acquaintance with you and Mrs Withers after what seems a rather long interval. I should arrive sometime between 12 and 1. I suppose there is some place near where the chauffeur could stable his steed.[43]

Later in June he would also ask the Richards whether he could drop in on them for lunch on his way to Eton.

It would seem that when Richards had sought that loan from Housman the previous December he had promised to repay it by April. Housman had not been receiving answers to his letters on Manilius and now putting two and two together, wrote on 14 July:

> I am afraid that the reason why you do not answer my letters is that you feel awkward because you said you would be able to repay my loan by April. But I never imagined that you would: I knew your sanguine temperament (due, in Herbert French's opinion, to an over-generous diet) far too well; and I write now to prevent you from afflicting yourself unnecessarily. I am not suffering any inconvenience, and the money would only be lying at the bank in my current account.[44]

A week later there came a tale of woe from Richards and Housman was having to write: 'very sorry to hear the tale of all your unmerited troubles: though "lassitude and inertia" are my normal condition, especially in this weather.' Housman may have suspected that Richards' money worries had brought him close to a nervous breakdown and so emphasised 'I hope you will not worry yourself about anything connected with me.'

Apart from the word 'tale' which has a rather unbelieving ring to it, Housman was being supportive and sympathetic, unwisely one might think:

> I intend to go to Paris for a week about September 10 and if that is about the time when you would be going to fetch Mrs Richards, of course I should like to go with you. I would not insist on your flying, as I could face land and sea with you for courier.[45]

He was obliged to be in Cambridge at the beginning of August 'for a meeting of the Classical Association, damn it; I am not a member, but they have chosen to meet here, and Americans are coming, and I am the only classical Professor of Cambridge who is able to deliver an address.' This would enable the gathering to hear one of his most significant papers, 'The Application of Thought to Textual Criticism.'

Housman had difficulty in pinning Richards down, flying or not flying, so it ended with Housman making a unilateral decision. 'As I did not hear from you by Tuesday evening I wrote and secured a passage to Paris by Messageries Aeriennes.'[46] After he returned Housman persisted, as a good friend would, and was soon inviting

Richards to join himself and another Trinity fellow, Winstanley, for lunch at the Café Royal on their way to view an exhibition of Max Beerbohm caricatures.

Housman was not becoming any more enamoured of publicity and gave short shrift to another writer who had approached Richards for an interview. 'Tell him that the wish to include a glimpse of my personality in a literary article is low, unworthy, and American. Tell him that some men are more interesting than their books but my book is more interesting than its man.' Housman was determined not to be a celebrity. 'Tell him that Frank Harris found me rude and Wilfred Blunt found me dull. Tell him anything else that you think will put him off. Of course if he did nevertheless persist in coming to see me I should not turn him out, as I only do that to newspaper reporters.'[47]

Richards was by now in a state of desperation and sought a lunch meeting 'tomorrow' with Housman. Housman was very straight with him:

> I wish I could be of real help to you in your troubles, which I am very sorry to hear of; but the worst of it is that you are not the only one of my friends who is in want of money. Besides your £500 I have lent £600 to others, £300 of which I do not expect to see again (and I do not mind if it is the same with your £500) and the last loan I was obliged to restrict and make it less than was asked. I possess much less than you probably suppose. As I have nobody dependent on me I have always spent nearly up to my income: and at this moment my wealth consists of about £300 in the bank, and £1,500 in investments which would fetch much less if realized, and the dividends which do not pay my income tax. Therefore, in view of my means and of other claims on them which may arise, I am not properly able to lend you even the least which you think enough for your immediate needs; and being despondent by temperament as you are sanguine, I do not believe that it really would be enough. Even if your calculations are right, accidents will happen, like your ill-health earlier in the year. Naturally your troubles make me unhappy, and I hope you will not increase them by vexing yourself about repaying the £500. I shall never think of it.[48]

Perhaps he thought he had been too hard on Richards. The next day he wrote 'I had one of my loans repaid yesterday, so I can send what you want, and I enclose two cheques for £125 0s 0d. each. I am glad things are going better.'[49]

All this speaks volumes for how Housman and Richards had grown close over twenty-five years and how absurdly generous Housman was. They could now take each other warts and all and move beyond the relationship of interdependent author and publisher to that of friends, which for Housman always had an element of unconditional affection about it. He was no soft touch; Grant Richards was his friend.

In October he was invited to stay with the Withers but could not: 'next week is full of prelections by candidates (ten in number) for the professorship of Greek [left vacant by the death of Henry Jackson], some of which I want to hear, and one of which I must,'[50] here referring to the lecture of his good friend Arthur Platt from University College. Housman wrote subsequently to the successful candidate A.C. Pearson, deftly finessing his reaction to the result so as to retain his own credibility.

> As Platt was after all a candidate, my sentiments were divided, and my joy is not unalloyed; but I told those electors who consulted me that I was glad it was they and not I who had to choose between you and that it would be very wrong if they chose any of the other eight.[51]

In a later review of Pearson's *Sophoclis fabulae* Housman described him as 'an acute grammarian, a vigilant critic, and an honest man', which coming from Housman has to be classed as fulsome praise. Later he let fall inside information to Sir Herbert Warren, his former tutor and supporter just ending his stint as Vice-Chancellor of Oxford University: 'I see that your accompanying note was about the candidates for our Greek chair. So in thanking you I will say that I think the right man was chosen, as Platt, whom I should put beside him, did not really want to leave London.'[52]

He also shared with Withers, his enthusiastic reaction to churches encountered on his way home from Stroud. 'I was arrested by the beauty of the church at Bloxham.' He had made it his business to meet the incumbent who had then directed him to further churches. 'It was a great treasure trove, as I had never heard of the group, though it appears that they are celebrated.'[53]

This was in some contrast to his reception of a photograph from Sydney Cockerell featuring the Rossetti brothers and Fanny Cornforth,

Dante Gabriel Rossetti's model, mistress and housekeeper. 'This is so very precious, that I return it instantly after showing it to Winstanley who shared my curiosity about Miss Cornforth. I am very grateful for the sight of it. It will often flash upon the inward eye which is the bliss of solitude.'[54] It says much for the range of Housman's interests that he could be arrested both by the beauty of churches and by the attractions of the artistic low life of Chelsea in the person of Fanny Cornforth.

An invitation from Maria Richards arrived inviting him to stay with them for Christmas. His five nights with them was notable for his part in a brush with the ecclesiastical authorities. To cut a long story short, a group of very badly performing carol singers had been calling at the Richards' house on and off for about a month and had been sent away with requests to come back at Christmas, when they would be rewarded. Reappearing on Christmas Eve, the carol singers were rewarded 'more than their deserts', whereupon they disappeared without finishing their carol, as did bottles of champagne Richards had placed in the snow to cool. Indignation followed and according to Richards, Housman produced a notice for the board at Little Cookham Dean Police Station with a duplicate in the church porch. Housman's notice read 'The carol-singers who, after being paid for their carol singing at Bigfrith on Christmas Eve, removed a bottle of champagne which had been placed in the garden to cool, are requested to return the empty bottle and cork.' Unfortunately, there had been a too rapid rush to judgement. On Christmas Day a letter from the vicar informed Mr Grant Richards that before writing his notice he should have found out something about the carol singers, because the church choir had for some years given up that practice. Subsequently the church warden protested at their having put a notice in the church porch. This prompted a round of point scoring by Richards who ended up slightly shame-faced: 'Nothing to be proud of, of course, but one is light hearted at Christmas!'[55] When Housman subsequently told Percy Withers about the champagne episode, he made no reference to himself or to the notice. As Withers had yet again been asking about new poems, Housman avoided telling him an outright lie: 'No, no more poetry, or at least nothing to speak of.' As if to divert Withers' attention he then added a semi-blasphemous comic verse in place of a postscript; a verse hardly likely to be seen as the funny side of things by Percy Withers, a Catholic. A recent change of popes had aroused Housman's inveterate antipathy to Rome:

It is a fearful thing to be
The Pope.
That cross will not be laid on me
I hope.
A righteous God would not permit
It.
The Pope must often say,
After the labours of the day,
"It is a fearful thing to be Me"[56]

PART XI

Last Poems
A Requiem for Moses Jackson

During April 1922, Housman was hard at work, creating as many as six new poems and bringing seventeen more into a finished state. He kept this industry hidden from Richards and instead concentrated on a debate of petty wine snobberies. 'I knew already, having been told, that it is wrong to have one's wine brought in a cradle, and now I know further that it is wrong to decant it; so in future I shall just have the cork drawn, and suck the liquid out of the bottle through a tube.'[1]

And then suddenly came the day Richards had been waiting for. Housman wrote on 9 April 1922: 'It is now practically certain that I shall have a volume of poems ready for the autumn; so I wish you would take what steps are necessary as soon as they are necessary.'[2] He was clearly working through the poems he intended to include and asked about the legal position of *Illic Jacet* which had already been published in *The Academy* in 1900. Ten days later he was asking for the deadline for sending Richards the complete manuscript and expressing a particular desire that the price should be moderate. Less than ten days after that he was firming up on a publication date.

Almost as an afterthought he wrote 'when you next print *A Shropshire Lad* I want to make two alterations.'[3] On this occasion they were not matters of punctuation but of wording. To change words after twenty-seven years seems strange, indeed suggesting that his gestating mind had suddenly decided that he now preferred other wordings which his notebooks show he had rejected almost a quarter of a century earlier. The changes were 'loose' for 'thick' in the third stanza of 'The winds out of the west land blow' and 'no more remembered' for 'long since forgotten' in the third stanza of 'Far in a western brookland'. As part of his preparation for selecting poems for *Last Poems* he must have been carefully re-reading *A Shropshire Lad*.

By the end of April he was approving a specimen page of *Last Poems*. He had been quite clear on the layout. 'The poems should not be run on, as originally in *A Shropshire Lad*, but each should start on a fresh page.'[4] By 19 June he was sending Richards his fifty-page manuscript. As usual, his views on the process were crystal clear: 'When it is printed, let two copies be sent to me at first, for correction. It will save the printers trouble if you tell them that they had better not try to improve my spelling and punctuation.'[5] On 10 July he returned his corrected proofs plus an additional poem 'The sloe was lost in flower' and asked for four sets of proofs, one for Mackail, one for Ker, one for another unnamed advisor and one for himself.

Life did not stop just because Housman was preparing another volume of poetry. J.B. Priestley, who went up to Cambridge in 1919, sent Housman a copy of his *Brief Diversions: being Tales, Travesties and Epigrams*, which included a parody of Housman, a 'Dedication for the Shropshire Lad' entitled 'To All the Gravediggers between Ludlow Town and Hughley'. It earned from Housman a dry 'Some of the parodies and other verses I read with great interest and pleasure in the *Cambridge Review*,'[6] a rather understated expression of approval but hardly a put-down.

He had promised to go to the Withers' for a long weekend: 'I should be interested and pleased to meet Gordon Bottomley,'[7] a poet and dramatist whose work had been included in *Georgian Poetry*. Housman said nothing then or later about other poets included in that group, particularly Lascelles Abercrombie, or Edward Thomas killed at Arras. His rapprochement with John Drinkwater, another Georgian, continued. A review of Drinkwater's poems in *The Times* had denounced him for plagiarism from *A Shropshire Lad*. Housman described this to Drinkwater as 'silly', which reminded him 'I never thanked you – or at least I think I did not, and indeed I usually put off writing letters till they do not get written at all – for giving me your *Seeds of Time* when you were last in Cambridge. I particularly admired the third poem.'[8] So while he could appreciate what he thought was good poetry, he was unconscious or careless about the Georgians as a group; the idea of groups of poets was alien to him.

Return from his visit to the Withers' occasioned a graceful thank-you. 'We made a capital run to Bletchley in little more than 50 minutes with the sun lighting the landscape and green leaves just

Figure 39 J. W. Mackail, classical
scholar, Fellow of Balliol College
Oxford, Professor of Poetry at Oxford.
One of the three people whose opinion
Housman sought on Last Poems. ©
National Portrait Gallery, London.

as it should. To-day it rains in Cambridge, and appropriate gloom
surrounds my emotions of regret, and of envy for Mr and Mrs
Bottomley.'[9] Mrs Withers had transformed his thanks into a *pas de
deux*. 'The marmalade has just arrived quite safe, and two pots when
I only hoped for one; and I am very grateful to you and Mrs Withers
for your respective shares in the gift.'[10]

When Hugh Anderson, Master of Gonville and Caius College, was
knighted, Housman wrote to Lady Anderson:

When these honours fall to my friends and acquaintances, I
always write to congratulate their wives, if I have the pleasure
of knowing them, because they are the persons who take most
pleasure in the affair; and so I send these felicitations to you in
particular, though I do not altogether exclude Sir Hugh.[11]

Housman had set his face against honours for himself, was pleased
for friends who received them but could never resist this kind of male

chauvinistic observation; to be expected then, but still frequently made today.

Although overjoyed that he had at last another set of poems from Housman, Richards demurred at Housman's title, *Last Poems*. He had a vivid recollection of his first reading:

> Then, for the first time and last time in my career, without, I am certain, any idea of being theatrical, but with a feeling that here was an occasion, *the* occasion of my life, I began to read the poems aloud. Their effect on me, and I think on my hearers, was instantaneous. I cannot, I will not, attempt to describe it. As each poem was read and returned to the envelope I became encompassed by the sad, haunting, tragic air that the book has and I felt uplifted into ecstasy by its beauty.[12]

Housman warned Richards: 'I cannot arrange the order of the poems satisfactorily until I know for certain which I shall include and which omit; and on that point, as I told you, I want to consult one or two people.'[13] And so he sent his manuscript to J.W. Mackail, marked 'Secret as the grave', writing 'I am bringing out a volume of poems this autumn: will you do me the kindness to look through them first? They are neither long nor many.'[14] Mackail agreed. Housman sent him the proofs and laid out his expectations:

> I want you to note anything that strikes you as falling below my average, and open to exception for any other reason. The piece I myself am most in doubt about is the longest; and I fear that is not its worst fault. You need not be afraid of stifling a masterpiece through a temporary aberration of judgement as I am consulting one or two other people, and shall not give effect to a single opinion unless it coincides with my own private suspicions.[15]

Mackail replied quickly and within a week of having sent him the proofs, Housman was reacting in an open and non-defensive way to his comments on fourteen of the poems. Housman himself seems to have been definitely pleased with three of his poems, had doubts about another four, and was happy to engage with Mackail on the wording of four more. He wrote most about 'Hell Gate', the longest poem. He was obviously equivocal about it; he did not think Mackail's suggestion of omitting certain passages would work and stoutly defended a succession of three 'ands', for which he gave precedents from Milton, and from Shelley, who Housman said had gone even further with five successive 'ands' in *Ariel to Miranda*.

Especially noteworthy was what he said about a poem on page 36 of his proofs, which 'dissatisfies me too, but not quite in the same way. The first and last stanzas came into my head; the middle ones are composed. I think the last stanza really requires that the poem should have five stanzas.' Here he was talking about the balance between inspiration and composition which he always acknowledged as a characteristic of his creative process, a combination of inspiration and perspiration.

For the moment that was as far as they could go and Housman asked Mackail to keep the proofs because he might wish to go back to him, 'when W.P. Ker comes back from the Alps, on whose summits he is now pirouetting'.[16] In the meantime Housman was turning his attention to the layout of the book, asking questions about the height of the page and so on, so that he would be able 'to map out exactly what page each poem or part of a poem will stand on'. He also asked Richards about procedure for drafting the contract and, tongue firmly in cheek, whether he should submit it to 'some society for the Protection of Authors against Publishers?'[17]

By 24 August he was writing from the Angel Hotel, Midhurst, asking Richards to get the corrected proofs into book form and announcing with mock solemnity: 'Silence may now be broken, as I am safely away from Cambridge and out of humanity's reach.'[18]

As for the announcement in print, he anticipated having 'to censure your fanfares'. He wanted a short announcement such as, 'I shall publish on – the only book of poetry written by Mr A.E. Housman since the appearance of *A Shropshire Lad* twenty-six years ago', or, perhaps better, simply 'Mr A.E. Housman's second volume of poetry'.[19] How Richards must have groaned. Nevertheless, his announcement in the *Times Literary Supplement* read 'Early in October I shall publish a new book by A.E. Housman. It will be entitled *Last Poems* (5/-).'

Housman followed up with a list of thirty-three names of people to whom copies should be sent including his brothers and sisters, Sophie Becker, Edith Wise, Mrs John Maycock, Alfred Pollard, Herbert Millington, William Rothenstein, Percy Withers, Witter Bynner, J.W. Mackail, Arthur Platt, W.P. Ker – quite a tally of friends.

Last letters

One friend was not on the list. On publication day 19 October 1922, Housman, now sixty-three, personally sent a copy post haste to Moses Jackson. He knew that his friend was far from well:

> My Dear Mo
>
> I have been putting off writing so as to be able to send you this precious book, published today. The cheerful and exhilarating tone of my verse is so notorious that I feel sure it will do you more good than the doctors; though you do not know, and there are no means of driving the knowledge into your thick head, what a bloody good poet I am. In order to intimidate you and repress your insolence I am enclosing the review and leader which the *Times* devoted to the subject. I may also inform you that the copy of the 1st edition of my other immortal work which I gave you is now worth £8 or more if you have kept it at all clean; and that the average annual sale is over 3000 copies. That is largely due to the war, because so many soldiers, including at least one V.C., carried it in their pockets, and thus others got to know of it and bought it when they came home. But it does not seem to stop bullets as the Bible does when carried in the pocket, so I have been disappointed of that advertisement, probably through the jealousy of the Holy Ghost. Of this new book there were printed 4000 copies for a 1st edition, which were all ordered by the booksellers before publication, so there is already a 2nd edition in the press. It is now 11 o'clock in the morning, and I hear that the Cambridge shops are sold out. Please to realise therefore, with fear and respect, that I am an eminent bloke; though I would much rather have followed you around the world and blacked your boots. The eminent poet would willingly have exchanged his fame and position for the chance of following his correspondent, in the humblest capacity, to the farthest corners of the earth.
>
> In June I flew over to Paris for a week as usual and late in the summer I spent a month at Midhurst in about the best part of Surrey, between the chalk downs and the Haslemere type of country. I motored through Godalming: Witley Common has been rather devastated by the Canadian camp there.
>
> Gerald writes to me now and then, and seems to be a wonder

in the way of industry and determination: both Oscar and Rupert evidently think a lot of him.

My very kind regards to Mrs Jackson.[20]

On 23 November Moses began his reply from his bed in Ward T of the General Hospital, Vancouver. It deserves also to be quoted in full:

My dear old Hous,
I got your letter and your egregious poems at home about a fortnight ago. I thought of heaping sarcasms on your brain products, as usual, but some of the pieces are good enough to redeem the rest. The Times critique was good, and its selection sensible, but the Observer, which the faithful Ward sent me, was still better. I hoped to see the Spectator, but it has not been sent along. The Morning Post is about the only other paper to count. The old woman's D.Telegraph and the screamingly radical press, with bosh writers like that A.G. Gardiner, don't count.

You certainly know how to end the book. But who is going to labour at collecting your Juvenilia from the 'Round Table' & elsewhere, and to exploit acute inaccuracies about them in the not far distant future? That thing that you published in some aesthetic magazine seems to me, in its disregard of all politeness towards possibilities in the unknown future, seems to me to contain nearly half the philosophy of your two books. You will be surprised at my remembering them so nearly, if I am not quite word-perfect.

Ave atque Vale
Goodnight. Ensured release,
Imperishable peace,
Have these for yours
While earth's foundations stand
And sky and sea and land
And Heaven endures.
When Earth's foundations flee
Nor sky, nor land, nor sea
At all is found
Content you, let them burn,
It is not your concern.
Sleep on, sleep sound!

It wants the poet to punctuate it. It deserved a place in the Shropshire Lad! It was the condensation of so much meaning into a few words – furiously unorthodox though it might be, that struck me.

Your 'Mercenary Army' bit is as skilful as anything in the book. It was a good deal quoted out here during the War.

Here is the 30ᵗʰ. [The letter was not written at one go.] No haggis. No whiskey. No nuthink.

The great Ward informs me that your sales have gone up to 17,000 at the time of writing. Your 'Tis little luck that I have had' can have no personal reference to the poet. [Moses misquotes the second quatrain of *Last Poems* XXVIII which begins 'Little is the luck I've had'].

I have also seen your portrait in *Punch*. Ridiculous as it may appear, there is just a faint indication of the shape of your head, and just a hint of an expression that I have seen on your mug once in a way. I suppose your boots are supposed to harmonise with the bucolic heroes you often immortalize, sleeping off their beer in lovely muck.

1 Dec. I am getting on fairly well in this hospital, but I will come out of it pretty soon now, well or ill, and finances won't run to these expenses. It is funny to be 'land poor', with severe depression in agricultural values. I have practically all that I originally paid £3,000 for in cash – land and stock etc. with lots of improvements, yet cannot even sell or even borrow £200 from a bank. The boys all hang together well, but it is an outrage for an older generation to weaken the younger.

We shan't go on at Applegarth as hitherto. The missus dislikes it. I dislike anything else. I will sell the whole or part, or put on a temporary mortgage or something. What I want is a partner, honest and fond of farming. We could easily make the place produce more than it has ever done. There must be lots who would do, if only I knew them.

Land sells worse now than ever. Most of the returned soldiers have gone out of their little lots, and relinquished their land to Govt., with the results that we land-owners have Govt. as dealers in ahead of us. Doubtful land will get up again in time, and then everybody will tumble in to buy. The correct thing to do is to wait, if one can. If I were a capitalist I would buy now. The disgusting thing is the way I have let you and Ward down. I will return what

I can, when anything comes in, but things shape up for my dying a hopeless bankrupt. Probably the sooner the better as I shall never return to my old self, and at the moment am just a burden to everybody. I apologise in dust and ashes.

I haven't your last letter here, but I remember an extraordinary exhibition about blacking boots! My most presentable boots are brown, requiring no blacking, Larry old chap. At home I wear boots of canvas & rubber composition, known as snagproof, as your choice is an absolute sinecure. But it would be fine to see you here, though no chance of the old amenities. No 15-mile walks to a good pub to consume cold ribs of beef 10" thick, pickled walnuts, and a quart of bitter, with a good tub of cream, & rich cream to finish. None of that in this beastly land, with their infernal prohibition.

G.W. Ellis stayed with us for some time a year ago. He had farmed in Alberta. He is rather a slacker, but well up in St John's recollections, so we could talk about many things.

Oscar, Bachelor of Applied Science, is now assaying at the big smelter at Trail, B.C. Gerald ran a motor boat up the coast as an Assistant Fire Ranger for the Forest Dept. in the Summer Vacation. He did so well that they promise him a better job for next summer, but he thinks he will go as a 'mucker' or labourer in the Britannia Mine, just for experience. He is going strong at the Univ. That institution has grown wonderfully.

I have seen the Spectator review of your emanations. The second paragraph seems to the point, some others less so. The last part of this musical thing for the Sunday Times seems largely rot. I did not see the review by Gosse the week before. If you read all the commentaries you must be pretty busy.

I hope your publisher will shoo the Americans off. While lying on my back here I have been exasperated to see how they publish well-known English books, curtailed with only a Yankee publisher's name on the title page, and make their ignorant readers think the author is a Yank. I dislike the arrogant brutes.

Gerald will be up presently & will post this. So here is to continued luck. Printing 'Jones of Jesus', 'Tennyson in the Moated Grange' etc. may bring you in a fresh fortune at the right time. 'First Poems'.

Goodbye

Yours very truly

M.J. Jackson[21]

Housman wrote back on 4 January 1923:

My Dear Mo,

I got your letter on New Year's Day. As you threaten to leave the hospital well or ill, I suppose I had better direct this to Applegarth, though I understand it is empty now, rather than to bed 4.

I was never more astounded at anything than at your reproducing my contribution to *Waifs and Strays.* I remember your reading it at Miss Patchett's and how nervous I felt. If I had known you would recollect it 42 years afterward, my emotions would have been too much for me.

On the copies of the new book already sold in England there will be due to me royalties of about £500. As I cannot be bothered with investments, this will go to swell my already swollen balance at the bank unless you will relieve me of it. Why not rise superior to the natural disagreeableness of your character and behave nicely for once in a way to a fellow who thinks more of you than anything in the world? You are largely responsible for my writing poetry and ought to take the consequences.

The American edition which is to be as like the English as possible, was published on Dec 1 and sold out in four days, but I don't know how many copies it consisted of. I am to have £300 from it in any case, and higher royalties than in England after 3000 copies have been sold.

A female third cousin of mine, whom I have never seen, has burst forth into song on this occasion and sent her poem to my brother. It describes how the devil paid a call in Cambridge on a friend of his (that is me) and explained that as the Rev. Robert Housman (that is my great-grandfather, known as 'the Lancaster evangelist') had saved some souls, he (the devil) wanted me to destroy an equivalent number; and wrote my poems to oblige him: the result being that the name of Housman is 'tarnished for evermore.' That name she fondly fancies, had hitherto stood for everything noble; which is news to me, and shows that the poor dear does not know as much about her grandfather as I do. Among other things, he invented a new religion and held forth in a chapel of his own, which he finally emptied by a sermon in which he described Potiphar's wife as an ill-used woman and Joseph as a cold-blooded young fool.

I was in Oxford about a month ago and saw Watson, very sleek and sleepy. The most noticeable change in the place since our time is that the trees in front of Magdalen school are gone, so that the façade of Magdalen chapel looks right down the High as far as Univ., and the effect is more stately if less rural. The trees in front of St John's are much diminished, and the Broad Walk in Christ Church Meadows is a thing of the past. Our lime avenue at Trinity, now 200 years old will soon follow it. Millington of Bromsgrove, who partly educated me, died the other day at 82. He had been suffering (or rather not suffering) from, senile decay, Aphasia and loss of memory are probably the stages by which I shall approach my end.

Yours very truly,

A.E. Housman.[22]

14 January 1923: Moses Jackson dies

But before Housman's letter reached him Moses died of stomach cancer. One wonders if when Housman read Moses Jackson's letter, he was at all struck by his own lack of perception of his friend, whose actual attitude towards his poetry seemed to be totally at odds with that of the Moses Jackson he had referred to in his dedication; the Moses Jackson whose almost exact memory of the poem published in *Waifs and Strays*, in March 1881, astounded him. For Moses to have remembered verses, not obviously constructed for easy memorising, was a measure of the impression they had made on him.

This final correspondence revealed a relaxed Moses, happy in his skin, able to deal openly with Housman, and a Housman unable to conceal his unbounded and unconditional generosity of spirit for Moses, yet uncharacteristically clumsy in his expression of it; falling into false heartiness rather than employing the polished and measured eloquence of his tribute to Henry Jackson. But Housman was now writing out of a heart full of sentiment, a mind overcome by emotions, rendering him powerless to summon up his linguistic skill; the same Housman who had been unable to control his emotion over *Diffugere Nives* in the lecture room. After forty years in the bottle his feelings had matured into friendship.

Three days later, on 17 January 1923, Housman wrote to their friend Pollard:

Jackson died peacefully on Sunday night in hospital at Vancouver, where he had gone to be treated for anaemia with which he had been ailing for some years. I had a letter from him on New Year's Day, which he ended by saying 'goodbye'. Now I can die myself: I could not have borne to leave him behind me in a world where anything might happen to him.[23]

Here was his epitaph on Jackson, acknowledging the allegiance of his life to which he had been always faithful. Who among us could have expressed the end of things so poignantly? And that *Goodbye* in Moses Jackson's last letter resonated perfectly across a lifetime with Housman's diary entry for Sunday 1898, 10.45 p.m. – 'said goodbye'.

At one time, the Jackson family believed that the death of Moses prompted Housman to write the fragment published by Laurence after Housman's death in *Additional Poems.* But having been begun in 1895 it had preceded Moses' death by at least a quarter of a century, a fact that does not, however, make its use inappropriate:

> Now to her lap the incestuous earth
> The son she bore has ta'en.
> And other sons she brings to birth
> But not my friend again

A poem that *could* stand as an unacknowledged epitaph to Moses Jackson was from the book of poems sent to Housman in November 1914 by Thomas Hardy. In his reply, Housman had especially commended 'In Death Divided', 'the second stanza of which is quite perfectly beautiful'.[24] Hardy's second and final stanzas expressed the final truth of things for Housman and Moses:

> No shade of pinnacle or tree or tower,
> While earth endures,
> Will fall on my mound and within the hour
> Steal on to yours;
> One robin never haunt our two green covertures.

> And in the monotonous moils of strained, hard-run
> Humanity,
> The eternal tie which binds us twain in one
> No eye will see
> Stretching across the miles that sever you from me.

Grant Richards was in no doubt about the quality of *Last Poems*. 'I have in my heart that *Last Poems* is an even better book than *A Shropshire Lad*'. He had a success on his hands. His own judgement was that he should print five thousand copies. Housman himself thought ten thousand, but by the end of the year Richards had printed twenty-one thousand.[25]

Housman's estimate of his market was better than Richards' but while he saw quite clearly that volume of sales was the best indicator of success, he seemed content to let his poems make their own way. He was happy that Richards should 'Brag about the sale as much as you like'[26] but he did not wish him to quote reviews in his 'weekly epistle'. Housman still shrank from personal exposure. When Richards was organising a celebration party Housman replied 'I would rather there were no one but you and Mrs Richards'.[27] In his *Housman 1897–1936*, Richards recalled that the celebratory dinner was held at the Carlton on 13 November when they were served saddle of hare 'for which Housman had a partiality'.[28] He made no mention of any other guests.

Last Poems: Critical reception

The public reception, measured by its reviews, was overwhelmingly favourable. Housman's voice was immediately recognised. Before long he was writing to Richards: 'The press-cutting agency sends me, with due delay, more notices than I want to see'.[29] The book was being widely reviewed bringing with it the problem every author has of how to armour oneself against unfavourable reviews. In the event, that was not something Housman had to cope with. So he could write to F.C. Owlett in 1924: 'It is very unreasonable for people to be depressed by unfavourable reviews; they should say to themselves "do I write better than Wordsworth and Shelley and Keats? am I worse treated than they were?"'.[30]

Many of his critics recognised that in *Last Poems* Housman was taking them down the same road as in *A Shropshire Lad* but it was a road they liked going down; an unsigned review in the *Times Literary Supplement* put it like this: 'Again the road beckons us into a land of radiance and sorrow, loveliness and briefness'.

Housman probably had no conscious intention to mislead his readers about the origins of this book of last poems but that is exactly what he did. On the face of it, his preface was clear, but only to those who did not read it closely and ask what it meant:

"CURIOSITIES OF LITERATURE."

The Muse. "OH, ALFRED, WE HAVE MISSED YOU! MY LAD! MY SHROPSHIRE LAD!"

Figure 40 The Punch cartoon which signalled
the publication of *Last Poems* in 1922.
Reproduced with permision of Punch Ltd.,
www.punch.co.uk.

I publish these poems, few though they are, because it is not likely that I shall ever be impelled to write much more. I can no longer expect to be revisited by the continuous excitement under which, in the early months of 1895, I wrote the greater part of my other book: nor indeed, could I well sustain it if it came; and it is best that what I have written should be printed while I am here to see it through the press and control its spelling and punctuation. About a quarter of this matter belongs to the April of the present year, but most of it dates between 1895 and 1910.

Housman spoke in riddles, leaving us to decide for ourselves the nature of the continuous excitement (agitation, ferment, fever, delirium?) and why it was unlikely to return; and to make sense of his inability to sustain (endure, bear?) it, if it did. We have already seen how he had found the emotional experience of writing his poetry the exact opposite of Wordsworth's emotion recollected in tranquillity; he had found the experience almost too painful to bear because its origins lay mainly in his loss of Moses Jackson to marriage and India and his personal reaction to Oscar Wilde's imprisonment. Five years later, when asked by an American what he meant by 'excitement', he replied, 'The excitement was simply what is called poetical inspiration.'[31] But one of his reviewers recognised more acutely what he had done: 'every line is a quintessence; he can pour his full passions, the molten metal of himself, into a quiet, restraining phrase and fix it forever.'[32]

Housman then wrote a sentence in his preface suggesting alienation from his own poetry. He seemed to elevate its least important components, spelling and punctuation, to be *the* critical element. This was Housman the scholar speaking, the man of dry-as-dust exactitudes. But as we now know, this scholarly exactitude did not extend to the composition dates of the poems. About them he was frankly forgetful and misleading. In April 1926 he wrote to an unknown correspondent: 'I have some times thought of attaching dates to the poems, so far as I can remember them.'[33] So he ended up minimising the number conceived during 1894 to 1895, when twenty-three of his forty-one *Last Poems*, well over half the volume, actually began their lives.

Of course, none of the reviewers looked closely at any of this and why should they? Housman had provided an introductory translation of an old French song to make his position clear: 'We'll to the woods no more,/ The laurels are all cut.'

One reviewer, the American William Rose Benet, elder brother of poet Stephen Vincent Benet, did touch on the mystery of Housman. 'We have read of him as an odd and 'cranky' personality – we can weigh the obsessions of his mind, calculate from the form and tone of his work its peculiar strains and stresses. But the intimate man remains a mystery.'[34] Such a thought did not occur to most of Housman's reviewers who had immediately recognised the essential homogeneity of his first and second volumes and found nothing radically changed, neither in voice, subject matter, nor philosophy. His readers were being given more of the same and they loved it. His friend Edmund Gosse wrote: 'It is the same voice; it is a continuation of the old theme, for the tone, which was so clear and personal in 1896, is as individual as ever in 1922. If there is any change at all, it is in the direction of a completer technical excellence.'[35] *The Cambridge Review* simply hailed a second coming, 'a true poet and consummate craftsman has repeated a triumph.'[36] J.C. Squire experienced a seamless continuity: 'Many of the 'new' poems are old; the more recent are not

always distinguishable from the others ... the book is an extension
of the first book, and it is as good.'[37] J.B. Priestley emphasised the
individuality of Housman's voice:

> A line from A.E. Housman is as unmistakeable as a line from
> Milton, Shelley or Wordsworth, and bears the same impress of
> the poet's individuality; and to me the difference between the
> modern poets and these three Titans, on this count of original
> force, is one of degree alone, for I hold him to be of the same
> imperishable kind.[38]

The *dramatis personae* of his poems were recognised as unchanged;
Outlook noted 'We proceed; and lads go to market, go sweet hearting,
are hanged or "list for soldiers". There is perhaps nothing in this part
of the book to equal the best of the Shropshire Lad, but also hardly
anything which might not have taken its place in that sequence.'[39]
Housman's world view and philosophy were perceived as unchanged,
the *Bookman* noting 'The attitude ... is dictated by the same
disillusioned or never-illusioned confrontation of the "sorry scheme
of things".'[40]

As with *A Shropshire Lad*, there were a few dissenting voices, but
they were lost in the clamour of praise. Clement Wood of New York,
lawyer, schoolteacher, and prolific poet, put it simply: 'Why did he
never grow up and out of the morbid wisdom of nineteen?'[41]

A year later in October 1923, F.L. Lucas, poet, novelist, scholar and
Reader in English at Cambridge, distinguished Housman from the
Georgian poets as 'one personality among so many echoing masks,
one reading of life, wrong maybe, but blurred and corrupted at least
with no optimistic emendations, and rendered into English of a purity
that English literature has not surpassed.' Lucas had attended one of
Housman's early lectures at Cambridge and so had an opportunity to
see the scholar-poet perform in his main occupation:

> With what expectation one waited in the Lecture Theatre of the
> Arts School amid an audience that seemed unworthily sparse, for
> the first sight of the poet – and in what perplexity one went away!
> Could this quiet, immaculate figure, setting straight, with even-
> voiced, passionless, unresting minuteness the jots and tittles of
> a fifth-rate ancient whose whole epic was not worth one stanza
> of his own – could this be the same? Only the lines about the

mouth with their look of quiet, unutterable distaste, only the calm, relentless, bitter logic, as of destiny itself, with which some sprawling German commentator was broken into little pieces and dropped into the void, seemed in the least recognizable features.

There was no doubt that Lucas admired Housman's poetry: 'these poems as Meleager said of Sappho's, are "few but roses." The poems of Catullus are likewise few.'[42] Another American, also writing in autumn 1923, wrote of a quality Lucas had detected – stoicism.

> On this side of the Atlantic, at least, pessimist is just one degree below bolshevist as a term of abuse. We dislike the fact, indeed shut our eyes to the fact, that in this world every religion, every culture, that stood the test of long years had in it a core of stoicism by which it endured even if it couldn't rejoice and triumph. And we are prone to confuse pessimism with stoicism.

This was the reviewer who also wrote 'The one faith that burns clear in his poems from first to last is trust in friendship.'[43]

Lifting the veil

It is ironic that Housman, ever extolling truth, preferring to camouflage the truth about himself, lifted the veil ever so slightly in *Last Poems* when he included a powerful and aggressive poem he had left out of *A Shropshire Lad*. It defies us to read it as other than an autobiographical statement, a *cri de cœur*, which he felt he could now publish thirty years after he had written it. In the climate of opinion of the 1920s, to complain about the laws of God and the laws of man and couple them together would not attract as much obloquy as it would have done in late Victorian England. His complaint was here in *Last Poems* XII:

> THE laws of God, the laws of man,
> He may keep that will and can;
> Not I: let God and man decree
> Laws for themselves and not for me;
> And if my ways are not theirs
> Let them mind their own affairs.
> Their deed I judge and much condemn,

Yet when did I make laws for them?
Please yourselves, say I, and they
Need only look the other way.
But no, they will not; they must still
Wrest their neighbour to their will,
And make me dance as they desire
With jail and gallows and hell-fire.
And how am I to face the odds
Of man's bedevilment and God's?
I, a stranger and afraid
In a world I never made.
They will be master, right or wrong;
Though both are foolish, both are strong.
And since, my soul, we cannot fly
To Saturn nor to Mercury,
Keep we must, if keep we can,
These foreign laws of God and man.

In the aftermath of publication John Drinkwater sent him a copy of his *Preludes* and Housman was happy to respond with *Last Poems*: 'I have written your name and mine in the book.'[44] With Edmund Gosse he went much further: 'I thought you were very nice about me in the *Sunday Times*, and I have copied out a poem for you as you wish. It is one of those I did not put into the book [and would remain unpublished till it appeared as XV in *More Poems* so Housman copied out *Tarry delight; so seldom met*[45]]; for I know you bibliophiles, and your passion for *'l'inedit'* irrespective of merit. Sir James Barrie wrote warmly. 'To meet you last night was a great thing to me. That was mainly what I journeyed to Cambridge for with Charles Whibley's kind help, and I am very glad I went. My admiration for your poems passes words.'[46] E.M. Forster, the novelist, who by then had published *Where Angels Fear to Tread*, *Howard's End* and *Room with a View*, wrote on 22 February 1923 to express 'thankfulness from the bottom of my heart for the poetry' and to express 'the wish that you may be happy.'[47] Housman replied: 'It is very kind of you to write, and I value what you say. I remember meeting you, and the circumstances; and so perhaps this letter may find you even though you withhold your address.'[48] Forster would write to Housman again on 28 March 1928: 'I don't know whether there is such a thing as impersonal affection, but the words best express the feeling I have had towards you, through your poems, for the last thirty years, and I ask you to pardon this expression of it.'[49] At the time of their meeting, Forster already had in manuscript his *Maurice* and *The Life to Come and other Stories* with their homosexual themes, but they would not see the light of day until the 1970s. Forster was homosexual but never disclosed the fact widely. He had first encountered *A Shropshire Lad* in 1907 and there and then wrote in his diary: 'Want to write to Housman', which he did that day from the Angel at Ludlow. Forster realised that Housman must have fallen in love with a man; he could feel that Housman's poetry mirrored his own adolescent development and feelings.

Forster did not meet Housman until he took the Clark Lectureship at Trinity in 1927 after Housman had turned it down. Forster recorded a conversation with Housman:

> Our most intimate conversation was on the subject of Paris. "When I go there," said the Professor with a twinkle "it is to be in unrespectable company." This was offered as a jest, and accepted as such, but so offered that I might make the mistake of accepting it seriously if I chose, which was intriguing. Well pleased with such progress, I ventured to climb the forbidding staircase which led to his rooms. They were sported [meaning closed] but I dropped a visiting card through a slit.

His early attraction to Housman grew with the years; he used quotations from *A Shropshire Lad* in his novels; for Forster, he was 'a light in the sky'. However, less than a year later when Forster sent Housman a newly-published copy of his collection of stories *The Eternal Moment* and 'wrote warmly and somewhat sentimentally' of the resemblance between one of his stories and one of Housman's *Last Poems* he was astounded by Housman's reply. He told a friend: 'It was absolutely hateful. I can't show it you or even quote it, for I was so disappointed and hurt that I destroyed it after one rapid perusal.' Forster's conclusion was 'I had been forcing the pace, I had tried for intimacy too soon, I had presumed, a mere novelist, to parallel myself with a poet. I had made a fool of myself and been snubbed.' There is just the possibility that Forster, misled by what he may have interpreted as a 'come hither' from Housman, had written to him in a way that was tantamount to a romantic approach. There was also another simpler explanation. When he had been giving the Clark Lectures in Trinity,

Forster committed the social sin of not dining sufficiently frequently in Trinity, which led him to write:

> This was the first time I had encountered the celebrated Trinity silliness, and it nearly knocked me flat ... What a college! What dons! Offended till death because I had eaten in Kings ... I thought he was annoyed with me because I had behaved as a small writer shouldn't behave to a great one. He was really annoyed because I hadn't behaved as a don should to dons.

When Forster eventually dined in Trinity, he recalled:

> to my horror Housman swept up, and without seeing me, sat down on my right. Constipated conversation ensued which ended when he turned his head away... choked by a piece of his own rubbish, and we never spoke again. I passed him on one of his afternoon walks, but we took no further notice of each other.[50]

Witter Bynner sent Housman a copy of his *Canticle of Pan*. Housman had to apologise.

> I am afraid you are not the only person to complain of my ungracious silence. The fact is that I have a strong tendency to postpone writing all letters; and so it often happens that they do not get written at all, because I have generally come to fancy that I have written them because I ought to have written them.

His reference to *Last Poems* which he had arranged for Bynner to receive was brief. 'Thanks for what you say about my last volume. The sale is larger than I expected, though I expected a larger sale than the publishers and the booksellers did.'[51] He seemed to try hard to diminish his book; he had told Percy Withers in advance not to allow his expectations to run away with him. Now he seemed barely able to disguise his ambivalence about the finished work, not, one feels, out of modesty but almost like a mother rejecting a child, the scholar rejecting the poet. 'Your generous enthusiasm is very nice, but I have not myself felt more than a faint pleasure in the success of the book which is not really a matter of much importance.' Even so, he could not totally hide the good feelings he got from recognition by other poets. 'I was pleased by letters I had from Masefield and others.'[52]

Focus on *Last Poems* had not inhibited Housman from leafing through later editions of *A Shropshire Lad* and then delivering a blast to Richards. '

> You must not print editions of *A Shropshire Lad* without letting me see the proofs. I have just been looking through the editions of 1918 and 1921, and in both I find the same set of blunders in punctuation and ordering of lines, some of which I have corrected again and again, and the filthy beasts of printers for ever introduce them anew.[53]

Nor was *Last Poems* escaping his eagle eye unscathed. 'On p. 52 they have removed a comma from the end of the first line and a semi-colon from the end of the second.'[54] When Richards proposed an errata slip he replied perversely: 'No ... the blunder will probably enhance the value of the 1st edition in the eyes of bibliophiles, an idiotic class.'[55]

Laurence sent him *his* latest book, *Dethronements: Imaginary Portraits of Political Characters, Done in Dialogue,* and earned a frank opinion: 'I do not think it one of your good books ... the falsification of history is quite awful.'[56] A few days later he returned to the fray: 'To represent Chamberlain as an injured man and Balfour as a man who injured him is like saying that Christ crucified Pontius Pilate.' There followed a lengthy thesis on the interactions of Chamberlain and Balfour which revealed that the witty and perceptive young St John's undergraduate was still alive and well, and helps us to realise what was lost when he left no observations on the college life of his time. It also gives us insight into what the fellows of Trinity enjoyed in his conversation – when he chose to join in. After providing this trenchant criticism he ended with a humorous 'Your affectionate brother (though I have received a press-cutting which authoritatively states we are not brothers).'[57]

Within two months of the publication of *Last Poems* Herbert Millington died and his death was marked by an obituary in *The Times*:

> He was a great teacher, vivid, stimulating, endlessly enthusiastic, and occasionally terrifying. Whatever else his lessons were, they were never dull. His vigour and driving force were remarkable, for, while he never spared himself, he paid others the high compliment of exacting from them the same standard of endeavour and achievement ... Upon sloth, meanness or insincerity, he had

no mercy. Even some, who were neither slothful, mean, nor insincere, suffered from the indiscriminating flame of his zeal for efficiency. But both masters and boys... willingly recognised the high motives that conditioned all his actions, and never concealed their admiration for his exhaustless energy.[58]

This obituary is almost a description of Housman; the fullness of time had shown how Millington had left his mark on his pupil.

Some months later he was amusing himself with something that was almost taking him back into the fantasy world of his comic verse. With a straight face, Housman reported to Richards that he had been asked by 'my old, dear and intimate friend Princess Marie Louise Victoria, who is furnishing the Queen's doll's house' to let twelve of his poems be copied small to form one volume for the library. So he had 'selected the 12 shortest and simplest and least likely to fatigue the attention of dolls or members of the illustrious House of Hanover'. There was to be a companion volume describing the contents of the library; his twelve poems totalled ninety-six lines of poetry. Thus his instruction to Richards: 'So do not send a solicitor's letter to the Queen (for the book is to be hers when it appears). The issue is to be 2000 copies in this country and 500 for America, and the Queen is to do what she likes with the proceeds.'[59]

Back in the real world, Robert Bridges seems to have touched on the possibility of yet another volume after *Last Poems*. Housman replied 'The title of the next volume will be *Posthumous Poems* or *Chansons d'Outre-tomb*.'[60]

He was feeling free to plan another trip to France, telling Richards

I shall cross to Paris on the 31st by Handley Page from Croydon at 4.30. I shall stay at the Continental for about 3 days, and then, I think, go by train to Le Mans and engage a car there, which will be cheaper than in Paris. My idea is to follow the south coast and come back by the north. Thanks for all your maps, books and other aids. If we are in Paris together, I probably should not be free in the evenings but should be during the day.[61]

When he arrived home he gave Kate an account of his motor tour of Brittany. As we might expect he was good at the travelogue, with the odd and surprising comment 'Carnac is almost as unimpressive as Stonehenge.' He had been delayed a day because the weather was 'too dangerous for the aeroplane to start: but on August 1 I had the best voyage I have ever had. We crossed the Channel 7000 feet high, higher than the piles of clouds which lay over both shores, and both coasts were visible at once, which I have not found before.' To add to the sense of how intrepid he was, he had just had a letter from 'photographers who were taking "for press purposes" photographs of ladies and gentlemen who are in the habit of flying between London and Paris, and they want to take mine as they "understand" that I have also had that distinction.'[62] Here was an exploit that could outshine most ordinary achievements, the actual experience of flying in 1923, of committing oneself to the air on take-off, the transcendent experience of being in another world above the clouds, the magic of the patchwork landscape below, and all the metaphysical angles of being in flight. None of this ignited a poetic flame in him, even though he may still have felt the ordinary emotions of apprehension, uncertainty and relief. The fact is that he seems to have experienced flying with a great sense of curiosity, awareness and calmness; it became food for his mind but not a trigger for poetry. Housman was not on the lookout for new poetic material. *Last Poems* proved that he was still fixated on the poetic world of *A Shropshire Lad* and all that had given rise to it.

Back to earth he was again trying to make policy on the use of his poems by others. He joined the Society of Authors. He refused consent to the BBC to broadcast readings from his poems. He told Richards on 23 September 1923 'I do not unconditionally prohibit the use of *Last Poems* as I do of *A Shropshire Lad*', a rather curious statement which suggested that he saw *Last Poems* as not having the iconic quality of *A Shropshire Lad*. Or maybe he was just being wilfully inconsistent. In Bridges' case he was not only willing to allow Bridges to reproduce two poems from *Last Poems* but was also willing to turn a blind eye to his inclusion of three poems from *A Shropshire Lad* in his *The Chilswell Book of English Poetry*. Housman told Richards why:

> I had better also tell you that I believe that he, (being Poet Laureate, and an unscrupulous character, and apparently such an admirer of my verse that he thinks its presence or absence will make all the difference to his book), intends to include three poems from *A Shropshire Lad* in his, though I have not given him my permission, because he thinks he has reason to think that I shall not persecute him. Well, I shall not; and you will please turn a blind eye too.[63]

Every now and then there were letters in his correspondence to remind us that he was still the Professor of Latin at Cambridge. However, out of a total of one hundred and forty-seven letters for the years 1922 to 1923 only eight (five per cent) were to fellow scholars: a letter to Andrew Gow on usage in Ovid and Catullus; to J.D. Duff on word meanings in Sophocles; to a Frenchman, Jean-Louis Perret, on manuscripts of Juvenal; letters to Andrew Gow on classical books he was to look out for and purchase on Housman's behalf; a letter to the Superintendent of the Nautical Almanac Office asking for answers to questions relating to zodiacal movements on 15 January, 49 BC, and 28 November, 50 BC, 'in what degrees of what zodiacal signs were *Saturn, Jupiter, Mars and Venus* situated?' (this was the only indication that Housman was hard at work on *Manilius V*); to Ernest Harrison, Senior Tutor at Trinity, with his comments on the use of certain words in Juvenal as interpreted by another scholar, and on metrical points arising from Harrison's own article on Aristophanes' *Frogs* in the *Classical Review*. The conclusion that one might draw from this is that Housman wrote relatively few letters to other classicists, there being little value in initiating correspondence with scholars from whom he felt he needed no help.

Workaholic though he was, he could keep his obsession for textual criticism under control. He was definitely not sending off letters in all directions merely to keep himself professionally in the eyes of others. His capacity for working efficiently and for managing his time was leaving him room for wining and dining, for keeping his written links with friends and family in good repair, responding to reasonable requests for his books to be autographed, his poems to be set to music and responding to requests for information and advice.

In November 1923 he heard from a man who would have much more to say about him in future. H.W. Garrod, fellow of Merton College, Oxford, had published an edition of *Manilius II* in 1911 which Housman had declined to review. Garrod had produced studies of major English poets, had published in 1912 *The Profession of Poetry* and had been elected Professor of Poetry at Oxford in 1923. He sent Housman a copy of his just published *Wordsworth: Lectures and Essays* and on 2 November Housman wrote 'many thanks for the gift of your Wordsworth, which I am reading with great interest and finding in it many things which I did not know.'[64] A day later he answered a letter from E.V. Lucas, a man of letters who had written to him about a poem which had appeared in *The Times*. Housman gave him a masterly demonstration of how to register a criticism without creating offence; he referred to the author as 'the poet in the *Times* whom I judge from his versification to be a very gallant soldier.'[65]

A member of The Family

By now Housman had been elected a member of another family, The Family, an exclusive dining club limited to twelve members of the university which met on alternate Fridays in term time, each member taking turns to give a dinner. Among its members were A.C. Benson, Master of Magdalene; S.C. Roberts, then secretary to the Cambridge University Press and lecturer for the English Tripos, and Sir J.J. Thomson, at that time Master of Trinity, formerly Professor of Experimental Physics, winner of the Nobel Prize in 1906, knighted in 1908 and awarded the Order of Merit (OM) in 1912. In his *Recollections and Reflections*, Thomson said of Housman: 'The dinners which he gave as a member ... had like everything he did, the air of distinction.'[66] S.C. Roberts remembered that when he was himself invited to join The Family

> an intelligent interest in food and wine was regarded as one of the necessary qualifications of membership and no one insisted on this more firmly than Housman, who, when he was host, designed his menus with great care. Under the mellowing influence of a good dinner conversation became quite easy. I remember his telling me that he had rather ruefully agreed to be a pall-bearer at Thomas Hardy's funeral. One of his companions was Galsworthy, of whose books Housman had a low opinion. 'He,' said Housman 'represents humanitarianism; I represent pessimism.'[67]

A.C. Benson chose to remember conversation in The Family rather differently in his diary entry following a dinner in 1923: 'Housman told me two of the most obscene French stories I have ever heard in my life – not funny, only abominable.'[68] That remark may say as much about the son of the Archbishop of Canterbury as it does about Housman.

A sea change was occurring in Housman's attitude to returns from his books, occasioned, it would seem, by Richards' failing to pass on his American royalties. 'I am going to write to Henry Holt & Co. to tell them to send my royalties direct to me in the future.'[69] The envelope was marked 'Private', but no more was said at that point. Although Richards had previously demonstrated unreliability on matters financial, Housman was evidently not willing to foment a rupture. But his next letter about the inclusion of poems in other people's anthologies and subsequent letters, were directed to the firm and not to Richards personally.

Housman was determined to maintain the integrity of his text; reproduction of his poetry would have become a game for any number of players, once he had given the freedom of his text to anthologists, setters to music and miscellaneous individuals. He saw them all as potential underminers of his text. And so he gave Ivor Gurney permission to set eight of his poems to music but 'with the restriction that no omission of lines must be made in any poem ... I have always refused to allow the printing of the words of poems in concert programmes.'[70]

He was rigid also in his unwillingness to give any further publicity to the light verse he had included in the paper on Erasmus Darwin he gave at University College and at Eton. The headmaster of Eton made what Housman regarded as a flattering request, that he should publish his own verse. Housman thought them inferior to *The Loves of the Triangle*, a parody by George Canning and others on Darwin's *The Loves of the Plants*. Housman said of his own verse: 'I think them so much inferior to *The Loves of The Triangle* that I am not willing to have them published. Do not tell me that there is much more vanity than modesty in this because I know it already.'[71]

In August 1924 it was time for family and friends, on this occasion staying at the Spa Hotel in Bath so as to be near to Kate. From there he was in contact with Bridges, seeking a bed for the night on his way back to Cambridge whence he would 'greedily be returning to urgent and agreeable work',[72] and with Alice Rothenstein, saying that there would be no chance of seeing her at Oakridge that year, giving her an account of how his own year had gone and poking fun at William: 'I have no doubt William will bring home some grave and weighty studies of Alps and Swiss peasants rendered invisible by rain. There has been a good deal of invisibility in England for the last month, but I hope you are well and none the worse for it.'[73]

A weightier interchange followed with J.B. Priestley who had sent him a copy of his *Figures in Modern Literature*, a collection of essays on nine authors including Housman. There was a slightly offhand flavour in Housman's reply: 'I can easily swallow all the flatteries brewed by you and F.L. Lucas' – who had written about Housman in an article

'Few but Roses' in the *New Statesman and Nation* – 'but I wish people would not call me a Stoic. I am a Cyrenaic; and for the Stoics except as systematisers of knowledge in succession to the Peripatetics, I have a great dislike and contempt.'[74] It was natural for Housman to be pedantic and to insist on terms being properly used but unnatural not to have acknowledged the ordinary lower case usage of the word stoic as 'a person having great self-control, or fortitude or austerity' which characterised Housman perfectly. Robert Bridges had bought a copy of Housman's *Manilius* and Housman's response was a health warning.

> I adjure you not to waste your time on Manilius. He writes on astronomy and astrology without knowing either. My interest in him is purely technical. His best poetry you will find in I 483-531, where he appeals to the regularity of the heavenly motions as evidence of the divinity and eternity of the universe. He has nothing else so good, and little that is nearly so good.

Housman seems to be talking dismissively when he says of his life's work 'My interest in him is purely technical.'[75] We should not take these words at face value; he found textual criticism fascinating and absorbing. His love for it was not only obsessive but deeply rewarding.

On 1 October 1924 Housman was back to writing direct to Grant Richards who had put out peace feelers in the form of an invitation. Housman would have none of it: 'As matters stand, it would cause me embarrassment to stay or dine with you.'[76] But he wished to remain friends with Richards and by 3 November was thanking Richards for a copy of Sacheverell Sitwell's latest poems which he found 'dull' and he had tried the first bottle of the Fernando VII sherry from Thame which he found 'excellent.'[77] But, as if to demonstrate his independence, he wrote a letter to Macmillan, the publisher. He told Macmillan what his policy had been.

> In the last twenty years I have produced several editions of Latin classics ... at my expense, offered to the public at less than cost price, and sold for me by a publisher on commission ... I am just completing an edition of Lucan which I wish to produce in the same way. The printers of my last three books, Messrs Robert MacLehose & Co of the Glasgow University Press are prepared to undertake the work; and Mr Charles Whibley has suggested to me that you may be willing to act for me as publishers on the

usual terms and to be the channel of my communications with the printers. As in 1895 you refused to publish another book of mine, *A Shropshire Lad*, under similar conditions, I did not think this likely; but he assures me you are now less haughty.[78]

This could hardly be classed as a seductive approach. In the event, Basil Blackwell published his Lucan in 1926. Nowhere in his book about Housman did Richards refer to that fact. Perhaps he had learned of it with relief.

When another fellow of Trinity, Alexander Higgins, Professor of International Law, asked him to look at his son's poetry one might imagine Housman's reaction, knowing how difficult it would be to avoid being cast as a coward or a flatterer. Housman wrote direct to the son, praised two poems which he thought were particularly good and was frank about some detailed dislikes. He explained:

I demurred when your father asked me to look through your poems, because I am always afraid of hurting young poets' feelings, and one of them once wrote back to say that he had put his verses in the fire; but your father assured me that you would not mind, and that my criticisms would probably be less hostile than his own, so I hope no bones are broken.[79]

The young man probably felt praised, helped and sympathetically advised.

On the last day of 1924 he wrote to Percy Withers in his frank and amusing way, being glad to hear

tolerably good news of your health, and to receive your Christmas reproaches ... It is true that I do not write to you, but then there are few people to whom I do, and never willingly. You write with ease, elegance and evident enjoyment, whereas I hate it ... I will remember you at midnight when I shall be drinking to absent friends in stout and oysters, which are very salubrious and which I take medicinally to neutralise the effects of Christmas. When you give Mrs Winslow's soothing syrup to a baby 'the little darling wakes up as bright as a button' and so do I on New Year's day.[80]

On that New Year's Day of 1925, Sir James Frazer was given the OM, so Housman enjoyed himself by addressing Frazer as 'My dear

Optime Maxime [best and greatest] my best congratulations to you on your birthday present ... Tell Lady Frazer that I think even she must be enjoying a brief moment of contentment.'[81] Sir Ernest Rutherford, a New Zealander by birth, had also received the OM, on which Housman was able to reflect: 'This is a sad day for poor old England, and will put new and unnecessary pep into the All Blacks ... if a Trinity Prime Minister had failed to do his duty he would have been unpopular in Trinity. Long may you live to enjoy your honour.'[82] Such graceful and good-natured congratulations were vintage Housman.

Yet another of Housman's rigidities was his refusal to countenance the publication of *A Shropshire Lad* and *Last Poems* as a single volume. Thus a report in *The New York Times* that *A Shropshire Lad and Last Poems* were now available in a uniform deluxe edition caused a flurry of letters from Housman to Henry Holt, Grant Richards and the Society of Authors. If the report proved to be true, Housman was determined to take *Last Poems* away from Holt. In the event, it had been a false alarm; what Holt were producing were companion volumes, which caused Housman no problems.

At this stage in his life Housman seems to have been feeling the self-imposed burden of his classical work. He told F.W. Hall, co-editor of the *Classical Quarterly,* 'I am busy finishing off my Lucan and also writing a review, a job which I always regret undertaking, as it absorbs a disproportionate amount of time, because I am so fearfully conscientious.' The review in question was of Pearson's *Sophocles* which Housman praised as 'much the best critical edition of Sophocles now in existence; the most complete and the most judicious'. There was also his final volume of Manilius: 'I ought to turn to at Manilius V, or the unfinished window in Aladdin's tower unfinished will remain.'[83]

Turns down the Clark Lectureship

On 22 February 1925, not long before his sixty-sixth birthday, it became clear that Housman knew his limits and was not afraid to declare them; he turned down Trinity's offer of the Clark Lectureship. The fact that he was asked reveals that the Council of Trinity judged that his celebrity as a poet made him appropriate, that he was recognised in the college for his considerable literary knowledge and that his college wished to honour him. Housman recognised the compliment that was being paid him and the friendliness behind it, but as he put it:

I do regard myself as a connoisseur; I think I can tell good from bad in literature. But literary criticism, referring opinions to principles and setting them forth so as to command assent, is a high and rare accomplishment and quite beyond me. I remember Walter Raleigh's Clark lecture on Landor: it was unpretending, and not adorned or even polished, but I was thinking all the while that I could never have hit the nail on the head like that. And not only have I no talent for producing the genuine article, but no taste or inclination for producing a substitute. If I devoted a whole year (and it would take no less) to the composition of six lectures on literature, the result would be nothing which could give me, I do not say satisfaction, but consolation for the waste of time; and the year would be one of anxiety and depression, the more vexatious because it would be subtracted from those minute and pedantic studies in which I am fitted to excel and which give me pleasure. I am sorry if this explanation is tedious, but I would rather be tedious than seem thankless and churlish.[84]

This is a Housman we do not see frequently, aware of an honour being done to him, truly humble, fully aware of his own limitations, honestly conscious as an excellent lecturer of the sheer toil, sweat and psychological weight of doing something to his own standards. He was, however, demonstrating moral courage; for him the Clark Lectures were not something he was willing to enter into lightly or wantonly.

Calls for his attention continued to come from many points of the compass. In spite of the weight of his workload, he was always apt to respond with grace, good humour and genuine concern to his many and diverse correspondents. There was a graceful testimonial to the Appointments Committee of University College in respect of Lawrence Solomon who had been his assistant there for ten years. 'I was particularly grateful to him for succeeding, where I always failed in making the students write decent Latin prose.'[85] There was contact with Andrew Gow on a textual matter that caused him to add 'No, I am not well, though in my case it is bronchial tubes and not a leg.'[86] Witter Bynner, who had asked him to do an introduction to his poems *Caravans*, received a friendly negative 'writing an introduction is what I would not do for anyone.'[87] Withers was a recipient of his concern: 'I am sorry to hear no better account of your health', adding 'Death and marriage are raging through this College with such fury that I ought

Figure 41 A.S.F. Gow, Fellow of
Trinity College Cambridge and
University Lecturer in Classics. Close
colleague of Housman and author of
A.E. Housman: A Sketch (1936). By
permission of the Master and Fellows
of Trinity College, Cambridge.

to be grateful for having escaped both'[88]; an American writer, Ridgely
Torrence, received a warm response for his *Hesperides*. Housman had
read the volume 'with admiration for its poetic impulse and for the
accomplishment of much of its verse. It has also more substance than
most modern poetry.'[89]

Housman was delighted on 27 June 1925 to hear that Andrew Gow
was being offered a teaching post at Trinity. 'I have always gone about
saying that you ought never to have been allowed to leave Cambridge,
and I am delighted at the chance of getting you back.'[90]

In July 1925 he again showed how generous he was. He answered
Kate's call for support with an immediate 'I can easily spare you
£200 and I enclose a cheque for the amount.'[91] Later in the year he
reassured Kate.

> There is not the least hurry about repaying me the £200. You are
> quite at liberty to look upon me as one of the ancient Gauls, who

were quite willing to lend money on a promise to pay it back in the next world: such was their belief in the immortality of the soul, until Christianity undermined it.'[92]

Not only that, he was also intending to meet the expense of her becoming a life member of the London Library, a thoughtful gesture towards a sister who was always *sérieuse* in pursuit of her own historical and genealogical researches. It was not surprising that on 9 April 1927 he would tell her 'I expect that at the end of your career they will put up a tablet in the Abbey and you will be known to posterity as the learned lady of Bath.'[93]

With Grant Richards things were almost back to normal:

> I have just been stopped in the street by an American lady who was yearning for the last work of your Mr Mais in the window of a shop whose door was locked. She seemed to want me to break the glass for her, but I persuaded her that there were other shops in the town.[94]

The same sort of mock drama with which he invested that situation was duplicated when he wrote to Laurence about his forthcoming visit to France, 'leaving behind me a nearly completed and in great part printed edition of Lucan with Basil Blackwell of Oxford. If the French kill me with one of these lethal railways of theirs, J.D. Duff of this college is to be asked to finish it and see it through the press.' He briefed his brother as if he were his executor and told him how things stood with Richards: 'Grant Richards has not paid me a penny of royalties on *Last Poems*, and has intercepted the first year's royalties from the American publishers. He also owes me £750 which I lent him four or five years ago.'[95] He was forgetting that he had not given Richards any sense that he wanted the money back, quite the reverse; but here it looked as though he was intent on giving him a nasty shock from beyond the grave.

He briefed Duff in a similar vein.

> As I cannot fly to every spot I wish to reach I shall probably perish in a railway accident; in which event you will receive a request from my executors that you would be so good as to finish off my Lucan; and I hope you will not refuse ... nothing remains to be done but the index, which I cannot compile till the book is in

pages. This of course is a nasty job, and when the engine is on the top of me I shall console myself with the thought that I have escaped it.[96]

In Paris on 19 September 1925 he wrote to Laurence who appears to have sent him the Hugh Kingsmill parody, 'What, still alive at twenty-two, /A clean upstanding chap like you.' He approved: 'The parody of me is the best I have seen, and indeed the only good one.'[97] He was now frankly recognising the commercial instincts, so evident in his brother and so absent in himself: 'An American named Keating wrote to me the other day and said he had bought a signed copy of *A Shropshire Lad* for £80. I suppose this is one of your commercial successes.'[98]

Back in Trinity, his young friend, the forty-year old Andrew Gow, was fast becoming a self-appointed adherent, in the first instance preparing a list of Housman's publications which he and two other friends arranged to have printed. Housman responded warmly. 'I am very much taken aback and my feelings are mixed; but however deeply I may deplore the misdirection of so much industry, it is impossible not to be touched and pleased by the proof of so much kindness and friendliness, and I thank you for it.'[99] He wrote likewise to the others involved – A.F. Scholfield, the University Librarian and former Librarian at Trinity, and D.S. Robertson, a classical fellow. This was evidence of the inroads Housman continued to make into the hearts and minds of the fellows of Trinity. In mid-1926 Reginald Gleadowe, formerly Slade Professor of Fine Art at Oxford, was commissioned by Trinity to do Housman's portrait. Nor was he forgotten at the scene of his failure in Greats; St John's College, Oxford, were intent on memorialising the connection between the college and this famous scholar and poet by commissioning Francis Dodd RA to do a portrait drawing of him.

Housman was now back to giving Richards the results of his researches into French provincial cooking, mentioning a good bourgeois restaurant in Pau in the Place du Casino, and the best thing he had come across, *Truite à L'Américaine* (with *écrevisses*). Somebody, he hoped not Richards, had told him that the local dish of Carcassonne was called *Soufassou*, but the locals had denied all knowledge of it and pressed cassoulet on him, which he correctly identified as a *plat* of Toulouse but 'hardly deserving its reputation.'[100] He twice fed on the isard, the chamois of the Pyrenees, and found it 'not very good.' Housman was showing himself to be a consistently adventurous eater.

Percy Withers' health had taken a turn for the worse following a visit to Italy and Housman tried to jolly him along:

> I have a book just coming out, but it is one of my serious works and you will not want to read it; nor will any mad millionaire pay £80 for it as one did the other day for an autographed first edition of *A Shropshire Lad*. My brother who has commercial talents, had bought the last six copies in 1898 and got me to sign them. I hope you will be consoled for the stiff price which, I gathered, you paid for your own copy ... I close this letter in order to go and dress for our domestic Feast, and as I guzzle and guttle I shall wish that you were here and had not taken leave of these agreeable vices.[101]

When he next wrote to Laurence to thank him for his latest book he retailed the latest case of mistaken identity. 'At our last Feast I had the new Dean of Westminster next me, and he said he had been long wanting to thank me for the amusement he derived from my writings, especially about Queen Victoria and her Ministers. So if I bring you money, you bring me fame.'[102]

16 March 1925: Arthur Platt dies

The aches and pains of his older age were overshadowed and put into perspective by the death of one of his best and oldest friends, Arthur Platt, who died on 16 March 1925 at the age of sixty-five. No letter of Housman's mentioning his death has come to light and no letter of condolence to his widow Mildred has survived, but a letter must have been sent.

Housman's first recorded mention of Platt after his death was in January 1926. Reginald St John Parry, Vice-Master of Trinity, was assembling Platt's writings and addresses for publication in *Nine Essays by Arthur Platt*. Housman was able to direct Parry's attention to Platt's time at University College.

> There is at least one address of Platt besides the Prelection, which well deserves to be published ... papers read to the students' Literary Society, some of which I heard, and they were very good

to listen to. How they would look in print I do not feel quite sure: but they were full of good stuff, apart from the fun ... I should not enjoy writing an introduction, but I would do it for his sake, and in the interests of scholarship and literature.[103]

In spite of any inner worries he might have had about doing justice to his subject this was a labour of love – sympathetic, empathetic, and full of observations which reveal as much of Housman as they do of Platt.

Platt like himself had been a lover of literature but there was a caveat. 'He knew better than to conceive himself that rarest of all the great works of God, a literary critic; but such remarks on literature as he did let fall were very different stuff from the usual flummery of the cobbler who is ambitious to go beyond his last.' Housman's closing coda was truthful and from a heart full of understanding of the carnage wreaked by time on memories:

His happy and useful life is over, and now begins the steady encroachment of oblivion, as those who remember him are in their turn summoned away. This record will not preserve, perhaps none could preserve, more than an indistinct and lifeless image of the friend who is lost to us: good, kind, bright, unselfish, and as honest as the day; versatile without shallowness, accomplished without ostentation, a treasury of hidden knowledge which only accident brought to light, but which accident brought to light perpetually, and which astonished us so often that astonishment lost its nature and we should have wondered more if wonders had failed. Yet what most eludes description is not the excellence of his gifts but the singularity of his essential being, his utter unlikeness to any other creature in the world.[104]

Housman had expressed this even more pithily and humorously years before, presumably in his University College days, in lines found among his preserved light verse:

Philology was tame and dull, and flat:
God said 'let there be larks' and there was Platt.[105]

16 March 1926: Housman's Lucan published

In January 1926 Housman's edition of *Lucan* was published, another milestone passed, another smaller companion monument accomplished. Unlike dear Platt, who had neither time nor inclination to create a monument that could last longer than mere memories, Housman was already well on the way to having a field full of monuments. An advance copy of his *Lucan* was to go to his Trinity colleague J.D. Duff; he wanted Duff to have a copy personally inscribed, J.D. Duff from A.E. Housman, a measure of the respect and reliance he placed in the pertinacious Duff.

Death came knocking at the door of Trinity and prompted by a letter from Percy Withers, Housman wrote to him about the sudden and easy death of Professor Lewis, how he had suffered 'false angina pectoris but had got better, and on the morning of the day of his death he wrote a letter and in the afternoon went to bed and was found dead.'[106] When Housman next heard that Percy Withers was laid up, he expressed himself 'much grieved' and advised him to follow the example of his own gondolier 'who had summoned me to his death-bed' and 'was quite revived by the summer weather.'[107] When he eventually received good news about Percy Withers' progress, he wrote that he had burst out into verse three of William Cowper's hymn 'God moves in a mysterious way', further evidence of his growing feeling of closeness to Withers,[108] and incidentally demonstrating that his professed atheism had made zero impact on his wish or capacity to quote hymns, or pepper his correspondence with Biblical allusions.

His little enclosed world of classical scholarship was again sharply illuminated in a letter to S.C. Roberts, secretary of the Cambridge University Press. Housman declined to do a report for the Press on a treatise on Catullus by O.L. Richmond on the grounds he had been instrumental twenty years earlier in getting his previous treatise on the pagination of Catullus' manuscripts turned down; Housman trod a very careful path between being honest about Richmond, yet showing awareness of how damage may be done to a man's reputation by unconsidered words. He went on 'If it is not impertinent I suggest that H.E. Butler might be asked for his opinion. I daresay the Syndics or some of them, know enough about the passions which seethe in the world of classical scholarship to understand that there is one person to whom the work should not be submitted.'[109]

Also illuminating was his handling of a minute scholarly matter. On a rare occasion when he took the initiative, he wrote to the Regius Professor, Alfred Pearson, seeking help: 'Is it good Greek to say...?' The point was the Professor of Papyrology at Oxford had sent Housman some 'new Callimachus from the next Oxyrhyncus volume, and I am making a manful pretence of knowing the language; but you see I require your assistance.'[110] Having got it, his acknowledgement was gracious 'Thanks for your letter. The number of good Greek scholars whom I have deceived into thinking that I know Greek is mounting up, and I add your scalp to Platt's and Headlam's.'[111]

Richards again in crisis

In autumn 1926, twenty-five years after his first bankruptcy, Grant Richards' business affairs were again in deep trouble. Housman wrote to him 'I think I ought to be included among your creditors. It is all very well to say that I shall not lose the £750 if you can help it, but it may easily turn out that you can't help it.'[112] A receiver and manager, Sir Maxwell Hicks, had been appointed and had contacted Housman as a creditor.

Coincidentally, Housman received a statement from Richards going back to 1921 showing that he was due £1,014 11s 8d from sales and royalties. Royalties on *Last Poems* amounted to £982 6s 10d, including £343 2s 5d specifically attributed to American royalties on *Last Poems* and the balance of £32 4s 10d to the minor sales of *Juvenal* and *Manilius*.

Housman asked a Cambridge solicitor, J.E. Few, to act for him, sent him Richards' statement and Few's partner submitted the claim: 'we do not know whether it is the intention to pay any of this money out of funds which may accumulate, but if so, we shall be obliged if you will let us know, as it seems rather a large sum of money for Mr Housman to lose.' To put these figures into perspective, Housman's official University stipend at the time was £1000 per annum. The receiver did not hold out much hope; debenture holders were first in the queue for payment.

At the end of November Richards launched a smoke and mirrors missive to Housman's solicitor, sending a copy direct to Housman. He said in plain terms that Housman was unlikely to receive anything after the debenture holders had been satisfied. Neither here nor hereafter was there any record of who the debenture holders were and what their joint claims amounted to. Richards went on to claim

> I believe I can make such arrangements hereafter as will make him independent in the long run of what he may get out of the present business of Grant Richards Ltd. When Mr Housman entrusted us with the publication of *Last Poems* I took care to safeguard his interests to the extent of arranging that at any moment he could take 'Last Poems' and entrust it to another publisher on payment of the cost price of such copies as were in stock – a small amount anyway.[113]

He went on to recite how the business would be reorganised under effective financial control of certain people who would bring in fresh capital. He offered the possibility of paying off some of the debt immediately in which Housman would take priority over other authors 'so far as I am able to secure priority.'

Richards portrayed Housman as being in a position to stand out for his own terms. But Housman was not in a mood to insist. He did not wish for change. He was not motivated by money and still clung to his friendship with Richards. Indeed, he was fully protected for the future in the sense that he could take his books where he pleased. Getting what he was owed by Grant Richards was another story; he appeared to be happy to write off what he was owed.

Housman had already said in a letter of 21 October 1926,

> I do not want to take the books away from your firm. The *vis inertiae*, no longer regarded as a true cause in the physical world, governs me all the same. I expected something of this sort, because it was hinted by a publisher who wrote to me a few weeks ago asking for *A Shropshire Lad*.[114]

On 4 November he told Richards 'Heinemann write to me saying they are thinking of taking over your assets and asking particularly for *A Shropshire Lad*. Before I answer I should like to have anything you may wish to say on the subject.'[115] He was himself punctilious in keeping Richards in the picture: 'I have been told that the scheme for the carrying on of your business by the creditors has fallen through, and therefore I shall have to close with one of the offers made by publishers for *A Shropshire Lad* and *Last Poems*.'[116]

By the end of November Housman had clearly decided not to pursue Richards for what he was owed. So when he received his copy of the letter Richards had sent to his solicitors, he replied on 30 November 'I don't think it has anything to do with Messrs Few & Wild, or any bearing on my presentation of my claims against the Company, which I made at the request of Sir Maxwell Hicks.'[117]

Housman continued to turn down approaches from other publishers, this time George Allen & Unwin,[118] until on 17 December 1926 he was able to reply to Richards:

> I suppose the new arrangement is satisfactory to you, and if so I am glad of it; and for my own part it is a relief not to have the bother of making new arrangements. But when the arrangements are complete I am going to exact royalties on *A Shropshire Lad* for the future as well as on the other book.[119]

So the worm, adapting to reality, had turned, but only a very little.

Sir Frederick Macmillan was another to turn when he wrote on 22 December 1926 offering to publish Housman's *Lucan* after all:

> I remember thinking at the time that this was possibly a case in which it would be wise to relax our rule, but I expect that what decided us not to do so was a phrase in your letter describing us as 'haughty' – an adjective that seemed then, as it still does singularly inappropriate ... It may be that it is too late, but this letter will at all events convince you that the quality of humility has not been omitted from our composition.[120]

Housman now wrote back 'I am much obliged by your amiable letter. The *Lucan* however was published last January, and is now nearly sold out, which testifies to such efficiency in the publisher as even you could hardly surpass.'[121] Housman was not about to recant.

The New Year of 1927 opened with his reflecting the results of his fame in his usual matter-of-fact way to Kate:

> My edition of *Lucan* of which you have not heard, but which appeared last January, has been selling just twice as quick as *A Shropshire Lad* did; and I am glad that some interest is taken in my serious works. I have suffered during the year from having to sit to two artists who were commissioned to make drawings of

me for my two colleges. Each thinks that the other has done it badly, and indeed I can hardly be like both.[122]

He could not refrain from letting Alice Rothenstein know that William

has lost his monopoly in my features, as I have been drawn this last year by two artists named Dodd and Gleadowe ... neither of them makes me look so nasty as the portrait this college bought from William ... But I have a beautiful and forgiving nature, and I wish him as well as you a happy new year in response to your wishes for me.[123]

By now they must have become used to Housman's hyperbole and their sociable natures deterred them from cutting him off. Perhaps William could see clearly that he need not take Housman too literally or too much to heart.

Richards was intent on mending his fences with Housman, offering him the use of their car. Housman replied that he did not need the car: 'the purpose for which I wanted one is now served by the number of motor omnibuses which take one out into the surrounding country and enable one to start walks at a distance, and for some time past I have ceased to think of a car.'[124]

He was soon on his usual warpath. 'I have just seen an edition of *A Shropshire Lad*, 1925, with a disgusting misprint, souls' for soul's on p 99; how many more I don't know. I have said again and again that new editions must be sent to me for correction.'[125] The same month he wrote a formal and business-like letter to Richards authorising him to reprint *A Shropshire Lad*, it being understood that 'I remain at liberty to take the book away from them at any time on paying the cost of production of existing copies.' He accepted a royalty of fifteen per cent, it being understood 'that this does not limit my freedom of action in the future.'[126]

So he was now explicitly holding a sword over Richards' head and by implication regretting his own previous commercial laissez-faire.

He was still attracting notice from outsiders who wished to hitch their wagons to his fame. When Cyril Clemens, president of the International Mark Twain Society, invited him to become vice-president of the Mark Twain Society, he neither accepted nor declined but added, 'The Elegy on Stephen Dowling Botts in *Huckleberry Finn* is one of the poems I know by heart.'[127] With its concluding lines somewhat reminiscent of Lieutenant-Colonel Mary-Jane, the poem appealed very much to the light nonsense side of Housman.

Dealing with tricksters

Not all Housman's correspondents could be classed as straightforward and he could be naïve in dealing with them. An American named James Leippert had an original way of getting literary men to write autograph letters to him, saying in Housman's case that his father had named him Alfred Housman, which in a manner of speaking was what he told all the poets on whom he worked the same trick. With Housman it worked, and Leippert reaped some written advice on versification. 'If you are going to be a poet, it will come to you naturally and you will pick up all you need from reading poetry.'[128] Another trickster, but of a rather different calibre, was Charles Wilson, 'The Pit Poet', from Willington, County Durham. He wrote to Housman at least ten times in that year, full of ploys to get answers from him. He sent a photograph of Keats' grave; he asked Housman to lecture to his students. He asked Housman to judge student essays about his poems. When he announced his intention to dramatise *A Shropshire Lad*, Housman threatened to prosecute him 'with the utmost rigour of the law'.[129] Housman quickly scotched Wilson's idea that his students would make him a birthday present. When a black pipe arrived, it was returned with a note, 'as I do not smoke it would be absurd for me to keep it'. By then Housman must have realised there could be no end to Mr Wilson. He administered what he thought would be a *coup de grace*: 'Now you must give me a rest; and in fact I am shortly going abroad for some time.'[130] Nothing could dent Mr Wilson's persistence and Housman continued to answer every letter from Wilson till the day he died, powerful evidence that once a correspondence is opened and is given encouragement, a relationship is created between the protagonists which encourages it to continue. Housman found it impossible to call a halt and answered Wilson's letters until he found it a physical impossibility to do so.

Yet when Professor Campbell, fellow and lecturer at St John's, Cambridge, and Professor of Greek at Liverpool University, had drawn to his attention a difference between Francken's edition of *Lucan* and Housman's own, he got a pompous reply: 'When will mankind begin to understand that I am more careful than they are, not less.'[131] Coincidentally, he was applying his carefulness to Platt's volume where he had added notes on cricket terminology and on cricketing characters from the past: 'my true object in adding the notes was to win a smile from Platt's beatified spirit and mitigate the tedium of Paradise.'[132]

He continued to demonstrate his paradoxical combination of total disregard for money-making with a constant thirst for accuracy. When Henry Holt sent him a cheque he commented 'I observe the item 20 dollars for use of poems ... I suppose this is for poems included in an anthology or set to music. I do not make any charge for such use in England, and I do not wish to do so in America.'[133] Most authors would simply have banked the cheque, but for Housman everything had to be right.

Burgundian odyssey with Richards

He had decided on his dates for Paris and on 13 August let Richards know that he would be in Paris at the Royal Monceau Hotel from 19 August 1927. It turned out that Richards, his wife and daughter were to be in Paris at the same time and so he wrote to him from the Royal Monceau: 'Of course I should be pleased to entertain Mrs Richards and Helene too, but would rather see you alone.'[134] And so Richards had gone to his hotel alone, and Housman had revealed the real reason for wanting to see him: to raise the possibility of their going off together to Burgundy; the only problem standing in their way being Richards' wife and daughter. Richards remembers Housman saying 'I'd ask Mrs Richards and Helene to come with us but you know my views about ladies; they are very well but not for a holiday in a car, an architectural, gastronomic, holiday.'[135] So they agreed on a lunch at Foyot's for the four of them, when Housman would broach the subject. The day arrived and aided by the surroundings, a sense of occasion, Chateau Yquem 1900 in a wine bucket for the ladies, Housman at his smoothest finessed the separation of husband from wife and daughter for a fortnight.

Richards would write of their holiday in his *Housman 1897–1936* under the very appropriate chapter heading 'Eating and Drinking our Way to Dijon'. They decided to travel in a car supplied by an English-American firm, Morgan, Booth and Pott, who operated from the rue Caumartin in Paris and who supplied their driver, Louis. Richards embroidered the sixteen pages of his chapter with details of the lunches and dinners they had during what must have been for both of them a quite magical, boys together fortnight. The list of the wines they drank totalled forty-five bottles, about three a day. Included among the many white Chablis and Mersaults were fine reds including Chateauneuf du Pape 1911, Romanée 1904 (the oldest wine they drank on the trip), Corton Clos du Roi 1915, and Clos Vougeot 1915. For Housman it was a wonderful opportunity to enhance his authority as *the* wine buff of The Family. A fortnight in Burgundy would enable him to fine-tune his appreciation of its wine, from the sublime of fine red burgundy to the very good, the rather everyday, and occasionally, the 'cor blimey' of unremarkable stuff masquerading, then as now, as Chablis.

It was also an opportunity to establish bench marks for Burgundian cooking at its best which they agreed was found in Dijon, chez Racouchot (Les trois Faisans) where they dined on caviar with chopped shallot, *consommé de volaille* and *coq au* Chambertin, accompanied by Clos du Roi 1915; and chez Bony (Le Chateaubriant) where 'Housman admonished me, if I ever wrote of the place, not to forget the excellence of the escargots, which had been sought for, a little before their proper season, specially for us; the onion soup – especially the onion soup – and a fish stew, *pauchouse*, into which as many ingredients entered as into *bouillabaisse*, carp, eel, tench, and pike being among them.' With that dinner they had 1915 Clos Vougeot again.

The trip revealed that Housman was always in charge, astonishing Richards at Auxerre by ordering two rooms with two bathrooms, 'a foretaste of the milord manner in which A.E.H. journeyed.' Housman established their habit of ordering a bottle of red and a bottle of white for lunch and generally only one bottle of red for dinner. And it was Housman who, turning up at the Hotel de la Poste in Beaune in his usual dark suit and small cloth cricket cap, being unwelcomed by a rather indifferent waitress, and having been presented with a poor choice of food and offered wine red or white, quietly consulted the wine list and ordered two bottles from its expensive end. This soon had the mâitre d'hôtel, the sommelier and the patron rushing around, producing a more imposing menu to match Housman's choice of wine, 1919 Mersault and Montrachet. In the end, they were served *écrevisses a la crème, pâté de foie gras maison* and *truffes-en-serviette*.

All this was in remarkable contrast to their meeting with Monsieur and Madame Perrier in the Jura whence they went from Burgundy.

Monsieur Buffa (the manager of the firm which had provided their car) had given them an introduction to Monsieur Perrier, a small watchmaker and jeweller, who would be able to help them in their enquiries about Arbois wine which they had drunk in Paris and were keen to try in its native region. Monsieur Perrier offered to take them on a tour around the region in his own little car and Mme Perrier would arrange dinner in the evening. Richards records of Housman: 'Visibly, he was pleased at the invitation. He did not wait for me to speak but accepted for us both ... Housman not only smiled his assent but he made it clear that the whole programme gave him pleasure.' Richards was very, very surprised by Housman's behaviour, which accounted for his exclamatory reaction 'Housman, the shy, the reserved Housman!' Their return trip to Arbois with Monsieur Perrier involved introductions to vineyard owners, restaurateurs, wine merchants and much tasting of Arbois, 'but for some reason or other we did not appreciate it as highly as we were expected to do.' However they spent a wonderful evening in the Perrier's little living room behind the shop.

> Madame did everything, ladled out the soup, which she had made with her own hands, and cleared away, and gave us dishes, also her own work, which were so admirable and so clean tasting that we almost forgot all the other food we had eaten on our journey. And Monsieur attended to the bottles ... a little forest of them ... they were of rare vintage and of rare quality ... We laughed and we talked and we ate and drank, and Alfred Perrier told us of his business and of his youth and teased his wife; and she told us how to her husband his cellar was more than a child; and I who have little French with which to talk sat silent and listened to my now interested and quite voluble friend. We did not stop very late in that little back room, but that was not because we had eaten and drunk too much. We had eaten and drunk enough! And then we walked back to our hotel in the light of the crescent moon, jolly and a little unsteady. We were neither of us any the worse for it in the morning. Thereafter we talked much of the Perriers, Monsieur and Madame, and thought that one day we would visit them again. I still hope to do so. Monsieur Perrier promised to visit Cambridge and London and to call on both of us.

Although Housman never mentioned the Perriers again in subsequent letters, Richards' description of their lovely evening and their delightful encounter makes it clear that what Richards said of Housman's reasons for accepting their invitation was so true: 'These he told me were people very much after his own heart.'

Richards had some misgivings about what he said about Housman in this chapter.

> Is one shocked that I have so frankly shown A.E.H. taking pleasure in, and spending much time on, what he ate and drank? Well he did so. His passion in life was, I should say, accuracy in Latin and in Greek, and he also had pleasure in architecture, but he liked his meals. Do not mistake me. He did not eat a great deal. When he was at table he was of the Edwardian school rather than that of Victoria or the Georges. Nor did he, save on the rarest occasions, drink too much. *He enjoyed.* That is the truth: he enjoyed, appreciated, was happy with good food and fine wine. Perhaps a further truth is that, having as Mrs Symons his sister, has said, gone so far to suppress other senses, he did strongly retain pleasure in his senses of taste and smell. Whatever else he denied himself, he saw no reason to deny the pleasure of eating and drinking. His spare, wiry frame was good evidence that he did not indulge to excess.

And perhaps there was another component which Richards himself experienced many times with Housman, the pleasure of companionship, inseparable from the pleasures of the table.

When Housman wrote to him later in October to thank him for his list 'of our wines in Burgundy and also for the reminiscences appended', he had a few points to make of his own:

> Your memory is better than mine in most respects; but I think that at Feurs what we had was two bottles of white wine (the first probably Pouilly-Fuissé and then half a bottle of Moulin-a-vent). The ballotine de pigeonneau at Chablis, as I remember it, was slices of cold paté. Do not forget the onion-cheese soup at the Châteaubriant.[136]

He also wrote to Kate, aware that his letter from Paris had been 'nothing but an egotistical note to inform you of my doings and intentions'; now he was putting matters right with domestic chit-chat about her sons and new people living near the Wises at Woodchester, and telling her of his upgraded experience of flying:

> I flew home by the new 'Silver Wing' aircraft, which is more roomy and steadier, and contains an attendant to supply you with cheese and biscuits and various liquors and to point out objects of interest on the route: also an emergency door in the roof which ought to be very tranquilising. But I did not enjoy it, as I had got ptomaine poisoning in Paris from stale fish, for the third time in my experience, and I am still rather out of sorts.[137]

The appeal of Housman's poetry had spread well beyond America; in August 1916 the Japanese journal *Eigo Seinen*, the Rising Generation, had featured an article on Housman by Professor Tokiboku Hirata, 'one of the pioneers in the studies of English Literature in Japan'. Besides being an admirer of Housman's poetry he had translated into Japanese many English novels including Thackeray's *Vanity Fair*, Dickens' *David Copperfield*, Wilde's *The Picture of Dorian Gray* and Hardy's *Tess of the D'Urbervilles*. Hirata had no difficulty in distinguishing differences in tone between Housman's poetry 'exceedingly quiet and introspective' and what he called the soldier poems by Kipling and the sailor poems by Newbolt. Now, a decade later in 1926, another Japanese, Dr Hojin Yano, published a first article on Housman, and travelled to England to pursue his literary studies. An introduction to Sydney Cockerell led to a somewhat casually arranged meeting with Housman who had responded to Cockerell's note that Yano would like to meet him with a jocular, chauvinistic reply typical of the Englishman of the time: 'I am generally in my rooms between 6 and 7 of an evening, if the son of Nippon likes to take his chance. At any rate he is not an American.'[138]

His Japanese visitor recorded that after a hesitant beginning, a very shy and nervous Housman began to impress with his 'brief manner of speaking and his definite answers without any hesitation'.[139] One surmises that they covered a lot of ground, not because Housman volunteered a lot, but because Dr Yano's enquiries are likely to have been typically Japanese in their ordering and thoroughness, qualities which would have stimulated Housman's willingness to collaborate. As far as the moderns were concerned, Yano noted that Housman didn't care much for the poems or the critical thought of T.S. Eliot, whose Clark Lecture on metaphysical poetry had 'praised Donne highly and seemed to pay no attention to other poets'. Housman had even felt encouraged to say something about his effect on younger poets: 'It does not seem to me that my poetry has effectively worked on younger poets, though I suppose that Drinkwater may have imitated both the metre and the subject matter in my poetry.'

Housman's enthusiasms had communicated themselves; Yano noted his 'extravagant' admiration for Constantinople and Venice, and his very high opinion of Matthew Arnold. That they met again three weeks later underlined not only Yano's pertinacity but also Housman's amiability and above all their compatibility in conversational style. They even got on to the subject of food because Yano discovered that *Barbue á la Housman* was served at the Tour d'Argent in Paris. Yano's reporting of this showed he had detected amusement in Housman's eye when he had expressed the hope that the restaurant would become a place of pilgrimage for scholars of English literature in Paris. This warm and revealing encounter between the reticent Housman, who had unbuttoned and relaxed under the thoughtful probing of the Japanese, shows the same Housman who enjoyed his encounter with the Perriers.

Next it was Sir James Frazer's turn to exhibit what Housman evidently read as British chauvinism. Asking Housman about usage of a word he had come across in a manuscript of Ovid, Frazer referred to the German scholar Wilamowitz as a 'sophist with an infallible instinct for getting hold of a stick at the wrong end'. Housman came to his defence:

> Where I come across him, in verbal scholarship and textual criticism, he is a very great man, the greatest now living, and comparable with the greatest of the dead .... last year one of my old pupils went to see him and Wilamowitz said: 'Although we Germans know that Housman is a rabid Germanophobe, we are unanimous in regarding him as the greatest authority both on Greek and Latin among the English-speaking peoples.' Unfortunately he was almost as wrong about my Greek at any rate as he is about my Germanophobia; but it is an amiable error.[140]

Housman had heard that Walter Ashburner was coming to Cambridge and invited him to dinner in Hall. The words he used, 'I hear with emotions which I will not attempt to describe because you can easily imagine them that you are coming to Cambridge,'[141] may have been indicative of something or nothing, a rather over-the-top greeting to a good friend or words carrying a personal and hidden meaning.

He was still steadfastly trying to control, where he was able, publication of his poems: 'I think that there are already far too many anthologies in the world, and I receive requests like yours once a month. I hope you will not be much vexed by this refusal.'[142] He was like a mother fearfully protecting her children.

In early December he acknowledged a package from Grant Richards' secretary Miss Hemmerde: 'The registered parcel has arrived with contents as described.'[143] In his *Housman 1897–1936* Richards explained that

> Housman had shown some liking for the work of Frederick Rolfe (Baron Corvo), and having in my hands for a little while in the autumn of 1927 a novel of his in typescript – a novel which at the time seemed to have little chance of publication for the excellent reason that it was full of potential libels – I offered to lend it to him.[144]

Within a week Housman had read the typescript and a couple of months later wrote 'When he depicts Italians or describes Venice it is delightful; the talk about himself I skip; the quarrels with other people show them in a better light than him.' Also in the package was A.J.A. Symons' biography *Frederick Baron Corvo* and another book *Dialogus* which was not described other than by Housman's comment: 'It is in decent Latin and the matter is mildly interesting, though it leaves me calm. I don't know if it is Corvo's; my passions would probably be more inflamed by his letters, which are what I thought you were going to send me.'[145] On this Richards notes that 'the letters' were 'A whole collection of autograph letters from Corvo to a friend in England, fantastic, extraordinary letters … offering the more than doubtful "delights" of Venice to a friend in England.' Or as Burnett puts it in his footnote, 'dealing in explicit terms with the Venetian homosexual underworld.'[146]

In January of the next year Housman returned to the subject. 'You did enclose two notes from Symons, which I have not kept, though the handwriting was very magnificent.'[147] On 29 March Richards sent Housman the promised typescript of the Corvo letters and at the time wrote 'I suppose I ought not to post it to you, but if by some mischance

I am prosecuted, I shall maintain that its literary interest to citizens connected with literature places me in a privileged position.'[148] Housman acknowledged receipt in a suitably discreet way, but on 24 April when he said he was about to return Corvo's letters, commented rather tartly, 'That sort of thing is not really improved by literary elegancies, and I have been more amused with things written in urinals.'[149] This strengthens one's view that pornography *qua* pornography might only have interested Housman as data and information but to make a real impression on him it had to be funny or witty.

The final days of 1927 brought the usual crop of family letters. He told Kate 'do not worry about the £200, especially as my income for this year has been accidentally increased by more than that through the payment of arrears of royalties; of which the tax-collector has taken ferocious advantage.' He gave her an account of his health:

> I am well, though Christmas makes me eat and drink too much and the snow does not allow me to walk it off but I am busy on several interesting jobs at once, which probably help to keep my liver in order. I was prepared for this winter, as I had just put a new and very efficient gas-stove, Sunbeam by name, in my bedroom, in place of an old and weak and wasteful one.

There was wider family detail to be passed on, detail about Jerry and his job, Jeannie and her two successive colds, and Laurence's new book.[150] In all of this Housman was the epitome of the ordinary man, the man on the Clapham omnibus. Except that in his letter to Basil there was a characteristically mock-heroic element.

> I have had a terrible shock from a telegram to-day from a London fishmonger. All the native oysters have been torn from their beds by tempest, and I shall have to eat the New Year in on Dutch. For me it therefore opens gloomily, but I hope that you and Jeannie will not find it saddened by any such calamity.

Basil was also told about his tour of Burgundy with Grant Richards and his new stove. Another piece of grotesquerie for Basil's delectation came in the shape of Clarence Darrow, the great American barrister noted for defending murderers. 'He had only a few days in England, but could not return home without seeing me because he had so often used my poems to rescue his clients from the electric chair. Loeb and

Leopold owe their life sentence partly to me; and he gave me a copy of his speech, in which, sure enough, two of my pieces are misquoted.' Housman's perennial generosity was once more in evidence: 'Don't trouble to acknowledge what my banker sends to yours at the New Year – unless he doesn't, as the Irishman would say.'[151]

1927 ended on a lovely note with a flattering compliment to Bridges, Housman placing him on a par with Lucretius: 'I am glad that the philosophical poem progresses: at present I am occupied with your rival Lucretius, on whom I am to lecture next term.' Bridges had referred to Arthur Platt, now identified by Housman as 'The man to whose essays I wrote a preface... my Greek colleague at University College, a dear and wonderful creature.'[152]

In the early weeks of 1928, he told Richards he was very glad to be a dedicatee of his next book *The Coast of Pleasure*. This had brought on memories of their wartime trip to the Riviera. 'But it was not only the fresh trout but the fresh truffles of the Gorges du Loup which dwell in my memory.' And another mention by Richards sharpened his taste buds further: 'the menu of Sorret is very appetising.'[153] Housman had become a gourmet; food and wine had joined his passions for travel and sightseeing by motor or aeroplane. Not surprisingly, a few months later he was writing to Richards: 'I expect to be in Paris, or perhaps at St Germain, for the fortnight June 5–19. Any chance of seeing you there?'[154]

Thomas Hardy's funeral

On 16 January 1928 he was among the great and good as a pall-bearer at Thomas Hardy's funeral in Westminster Abbey. Richards quoted the *Manchester Guardian* account: 'In stillness the clergy and the mourners took their places. One saw splendid copes of purple, cloth of gold and crimson flowing up into the sanctuary. Then the coffin was laid on the bier, and one saw the ten famous pall bearers holding the fringes of the pall.'[155]

The death of others tended to bring out the best in Housman which showed when he had to condole with Lady Gosse on the death of her husband, which he did with dignity, simplicity and avoidance of sententious abstractions: 'I met your husband last January at Hardy's funeral, when he seemed as young as ever. In common with all the friends who will miss his delightful conversation and companionship, I know and feel what the sorrow of your bereavement must be.'[156]

It must have struck him forcibly how fortunate he was that writing poetry was his secondary occupation, that he was not dependent on the vagaries of journalism for a living and that the main pillar of his economic well-being was classical scholarship where his publications could be self-financed and their modest sales buoyed by his poetic celebrity. Nor was he given to excesses of conspicuous consumption, always living within his means which were sufficient for a bachelor to be generous when the spirit moved him. Here he was collaborating with Sydney Cockerell on a letter to the Committee of the Royal Literary Fund, supporting an application by Edmund Blunden for a grant. Housman wrote a characteristically restrained but credible letter and the happy upshot was that Blunden was awarded £500 in February 1928. The sweet Housman is seen in his reply to Blunden's letter of thanks. 'I am very glad if I have been of service to you, for "Evening has brought the glow-worm to the green, And early stars to heaven, and joy to men" are two of the more enviable lines I have come across for a long time.'[157]

The issue of Richards' new business surfaced yet again and Housman wrote:

> As to *Last Poems* and your new business, I am not so confident as you seem to be about the latter. When I last heard, the arrangements were due to take place in November, and here is January. I don't know who your capitalists are, but I do know that if I were a capitalist I should not set you up as a publisher but engage you as a courier, salary unlimited. Not hearing from you before the end of the year I had drafted a letter to Richards Press about *Last Poems*; and it would have gone if your letter had not just now arrived. They have behaved quite properly to me as far as I have observed, and I will not do anything uncivil to them.[158]

His deftly expressed assessment of Richards' abilities was right on the mark.

There was also the gem of his heavily ironic letter to William Rothenstein who had the bright idea of painting the ten pall-bearers at Thomas Hardy's funeral: the Prime Minister Stanley Baldwin, Ramsay MacDonald, Sir James Barrie, John Galsworthy, Edmund Gosse, Rudyard Kipling, A.B. Ramsay (Master of Magdalene College), George Bernard Shaw, E.M. Walker (Pro-Provost of Queen's College, Oxford) and Housman.

> If you get the consent of all the nine others, I will not stick out. But you are much too great an artist to catch a likeness. Of course I do not know what I look like myself, but my acquaintances do not recognize me, so much are my traits ennobled by your pencil. Also I am much exhausted by having sat for two drawings for my two colleges in the last year, mutually much disapproved by the two artists. Also the languor of extreme senility makes me more averse to locomotion. Also a journalist present in the Abbey says that my person proved as polished as my verse, after which I desire forever to be invisible.

Nevertheless he looked forward to seeing William in Cambridge in March and mentioned having met his son, a guest at the Trinity High Table.'[159]

Enquiring about how many copies of *Last Poems* had been printed and how many were in stock he was told 21,000 had been sold and 1,647 remained. So in six years his poems had sold at a rate of more than 3,225 a year, a very respectable sales record indeed. He would also learn later in the year that the last copy of his *Manilius I* had been sold. Richards Press was doing very well out of him. Although the friendship between Richards and Housman was real, founded on mutual interests and a definite compatibility, it was also a friendship with a distinct utility element for both parties. Housman seemed to be trying hard to keep separate their friendship and their business relationship, adopting a method of reporting to Richards what he had said to the Richards Press: 'But I have not unsettled their minds by foreshadowing transfer, and I am not inclined to do so till your prospects are clearer. They send me royalties and accounts fairly regularly.'[160] Housman was also keeping tabs on things.

As we have seen he was generally amiable and complaisant, but he was very sharp indeed with William Leonard, Assistant Professor of English at the University of Wisconsin.

> The packet containing (I suppose) the book has arrived, but I have handed it back unopened to the Post Office for return to you. I told you that I would not copy the poem; the request is one which I myself should not make, and I am not inclined to accede to it when it is made to me. I suppose you thought that the magnificence of the binding would melt my heart; but you see I have eluded that snare.[161]

Margot, Lady Howard de Walden, received a similar rejection but without the sharp edge: 'I am flattered by your request, but I do not read poetry in public nor even in private.'[162] The editor of *The Spectator*, Evelyn Wrench, obviously wanting something from Housman, prose or poem, also received a dusty reply: 'but to make me write you must use intimidation as well as bribery.'[163]

Rothenstein had returned to the fray on his projected pall-bearers picture, but Housman was still intent on outflanking him. 'I have some slight reason to think that you will not capture all your 10, and I feel you mean to use me as a decoy: "the churlish recluse A.E. Housman has consented, how can you or anyone refuse?"'[164] Humorous exaggeration was a means of self-defence. This was apparent in what he wrote to Sir James Barrie: 'I hear that you are coy to Rothenstein. I also do not want to sit (the more so because I have suffered enough from his pencil for one lifetime), and if you will stand firm, so will I. The Master of Magdalene likewise is reluctant, but is consulting his Oxford colleague.' He added 'Though Rothenstein cannot draw a likeness, he has a pretty wit, and told Shaw that the secret of his health at his age must be that he has been able to extract ultra-violet rays from lime-light.' [165] In the end, Rothenstein had to tell Housman that Barrie had refused and quick as a flash Housman leapt at the opportunity to say 'I now shall also refuse, as I warned you. I am also grateful for your mot about Shaw.'[166]

On 28 February 1928 he was writing to the Richards Press from The Evelyn Nursing Home in Cambridge. His letter said nothing about why he was there and for how long, but merely communicated 'I do not intend to reprint either the Juvenal or the Manilius.'[167]

Within a week he was back in Trinity where he received from T.S. Eliot a copy of Wilkie Collins' *The Moonstone*, which Eliot had edited. Housman was a great reader of detective stories and his reply displayed deep knowledge of the works of this writer, thought of today as the first writer of detective stories.

The Woman in White the best, chiefly on account of the two characters you mention; and I put *No Name* very high, for the art with which trivial incidents are made to cause intense and painful excitement. I am glad you have a good word for *Poor Miss Finch*. *Armadale* I never took to; he cannot manage the supernatural; and I was not young enough when I read it.[168]

His knowledge probably surprised Eliot, but there was no follow-up on either side.

It was one of Housman's likeable characteristics that unless individuals were asking him to do something he did not want to do, he was always tolerant. A Mr Finkelstein sent him two poems which were sufficiently pleasing to prompt Housman to write 'I think myself that *A Shropshire Lad* is better on the whole than *Last Poems* but Mrs Wharton and Mr Masefield are of the contrary opinion.'[169] Percy Withers had obviously complained at not receiving a Christmas letter. Housman, possibly a mite irritated about being thus traduced, promptly placed the responsibility on Withers himself.

> If you wanted a letter at Christmas you did not go about the right way to get it, for you told me that my letter in autumn was the only one I had ever written to you except in answer to one of your own; and this so filled me with the consciousness of virtue that I have been resting in contemplation of my merit ever since.

This obviously insincere and bluffing reply showed that Housman was not to be nagged about his letter writing, but neither did such a minor crossing of swords inhibit him from choosing dates for a visit to the Withers, or from indulging in their shared interest in weather recording, although Housman's sword was still at least half out of its scabbard:

> This is not a late spring. Till the cold set in after Easter it was quite an early one; but there have been so many early springs in the last 15 years that people have forgotten the proper times for leaves and flowers to come out. For twenty years or so from 1887 onward I have noted these things in a diary, on the strength of which I inform you that the lilac usually comes into bloom on May 7; and it is opening now by Magdalene Bridge, though I admit that it is always early there.[170]

By contrast, he was dealing with letters from America on more weighty matters. It would seem that Seymour Adelman had heard from somewhere a definition of poetry ascribed to Housman, who replied on 6 May 1928:

The words of mine which have reached your ears may be something like this. I can no more define poetry than a terrier can define a rat; but he knows a rat when he comes across one, and I recognise poetry by definite physical sensations, either down the spine, or at the back of the throat, or in the pit of the stomach.[171]

When another American, Harold Allison De Rue of Princeton University, wrote to him in the same month, not about his definition of poetry but about his production of it, he received a precise answer borne out by the facts of Housman's life: 'Lack of poetical inspiration is, and always has been my normal condition in normal health. I have very seldom felt any impulse to write poetry, and it has never lasted long except in 1895, when I had a relaxed sore throat.'[172]

Refuses an honorary doctorate from his alma mater

When the registrar to the University of Oxford wrote to say that the university was proposing to confer on him the degree of Doctor of Letters, Housman's draft reply indicated a careful searching for words and phrases with which to decline this honour. He was expecting his university to accept his bafflingly opaque excuse 'in pursuance of a resolution taken long ago, and for reasons it would be tedious to enumerate, and perhaps not quite easy to formulate'. He expected Oxford to accept his custom of declining honours from other universities, as applicable also to his alma mater: 'I only ask that neither ingratitude nor lack of appreciation may be inferred from my action, as they are indeed far from my mind.'[173]

Housman knew that failure at Oxford had been his own fault but it was still possible that in some obscure way he harboured resentment for the humiliation he had suffered there more than fifty years previously.

Encore Paris

Come June, Housman was staying at the Pavillon Henri IV at St Germain-en-Laye at the western edge of the city. This hotel was well outside Richards' price range and according to him, 'One of the most expensive hotels in France.'[174] Housman wrote to Richards with his usual open-handed generosity. 'If it were convenient for you to stay at St Germain as my guest I should be delighted; and Louis [the driver they had employed on their Burgundy trip] should be able to take you in and out of Paris, unless your business interviews there were too numerous or inconveniently fixed.'[175] In the event Richards stopped not two nights but four which produced a reprise of their time in Burgundy.

> It was on the evening of my arrival that, dining at the Pavillon Henri Quatre, which, by the way, was an old haunt of Housman's, and finding that we were to drink red Burgundy with a lobster dish, I asked him if he paid no attention at all to the convention which I thought forbade, in almost all circumstances, the drinking of red wine with fish. 'That doesn't, as far as I am concerned, apply to Burgundy', he answered; 'Burgundy is strong enough to stand up to anything.'

There was a trip out to Chartres where Housman was disappointed with lunching in the shadow of the Cathedral; another not totally successful choice was a dinner in Montmartre at a place recommended by some Cambridge don, and on this occasion 'Housman went off after dinner to keep some engagement and I returned to St Germain.'[176] Housman had previously warned Richards, 'I should like as much notice as possible, to arrange about having evenings free.'[177] But Housman never gave the merest hint of what else might be occupying his evenings. He gave no names of people, academic institutions, nor any indication of entertainments, high or low. Richards recorded that on the following day they walked in the forest, lunched at Maisons-Lafitte and

> went on to a more distant forest. In such ways my host knew not fatigue; each day had to be full. We dined at our hotel. And on the next, my last day, we drove, the choice being left to me, to Vernon and on to Les Andelys where, because of the excellence of its paté, we lunched at the Chaine d'Or. But alas! As it was a Monday there had not been time to replace the patés that the week-end visitors had finished off, and we did not do so very well ... During all the four days Louis and the car were at my disposal. Housman was always that kind of host.[178]

Once back in Cambridge, another letter from Seymour Adelman was the first Housman answered. Adelman was writing to Housman about Oscar Wilde. Housman replied: 'A Shropshire Lad was published while Mr Wilde was in prison, and when he came out I sent him a copy myself.' We know that Wilde wrote to Laurence Housman in 1897: 'I have lately been reading your brother's lovely lyrical poems, so you see you have both of you given me that rare thing happiness.' Housman seems to have been asked by Adelman for his opinion of Wilde's *The Ballad of Reading Gaol*; he got a straight reply: 'Parts of *The Ballad of Reading Goal* are above Wilde's average, but I suspect they were written by Lord Alfred Douglas.'[179] No signs there of hero worship for Wilde.

Crosscurrents in Housman's dealings with Richards were again being felt, exacerbated by Geoffrey Keynes' discovery of a misprint in the 1927 edition of *A Shropshire Lad*, and by Housman's subsequent discovery of more errors in the 1926 and 1927 editions. Housman's mood was black and probably caused an unfortunate phrase in a letter he wrote to Richards. 'You will be amused to hear that careful Louis knocked down a small girl.'[180] Richards himself was in the firing line. 'At the present moment my feelings towards you are much embittered by the discovery that your last small edition of *A Shropshire Lad* contains 15 errors, some of them filthy.'[181]

The bigger question of who was to publish his books in future was once again in the air. Housman told the Richards Press that he had received approaches from other firms:

> indeed more than one, who want me to transfer my books to them … I am offered certain monetary inducements, and prospects of pushing the sales of the books are held out, these do not weigh with me, and I should not do anything I thought likely to injure you or your feelings. Still the present bother about correcting and reprinting, which has been brought on you by no fault of your own must be rather unwelcome to you.[182]

A week later he had also concluded, in answer no doubt to specific questions, 'I have no wish to transfer my books elsewhere, nor do I desire an increase in royalty; a poet, says Horace, is seldom avaricious. We will therefore go on as heretofore.'[183]

What had Richards been up to? He had evidently written a long letter to Housman which caused him to reply 'If I did not know how easily composition comes to you, I should be sorry to have caused you to write so much. It has interested me to read it, but the utmost I can say is that if the Richards Press change their title to Grant Richards

Limited I shall regard this as a shabby act and take the books away.'[184] What this was all about is now unknowable but the fact was that for more than a year there were few letters to Richards personally and it was only in September of the following year, 1929, that France and food ended a period of coolness between them. But it may well have been that during that period Housman had been giving priority to his work on *Manilius V*. It is easy to forget the frustrations and challenges which that could provide, with many moments of depression as well as elation. And it is easy to see also where his concise letters came from; they were a necessity imposed on him. Keeping in contact with others, answering letters from others, had to be compatible with conservation of time and energy for his work and keeping interruption to a minimum.

So when S.C. Roberts of the University Press sought advice yet again, this time on a projected new edition of Catullus by John Carter, Roberts did not receive a two page essay but an opinion reduced to essentials with a concise bottom line: 'And I get the impression that he wants to cater for dilettanti, which, as a pedant, I cannot approve. But many people do not approve of pedants, and we must live and let live.'[185]

In October 1928 another would-be anthologist, A.J.A. Symons, bibliophile and biographer, received short shrift. Housman, aware that Symons, a dandy and bon viveur, was founder with Andre Simon of the Wine and Food Society, carefully angled his suggestions as to how Richards' should reply.

> He may be consoled, and also amused, if you tell him that to include me in an anthology of the Nineties would be just as technically correct, and just as essentially inappropriate, as to include Lot in a book of Sodomites; in saying which I am not saying a word against sodomy, nor implying that intoxication and incest are in any way preferable.[186]

Housman added a note, 'If Mr Symons ever feels sad, he ought to be able to cheer himself up by contemplating his handwriting.'

He thanked Richards shortly for *A Handbook on Hanging*: 'The writer seems to be rather a buffoon', on which Richards remarked 'Unlike the rest of the world who had read it, A.E.H. did not like it.'[187] The book is still in print, updated but essentially unchanged from its first edition. It cannot have been welcome or pleasant reading for a man with a deep horror of execution by hanging. Housman chose the word buffoon to describe the author of this macabre, albeit ironic work; Housman was not responsive to irony on this subject. He wrote of the act of hanging and its horrid process in his poem, *Eight O'Clock*

> HE stood, and heard the steeple
>   Sprinkle the quarters on the morning town.
> One, two, three, four, to market place and people
>   It tossed them down.
> Strapped, noosed, nighing his hour,
>   He stood and counted them and cursed his luck;
> And then the clock collected in the tower
>   Its strength, and struck.

H.W. Garrod, formerly Professor of Poetry at Oxford, sought permission to quote from Housman in his *The Profession of Poetry and Other Lectures (1929)*. Housman wrote: 'I do not think that one ought to interfere with critics' quotations, unless they are immoderate, and I shall certainly not exercise any right I may possess to prevent you from printing entire the four poems you mention.'[188] Garrod seems not to have given Housman any indication of the context for the quotations in the book he would publish in the next year. Ever incurious, Housman did not ask him.

Kate inherits

Kate had at last benefited from their Brettell connection. In 1928 she inherited the estate of 'Uncle Joe', the Rev. Joseph Brettell Housman, following the death of his widow. This brought her a large house in Exeter and £14,000, making her a very rich lady. Kate quickly sent Housman a cheque for the £200 she owed him, which he acknowledged in his best Olympian manner: 'I do not remember that you gave me an I.O.U., and if you did I am not likely to have kept it. I am glad you have come to comparative opulence and that you like your last new mansion.'[189] Kate was very interested in their family's history, unlike Housman, who from time to time made comments on various family characters, be they Brettells, Holdens or Housmans, but never himself showed the slightest wish to dig deeply into the family history. In fact, his last letter to Moses Jackson indicated that he probably knew more about some of his less orthodox forebears than he was prepared to let on. The inheritance had made Kate financially secure and more than equal to her surviving brothers and sister; she had now got what she had long believed to be her due. Her personal standing was now fully secured and she no doubt relished the thought that she would have money for *her* children to inherit.

PART XII

Last Things

When Housman wrote to Robert Bridges on 28 December 1928, the feast of the Holy Innocents as he called it, he informed him 'I am myself engaged on one of my serious works, the fifth and last volume of Manilius. It ought to be out in a year's time, and then I shall have done what I came on earth to do, and can devote the rest of my days to religious meditation.'[1] Some chance, you might say.

On the same day, he had rapidly to come down to earth to deal with Percy Withers who, judging from Housman's reply, was feeling left out. Housman deftly turned the tables on him: 'Christmas generally brings me a certain amount of abuse for being a bad letter writer, but nobody else makes such a moan as you do; so I suppose your feelings towards me are especially tender.'[2] Having smoothed ruffled feathers, Housman told him about his stay at the 'luxurious Pavillon Henri Quatre', his motor tours around Paris, his summer stays in south-west England, the many fine abbeys and churches he saw there, and their architectural detail.

A couple of days later he exhibited the caring side of his character. A.C Pearson was about to retire as Regius Professor of Greek. Housman, an elector for his replacement, was thinking about Pearson's feelings and wanted to help smooth his transition into retirement:

> I cannot let the year run out without wishing you a happy one to follow, and hoping that your sense of well-being will be as much increased by relief from duties as mine would be. I am glad that Cambridge has seen you, though for a few years, in the chair of Porson and Dobree. I hope that you approve of the successor we have given you: I suppose he is what would be called a safe choice.[3]

The Richards Press had been trying to lure him into limited editions of his poetry with a promise of financial gain. Housman reacted with a deep visceral rejection of money grubbing: 'I have a dislike to limited editions. I know there is money in them, but I cannot stoop.'[4] Possibilities for limited editions were being offered from other directions; he refused to be a party to an edition of signed copies proposed by the Windsor Press of San Francisco. Surprisingly, he gave in to the Alcuin Press of Chipping Camden, but even so, this had to be on the understanding that their limited editions of *A Shropshire Lad* and *Last Poems* bore the imprint 'Printed at the Alcuin Press and published for the Press by The Richards Press Ltd.' He was anxious not to ruffle feathers: 'They have no rights over the books, and it would be feelings and nothing more, but still I do not like injuring even feelings.'[5]

Housman refuses the Order of Merit

This concern for feelings did not extend to those who wanted to confer honours on him. On 23 February Housman refused King George V's offer of the Order of Merit, 'In recognition of your valuable work as a Classical scholar and in the ranks of literature.' His refusal was clear but his rationale dauntingly opaque. He wrote to Lord Stamfordham who had conveyed the King's offer:

> With all gratitude for His Majesty's most kind and flattering wish to confer upon me the Order of Merit I humbly beg permission to decline this high honour. I hope to escape the reproach of thanklessness or churlish behaviour by borrowing the words in which an equally loyal subject, Admiral Cornwallis, declined a similar mark of the Royal favour: 'I am, unhappily, of a turn of mind that would make my receiving that honour the most unpleasant thing imaginable.'[6]

He was being tricky, quoting the precedent of Admiral Cornwallis whose motivation a hundred and thirty years earlier for refusing the Order of the Bath from George III would be totally obscure to anyone not deeply steeped in the naval history of the Napoleonic wars. On this occasion Housman seemed to have run out of tact.

A remarkable story in connection with his rejection of the OM was recounted by Grant Richards in his *Housman 1897–1936*.

Richards said that Housman had told him he had spent an hour or two of that day writing a suitable refusal of the OM because it was to be offered when a vacancy occurred. Now in April 1930, when they were walking along the Strand to dine at Boulestin's, Richards remembered that a vacancy had in fact occurred and thought to ask Housman whether it had been offered and had he declined. Richards goes on: 'He paused, looking at me with a face of rage. "What the hell has that got to do with you?" he ejaculated, and then, in a second, resumed his progress.' Richards recollects replying: 'Nothing of course. But as you told me about it yourself and told me that you would refuse it when offered, I don't see that my half-question was out of the way.' He added 'it was a sudden anger, gone almost as soon as it came'.[7] Arguably the target of Housman's outburst was not Richards but himself. He had been caught out by his intimacy with Richards which had tempted him into confiding too much in him. Possibly more reliable as a witness was Joan Thompson, daughter of J.J. Thompson, Master of Trinity from 1918 to 1940. She wrote in an appendix to Richards' book:

> Though he did not often talk about himself, yet he would sometimes do so, concealing the fact behind the fiction that he was alluding to a third person. On one occasion he was discussing with a friend [herself?] a recent award of the Order of Merit, and he mentioned one or two distinguished people who had declined this honour. His companion well knew that it was supposed he had himself declined it, and she said she wondered why anyone should wish to refuse that particular honour for great ability. Housman instantly informed her at length of the various reasons that prompted such an action. He did not disclose that he had done so himself, but remarked, half wistfully, at the end, 'You know, it is really a great distinction to have refused the OM.'[8]

Housman seems not to have needed the reassurance that honours gave of being liked, or admired, or respected. Part and parcel of his nature was to over-value himself and to have an excess of self-respect. He wished to remain a free spirit without obligation to anyone, except, of course, in Trinity, where his sense of obligation to the college had increased with time, and with the growth of respect for him by its Master and fellows.

To turn down an honour could be more self-regarding than to accept one. Cornwallis had been aware of that danger and in a second letter had added, 'I shall endeavour to suppress my Vanity by not making it known that such a distinguished mark of His Majesty's favour was intended.' Housman did not behave like Cornwallis. Harold Nicolson recorded meeting Housman at a dinner party in September 1931 when their host mentioned after Housman's departure that he had refused the OM.

Housman might also have wondered whether he had been in the running for appointment as the next Poet Laureate. Had there been gossip about him in high places? Had he been on the list and struck off? When the Liberal Cabinet Minister Earl Beauchamp fled to America in 1931 because his homosexual activities had come to light, George V was reputed to have said 'I thought men like that shot themselves.'[9] In May 1930 Housman wrote to Laurence: 'No, I was not given the chance of being Laureate. I thought Masefield the right choice, as all the other good poets are too obviously unsuited for the official duties.'[10] He probably included himself, given his unwillingness to write to order, a necessity in this post.

The other part of that OM episode with Richards had been a congenial and acceptable invitation from Boulestin to dine at his restaurant in Southampton Street. Housman had been at pains to ensure that his host understood how much he appreciated the invitation. Richards had tempted him with the thought that Boulestin had in his cellars 'some of that very, very rare, almost legendary, white Haut Brion, of which so few bottles leave the Chateau that each is numbered just as if it were a copy of a special large-paper edition of a book by Oscar Wilde or some other poet of the "nineties".' There were four of them. 'At that memorable dinner ... we drank a bottle of that Haut Brion.'[11] Housman's scale of values, priorities and enthusiasms had been neatly expressed that evening.

26 March 1929: Housman's seventieth birthday

On Housman's seventieth birthday, 26 March 1929, Laurence Housman read from his brother's poems on BBC radio. Housman had not been too sanguine. 'Only the archangel Raphael could recite my poetry properly, but I have no doubt you would do it quite nicely... but I understand that I incur no obligation to do the same for you on your 70th birthday.' And he added a warning:

You had better select with care. The financial expert who had reorganised Grant Richard's business for his creditors thought he would like to read *A Shropshire Lad*. He did, or as much as he could; then, in his own words, 'I put it behind the fire. Filthiest book I ever read: all about rogering girls under hedges.'[12]

He was not able to resist commenting to Percy Withers: 'I understand that Laurence did not read me very well, dropping his voice too much at impressive points.'[13]

When the Master sent congratulations and added how well he looked, Housman played along with a pretty story: 'One day when I was just turned 40, I was walking along and brooding on the fact, when a passing carter of some 25 summers said "What's the time young fellow?" A spring of joy gushed from my heart and I blessed him unaware.'[14] Later, in June, he was writing perhaps a mite more authentically to his friend Herbert Foxwell: 'I give myself the pleasure of sending you my best congratulations on your attaining the age of 80, and I think I may quite properly wish you many happy returns of the day to such a juvenile octogenarian.'[15]

Housman's connection with the Jackson family had continued. He heard from Moses' sister, Margaret Jackson, that their younger brother Victor had died. Housman retained a clear memory of him. When he had called at the family home in Ramsgate in August 1889 to see Adalbert, who was away in Essex, Housman had stayed overnight. Victor, then a lad of fourteen, 'was deputed to show me the way to the station, and imparted to me a great deal of knowledge, as I believe was then his habit.' Then echoing something she must have said about Moses he went on: 'I am glad to think that my dear Mo enjoyed his life at Applegarth so much. I hear at intervals from Gerald and sometimes from his mother. My kind regards to any of your sisters who are at Ramsgate.'[16] He set out in July on a motor tour which took in Tardebrigge and Woodchester and beauty spots such as Chipping Campden, Bourton-on-the-Water and Sherborne, 'where I found the interior of the Minster much finer than I had any idea of'. He had also found the Wise daughters in poor health. He had called in on Basil and Jeannie. 'I thought Basil looking older – his hair whiter'. All this he took as a portent of things to come for Kate and himself. 'My turn next, then yours.'[17]

France was calling again but he told Richards, 'I am deserting the air on this occasion, because my life, until my Manilius is quite finished, is too precious to be exposed to a 1/186000 risk of destruction, even though they have killed their proper quota for this year.' Scattering French accents like ill-directed confetti he outlined his itinerary: Poitiers, Angouleme, Perigueux, Cahors, Gorges du Tarn, Le Puy and perhaps round through Burgundy again.[18] Hoping to catch up with Richards, he sent him a postcard telling him when he would arrive at Autun and, failing a meeting there, when he was due in Paris. Richards' lumbago prevented any meeting at all and he had to be satisfied with a lengthy food and wine report which showed that Housman had discovered the other side to French provincial cooking.

> Food not varied or inventive, especially soup ... the best meal was at the Gastronome at Clermond-Ferrand... In Paris I was not best pleased with the Belle Aurore, where they made me ill, perhaps with the very poor caviar ... The Grand Veneur is good, though its *plats regionaux* are not an exciting selection ... At the place in the Place St. Michel I was disgusted with a pretended Sole Normande smothered in mushrooms, of all things in the world, and tasting exactly like the usual sole de la maison of a Parisian restaurant. The best cooking that I found was at the Escargot. Avoid Clos de Vougeot 1915: for some reason it has turned out badly, as did Lafite 1900.

It all sounded as though his love affair with France had gone through a rough patch. However, he had been happy with his transport: 'a car less liable to sudden illness than the one we had two years ago, and a chauffeur whose strong point, like Louis, was smiling, not finding his way nor knowing north from south.'[19] As always Housman had been pleased by fine scenery, this time beyond Perigueux, and a fine cathedral at Rodez. For him *la belle France* still had its many-layered magic.

When Charles Williams, novelist and reader for the Oxford University Press, showed interest in Housman's University College Introductory Lecture, Housman revealed that he had often thought of printing it together with his Cambridge Inaugural and the lecture he had given to the Classical Association, *The Application of Thought to Textual Criticism*. The obstacle to this scheme was the fact that he had included in his Cambridge Inaugural a line from Shelley commonly quoted as 'Fresh Spring, and Summer, and Winter hoar', the line praised by Swinburne. In his lecture, Housman claimed that what Shelley wrote in his own hand was 'Fresh Spring and Autumn, Summer and Winter hoar', so the line on which Swinburne had lavished so much praise was the verse not of Shelley but of a compositor – a misprint. Housman's thesis was that the aim of science was the discovery of truth, the aim of literature the production of pleasure. In this case the application of science, that is examination of the manuscript evidence, produced the truth, and the literary approach of Swinburne produced one man's aesthetic judgement. Unfortunately, Housman was subsequently unable to trace his source nor find any manuscript to support his contention, hence his unwillingness to have the lecture published.

The Oxford University Press sought guidance from a 'Shelley expert', Roger Ingpen, who declared that Shelley's fair copy of the stanza did include the line in the familiar form which Housman had been dismissing as a compositor's error. So the manuscript had proved Housman wrong and Housman had to accept he was wrong. But that was not the whole story. Further manuscript research enabled John Carter and John Sparrow to demonstrate in an appendix to their 1969 edition of Housman's Cambridge Inaugural, which John Carter had entitled 'The Confines of Criticism', that Ingpen's report had been 'incomplete, misleading and inaccurate', and that there was a big gap in the line in Shelley's revised version and also in Mary Shelley's fair copy of it, but critically the line always began 'Fresh Spring and Summer' and ended with 'Winter hoar'. Putting 'Autumn' in the empty space would not have produced Housman's line. There was no evidence to show that the poet had been intent on altering the sequence of the seasons. So Housman as a scholar was right not to publish his own version because he could not verify what he had said. Whether Housman was right in his confident assertion that the line should read 'Fresh Spring and Autumn, Summer and Winter hoar' was quite another matter. On the face of it he was still wrong.

Ever generous Housman

Basil's health and approaching retirement prompted another of Housman's generous impulses and he probed Kate on Basil's financial position.

> I remember your telling me last year that you had offered to share with him what you inherited from Uncle Joe, and I suppose

there is room for hope that the County Council will award him
something of a pension. But as you know more of that household's
affairs than I do, I wish you would tell me how much I ought to
add in future to the £50 per annum I now send them.

Mentioning Basil prompted Housman to comment on his own health:
'Perhaps I had better tell you that the doctor, whom I made overhaul
me when I turned 70, says that my heart is not as stout as it was and
ought to be; and I found this out when climbing the Puy de Parioux,
about the height of Snowdon, on a hot afternoon.'[20]

Unlike their author, sales of his poetry were still capable of scaling
the heights; he gave permission for the Richards Press to print another
7,000 copies of *A Shropshire Lad* and 5,000 of *Last Poems*. Although
his own poems were proving themselves to be good little earners,
he rightly ignored his own literary success when he counselled an
American admirer, Mr Rubin:

> Assuming that you have to earn your living, I advise you to
> follow chemistry or any other honest trade rather than literature,
> which, as Scott said, may be a good walking-stick but a bad
> crutch. It cannot be depended on. Maurice Hewlett, when his
> novels were selling well, threw up a post in the Civil Service,
> intending to live by his pen: the public ceased to read his novels,
> and he died in poverty. And of all the forms of literature, poetry
> is the straightest way to starvation. There is one living poet who
> boasts he lives on the proceeds of his poetry, but he is a bad one.
> Moreover poetry is not a job to fill all one's time, and poets like
> Wordsworth and Byron, who were always writing, would have
> done better to write less.[21]

This was hard-headed practical advice confirming that he had never
had an overwhelming urge to be a writer, never an urge to be a poet.
Although he was a man who had found himself writing poetry from
time to time, and who could at will turn on the tap of his nonsense
verse, he never thought of himself as a professional poet or wanted
to be one. He had been inspired by Munro to be a textual critic and
thereafter had followed his own star.

Among his characteristic batch of New Year letters to family and
friends at the end of 1929, we learn that Helene, Grant Richards' step-
daughter, had 'looked in last term with her husband and a brother-

in-law who writes poetry'[22]; Housman cannot have presented too formidable an aspect to her. Jeannie Housman learned that 'Laurence was here some weeks ago, engaged in some villainy connected with the League of Nations. Of course I did not go to hear him, but he looked in on me, and seemed very well. I daresay you saw the photographs of him and his home in *Country Life* or whatever paper it was.'[23] He was giving a good impression of being frankly dismissive of his brother's campaigns. Much more to his taste were Mildred Platt's efforts in brewing sloe gin. 'I do not think I have any friend trustworthy enough to convey it to me without taking a swig,'[24] so he proposed to collect it himself when next in London. In the event he confirmed in early February: 'The intoxicant has arrived. As you advised me to keep it till March, I have not opened the bottle, and am therefore in a condition to express my gratitude legibly and grammatically.'[25] He had a happy knack of inflating the value of gifts with his colourful hyperbole.

Grant Richards was keeping him supplied with what Housman referred to as 'improving literature', this time *Lady Chatterley's Lover*, that earthy and explicit story of sex across the social divide, banned in England as obscene. 'I return D.H. Lawrence, with thanks for your perilous enterprise on my behalf. It did not inflame my passions to any great extent, but it is much more wholesome than Frank Harris or James Joyce.'[26] Housman was attracted by Richards' offer to let him see *Le Troisième Sexe*, 'the more so since I thought that Willy had drunk himself to death long ago and this was the reason why Colette was going on without him.'[27] Less than ten days later it was a case of 'I return Willy. A lot of second-hand stuff: such as scandal about Frederick the Great from the spurious Matinees, when he might have gone to Voltaire.'[28] Housman was referring to *Les Matinees du Roi de Prusse*, a pamphlet discussing the homosexual activities of Frederick the Great. Apart from the scholarly and scientific tomes in his library, Housman appeared to be well acquainted with less scientific literature. It would seem that this flow of 'improving literature' to Housman was generally a matter of Richards' taking the initiative rather than demand from Housman, who nevertheless made no effort to turn off the supply tap.

In March Housman made a surprising and mysterious request to Scholfield of Kings: 'Could you and would you provide me with means of admission to your College chapel for the afternoon service next Sunday?'[29] Was Housman thinking of something he needed to verify from evensong, or had he always liked evensong and felt an urge to experience again feelings from his youth, or was he thinking of his own Nunc Dimittis, possibly not too far distant?

Also in March, he heard again from Charles Williams who had now sent Housman a copy of his own *Poetry at Present,* in which he said at least two illuminating things about Housman. He described the genesis of *A Shropshire Lad* and *Last Poems,* which he found 'perfect in word, perfect in spirit', as arising 'from a depth of bitter resignation', and later that 'Mr Housman, who has no concern for romantic love except as a keen and often thwarted delight, has restored the love between friends to something approaching its right place'.[30] Housman was not to be drawn by Williams' exercise in insight and empathy and replied, 'The chief criticism I have to make is that you praise us all too much', quickly diverting Williams' attention elsewhere: 'I have given you a great deal of fruitless trouble about Shelley',[31] and then by giving him chapter and verse on the origins of *Nous n'irons plus au bois* which he had printed as a Prelude to *Last Poems.* Housman was not to be tempted into indiscretions.

Housman was never one to adopt conventional phrases when writing about people he truly valued. When Robert Bridges died, Housman wrote to his widow:

> but of your husband's departure it may be said, if of anyone's, that nothing is here for tears, nothing to wail or knock the breast. A fortunate and honoured existence is ended in the fullness of time; life did not long outstay strength; and his poetry, though the vulgar could never admire it rightly, did at last win him fame even among the vulgar. For myself, I do not suppose that there is anything which I have read oftener than the first four books of *Shorter Poems.*[32]

Flying again

By 22 April, all but the index of *Manilius V* had been completed and with that behind him he could contemplate a happy return to flying. As he told Kate, 'If I do not come home alive, my book V of Manilius, all written and mostly printed will be seen through the Press by a Fellow of this college named Andrew Gow'.[33]

In Paris he met Edith Wharton, the American novelist, author of *The Age of Innocence* and *The House of Mirth.* She loved Housman's poetry, a passion she shared with another fellow of Trinity, Gaillard

Lapsley, who had been her friend for thirty years and would be her literary executor. She already knew Housman's poetry but when Lapsley sent her a copy of *Last Poems* she says she 'gulped it down in my coarse carnivorous way; & then returned & lingered with slow delight. I'm sure it's far above the Shropshire Lad; not only in sudden lifts, but continuously... the depth and not the tumult of the soul, has come again ... Please tell Mr Housman so...Thank you a lot for a precious present.'[34] Towards the end of the year in which Housman died she wrote to Lapsley:

> You probably noticed that the reviewer in the Lit Supp. pronounced him, in private life, to be 'prim & grim'... I was tempted to deal with the 'grim & prim' in a letter to the Supp., but as my offerings to Times & Supp. are always rejected, I refrained. But what an age of mental darkness we are living in![35]

When Housman introduced himself to her in Paris in 1930 it was with panache. He would come to visit her under his own steam 'as I have a tame motor and the chauffeur is supposed to know all about the environs of Paris. The correct pronunciation of my name is Oozman: at least when I gave it so to the commissionaire here, he said "vous parlez français très bien, Monsieur".'[36] This ready capacity to set the stage had been in evidence a month earlier. Accepting an invitation to dine with Foxwell at a feast in St John's he replied, 'It will delight me to dine with you on the 6th. The Evangelist, I must remind you, was too tough to be martyred, and throve on boiling oil; I expect to receive some of his healthy vigour from his commemorative feast.'[37]

Another American meeting was with Cyril Clemens, president of the International Mark Twain Society, who had offered Housman the office of honorary vice-president of the Mark Twain Society. It must have intrigued this American to read in Housman's reply 'The elegy on Stephen Dowling Botts in *Hucklebury Finn* is one of the poems I know by heart.'[38] Thus when Clemens visited England in the summer of 1930 and visited Cambridge, Housman welcomed him and his companion and they dined together in Hall. Subsequently, Clemens provided a fascinating written portrait of Housman, moreover one that was given to Housman to read and correct. It strikes one as both authentic and accurate. It provided a sense of the authority conveyed by Housman as a measured person, and his instant likeability:

> In appearance Housman was a striking man – one who would stand out in any crowd – five feet, nine inches tall, with hair turning grey at the temples; a fine Roman nose; keen piercing, kindly, grey eyes; and seventy-one years of age. His smile was of rare sweetness, and the twinkle in his eye gave evidence of a keen sense of humor. I shall always remember the stately manner in which he walked across the quadrangle to the dining hall.[39]

Over dinner their conversation was wide ranging. They talked about aeroplanes and flying. Clemens told a story of a hundred and fifteen-year-old Turk who, reaching America, told a reporter that he attributed his long life to the fact that he had always lived in Turkey where drinking was prohibited. Housman commented: 'He was complimentary to America and not true to Turkey' as he held a glass of rare white wine up to the light, 'for there are a great many Turks who do enjoy wine.' Housman gave his opinion on American literature and authors he enjoyed like Sinclair Lewis, Theodore Dreiser – who had sent him copies of his books – and Edith Wharton who he admired and of whom he said 'I have known her for a number of years, I saw her the last time I went to France ... she lives in one of the suburbs of Paris ... an old fashioned house with the prettiest garden I have ever beheld.' The Master kept the literary ball rolling by asking Housman about 'the funny author whom you had us all reading a while back.' This was Anita Loos' *Gentlemen Prefer Blondes* sent to Housman by Grant Richards. Housman admitted:

> before I knew it everyone in the University was reading it, and thereafter the delightful work became popular throughout England. You see even a staid and sedate professor of Latin knows how to enjoy the lighter things of literature ... Many years spent with Manilius, Lucan, and Juvenal have perhaps quickened my sense of humour.

Dinner over they adjourned to the Combination Room where Clemens could not help being impressed by the low ceiling with its scrolls and traceries, its Tudor fireplace nearly as large as the one in the dining hall, finely shaped windows, portraits, a mahogany table whose top was so brightly polished that one could see the beautiful ceiling reflected. In the relaxed atmosphere they conversed happily on subjects as diverse as their choice of books for a desert island;

the sense of humour of the French, Germans, Italians, and Spanish; England's reception of American jokes, and the best of Mark Twain where Housman recited there and then the concluding stanza of Stephen Dowling Botts, drowned in the well:

> They got him out and emptied him;
> Alas it was too late;
> His spirit was gone for to sport aloft
> In the realms of the good and great.

After sampling Hall and the Combination Room, Housman took his guests to the ancient college bowling green sloping down to the Cam. Clemens reflected 'In these surroundings of blessed peacefulness our talk was of the different cathedrals of England and of the Continent.' Housman 'told me how much he loved the cathedrals of England and France. He expressed an especial fondness for Chartres Cathedral in France and Lincoln in England.' Back at the door of Housman's rooms, 'before I could bid my host goodbye, he said with true English hospitality, "You must come in first, and get a whisky and soda."' Once inside, and while Housman went in search of their drink, Clemens had a chance to cast his observant eye over Housman's room. He saw 'all the available wall space taken up with book-cases, literally bulging with books … At one side of the window stood the desk, covered with manuscripts and letters. Nearby was the fireplace with its stone mantel on which appeared the books that their owner used more frequently.'

Clemens' account of time spent with Housman is rare. He was an articulate man with wide sympathies who valued the experience. He had his account authenticated by Housman, leaving notes of what Housman had changed. Housman provided his exact height and deleted anything he did not consider accurate. Clemens issued an immediate invitation to Housman to take tea but Housman, on the eve of departure, had to decline, 'so I will wish you goodbye and all success.'[40]

This image of Housman's genial reaction to Clemens was shattered by what Housman wrote to Walter Ashburner on 27 December 1930:

> Connected as you are with Italy, England and the United States, it may interest you to learn that Mussolini and I are honorary vice-presidents of the Mark Twain Society. In company, I ought to add, with less distinguished persons. A cousin of the author's,

a Mr Cyril Clemens, a very vacuous young man, has been going about Europe this summer establishing 'centres', and stayed here for some time trying to improve his mind.[41]

Accounts of Housman can tell us as much about the person writing the account as they do about the subject. Harold Nicolson recollected in his diary for 26 September 1931, how he had gone down to Cambridge with 'old Gaselee' (Sir Stephen Gaselee, a fellow of King's College and librarian at the Foreign Office).

> We walk about the colleges... We dress for dinner. Black tie. We assemble. A.E. Housman and a don disguised as a Shropshire Lad. We have 1789 Madeira and Haut Brion and tripe and oysters and grouse-pie and mushrooms. The firelight flits on the silver of the smaller combination room and there are red shades, highly inflammable, to each candle. Housman is dry, soft, shy, prickly, smooth, conventional, silent, feminine, fussy, pernickety, polite, sensitive, tidy, greedy, and a touch of a toper. 'What is this my dear Gaselee?' 'This is Estrella 1789.' 'A perfect wine.' Yet not eighteenth-century and still less 1890. A *bon bourgeois* who has seen more sensitive days. He does not talk much except about food. And at 10.30 he rises to take his leave. All his movements are best described in such Trollope expressions. Gaselee tells me afterwards that MacDonald had offered Housman the O.M. and that he had refused. A gymnophobic attitude on the part of the old poet. The other don whose name I never heard, tells me that Housman was at school in Worcestershire and that it was to him an unhappy school. Shropshire meant the unattained and liberated. He had scarcely been there. It was known to him only as an occasional jaunt. He made topographical mistakes in the poems. That is why he is so sensitive about being asked Shropshire questions. An interesting evening. A strange island in the flux around me.[42]

There was indeed flux around Nicolson's life that day. He had resigned from the Foreign Office in late 1929 and joined the *Evening Standard* on 1 January 1930. That was one kind of flux but another kind may have been uppermost in his mind, the flux occasioned by his relationship with his wife Vita Sackville-West. That morning she had left for a hiking tour in Provence, causing him to ponder in the train and in his diary on the glue that held them together.

Although now a seventy-year-old, Housman's work rate and powers of concentration were still extraordinary. On 10 September 1930 he sent back the entire page proofs of *Manilius* and promised the index within a week; in fact, the index of thirty-one pages took him only four days – the mind boggles.

His own work rate and his own capacity for accuracy probably caused much of his continued irritation with printers:

> To make printers understand that they must not make corrections on their own initiative, you might point out to them the stupid 'correction' their reader has made on p. xxvii, which I have had to scratch out. With perfect confidence, without even a query, he has put a full stop in the middle of a sentence.[43]

Manilius completed

Housman's mood reached a low point around the end of 1930. To Kate he wrote, 'The last volume of my great work is now published, and now perhaps I shall have leisure to improve my mind and prepare to meet my God.'[44] To Jeannie he was more dramatic in his characteristic serio-comic way: 'I have just published my last book, so I am ready to die tomorrow … as I shall now have no important work to bother about … However, I am all right at present, and taking my food nicely.'[45] The lowest point was mirrored in a letter to Percy Withers on Boxing Day.

> Rutherford's daughter, married to another Fellow of Trinity, died suddenly a day or two ago. The wife of the Emeritus Professor of Greek, who himself is paralysed, has cut her throat with a razor which she had bought to give her son-in-law. I have a brother and a brother-in-law both seriously ill and liable to drop dead any moment; and in short Providence has given itself up to the festivities of the season. A more cheerful piece of news is that I have just published the last book I shall ever write, and that I now mean to do nothing for ever and ever.[46]

Notwithstanding that gloominess, his sense of humour was far from deserting him, telling Richards that 'It would be absurd to send a copy of Manilius V to *The Listener*',[47] and telling Petica Robertson, wife of the Regius Professor of Greek, 'I have to thank you for another pound of the priceless (in every sense) sugar. Sir Robert Walpole said that women who will not take money will take diamonds; so I am saving up,'[48] and to R.W. Chambers: 'Did you ever hear of the newspaper which reported an address of mine "On the application of thought to sexual criticism?" '[49]

The first day of 1931 had found Housman using his usual formula for congratulating the wives of friends who had been knighted. This time it was William Rothenstein, who was reaping the reward for his artistic endeavours and the multiplicity of his contacts. He wrote to Alice what he was accustomed to write to all the wives:

> When anything of this sort happens to a friend of mine, I always write to his wife ... because she is the person who is chiefly concerned and who takes most pleasure in it. I therefore send you my warm congratulations (from which I do not altogether exclude Sir William), and my earnest hope that you will not be stuck up.[50]

In early 1931 there were further obscure rumblings of change at the Richards Press because Richards sought an audience with Housman who replied: 'I have not heard anything about the Richards Press. Certainly I should be ready to see you and pleased to have you here.'[51] Richards went to Cambridge and the upshot was a letter from Housman to Walter Makin, manager of the Richards Press: 'The Richards Press has always treated me very well and I have no inclination to seek another publisher; but if it is made over to or merged in another firm, I shall prefer to transfer the books to their former publisher Mr Grant Richards.'[52]

Time and celebrity had brought him books of poetry, gifts and well wishes from unknown people, and were now bringing scholars who wished to write about him and his work. He wrote to L.W. Payne, Professor of English at the University of Texas: 'In spite of your courteous and amiable letter I will not assist or encourage young men to write theses on "The art of A.E. Housman" ... I have received a good many similar enquiries and have answered them much in the same way; so do not feel hurt.'[53] Professor Camille McCole, who was producing a book with Andrew Smithberger, *On Poetry*, got from Housman his famous non-definition of poetry: 'I am afraid I can no more define poetry than a terrier can define a rat. We can both recognise the object by its effect on our senses. For instance, if a line of poetry comes into my head while I am shaving, the hair bristles on my skin, and I have to stop.'[54]

With Arnold Rubin, Housman seemed to be fighting a rear guard action to be seen as a scholar and not a poet:

> As you ask about my doings I may say that I have published the 5th and last volume of my chief work, an edition of the Latin astrological poet Manilius. I do not send you a copy, as it would shock you very much; it is so dull that few professed scholars can read it, probably not one in the whole United States. But I rank much higher among English scholars than among English poets.[55]

Praefanda

At the end of December 1931 Housman was evidently reading the proofs of Henry Stuart Jones' revision of Liddell and Scott's *Greek-English Lexicon*. Housman was bringing his learning to bear not on astrological but on sexual terms, giving Stuart Jones references for the true meaning of the Greek word for *fellare* and that it did not also mean *cunnum lingere*, which Housman did not translate, feeling no need to go beyond the Latin equivalent of the Greek word. Similarly, when he nailed down another Greek word as meaning 'precisely *cinaedus*', he again avoided the English equivalents which would probably have been 'catamite' or more popularly, 'rent boy', not in Housman's view to be confused with *pedico*, a 'sodomite'. He added a typically sardonic observation, 'To-day by the way, is the Feast of the Holy Innocents.'[56]

His proof reading may have prompted Housman to submit to the *Classical Quarterly* a paper called *Praefanda*, which dealt at more length with sexual terms employed by Latin authors. This paper was unusual being totally in Latin; it had no introduction to explain its purpose, or to indicate what type of textual issue it dealt with. Its subject matter was textual commentary on eighteen short extracts from sources as diverse as Catullus, the Priapeia, Seneca, Persius, Carmina Latina Epigraphica, Martial, Suetonius and Apuleius. The only complete translation of the whole paper available to date is that produced by James Jayo in 2001 and published by the Trustees of Boston University in its periodical *Arion*. This rendered all the sexual terms into very explicit North American demotic. It also translated the Latin extracts and Housman's Latin commentary in the same style, providing graphic descriptions of sexual congress between two, three or more people, male and female, sufficiently explicit and titillating to be classed as pornography. Even in 2015 many English and American readers will find the Jayo translation gratuitously offensive. Those who wish to make their own judgement may easily consult *Catullus 16* in *Wikipedia*.

It was not surprising that some members of the 1931 management board of *Classical Quarterly*, were sufficiently repelled by the paper to urge its rejection, notwithstanding that its author was the university's Professor of Latin and none of the Latin terms were actually translated. Perhaps the content of the paper convinced them that it was less concerned with scholarly issues than with a self-indulgent romp through some of the smutty passages of classical literature. One is bound to question Housman's motivation in writing such a paper. Was it in some way thrilling and personally cathartic, or was it simply an example of his single-minded pursuit of meaning in every nook and cranny of Latin literature? Housman was always happy to read work classed as pornography and as a voyeur may have witnessed some of the actualities of sexual congress in Paris.

When Reginald Hackforth, a fellow of Sidney Sussex College, Cambridge, and editor of the *Classical Quarterly*, wrote to convey rejection of the paper, a rather big step for him to take with a man of Housman's standing and reputation, Housman received the decision with an air of unconcern, at the same time putting himself in the right, 'The average Englishman is a sexual monomaniac; and if you and I have escaped the taint we may be thankful.'[57] Apparently the paper, originally accepted, had suddenly been rejected, possibly at the instigation of two members of the management committee. One of them, D.S. Robertson, Regius Professor of Greek and also a fellow of Trinity, received the next day the mildest of rebukes from Housman: 'I hear from Hackforth that I have been causing you some trouble and perhaps polluting your mind.'[58] In spite of seeming to give in graciously, Housman was not at all deterred by rebuff from the *Classical Quarterly*, and published *Praefanda* later in the same year in the German periodical *Hermes*, but still in Latin.

After more than twenty years as a fellow of Trinity, Housman did not feel he had to be as careful as in his early days. He could now afford to ignore tittle-tattle in the university, where he had by now gained a reputation as gourmet, intrepid air traveller and Europhile. This latest example of self-direction was also an echo of his pursuit of

Propertius rather the Greats syllabus. Housman was his own man and in most things a law unto himself.

More slashing invective

In the aftermath of his controversy with Postgate he had himself not been above writing sneeringly about him: 'Dr Postgate is both sanguine and stubborn and if once he gets hold of the stick by the wrong end he does not soon let go.'[59] In his subsequent paper, 'De Nihilo':

> Dr Postgate's willingness to teach is great and obvious, yet I do not find him very instructive. An air of ripe and penetrating judgement is never absent from anything that he writes, but I sometimes miss the substance and I cannot reconcile the strength of his anxiety to seem superior with the faintness of his endeavours to do so.[60]

In 1921, J. van Wageningen was in trouble over the manuscripts of *Manilius*: 'The truth was stated, before my time, by Jacob; Mr van Wageningen presumes to contradict us both, relying on his own defective eyesight or superficial observation or inexperience in reading MSS.'[61] This was the scholarly equivalent of jeering at football matches 'Get a pair of specs, ref!'

In 1924 he vented his spleen in a review of Professor E.T. Merrill's *Catulli Veronensis Liber* and went close to attacking his motivation: 'His main purpose in withholding indispensable information is to find room for a long record of conjectures which dishonour the human intellect ... The book teems with suggestio falsi ... Such deficiency in craftsmanship or care or sense is not distinguishable by its consequences from malice aforethought and an intent to deceive.'[62]

Two years previously he had shown the other side of the Housman coin in his famous paper 'The Application of Thought to Textual Criticism'. His definition of textual criticism was simple and clear: 'the science of discovering error in texts and the art of removing it.' This he saw as a matter of reason and of common sense. He offered reasons why thought was not sufficiently applied:

> They get rules by rote without grasping the realities of which those rules are merely emblems, and recite them on inappropriate

occasions instead of thinking out each problem as it arises ...
It is only a minority of those who engage in this study who are
sincerely bent upon the discovery of truth.

Housman dwelt with notable insight on the pathology of critics,
their prejudices and personal preferences. He argued that the terms
of textual criticism were 'deplorably intellectual; and probably in no
other field do men tell so many falsehoods in the idle hope that they
are telling the truth, or talk so much nonsense in the vague belief that
they are talking sense.' He cited chemists and doctors as able

> to bring their opinions to the test of fact, and verify or falsify their
> theories by experiment ... our conclusions regarding the truth or
> falsehood of a MS reading can never be confirmed or corrected
> by an equally decisive test; for the only equally decisive test would
> be the production of the author's autograph.

He concluded:

> To be a textual critic requires aptitude for thinking and willingness
> to think; and though it also requires other things, those things
> are supplements and cannot be substitutes. Knowledge is good,
> method is good, but one thing beyond all others is necessary; and
> that is to have a head, not a pumpkin, on your shoulders, and
> brains, not pudding, in your head.[63]

His five volumes of *Manilius* published successively in 1903, 1912,
1916, 1920 and 1930 reflected a continuation of these attitudes, both
constructive and aggressive.

Certainly, the greats of the past, Scaliger and Bentley, were
dealt with in a spirit of even-handed respect but lesser lights were
not so fortunate. Elias Stoeber who had reprinted and provided a
commentary on Bentley's text was mauled: 'Stoeber's mind, though
that is no name to call it by, was one which turned as unswervingly to
the false, the meaningless, the unmetrical, and the ungrammatical, as
the needle to the pole.'[64] Baehrens was put in his place: 'Baehrens, a
man of vast energy and vigorous intelligence but of unripe judgement
and faulty scholarship, who with one hand conferred on the Latin
poets more benefits than any critic since Lachmann and with the
other imported ten times as many corruptions as he removed.'[65]

By the time he got to the publication of his final volume of *Manilius* in 1930 nothing much had changed. Housman was still playing up to his public image. He wrote of 'the natural disrelish of mankind for the combination of a tedious author with an odious editor' as accounting for low sales of Manilius. 'Of each volume there were printed 400 copies: only the first is yet sold out, and that took 23 years; and the reason why it took no longer is that it found purchasers among the unlearned, who had heard that it contained a scurrilous preface and hoped to extract from it a low enjoyment.'[66] It is evident that Housman had not significantly mellowed; his comments could still be in the nature of low personal abuse, as in the case of the now dead Ellis. 'The corrections of Ellis [to Breiter's edition] were rather more numerous, and one or two of them were very pretty, but his readers were in perpetual contact with the intellect of an idiot child.'[67]

However, in dealing with H.W. Garrod, who in 1911 had produced an elaborate edition of the second book of Manilius, he simply said 'I declined to review it on its publication leaving it a fair field in which it received no competent criticism.' Housman gave Garrod a mixed review as an editor of Manilius:

> Mr Garrod brought to his task activity and energy, a brisk intelligence, and a strong desire to shine. His work ... was the fruit of independent investigation, diversified reading, and genuine industry ... His conjectures were singularly cheap and shallow, and his impatience of the more circumspect emendators such as Bentley, broke out at [line] 689 in insolence ... I have counted more than 60 positive misstatements ... The commentary, which is full and mainly original, contains much more truth than error that the only readers who can use it with safety are those whose knowledge extends beyond Mr Garrod's ... it cannot be said that Mr Garrod's attainment in scholarship corresponds to his pretensions.

However, Housman drew attention to German admiration for Garrod's work, adding that 'There were no such bouquets for me; and perhaps the reader will do well to consider how far my judgement of Mr Garrod's performance may have been warped by the passion of envy.'[68]

That may well have been the case and it may well have been that Housman did not wish to trade insults with Garrod, by then Professor of Poetry at Oxford. In his *The Profession of Poetry & Other Lectures* published the previous year (1929), Garrod had written a penetrating critique of Housman and his poetry, including the words 'Life has done him some injury; the nature of which I am not curious to inquire beyond what his poetry tells us about him ... His poetry is wrung from him, as from so many poets, by some pain of life.' Garrod had also referred to Housman's 'false pastoral', his 'sham masculinity.'

And then there was Garrod's final judgement on Housman:

> What matters, and what will outlast curiosity, is the pure and cold art of his good work. But we are human creatures; and this enigmatic figure – one of the most notable of our time – this enigmatic figure, lonely, irresponsive, setting us so many questions and answering none of them, crediting none of us with truth or intelligence, but allowing us to make what we can of the fire and ice that contend in his nature, the Byronic and the donnish – we may be forgiven if we look at him a little like men who have forgotten good manners. It is his fault if we stare.[69]

If Housman ever read Garrod's words, and it would have been surprising had he not, we can readily appreciate how he could have had no wish to start a conversation let alone an argument with such a formidable commentator. The subjects likely to be for debate would be too dangerous for Housman and some of Garrod's words make it a near certainty that he had read Housman's dedication to Moses Jackson and had interpreted it for himself. Housman generally ignored a basic truth of life: aggression begets aggression. But on this occasion he seems to have wisely refrained from engaging in further controversy.

In that final volume of Manilius Housman took up again the qualities required of an emendator:

> Judging an emendation requires in some measure the same qualities as emendation itself, and the requirement is formidable. To read attentively, think correctly, omit no relevant consideration, and repress self-will, are not ordinary accomplishments; yet an emendator needs much besides: just literary perception, congenial intimacy with the author, experience which must have been won by study, and mother wit which he must have brought from his mother's womb. It may be asked whether I think that I myself possess this outfit, or

even most of it; and if I answer yes that will be a new example of my notable arrogance. I had rather be arrogant than impudent. I should not have undertaken to edit Manilius unless I had believed I was fit for the task; and in particular I think myself a better judge of emendation, both when to emend and how to emend than most others.[70]

It was at this point that he announced his own brilliance. He related how he had encountered for the first time a stanza of Walter de la Mare's 'Fare well' including the line 'May the rustling harvest hedgerow' in a newspaper review of the poem. 'I knew in a moment that Mr de la Mare had not written *rustling*, and in a moment I had found the true word. But if the book of poems had perished and the verse survived only in the review, who would have believed me rather than the compositor?'[71]

Significantly, he did not reveal that what de la Mare had written was *rusting*.

He ended this massively egocentric parade of learning by bracketing himself with Scaliger and Bentley: 'the reader whose good opinion I desire and have done the utmost to secure is the next Bentley or Scaliger who may chance to occupy himself with Manilius.'[72] His belief was clear. Only somebody of the quality of Bentley or Scaliger was likely to be able to improve on his own Manilius.

The strain of invective in his writings was evidently pathological, found also in a succession of entries in his notebooks X and Y, and marginal comments in books he had read.

Dating from the periods 1903 to 1915 and 1930 to 1933, his notebooks contain a series of statements, some with anonymous targets.[73]

I could train a dog to edit the Classics like Mr—
The standard of honour among classical scholars is not high but Mr—here falls below it

Truth is generally odious; but demonstrable truth is more than odious, it is infuriating.
The spirit is willing but the mind is weak.

Most of Ellis's conjectures have no other origin than infirmity of mind. They might have been proposed by an idiot child.

> Jowett's Plato: the best translation of a Greek philosopher which has ever been executed by a person who understood neither philosophy nor Greek.

> My honesty is the best known and most disagreeable of all my qualities.

> I do not enjoy despising inferiority. I would rather forget it: why will inferiority thus trail its coat under my toes?

Marginal comments made in books he was reading were often violently expressed. A survey by Paul Naiditch indicated that his commonest descriptors were 'you lie', 'no', 'liar', 'silly', 'ass' and 'ugh'.[74]

What he wrote in his notebooks and wrote in the margins of books was for his eyes only, yet it is all direct evidence of a subterranean cynicism and violence in his emotional reactions to individual scholars. Laurence Housman was probably more than half right when he wrote in *John O'London's Weekly* in 1936, 'there can be no doubt that he did greatly enjoy writing and saying bitter and contemptuous things... and he had in his note-book pages stocked with phrases which were apparently waiting a suitable victim to whom they might be applied'.[75] W.H. Auden described them as 'thunderbolts of poisoned invective'; his biographer Watson as, 'a compilation of waspish epigrams and demolishing phrases – a malevolent catalogue of quips and insults directed at no specific target but kept in readiness for a suitable occasion'.[76] Although his latest biographer, Richard Perceval Graves, described what Laurence said as a myth, the documentary evidence suggests that Laurence Housman's view was valid, even though Housman's actual use of his notebook material seems to have been scanty.

Housman's attacks on other scholars lie along a continuum from contempt, sometimes coated with wit, to slashing personal abuse. The issue is not whether Housman was 'sincere', or whether we approve or disapprove of his arrogant self-satisfied words, or whether they can be justified by his personal crusade for truth and honesty, or even whether they were normal coin among academics. Housman prided himself on the fact that his work was always evidenced yet on a few occasions he went so far as to attack another scholar for his supposed motivation, which by definition could not be evidenced and was just so much opinion. In those cases Housman failed to live up to his own standards. It is also evident that he was very easily aroused to moral outrage and anger. And for a man who had plenty of native humour and wit at his disposal it is surprising that he chose to attack and wound.

His environment may have intensified his unawareness and self-satisfaction. He had no well-educated partner to read his work and counsel him. He had no set of lively, highly intelligent and iconoclastic students to teach (shades of his youthful self) because his duties at Cambridge did not include undergraduate teaching. He could be as solitary and insulated as he wished.

Many of his eloquent and persuasive paragraphs seem to have a life of their own. His slashing style of invective seems to feed on its own eloquence and vitality. For a man who was apparently so disciplined, so careful about the exactitude of what he said, some of the paragraphs in question suggest a kind of possession, a characteristic shared with his nonsense verse. In a sense he was again being taken charge of, probably by his intense dislike of certain individuals. And it is part of our common experience that we do not always think before we speak. Despite his strictures about what scholars need to have on their heads, the occasional pathology of Housman's writing seems to be writing without thinking.

3 May 1931: Sophie Becker dies

Just before a visit to the Withers in June, a link with Housman's earliest years was broken. On 3 May 1931 Sophie Becker died in Wiesbaden at the age of eighty-seven. No family correspondence marking the event has survived and it seems to have provided no spur to communication between Housman and surviving members of the Wise family. In startling contrast, Percy Withers recounted in his *A Buried Life*, published some five years later, that during Housman's visit to Souldern, they were discussing 'friendship', when Housman made a totally uncharacteristic confession. According to Withers, Housman said that he 'never possessed but three friends – all, it is significant, associated with youth or early manhood'. He had continued:

> They were all now gone, and a note of exultation came into his voice as he spoke of his thankfulness for having outlived them. With a tenderness of passion utterly undisguised he went on to tell of the last of the three friends – a woman – recently dead.

His voice faltered, his whole frame seemed shaken, as he told the brief story. He had loved and revered her from youth. In the earlier years companionship had been close and constant. Then distances and the exigencies of occupation had rendered meetings few and difficult, and of late years they had never met, he said bitterly, as a consequence of her having returned to her home-land Germany, to end her days. The story closed with a thank God he had lived to know her safely laid to rest. He added – and for the first time his voice strengthened to a triumphant pitch – how comfortably he could meet death now his three friends were at peace.

This declaration was accompanied, in Withers' words, 'by the physical manifestations of a faltering voice, a flushed face, and an agitation of frame that gave the impression of a seething force restrained only by the exercise of stern self-discipline'.[77] This phenomenon gave some credence to an observation Withers' wife had made seventeen years previously. Whereas the sadness of Housman's expression in repose had brought to Percy Withers' mind Browning's phrase 'sad as mortality', it had caused Mrs Withers to conclude 'That man has had a tragic love affair'.[78] The extraordinary outpouring of Housman's emotion seemed to bear out Mrs Withers' judgement. Yet the only surviving evidence of a relationship between Housman and Sophie Becker is in the form of references to 'Miss Becker' in Housman's letters to the Wises and in their visitors' book; in the likelihood that she helped him when he was learning German as a schoolboy; in the likelihood that he was the A.E. Housman who had won a competition for translating Goethe's poem *Der Fischer* in the *Monthly Packet* of November 1875 with encouragement from Sophie Becker. In his *A.E.H.* Laurence Housman wrote sympathetically about her:

> At the home of his Woodchester friends, the Wises, with whom –
> so long as they lived – he remained in constant intimacy, he met
> his most life-long friend, a German lady named Sophie Becker.
> She was his senior by about fifteen years; and was governess-
> companion to the two daughters. When in late middle age she
> returned to Germany, he continued to correspond with her; and
> when, a few years before his death, she died at the age of ninety
> [*sic*], he expressed satisfaction at knowing that the last of his most
> intimate friends was safely out of a troublesome world.[79]

Laurence added tellingly:

> This I think was one of his most comfortable friendships: I remember her coming to stay with us in 1874 – a dark and rather plain woman, but sharp, shrewd, sensible, and brightly humorous, just the right corrective (so far as it could be corrected) for the melancholic tendency which grew on him during his adolescent years.

Hers were just the sort of qualities likely to appeal to Housman. Withers later made a brief reference to the episode in an article for the *New Statesman and Nation* in May 1936 and subsequently received a letter from Housman's sister Kate; she was at first inclined to brush the matter away – 'it must relate to a youthful infatuation, of which the family had full cognizance at the time, and knew it to have been soon and harmlessly outlived'. However, when Withers produced additional information about the lady in question, Mrs Symons remembered more about Sophie Becker, remembered too her brother's adolescent attachment, but had never for a moment suspected that a vestige had survived the first onset. Mrs Symons confessed 'she had no idea the acquaintance had been maintained, even tenuously'. In the same letter she expressed amazement that her brother 'had ever been able to open his heart to any mortal soul'.[80] Laurence subsequently told one of Housman's early biographers, Maude Hawkins, that he had found among his brother's papers a letter from Sophie to Housman which he had kept for fifty years; it began 'Dear boy' and ended 'Your affectionate friend', which may be taken either at face value, or as a coded message of deep affection. Unhappily the remaining contents of the letter are unknown and no letters from Housman to her have survived.

Sophie Becker had replaced his dead mother at a critical moment in Housman's life and had made an indelible impression on his heart; not surprisingly, his pre-adolescent attachment continued into his earliest Oxford days, when Sophie sent him socks and he sent her via Mrs Wise a cloakroom ticket (why a cloakroom ticket remains a mystery) and 'also a poem in her own beautiful language; please tell her this otherwise perhaps she may not know it'.[81] It seems very reasonable to assume that any potential ripening of this early bond was interrupted when Housman was impelled by nature to make Moses Jackson the centre of his emotional longings. But painful though that may have been, it could hardly have accounted for the maelstrom of emotion that Withers witnessed. Housman's outburst at Souldern suggested some form of profound inner conflict, possibly compounded with guilt and mixed with rage and despair, that all roads to love had been denied to him. Some mixture of those elements is the only reasonable way to explain his words and behaviour. The alternative would be to accuse Withers of exaggeration, of over-writing the scene to enhance his own importance, or that Housman was play acting in order to exaggerate the importance of a woman in his life.

Certainly, Grant Richards took great exception to Withers' description of the encounter because there had been

> no parallel, no approach to a parallel in my experience – nor in that of my wife, who had many solitary talks with him. It is true that, less venturesome in inquiry, less actively curious in fact, I never thought of going out of my way to disturb the depths or to invite confidences, and perhaps my nature does not attract intimacies of the kind of which Dr Withers writes; but it is certainly true that neither my wife nor I ever saw any signs of such mental disturbance as described in the sentence I have quoted. Nor did we experience the sight of 'a face wrought and flushed with torment, a figure tense and bolt upright as though in an extremity of controlling pain or anger, or both' to quote a sentence not from *A Buried Life* but from Dr Withers's kind contribution to this book [*Housman 1897–1936*]. Annoyance, yes; bad temper of a kind, yes now and again; anger, very occasionally, as when I asked him about the O.M. – but agony, torment, no, never.[82]

Neither of these two men strikes one as a totally reliable witness. Richards had a selective memory and needed to defend his own image of Housman. Withers seems to have been a collector of literary lions with a tendency in this case to exaggerate the effect he had on Housman and their level of intimacy. And it would not have been beyond Housman to exaggerate his feelings for Sophie for purposes of self-protection. But whatever the truth of this episode, it would still be perfectly possible for Housman to carry forward a powerful and truthful remembrance of that first emotional impact when his desperate need to be mothered was met by Sophie Becker. Remembrance certainly, but Housman evidently made no attempt to keep alive his connection with her. The conventional Housman could not be a man of romantic gesture, especially given that Sophie was of a different class, status and nationality. When he wrote to Walter Ashburner in June 1903 inviting him to dine at the Café Royal, Ashburner had just told him of a visit he himself had recently made to Wiesbaden. Housman replied calmly

> I hope everything went well at Wiesbaden. It is a place I am often incited to go and see, as a lady lives there who is one of my oldest friends; but Germany does not attract me so much as other places, and I hate the thought of having to learn up phrases of conversation and the names for common objects in a third continental language.[83]

According to Withers, Sophie was identified as one of three 'friends'; the first was certainly Moses Jackson and the other most probably his brother Adalbert Jackson. Both inspired poetry. Moses Jackson was the prime cause of *A Shropshire Lad*; Adalbert was the subject of *A.J.J.*, later resurrected by Laurence for *More Poems*. If Housman meant what he said to Withers about Sophie Becker, it is reasonable to assume that she too may have inspired a poem. There is in fact no poem entitled 'S.B', and without such a signpost it is a dangerous game to ascribe one to her inspiration; we know nothing about Housman's actual adolescent experience of her or how in poetic terms he would choose to present it.

Linda Hart has suggested *Oh see how thick the gold cup flowers* as a possible poem: 'Housman's imaginary youth woos a woman of no specified age. But she seems to be wiser and more mature than the youth; she seems to be in charge of the situation. She seems to be teasing him, humouring him – but at the end she says 'good-bye'. Three times she refers to him as 'young man'. Hart concludes 'The more I read *ASL V*, the more I think it had to be written by a young man who had known at first-hand about adolescent love for an older woman.'[84]

The first and last stanzas of the poem say it all:

> OH see how thick the goldcup flowers
>   Are lying in field and lane, with dandelions to tell the hours
> That never are told again.
>   Oh may I squire you round the meads
> And pick you posies gay?
>   — 'Twill do no harm to take my arm.
>   'You may, young man, you may.'

Oh, look in my eyes, then can you doubt?
  — Why 'tis a mile from town.
How green the grass is all about!
  We might as well sit down.
— Ah, life what is it but a flower?
  Why must true lovers sigh?
Be kind, have pity, my own, my pretty,—
  "Good-bye, young man, good-bye."

This poem implies an alternative and more prosaic, albeit realistic, version of Housman's relationship with Sophie Becker, and one that requires a straightforward reading of her 'Dear boy' and 'Your affectionate friend' salutations. This poem is a realistic report of amiable controlled romanticism; parting prompts no expressions of pain.

It is worth noting how far Housman had come in his seventy plus years. The essential Housman had been formed by nature, nurture and the opening circumstances of his life. The subsequent circumstances of his life had been arguably equally formative. His reaction to failure at Oxford, his reaction to his sexual difference, the outcome of his attachment for Moses Jackson, intensified his concentration on textual scholarship. At Trinity, growing satisfaction with his institutionalised way of life, growing confidence that he was in a place where his contribution was valued, encouraged him to indulge his enthusiasms for travel and for good food and wine. These widening influences, and the impact of his celebrity, were making him a more flexible person, and prompting him to show more of his empathetic and sympathetic characteristics. But he never lost the motive force that textual criticism had given to his life

When Lascelles Abercrombie sought a contribution to his *New English Poems: a miscellany of contemporary verse never before published*, he received not a curt reply but a relaxed and witty turn down: 'My last poems have already been published, and a posthumous poem would be premature. My barrenness is so well known that my absence from your miscellany, to which I wish all success, is not likely to cause remark.'[85]

Some things had not much changed. He remained congenitally incapable of self-publicity. Unlike T.E Lawrence who professed to dislike it but sought it and got it, Housman did not seek publicity and mostly did not get it. Among some there was a natural tendency to be excited by his reticence which sharpened their wish to penetrate behind it.

Louise Morgan, editor of the London *Everyman*, had sent Housman a copy of her interview with W.B. Yeats, no doubt as bait, but received only a polite 'I am grateful to you for sending me the interview with Mr Yeats, but not even gratitude will induce me to be interviewed myself.'[86]

Also unchanged was his behaviour in large groups of strangers. In August 1931 he made his only visit to Scotland, invited by Owen Smith, the Chairman of Hay's Wharf and a former member of Trinity College's Finance Committee to join a house-party of seventeen guests in his seventy-five-roomed mansion on the Ardtornish estate in Argyll. It was a party composed mainly of relations though Henry Tonks, formerly Slade Professor of Art at University College, came to dinner. Housman knew him well and the previous year had written to wish him a happy and contented retirement. Tonks found him 'shy and constrained.'[87] Another guest walked with Housman and found him dressed as 'a completely town person'. Neither at home in the drawing room nor on the grouse moors, he made no great impact. His thank-you letter to his hostess was adequate but not exactly enthusiastic and unlikely to prompt a further invitation; it featured his train journey home. He was indeed a celebrity but, alas, for social purposes a non-performing celebrity.

Back in Cambridge he displayed an actual if rarely employed capacity for extensive and unreserved praise when he commended Hugh Stewart, Professor of Latin at Leeds University and now Principal of University College, Nottingham, for his review of *Manilius V* in the *Classical Review:* 'I must pay a tribute not only of gratitude but of admiration and almost of awe to such a combination of care, patience and altruism.' Stewart had finally expressed the hope that Housman would produce an edition of Horace or at least of his Odes but the old warrior seemed to be losing his will to prove himself right: 'Several people want me to produce an edition or else a text of Horace's odes: a text perhaps I may; but it is about time that I gave up writing and tried to improve my mind in leisure.'[88]

The crisis in the economy

1931 saw the peak of the economic crisis and Ramsay MacDonald headed a coalition government. Housman took the rather extraordinary step of donating £500 to the Exchequer for which he received a letter of thanks from Neville Chamberlain. But life in Trinity went on much as usual. He wrote to Withers:

Some of our feasts are suppressed for the sake of economy (i.e. that waiters may suffer from lack of employment and our champagne may go bad in the cellar) but not the Christmas one. I have had my annual milk punch at Jesus and am expecting my annual stout and oysters on St Sylvester's day, after which I shall be able to face another year of life. Also I have lately had a blow-out at the Fishmonger's Hall.

He ended on an expansive note: 'Whether you are in palace or cottage I shall be very glad to come and see you in the summer.'[89] As we have seen, Housman was a generous man and when Kate asked him for an old suit and underclothes for an unemployed gardener in Bath, Housman was ready to oblige. For him charity began at home: 'I keep my benevolence for cases that I know about; as for distressed miners, who have twice tried to starve me, let them starve. My fear is that the suits may prove too tight. He must be restrained from writing me a nice letter.'[90] Five days later he added 'I hope the vests don't tickle him as most vests do me.'

His regular correspondent, Charles Wilson, lived at Willingdon in the economically deprived and depressed north-east of England. Housman surprisingly opened up to him on the subject of class: 'My feelings are much the same as Huxley's; but in my case school is not the cause, for I was quite uninfluenced by my school, which was a small one. I think the cause is in the home. Class is a real thing: we may wish that it were not and we may pretend that it is not, but I find that it is.'[91] In effect, he was endorsing Laurence's opinion of the social and political attitudes with which they had all been brought up and which Laurence spent his life rebelling against. By comparison, Housman seems to have been more deeply imprinted by his upbringing and more conformist and politically conservative by nature, borne out by his attitude to striking miners but denied by his generosity to individuals. The growing intimacy with a man he had never met but had frequently corresponded with led not only to remarks on class but prompted an expression of sympathy: 'I am sorry to hear of your mother's state of health.'

He also told Jeannie about the impact of the country's economic situation on life at Cambridge: 'Most of our Feasts have been put down to make a show of economy, the chief result of which, if it goes on, will be that the champagne will go bad in the cellar instead of being drunk.' He also enclosed for Basil 'the only existing portion of my second work of fiction', *Fragment of an afternoon with the Royal Family*, a sketch in verse and prose 'recounting an episode in which the gardener's boy had climbed into the boudoir of the princess and the two are engaged in conversation.'[92]

Although he could mobilise his innate generosity to help Kate's gardener and his innate sense of responsibility to contribute financially to the Exchequer in times of war and economic depression, and although there were many like him who did not empathise at all with striking miners, it is also noticeable that he experienced nothing like the 'tornado of emotions' the General Strike of 1926 had caused in the war hero Siegfried Sassoon who was 'prompted by the urge to help other outcasts like himself.'[93]

PART XIII

Paris 1932

1932 could be called the year of the great mystery but it began ordinarily enough. Housman had been approached by the syndics (a committee whose job it was to advise on and approve publications by the Cambridge University Press). They wanted to publish his *editio minor* of Manilius. All that remained to be done was a short preface, but he had other desiderata: 'I have ideas of my own about size of page and print and I also want it to be fairly cheap.'[1] Although meetings were made possible by proximity it took less than a month for war to break out between Housman and the university printers, and for Housman to be complaining to Sydney Roberts, secretary to the Press, that his 'overpaid underlings refuse to print my apparatus criticus as I wrote it, and insist on running together lines which I carefully separated, as well as certain signs not of a size corresponding to the type size such as that for omega.'[2]

Coincidentally, Jack Kahane of the Obelisk Press in Paris had asked to produce a deluxe edition of *A Shropshire Lad*. Richards described Kahane as 'a writer of semi-improper novels' and 'a publisher of more or less pornographic stuff.' Housman was clear: 'You correctly suppose that I will have no more editions de-luxe,' but 'talking of pornography, you have been remiss about promising me a sight of Frank Harris's last two volumes, for I understand that there are four in all, and I have only seen two.'[3]

At the end of January, he was empathising with Kate about her husband's death.

> To me he was a kindly and companionable friend; and your long married life must have been in essentials a happy one, and has ended as in the course of nature it should, by the survival of

the younger. In the manner of death we must agree that he was fortunate indeed, and there are many consoling thoughts to heal this sorrow in the course of time.

Kate had decided to move, possibly to Exmouth. Housman was sympathetic: 'I hope you are tranquil and not depressed.'[4]

To this sign of the passage of time was added another. In 1922 Housman had declined an invitation from D.B. Harden of the Classical Reading Society with the words: 'It is only a year since I had the pleasure of attending a meeting of the Classical Reading Society. Spare me a little that I may recover my strength. Social intercourse with human beings, however agreeable, is exhausting, and I cannot make a habit of it.' But Housman had added as a throwaway line: 'perhaps ten years hence, if the world lasts'. Amazingly, Harden must have set up a 'bring forward' for ten years hence and now in 1932, repeated his invitation. Housman saw he had been caught and gave in gracefully. 'I had hoped to be dead when the ten years were out; but as like Peleus and Cadmus, I have lived too long, and as I am sure your intentions are kind, I have made a note of the date.'[5]

Housman had evidently learned lessons from his experience with the Richards Press and was being more business-like with Sydney Roberts. 'I mentioned in one of our conversations that I wished to keep the copyright and to receive as royalty anything that I might receive, and you offered no objection. I return herewith the two copies of the form.'[6]

His celebrity was making him a target but when it came to an appeal to preserve Stonehenge, he demurred: 'for various reasons I do not wish to sign it, one of them being that I do not rate my own political sagacity high, and another that men of letters however competent in such matters they may actually be, are not so regarded by the public.'[7] Once again he was showing no wish to be recruited into the ranks of the great and good or to maintain a high public profile.

Nevertheless, flattery, hero worship and gifts continued to come his way. He told a Mr Dooher: 'I wish that writers would not dedicate books to me nor describe me in public as the greatest of living poets, which you cannot possibly know to be true. I do not copy out poems for anyone, so you must try to get what poor satisfaction you can out of my autograph.'[8] When the Bombay House branch of Longmans Green and Co sought permission to reprint 'Epitaph on an Army of Mercenaries' in an anthology for the use of schools in

India, Housman gave Richards a pithy reply. 'No the Hindoos should behave better!',[9] showing he was aware of changing Indian attitudes to the Raj. This was the year in which the Indian Congress would be declared illegal and Mahatma Gandhi imprisoned; characteristically, Housman did not expound on any of that.

Laurence offered him an opportunity to write an essay on Coventry Patmore for *Great Victorians*. Housman had some feeling that he ought to accept: 'But it would give me more trouble than you can imagine, whereas I want peace in my declining years; and the result would not be good enough to yield me pride or even satisfaction.' In any case Housman had a violent antipathy to Patmore resulting from his 'nasty mixture of piety and concupiscence', although he was prepared to acknowledge 'his essay on English metre is the best thing ever written on the subject'.[10]

Cyril Clemens sent him the piece he had written about their meeting which Housman now returned: 'I have corrected or marked the most inaccurate of your inaccuracies. I do not know why Americans are so fond of writing – and apparently of reading – about personal matters; but it seems to me to be a national characteristic and it makes me unwilling to meet them, though they are always so kindly and friendly.'[11] His American postbag brought him letters and requests of all shapes and sizes. Some like Sylvia Meech, a lady from Texas, got a one line answer: 'I am afraid I have never written any garden verse.'[12]

But it was not all a question of letters from unknowns. After four months, he was back in contact with Percy Withers offering dates in early July for a visit to them at Souldern. From there he could go on to Worcestershire. 'I myself am conceited at the moment because I have just made my annual visit to the dentist and he found nothing to do.'[13]

Likewise he was back in contact with the Rothensteins after an interval of well over a year. This time it was with William who had sent him a copy of his *Men and Memories: Recollections of William Rothenstein 1900–1922* in which he had printed Housman's parody of Frances Cornford. Housman's reaction to Rothenstein's book was unqualified: 'I am reading and enjoying your book. I suppose it is being a painter that makes you able to retain your experiences so distinctly and reproduce them with so much life.'[14] He hoped to see him soon in Cambridge and offered dates. One senses warmth in his words. And he now knew about Alice Rothenstein's nickname Noli given her by two admiring female poetesses, the Michael Fields, who saw her as a delicious, loveable, *Noli me tangere* sort of woman.

Paris and forbidden pleasures?

The mystery began when Housman wrote to Grant Richards on 18 May 1932:

> I shall be in Paris at the Continental from May 29 to June 14. I cannot offer you anything of an invitation, for I shall have a friend with me who would not mix with you nor you with him; but if by chance you should be there I hope you would come to dine or lunch with me one day.[15]

One asks how on earth could a friend of Housman's be unmixable with Grant Richards, a gregarious, worldly and sociable publisher? 'Friend' was a word open to a number of interpretations, yet Housman wrote as he did, without qualification or explanation, seemingly unaware of how his blunt words might be received, or the questions they might provoke. Richards, himself a man of the world, might have thought he knew exactly what Housman meant by the word 'friend'.

The 'friend' was not a fiction and Housman was completely open about him. He or somebody like him would reappear on three subsequent visits to France, for example in August 1933 when he told Percy Withers 'I expect to have a French companion, though not one of much education, and, though amiable, he may be bored.'[16] Just before his departure he wrote again to Kate: 'I shall have with me a French companion, a nice young man, not much educated, who regards me as a benefactor.'[17] By the time they reached Blois, Housman was unwell, and more information was volunteered: 'I am weak and low, but my companion takes all trouble on his shoulders, and really does not seem to be bored.'[18] The next year, 1934, the pattern was repeated. In 1935, he made no mention, either to Kate or Withers, of a companion or friend on his trip to Lyons, Grenoble and Annecy, but in a letter to Lady Frazer he reported 'I had a pleasant tour with a helpful companion.'[19]

Given his passion for linguistic accuracy it is very surprising to find Housman using the words 'friend' and 'companion' as if they were synonyms. And, none of his correspondents asked Housman how they had got on together, perhaps because they were politely incurious, perhaps because they thought they knew what his words implied and were happy to leave stones unturned; or they were simply being self-protective, knowing full well that Housman would not react at all kindly to being quizzed about what could be regarded as a perfectly normal arrangement.

The 'friend' who accompanied Housman must have come from somewhere. Most likely he had been recommended by the Anglo-American firm of tourist agents under Monsieur Buffa, 'a brilliant and knowledgeable Frenchman' from whom Grant Richards had hired a car and driver when he and Housman toured Burgundy together in 1927. But other French sources of recommendation cannot be entirely ruled out. Much earlier, in 1921 when Housman was intending to stay at the hotel Continental for a week, he wrote to Richards of having to send short notice of his imminent arrival to 'my friends and acquaintances there', about whom he characteristically said nothing more.[20] His 1933 companion was described as 'young' and was said by Housman to regard him as a 'benefactor' and was clearly without intellectual pretensions. Otherwise the adjectives used to describe him were 'amiable' and 'helpful'. He was not described as 'good looking', although Housman had shown himself to be aware of people's looks, having written to Witter Bynner that 'Kimball Flaccus impressed me as a very agreeable and good-looking young man.'[21]

The clear impression is that his companions were indeed younger men, their existence suggesting a growing need within Housman to mitigate his solitariness and the lonely tedium of eating alone, and to have help with the practicalities of touring in a foreign country. For the companions, free sightseeing, free meals, an opportunity to practice English, plus the expectations of a big tip could have been the incentives, hence the 'benefactor' description. There was, however, no record of any of them having been paid, not in itself proof that they were not paid. The reason for keeping his 'friend' and Grant Richards apart in 1932 is unknown. The simplest and most obvious explanation is that Housman did not wish to invite an unknown person, classed as an employee, to join them as an equal. One of the companions has been identified as Gaston Roy who seems, like Andrea, to have thought of Housman as a source of income because he pursued Laurence Housman after Housman's death. Laurence then disclosed to Andrew Gow:

> He professes unalterable grief – but as I expected – asks for money, assuring me that A.E.H. promised to remember him in his will. This I don't believe; so I am not sending any, but I am indicating

that I am well aware of his previous importunities, which Alfred sometimes met with difficulty, and I think occasionally with reluctance.[22]

This suggests that the lordly air, noted by Richards in Burgundy, may have encouraged some continentals to take him for a ride. His native generosity and the value of the pound did the rest, although some might conclude that Laurence's words implied a 'try-on' such as attempted blackmail.

However the ambiguities surrounding his 'friend' or his 'companion' are as nothing compared with the small piece of card found more than thirty years after Housman's death among books given by Sir Basil Blackwell in 1970 to T.F. Higham, a fellow of Trinity College, Oxford, and now in the possession of St John's College, Oxford. Inscribed in pencil, beyond doubt in Housman's hand, is the following list which has been shown conclusively to relate to this 1932 visit:

Monday	9	Max
Tuesday	9	Boxeur
Wednesday	0	
Thursday	3	Marin 1
Friday	9	Danseur
Saturday	0	
Sunday	3	Nicois
Monday	0	
Tuesday	9	Marin 2
Wednesday	0	
Thursday	3	negre
Friday	10	danseur
Sat	0	
Sun	3	danseur
Mon	10	danseur 2

Written up the right hand side of the card are the words '10 in 15 days'.

An immediate, simple-minded reaction is that these ten characters must be male prostitutes. Boxers, sailors, dancers, or people masquerading as such, are the kind of characters we might expect to find. Housman's list, albeit rather theatrical, is expressed in correct French masculine singular nouns, with one proper name, Max; they are: sailor (marin), dancer (danseur), man from Nice

(Nicois), negro (negre). There seem to have been two different sailors and two different dancers. The simple annotation '10 in 15 days' may strike some readers as being less of an arithmetic fact, more an exclamatory boast.

The men appear to be being compared, but exactly what was being compared is unknown: their charges, the nature of the services they rendered, or the pleasure they gave? Or were the numerals indicative of the number of encounters, their duration, the hour they took place, the address at which they took place, or, as Jeffrey Scott recently suggested in the *Housman Society Journal* of 2014, the numbers of three Parisian arrondissements. Or did the numerals relate to something entirely different, for example, to the number of hours the companion spent with Housman on those particular days?

It stands to reason that although the numerals may have many possible interpretations only one meaning could have been intended by Housman.

The card has been the source of mystification and speculation for thirty-five years. Paul Naiditch's 'Housman in Paris' in his *Problems in the Life and Writings of A.E. Housman* has established beyond doubt that the visit was in 1932, and that the numerals could not represent prices.

Numerous explanations have been put forward, attacked and defended in the *Housman Society Journal*. In 2013 David McKie, a fellow of Robinson College, Cambridge, proposed that the card was a dream diary prompted by the visual impact of vivid images of Parisian music hall characters.

To be fair to Housman, the matter cannot be left where it is. We need to know the truth about that piece of card because it will tell us whether the more tolerant climate of France did or did not lead to changes in his behaviour.

We have clues but no details on the card itself as to where events might have taken place. Ten years earlier in a letter to Grant Richards on 22 May 1922 Housman wrote:

> I am very much touched by your solicitude for the corruption of my mind, and I eagerly expect the new Proust. I rather gather from your epistle to the world last Thursday that your Mr Ronald Firbank is a bit in the same line. I never heard of Jean Coctreau, [*sic*] but do know something of the Paris bains de vapeur (or vapeurs as Mr Van Vechten says). I am flying to Paris (though

not necessarily to these haunts of vice) on June 1 and shall sleep in London the night before, Hotel Victoria, Northumberland Avenue; so perhaps we might manage to dine together.[23]

The Carl Van Vechten referred to by Housman was a writer, photographer and literary executor of Gertrude Stein, was twice married and was either homosexual or bisexual. Housman's teasing and light-touch approach to the sex lives of Proust and Firbank was coupled with his knowledge of the *bains de vapeur* (steam baths). According to Graham Robb in his *Strangers: Homosexual Love in the Nineteenth Century*, 'In Europe and America, bathhouses offered sex and companionship and were usually much safer than brothels ... The Bains de Penthièvre in Paris which flourished in the 1890s, remained in business until the late 1960s. Procedures were sufficiently similar from one country to the next to be understood by any visitor. In pre-Revolutionary St Petersburg, for example, customers were shown an album of miniature photographs so that they could choose their attendant and his style of dress.'[24] If the Bains de Penthièvre was similarly capable of producing attendants dressed up as the characters on Housman's list, they were a very possible venue for the events of 1932.

We can learn much more from the photographer Brassai's book, *The Secret Paris of the 30's*. It provides other options for venues for Housman's cast of characters. Brothels such as Le Sphinx or Le One Two 'not only offered the regular forms of sex that could be bought all over the city, but specialised in "shows" or "spectacles" constructed to the whim of clients, who dined well in the attached restaurants.'[25] Such 'Houses of Illusion' were all-purpose, equipped to deal with tastes, needs, obsessions along the full length of the sexual spectrum, from voyeurism to flagellation, to every kind of mutual sexual experience, including exotic forms of athletic coupling. These were among the places which also catered for exhibitions of sexual activity for clients who wanted to sharpen their own appetites, or who wished to witness but not necessarily participate in sexual activity; another way for Housman to view his sailors and dancers in action, one might add, visual images every bit as likely to impress themselves on his imagination as characters seen in a music hall.

The numerals are *the* puzzle. Only three were used, 3, 9 and 10, that is apart from 0 whose use has also to be explained. The numerals 3, 9 and 10 are a constant and have been shown to make no sense as prices in pounds sterling or in francs. Housman got seventy-nine francs for his pound sterling. Again Brassai is an expert witness on prices in high-class brothels: 'Around 1900, prices in these houses ranged from ten to forty francs. At the Chabannais, the price of a trick, drinks and tips included, was at least fifty francs. At the Moulins – frequented by Toulouse-Lautrec – you could get away with twenty francs.' It seems that in an ordinary whorehouse the charge was a mere two francs. Marcel Proust, who probably knew what he was talking about, wrote in *A La Recherche du Temps Perdu* that the Duc de Guermantes offered Morel fifty francs to spend the night with him at a brothel in provincial Mainville in Normandy. Thus 3, 9 and 10 are not credible as prices in francs for any establishment Housman was likely to go near, let alone be seen in. However, bathhouse charges amounting to a total of 68 francs for ten occasions is a credible possibility, although the considerable and regular variation in charges per occasion would still require explanation. So far, actual bathhouse prices of the period have not been identified.

There is so far no evidence to suggest that 3, 9 and 10 were part of a widely used and understood code for particular sexual experiences. Numbers did not feature either in the sex diaries kept by John Maynard Keynes or the so-called 'Black' Diaries of Sir Roger Casement. Housman's own diaries were innocent of any records of his sex life. And although three numbers would have been sufficient to cover standard sexual experiences, they would not have been sufficient to cover such stimulants to sexual excitement as flagellation, masochism, fetishism and voyeurism, all means of arousing sexual excitement and producing orgasm, and all available in Paris where the customer could get what he felt he needed.

It has been suggested that 3, 9 and 10 could refer to the number or duration of sexual encounters or as indicators of performance. Housman was a seventy-three-year-old man accustomed to living a quiet, cloistered existence. Sexual excitements would have had to be at the lowest end of demands for sexual energy or '10 in 15 days' would have constituted an exhausting sexual marathon; even if the spirit were willing most likely the flesh would be weak. As performance or satisfaction indicators, scores of 3, 9 and 10 employ too small a part of a simple one to ten scale to be at all credible.

The possibility that the numerals were addresses is credible. According to Brassai, many brothels were indeed identified by 'a gigantic number in the style of the period, art nouveau, cubist, art deco: Number 9, Number 26, Number 43, Number 122 were all famous.'[26] There is a photograph of Number 4 in his book, and a

Number 14 is mentioned. It would be irrational to think that there could not be a Number 3, a Number 9, or a Number 10.

Alternatively, the five zeros could represent days on which Housman's companion did not work and the numerals 3, 9 and 10 could be the hours worked or his pay for that day. A total of sixty-eight hours is certainly feasible for hours worked, but not feasible for the companion's payment because sixty-eight pounds sterling, as Naiditch has shown, would have been ridiculously high, the equivalent of six thousand francs. On the other hand, a payment of sixty-eight francs for nine or ten days' work would hardly be sufficient to classify Housman as a benefactor.

Out of all of this we have to ask what real evidence do we have? The card exists and is in Housman's hand but those are the only two facts. The cast of characters *could* have been found in the *bains de vapeur*, or in one of the multi-purpose brothels, or in a music hall, or indeed in a solo performance by his friend/companion or some other person dressing up in the privacy of Housman's hotel room. There is no direct evidence that any of these was the case. And although the account for his use of the car and driver mentioned some specific places, there was no mention of evening destinations like music halls, or particular arrondissements in Paris such as Montmartre, for which Housman could, of course, have used taxis or the Metro.

And so we have to turn to what we know otherwise of Housman. If hard evidence is negligible what is the soft evidence? Here was a man governed by reticence and discretion whose life was driven by his mind, not his biology. He has never yet been identified in gossip or memoirs as a member of any homosexual coterie in Cambridge, a place that was widely recognised at the time as a hotbed of homosexuality.

There is no evidence that when Moses Jackson went out of Housman's life in 1889 Housman's profound attachment and idealisation of him was transferred to any other person. Indeed, far from seeking other partners, the evidence is that Housman did his best to cling to his idea of Moses, maintaining friendly and helpful relations with him, his wife and his family. As long as he lived, Moses Jackson remained the central focus of Housman's feelings and fulfilled his needs for emotional attachment. By 1932 Moses had been ten years in the grave but his presence was still felt and Housman's connection with his family still maintained. It is a reasonable assumption that Housman's never powerful sexual needs would have been slowly diminished by age, his ferocious work habit, his disposition to celibacy and the satisfaction of whatever sensual needs he had by eating and drinking. Of supreme relevance to how he was likely to behave in Paris was that heartfelt annotation, 'This is me', written against T.E. Lawrence's personal statement that he shrank from human contact and intimacy. It would have been anathema for Housman to have had to strike up conversations with unknown men (as opposed to waiters, sommeliers and patrons of restaurants), or to have ventured into groups of strangers, to say nothing of the actual impact of a succession of sexual experiences in strange surroundings, indulged in with strange people in alien circumstances. It is highly questionable that he could have welcomed being manipulated by a bathroom attendant in fancy dress.

So it is unlikely to vanishing point that Housman underwent a Jekyll and Hyde transformation on crossing the Channel and indulged himself in ten days of sexual adventure. Housman spent this holiday in and around Paris, the broad outlines of his drives being recorded in the account of his daily mileage together with details of lunches and dinners at various restaurants during the period.

He seems to have set himself up as a one-man *Good Food Guide*. On 31 May he began his account of further encounters with French cooking in a series of letters to Grant Richards. The first dealt with the Ecu de France, 'which is good and evidently very successful, rather uncomfortably crowded after 8 ... sole with mushrooms, certainly very good, though it is not a mixture I approve of ... deadly dull, boiled or stewed fowl with mushrooms again ... and the hard uneatable parts of artichoke leaves ... The patron stands over the waiters while they serve one, in a menacing manner. When I started to order Burgundy the sommelier insisted on Chambolle-Musigny 1921 which was most excellent.'[27]

Three days later he damned Les Tilleuls at Bougival: 'Situation perfectly beautiful, wine quite good, cuisine mediocre, service atrocious. Benedictine poured out in bucketfuls does not atone for badness and coldness of coffee.'[28]

A week later he had eaten his way through another five restaurants, Boeuf a la Mode, Marins, Mon Pays, Korniloff and Gaschy. Two days later he sent Richards his reports on three others. Le Progres with a rather smart address, 195 Avenue de Neuilly, he damned outright:

> horribly noisy with trams and other traffic, it is about the most
> expensive restaurant I ever was in. It has a special wine-list of

grands crus, running into three figures; and if there is a fool on earth who wants to pay 65 francs for a glass of Chartreuse, he can do it here. Cuisine good; service hardly sufficient and not in the least *soigné*. I cannot imagine how it subsists.[29]

He had gone further afield to Chartres where he reported that 'L'Homme has lost its renown, and one is told to lunch at La Providence in Jouy, a few miles this side of Chartres.'

After his return to Trinity he was still in restaurant inspector mode: 'The chief discovery I made in Paris was a new Bearnais or Bordelais restaurant Albert Galen, 36 Boulevard Henri Quatre: very good and plentiful; and everything which should be hot is piping hot.' Below his signature he added another: 'A tiny, crowded, rather plebeian restaurant called Nine after its proprietress, 34 rue Victor Masse is Marseillais, and has the best bouillabaisse I have ever eaten outside Marseilles.'[30]

Although we know how ferociously energetic Housman could be when working at his scholarly tasks in Cambridge, this programme of constant eating and drinking calls into question his stamina and capacity for much else. It makes very plausible David McKie's proposition that Housman switched off in the evening, visited the music hall and had dreams of vivid characters he had seen there. Unfortunately, while there is abundant evidence that Housman was a great aficionado of the London music hall, frequently entertaining friends there, he never mentions that he visited music halls in France. He made no mention of them in correspondence with William Rothenstein who had written so vividly about the Moulin Rouge and its cast of exotic characters in his *Men and Memories 1872–1922*, which Housman so much admired. He made no mention of music hall acts, songs or ditties that caught his fancy, which must have been the case if the experiences had been sufficiently vivid to dominate his dreams for ten nights. This alleged dream sequence seems to imply photographic impressions left on the brain by vivid experiences. No other evidence has been produced for the existence of such a phenomenon, a distinctly different category of dreams from those prompted by subconscious desires as suggested by Freud.

We can also recall that in recording a meeting in Paris with Housman five years earlier in June 1928, Richards wrote that after dining together at Le Clou in Montmartre, 'Housman went off to keep some engagement and I returned to St Germain.'[31] It was not in Housman's nature to enlighten Richards further and he did not. So either he had an undisclosed agenda for the rest of the evening or had a previously arranged engagement or simply fancied a solitary and silent walk after their convivial dinner. But we also know that Housman knew Paris well and that over the years had built up a range of contacts of whom he has left not the slightest trace. So although it may be tempting to think Housman led a secret life in Paris, there is absolutely nothing other than this kind of circumstantial evidence to support it.

A different kind of clue is provided by the fifty books in English, French and German classified by Paul Naiditch under Erotica/Sexual Studies. They may have been acquired to help him research the nature and boundaries of his own sense of difference but insofar as they included books on flagellation, sadism, masochism and fetishism, these particular books may have been acquired because he felt a lively and active interest in one or more of those subjects.

We have also seen that in the previous year, 1931, he had produced his paper *Praefanda* which dealt with textual problems relating to sex vocabulary in Latin poets. On that occasion Housman had gracefully absolved himself of the Englishman's obsession with sex, yet *Praefanda*, the books in his library and his correspondence with Gosse and Richards were together suggesting a certain interest, certainly in flagellation and what he himself classified as 'pornography'.

Housman lived a solitary, introverted, institutionalised existence punctuated only by lectures and meals, fertile ground for promoting odd behaviour and possibly sexual fantasies which he could exercise alone in his study by turning pages, or by looking at exciting pictures.

Housman was certainly not a prude. He was a great frequenter of music halls, notorious for songs of gross innuendo, 'naughty but nice' being a phrase he picked up there and implanted in one of his verses. There was gossip that he liked dirty stories. When Stanley Baldwin went to Cambridge for the opening of the Mond Laboratory, he reported to Thomas Jones, Deputy Secretary to the Cabinet, 'I dined with a club called, 'The Family'– Housman, poet, there, most unclubable man. I could get nothing out of him. Was told after I could have drawn him with obscene stories, but I gave them up when I left Harrow.'[32] And there was A.C. Benson's recollection that at a dinner of The Family, Housman had told the most obscene story he had ever heard.

Housman's friendships with Grant Richards and Herbert Foxwell suggest that he may have been drawn to the company of men who were his opposites, who were extrovert and who lived relatively uninhibited lives. Grant Richards, seen by those who have written about him as the complete gentleman and man about town, supplied Housman with reading material banned in England, like *Lady Chatterley's Lover* and Frank Harris' *My Life and Loves*. Herbert Foxwell, as we have seen, was an economics don with an adventurous love life which may have provided some piquant conversation on the twenty-two occasions he and Housman dined together between 1911 and 1933.

However, a liking for risqué entertainment, an enjoyment of dirty stories, a liking for associating with men of the world can also be seen as a subconscious wish to be more like them. It would not be surprising if his repressed childhood, the death of his mother, the trauma of being circumcised when adolescent, the discovery in late adolescence of himself as different, his cloistered and generally solitary existence as a scholar and poet, had all contributed to tastes he wanted to indulge in. But they did not have to be more than voyeuristic experiences, implied in the photographs Laurence uncovered after Housman's death and about which he made his gnomic statement: 'I found other things among his papers, which did him no discredit, but told me clearly the direction of his interest in beauty of human form.'[33] This could at worst suggest he came across pictures of naked men, classical or otherwise.

Classicist Shackleton Bailey's theory about the Paris card was 'My own guess is that it was part of some private game or fantasy, or a combination of both.'[34] This startling theory has not been as deeply examined as it deserves. One of the salient things about Housman was his attitude to truth. He declared 'It is only a minority of those who engage in this study who are sincerely bent upon the discovery of truth ... the amount of subconscious dishonesty which pervades the textual criticism of the Greek and Latin classics is little suspected except by those who have had occasion to analyse it.'[35] He famously declared 'the love of truth is with most people the faintest of passions.'[36] This constantly declared passion for truth and hatred of falsehood suggests that he may have been like the preacher who is hot on morality but whose own conduct leaves something to be desired. Housman's passion for truth had to live alongside other elements in his nature, his habitual secrecy, his instinct to tell others no more than they needed to know, his frequent veiling of his thoughts in irony and ambiguity, his frank enjoyment in his talent for skit and nonsense verse tantamount to holding up a distorting mirror to nature. Housman could also play games. He had been wilfully obscure with Stamfordham over his reasons for refusing the Order of Merit. His famous claim that he knew immediately that the word 'rustling' in a newspaper review of Walter de la Mare's *Farewell* was wrong was not accompanied by the right word, nor did he provide any basis for preferring it. A year later in 1933, when researcher Maurice Pollet quizzed him, Housman simply ignored questions he did not wish to answer. In 1933, parts of his Leslie Stephen Lecture would be teasing and ironic. The combative and aggressive way in which he penned comments on other textual critics suggest a man whose passion for winning and finding an outlet for his anger were together greater than his passion for truth. The fact that he usually out-manoeuvred or reduced his opponents to silence meant that he generally won, although he had not necessarily done so in the case of Postgate and Propertius.

There may be another curious parallel with T.E. Lawrence. Housman had read *Seven Pillars of Wisdom* and doubtless Lawrence's account of being assaulted in Deraa and sodomised by the Turks. Lawrence's biographer Mack wrote 'The wish to make himself known stands for Lawrence alongside the desire to hide or deceive; unusual candour and factual honesty exist side by side with secrecy and distortion.'[37] Lawrence's own accounts of the incident in various editions of *Seven Pillars of Wisdom* and in letters never describe what actually happened.

Nor had Housman in this case made his card unequivocally intelligible. He could have made it so by adding symbols like frs, £s, hrs, mins, or o'clock or other notations to make his meaning crystal clear. But if it was a private game, why was Housman playing it? Why was he doing a Lawrence of Arabia? Why was he revealing yet hiding? The only two intelligible messages it conveys are ten nouns and the summary statement, 10 in 15 days.

After his death Housman would entrust Laurence with his papers and allow him to publish poems he judged to be up to his normal standard. Housman did not take Laurence at all seriously as a writer, did not have regard for the quality of his intellect or his feel for language. Laurence was the last man he should have trusted with the job of literary executor, *except* that Laurence was homosexual and would find and publish the poems Housman himself had deliberately not published in *A Shropshire Lad* or *Last Poems*. The choice of Laurence as his literary executor is tantamount to proof that

Housman wanted those poems and the autobiographical clues they contained to see the light of day but he simply could not bring himself to make that absolutely clear. After his return from Paris, a 'college student', Virginia Rice, asked him whether *Last Poems* would be his last collection of poems. He replied, 'Not necessarily the last but the last volume which will appear in my lifetime.'[38]

However, Housman knew that Laurence's footnote to his *Echo de Paris*, published in 1923, was proof that he was right in placing his posthumous work in Laurence's hands:

> Obscurantists may still insist on treating as an acquired depravity what medical research has now proved to be an involuntary or congenital deflection from a normality which exact sciences find it harder and harder to define ... a surviving superstition of our own time has been that false and foolish moral insistence on regarding certain maladjustments of nature as something too horrible to be mentioned, and of putting the victims thereof in a class apart, rather lower than the ordinary criminal.[39]

This was the essential Laurence Housman, expressing a free-thinking, open-minded view of life. His elder brother had always felt the necessity for conformity and reticence, except where his comic works enabled him to distort and mock, or on other occasions when his self-control fractured and allowed his poetry or his aggressive anger to vent themselves.

There is no doubt of the card's existence. It is still kept in the library at St John's. There are explanations for its cast of characters, some more plausible than others, but there is no convincing evidence for the meaning of 3, 9, 10 and 0, or 10 in 15 days. As to purpose, it could have been used like any piece of pornographic material to bring to mind previous sensations its owner wished to repeat, or it could have been jottings intended to prompt future nonsense verses based on exotic characters, or as a simple and innocent record of an intriguing dream sequence, or, as suggested by another member of the Housman Society, a record of winnings from lottery tickets bought in Paris, or a list of unrelated things he wanted to jot down and remember, none of which were meant to be connected.

Whether the card was game or spoof or a disguised message for his brother, Housman lost interest in it. Instead of preserving it for his brother to find, Housman seems finally to have used it as a bookmark.

All the soft evidence derived from what we know of Housman's behaviour is overwhelmingly against a holiday of significant sexual adventure; the actual realities of his visit to Paris in 1932 lay in his flying, his motoring, his sightseeing, his eating and drinking.

Thus can we judge E.M. Forster's observation in 1936, 'One wishes he [Housman] could have enjoyed the happy highways which he resigned in the body and possessed so painfully in the imagination, but he was not destined for pleasures. Perhaps he had a better time than the outsider supposes. Did he ever drink the stolen waters he recommends so ardently to others? I hope so.'[40] This was a case of Forster wanting for Housman what Forster wanted for himself; he was not to know that his own principles of pleasure, free love and promiscuity did not rule Housman.

Back in Cambridge, a letter to Kate showed him full of 'the great improvement which had been made in the aeroplanes in the last twelvemonth, in size, steadiness, freedom from noise, and even to some extent in speed. The science also seems to have progressed: when I began, pilots had to fly below the clouds, because if they flew above them they lost their way; but now they fly *through* them and keep their bearings all right...and (on the 'silver wing', the most expensive machine – though the fare is only £5 10s 0d –) you can have a large lunch served if you want it.'[41]

He reacted characteristically to Professor Fobes of Amherst College, Massachusetts, who had sent him a book printed in a Greek font he had himself devised. 'I am not altogether a worthy recipient, for I have no more appreciation of what typographers call beauty than of the "elegance" of a mathematical proof or the points of a bull-terrier; and moreover I seem to find that thick type prevents men from reading quickly.'[42]

Arnold Rubin was after him again for a contribution to his magazine, and received a frank reply. 'A contribution from me is something that many magazines have asked, and none, within human memory, obtained. I do not remember that any of them suffered in consequence, and I do not suppose that yours will either.'[43] Nor was there to be any poem in his own hand for Houston Martin. 'It is now a great many years since I began to refuse requests for poems written out in my own hand, and therefore you must not mind if you receive the same answer as many others.'[44]

He seemed to be unruffled by yet another call for funds from Richards and sent a cheque for £200 at the end of July 1932 'which will do me no immediate injury. But it seems to me that you are likely to get into new difficulties if you order your finances in such a way that to be disappointed of *pre-payment* for a book has such dire results.'[45] Possibly as a means of thanking Housman, Richards proposed to arrange Housman's miscellaneous modern library. 'These modern books of his were in horrid disorder and all over the place,'[46] but it was not until September that they were able to agree dates for him to do the job. At the same time, Housman was looking to offload nine volumes of *Bibliotheca Germanorum Erotica et Curiosa* 'which I had ill-advisedly applied for', advising Scholfield at the University Library: 'Will you send a stout fellow to fetch them? There are nine volumes, of the shape and size of Pauly-Wissowa, but much thicker.'[47]

Demonstrating the family togetherness that had developed in his childhood, Housman had also been doing the rounds of family and friends at Tardebigge where he squeezed in a meeting with his nephew Denis, a stay with the Withers and a visit to Laurence and Clemence, now settled at Street in Somerset. He was working quietly: 'September is a month when I always feel industrious, and a pleasant month in Cambridge.'[48]

1 December 1932: Brother Basil Housman dies

When Basil Housman died at the beginning of December 1932, Housman wrote openly to Percy Withers. 'He was my favourite among my brothers and sisters, and the most normal member of the family.'[49] These few words speak volumes about Housman's reflections on his siblings. Basil was his favourite because they had the great bond that comes from being able to laugh at the same things. Believing Housman would be going to the funeral, Withers had offered him a bed and was probably surprised to hear 'I am not going to my brother's funeral, as it would be difficult and they do not press me to come.' Housman had felt able to participate as a pall-bearer at Thomas Hardy's funeral in Westminster Abbey. On this occasion, there were practical difficulties relating to his university duties but the great liking and respect he had for his brother may have been outweighed by reluctance to be part of a family funeral, when all the conventional expressions of grief and pious thoughts surrounding death would have been so out of key with his own philosophy. He was his usual self when he sent Kate a copy of the 'Bromsgrovian' containing Basil's obituary: 'you will notice blunders.' He was again being reminded of his own mortality and Kate received an up-to-date bulletin on his own health. 'In the course of this year I have grown older, which shows itself in my walking powers. After five or six miles, though I do not get tired, my legs tend to act sluggishly. My heart according to the doctor is going on all right.' He did not seem at all daunted by the onset of the festive season. 'I have to eat two Christmas dinners on Christmas Eve and a third on the Day itself.'[50]

At the end of 1932 Richards became concerned about Housman's health

> and consequently, about the Spartan nature of his immediate surroundings. His bedroom was narrow and austere in the extreme; there can have been no undergraduate in college who did not have at least as great a degree of comfort. It was dark and cold, or it gave that impression, and I could not help contrasting it with the degree of comfort to which he was inuring himself on his visits to France. Returning to London I summoned up courage to write and remonstrate with him, scolding him about this thing or that and making suggestions. [51]

He replied quickly: 'I am touched by your concern for my health and disapproval of my habits, but your picture is darker than the truth. The fire does not usually go out, nor is the bed to which I retire a cold one, as I keep my bedroom so warm with a gas fire that I do not even have to use my hot-water bottle.'[52] Richards felt he could only reply 'I am relieved', but realised he was up against an old man who did not wish to change his habits and besides, he had to admit to himself, 'the Colleges at Oxford and Cambridge were not built with any approximation to modern ideas of comfort and sanitation.'[53]

A Christmas present from Rosa Jackson

In the intervening years the Jackson family had suffered grievous blows. Hector, having survived three years of war, was knocked off his bicycle in Vancouver in early 1920 and died a week later without recovering consciousness. Three years later Moses himself died. When Rosa had regained health and strength after her two bereavements, she returned to England. Rupert was settled with his French wife in a County Durham medical practice. Gerald and Oscar were keen on pursuing their careers. There was nothing in British Columbia for Rosa.

Housman's contact with the Jackson family did not wither. He was an assiduous godfather and in regular contact with his godson Gerald from 1925 onwards. Now in December 1932, ten years after Moses' death, Rosa sent Housman a present – Moses' paper knife. He replied:

Dear Mrs Jackson
I am very grateful for your kindness in giving me the paper knife which belonged to my dear friend, and I shall treasure it to the end of my days.

My advancing age shows itself chiefly in my not taking such long walks as formerly; but otherwise I go on without much change for the worse. That however may soon come, as I have to eat two Christmas dinners on Christmas Eve and a third on the day itself.

I wish you a happy time among your family, and please convey my best wishes both to those now around you and those whom you are expecting.

I remain yours sincerely
A.E. Housman[54]

Godfather Housman

Housman had not been able to persuade Gerald's father to accept his £500's worth of royalties and alleviate the Jackson family's financial hardships but when he wrote to Grant Richards in 1933 that he was unable to help him in *his* financial difficulties he gave as one of his reasons: 'I am finding £450 a year for the education of a godson, and this will go on for four years.'[55] Housman had found his own way of helping the family and Rosa may have had Housman's generosity to Gerald in mind when she sent Housman the paper knife. His quiet words 'I shall treasure it to the end of my days' were a measure of the place Moses still occupied in his heart.

In fact, we now know from a group of hitherto unpublished letters that Housman was an assiduous godfather. His first surviving letter to Gerald had been in November 1925 when Gerald outlined his forward plans. Housman's response had been ready and generous: 'If you find yourself at all straitened for money at the university I hope you will apply to me. A little often makes all the difference between comfort and discomfort.' He was expansive too about a recent trip to the Pyrenees, the places he visited, the flying across the Channel. He

Figure 42 Gerald Jackson, game hunting in Rhodesia. By permission of the Jackson family.

had no inhibitions about telling Gerald 'I had a French friend with me, one of those delightful people who enjoy making arrangements, taking rooms, using telephones, and all the things that I hate, so I had no trouble – But like most Frenchmen he would not walk, and required a pony or donkey if the way was rough and steep.'[56] In May 1927 Gerald informed him of his intention to take a research degree and possibly go on to Cambridge; Housman was both welcoming but practical about his own capacity to give advice: 'Of course I should be glad to see you here, but it is no good asking my opinion and advice which are valueless, as I stick to my job and know hardly anything about research studies here.'[57] Between 1929 and 1935 Housman wrote, on average, seven times a year to Gerald. He wrote ten times in 1933 and three times in 1936 before he died, a frequency that ranks him closer to a parent than a godfather. In 1930 he wrote six times, this being the year in which Gerald was arranging to go to Cambridge after two years of fieldwork as a geologist in Northern Rhodesia, followed by study at the Royal School of Mines and a doctorate at Imperial College, London. Two terms at Cambridge would enable him to undertake specialised mineralogy and revise his thesis.

Housman's letters invariably began 'My dear Gerald' and always ended 'Your affectionate godfather A.E. Housman.' His letters were invariably relaxed and tactfully paternalistic when he had advice to give. They confirm an easy and inclusive relationship with the whole family. We read that in 1927 'The eclipse of the sun on June 29th has evidently been arranged by Rupert, and Hartlepool is to be the most eclipsed spot.'[58] In one of February 1928 he mentioned Gerald's mother Rosa who had evidently expressed worries about the likely curtailment of Gerald's Rhodesian fieldwork. Housman mentioned seeing Oscar in Cambridge: 'I thought him much changed since the war.'[59] Writing to Gerald in Northern Rhodesia it was a case of 'I hope both you and Oscar are well.'[60] In 1929 he wrote of having missed seeing Rupert: 'I expected to see Rupert last term, as he was coming up to a College Feast for men of his period; but just on eve of it the Master of the College went and died, so it had to be put off.'[61] Letters to Gerald in Rhodesia were seamed with humorous allusions, hoping he would not fall out of his aeroplane on to geological objects, however attractive; hoping his new rifle had protected him from lions and buffaloes; referring to snapshots in *The Times* of lions in the jungle in one of which they were eating something which he feared might be Gerald, till he saw its prey was more like a zebra. Frequently he drew attention to what he thought was Gerald's mishandling of English, which in his paper to the Geological Society was 'like the English army at Bannockburn, gay yet fearful to behold.'[62]

Once returned to England, Gerald had family obligations which Housman understood: 'If you are inclined to come for a day or two I should be very glad to see you. But perhaps your term is over and you are off to Hartlepool or some other distant spot.'[63] In October 1930 he learned that other financial support for Gerald had been forthcoming. 'It is a great and good thing that the Company has made you a grant, and you ought to be pleased with yourself.'[64] By 7 November 1930 Gerald had rooms in New Court, Trinity College. The ever-punctilious Housman had to write: 'When once you are admitted it will not be possible for me to ask you to the High Table, so will you come and dine with me in Hall on Monday, the first day I have free: and I will ask Winstanley [the Senior Tutor] to put off your fall in the social scale till afterwards.'[65]

Housman was always concerned to be kept up to date with Gerald's financial needs for fees and living expenses. He told him he intended leaving him £300 in his will but besides being a thorough father figure in the financial sense, he was motherly in his anxiety that Gerald should not work himself too hard, should not go 'starving yourself or depriving yourself of proper amusement', counselling him about career choices when he wrote in the dire economic circumstances of 12 March 1935. 'I think it would be a pity to break off your medical education unless a really good offer in the mining world comes along.'

In January 1931, expecting a protest from Gerald about his having settled his termly bill, he was prompted to utter a rare articulation of his feelings for Gerald's father.

> It may annoy you to hear that your College bill for last term is paid; but do not stick your heels in the ground and be nasty. If you could have any idea of what my feeling for your father was and still is you would not grudge me the pleasure.[66]

Housman was again speaking from the heart. His words *was and still is* (my italics) underline yet again the enduring nature of his deep attachment to Moses Jackson. They chime with words he had written to Moses himself in 1922, with the poignant words he had written to Pollard in 1923, and with those he wrote to Rosa on her gift of the paper knife in 1932. His words and their meaning cannot be doubted and are a formidable obstacle for those who allege debauchery in Paris.

PART XIV

Academic apotheosis and swansong

January 1933: The Maurice Pollet questionnaire

Richards described the Frenchman Maurice Pollet as 'an admirer and student' and his questionnaire as 'very alarming in its length and in its gimlet qualities'. Pollet had brought it by hand to Richards' office but Richards, knowing his Housman, had been extremely careful in taking it from him. 'I have led him to expect no specific answer from you – that is to say, I have not encouraged him to expect too much.' He made no recommendation on whether Housman should or should not reply. 'I can smooth the matter out even if you make no reply to him at all. If you do make any kind of reply, I suggest that you should make it through me. I can give him any kind of message. I can, if it is desired, choke him off.'[1]

Knowing of Housman's unwillingness to be interviewed and reluctance to answer personal questions, Richards was mightily surprised by Housman's response. Without further fuss Housman completed the questionnaire and returned it to Richards. 'I thought that for the sake of posterity I might as well answer some of the young man's questions.'[2]

His attached letter to Pollet gave his justification for answering. 'As some of the questions which you ask in your flattering curiosity may be asked by future generations, and as many of them can only be answered by me, I make this reply.'[3] The fact is he replied clearly and fully to biographical questions but dealt less fully with questions relating to his motivation as a poet or meanings and intentions in his poems. He was lifting the veil but again, only slightly. Yet this remains the only occasion on which Housman would ever answer questions as probing as these.

Only one of his answers was demonstrably incorrect; he correctly described his father's family as Lancastrian in origin but his mother's family was not Cornish; they had been East Devonian for generations. On religion he was categoric. 'I was brought up in the Church of England ... which is much the best religion I have ever come across. But Lempriere's *Classical Dictionary*, which fell into my hands when I was eight, attached my affections to Paganism. I became a deist at 13 and an atheist at 21.'[4] He also admitted to his interest in astronomy: 'almost as early as I can remember; the cause I think was a little book we had in the house.' He mentioned his early versifying: 'I wrote verse at eight or earlier, but very little until I was 35.'[5]

About the impact of his Oxford years he was brief but unguarded: 'Oxford had not much effect on me, except that I there met my greatest friend.'[6] He played down his connection with Shropshire, reducing it to a sentimental feeling 'because its hills were our western horizon.' He confessed that topographical details 'are sometimes quite wrong.'[7] Pollet's question ' Did you more or less regularly, always go back to Shropshire?' was avoided; clearly he did not want to be specific about just how little time he had spent there.

Questioned about The Shropshire Lad he said 'The Shropshire Lad is an imaginary figure, with something of my temper and view of life. Very little in the book is biographical,'[8] a view we have already questioned.

He was categoric that while he may have been unconsciously influenced by Greeks and Latins the chief sources of his poetry of which he was conscious 'are Shakespeare's songs, the Scottish Border Ballads, and Heine.'[9]

Housman avoided a question referring specifically to change and evolution in themes of soldiers and war and whether that was caused by the Great War and the antimony between friendship and heroism. All he said was that "'Oh stay at home, my lad and plough" was written years before the Great War, and expresses no change of opinion only a different mood.' He added 'The Great War cannot have made much change in the opinions of any man of imagination.'[10]

Pollet hypothesised that the poem 'Be still, my soul, be still' had followed a particularly sharp crisis of pessimism and linked it with the next poem 'Think no more lad.' In response Housman avoided interpretation of the poems, merely producing a statement of his philosophical position: 'I have never had any such a thing as "a crisis of pessimism". In the first place I am not a pessimist but a pejorist (as George Eliot said she was not an optimist but a meliorist); and that is owing to my observation of the world, not to personal circumstances.'[11]

Pollet probed further: 'are there not, besides, very precise occasional causes to that deep crisis which I suppose to have taken place at a certain time?' This was dangerous territory, which Housman avoided by separating his poetry from his emotional life:

> I did not begin to write poetry in earnest until the really emotional part of my life was over ... my poetry, as far as I could make out, sprang chiefly from physical conditions, such as a relaxed sore throat during my most prolific period, the first five months of 1895.[12]

Then came a question even closer to the bone: 'Have you ever disclosed the names of some of those friends of yours who are made the subject of some of your poems; and if not, do you think that you would, as it were, give them away, in handing their names to the public?' Housman simply ignored the question.

In his final question Pollet went on what amounted to a speculative fishing trip, asking Housman for his opinion on two schools of philosophy, the Stoics and the Epicureans, and ten named writers, Villon, Pascal, Verlaine, Leopardi, Calderon, Edward FitzGerald, Thomas Hardy, and three German philosophers, Kant, Schopenhauer, Hartmann. This trawl for enthusiasms and unguarded comments produced a clear answer:

> Pascal and Leopardi I have studied with great admiration; Villon and Verlaine very little, Calderon and German philosophers not at all. For Hardy I felt affection and high admiration for some of his novels and a few of his poems.[13]

Since Housman said he had studied Pascal and Leopardi with great admiration it is worth asking what he might have admired in them. Presumably what Housman admired were Blaise Pascal's *Pensées*; it is most unlikely that he was at all interested in Pascal's important contributions as a mathematician.

Pascal was a convinced Christian with 'an uncompromising commitment to Christian truth'.[14] His purpose was to defend Christianity as a revealed religion, not a position that would have at all appealed to Housman the atheist, though he might well have been intrigued to match his own intellect against that of Pascal whose *Pensées* were complex, intellectually demanding, wide ranging in their scope and closely argued, providing just the kind of strenuous mental exercise Housman enjoyed. They occasionally reflected his own views on the human condition. Reading Pascal would also have given him plentiful opportunities for polishing his own capacity for academic polemic, casuistry and sophism.

Giacomo, Count Leopardi, an Italian poet whose most celebrated work *I Canti* (Songs) appeared in 1831, has been described as a poet of 'cosmic pessimism', was admired by Schopenhauer as 'the supreme contemporary poet of human unhappiness', and by Nietzsche who coupled him with Pindar as 'poets who think'. Housman would have found many resonances with his own life view in Leopardi's poetry and would have been enchanted by Leopardi's lyrical yet clear and economical poetic voice. Leopardi's biographer Iris Origo spoke of the poet's deliberate restraint, economy of expression and surprisingly small vocabulary. A passage from *Le Ricordanze* in Galassi's translation harmonises with Housman's 'blue remembered hills':[15]

> E che pensieri immensi,
> Che dolci sogni mi spiro la vista
> Di quell lontano mar, quei monti azzurri,
>
> [And what immense ideas, what tender dreams the sight
> of that far sea inspired in me, those blue hills I can see]

Leopardi placed no boundaries on outright subjective expression of his personal feelings; he wrote about his unhappy love affairs, his solitariness, his alienation from the whole process of living; a poetry that is more richly autobiographical than Housman's. Leopardi, a hunchback, felt himself an outsider, different and rejected. But unlike Housman he acknowledged and was aware in his poetry of the illusions that made life worth living. This, perhaps, is why the *Canti* end with a touching command to pursue one's illusions, to live and love life as it occurs:

> Commit to present pleasure
> Your brief life.

Housman's affinities with both Pascal and Leopardi are crystal clear, the one feeding the scholar's mind, the other his mode of expression.

A wholly surprising thing is that Housman gave no reaction at all to the name of Edward FitzGerald and his *Rubaiyat of Omar Khayyam.* First published in the year of Housman's birth, 1859, FitzGerald's translation of the eleventh century verses of the renowned Persian mathematician, philosopher and poet was the height of fashion in late Victorian and Edwardian times and like *A Shropshire Lad* is still in print. It is inconceivable that Housman would not have recognised his name in 1933; FitzGerald died about the time the young Housman entered the Patent Office. Perhaps he ignored the *Rubaiyat* as beneath his notice, a mere popular translation from a language he himself was not familiar with. Yet in 1989, *A Shropshire Lad* was put forward by one editor as the 'true and immediate heir'[16] of FitzGerald's poem. The feel of Housman's poetry is akin to that of FitzGerald; the feel of 'With rue my heart is laden for golden friends I had' is very much that of FitzGerald's 'The moving finger writes and having writ moves on'. Housman's 'Wake: the silver dusk returning/ Up the beach of darkness brim' reminds one of FitzGerald's 'Awake! For Morning in the Bowl of Night/ Has flung the stone that puts the Stars to Flight'.

But whereas in the *Rubaiyat* there are consolations –

> Here with a Loaf of bread beneath the bough,
> A Flask of Wine, a Book of Verse — and Thou
> Beside me singing in the Wilderness—
> And Wilderness is Paradise enow.

there are no such consolations in *A Shropshire Lad.*

The writers Housman chose to identify all resonated with his own position, whether it was Pascal portraying all of us coming under sentence of death turn by inexorable turn, Leopardi seeing even the pleasures of life as fraudulent, or Hardy's portraying human beings as victims of uncaring chance or malevolent deity: 'Like flies to wanton boys we are to the Gods. They kill us for their sport'. Evidently Housman had not been prompted by Pollet to think back to his Oxford days and his youthful enthusiasm for Matthew Arnold. Housman's declaration to Pollard that Arnold's *Empedocles on Etna* contained 'all the law and all the prophets' was a more powerful statement than anything he said to Pollet about any other writer.

However, Housman ensured that factual information was placed on the record without encouraging fanciful interpretations of his poems or their connection with himself.

Pollet returned to the scene in September when he sent Richards a copy of his essay for Housman to see. Housman's reaction was positive: 'M. Pollet's essay, which I return, is certainly complimentary, and is not silly, and I should raise no objections, "momentous", or otherwise, to its publication in an English paper, though I imagine he would find this difficult, and have no wish that he should succeed.'[17]

Pollet's paper was eventually published in September 1937 in *Etudes Anglaises.* His remarkable success in persuading Housman to collaborate was a compound of Richards' careful introduction, the intrinsic merits of the questionnaire and the total control placed in Housman's hands. What it also reflected was Housman's acceptance that his increasing age and celebrity required some attempt to produce basic facts about himself. Characteristically and remarkably, he took no positive steps to enhance his reputation or to create myth and mystery.

The Leslie Stephen Lecture

In March 1933 Will Spens, Master of Corpus and Vice-Chancellor of the university, persuaded Housman to give the Leslie Stephen Lecture. Stephen, who had died in 1904, had been the first editor of the *Dictionary of National Biography* and father of Virginia Woolf. The lecture was first given in 1905 and had to be on a literary subject, 'including therein criticism, biography and ethics'.

Just before he set to work on his lecture he made two interesting statements about the relative merits of own poems, one to Houston Martin who had written to him on his birthday: 'I could not say I have a favourite among my poems. Thomas Hardy's was XXVII Is my team still ploughing in A Shropshire Lad, and I think it may be the best, though it is not the most perfect.'[18] A second to Gerald Bullett, editor of *The English Galaxy of Shorter Poems*, who had asked to print a number of poems from *Last Poems*: 'I am glad you have chosen V [Grenadier, 'The Queen she sent to look for me'], which I suspect of being the best piece in the book.'[19]

Contemplating work on his lecture, he wrote to sister Kate on 17 March 1933. 'As this must be on a literary subject it will give me a great deal of trouble to compose, and I shall not enjoy myself in the vacation, which began yesterday.'[20] In the Trinity garden, the crocuses – the chief spring show of Cambridge, especially magnificent that year – were now past their best as Housman set about deciding how to structure his lecture. Eleven days later Housman refused an invitation to visit Grant Richards: 'Until I have broken the back of that infernal lecture I have no time for anything else.'[21] A mere month later, business-like as ever, he was writing to Sydney Roberts, secretary to the Cambridge University Press, returning agreement forms for publication of the lecture, questioning a possible violation of copyright involving one of his quotations, asking for a deadline for his manuscript and requesting a printed copy for his own use when delivering the lecture on 9 May.[22] On 26 April he sent Grant Richards a note to ensure his admission to the Senate House.

At five o'clock on the 9 May 1933 Housman began his lecture in a packed Senate House, gaudy with academic dress. His lecture would turn out to be a major autobiographical document, a public revelation of a Housman few could have imagined existed. The lecture would also turn out to be Housman's academic swansong. Ironically, this final appearance on the big academic stage would not be related to classical scholarship, the matter to which he had devoted his life. His public persona had moved on; he had become more famous for his poetry than for his work as a classical scholar. Those instruments of celebrity, the print media, public emotion during and after the First World War, had become more powerful in moulding Housman's reputation than learned journals. It was a measure of his reputation and of changing times that he had been asked to deliver the Leslie Stephen Lecture; his theme, *The Name & Nature of Poetry*.

We should not mislead ourselves into imagining that Housman took to the stage as a professional poet talking about poetry or remotely thought of himself like that. He knew what he was; a textual scholar who happened to have published two volumes of poetry. He would not sail under false colours.

Writing eight months later in January 1934 in *The Criterion*, Ezra Pound wrote at the beginning of his article, 'Mr Housman at Little Bethel', 'This volume has reached me with a friend's note stating that it has "upset a lot of the Cambridge critics".'[23]

Guy Burgess told Michael Burn, poet and writer who subsequently won the MC for his part in the St Nazaire raid, how 'the university had been roused into a frenzy by the Leslie Stephen Lecture'. That afternoon, when he persuaded Burn to climb a college wall 'in order to look down into a garden where, in deckchair and panama hat, Housman himself sat reading', Guy Burgess nastily described the Cambridge of his time as 'an arcane world in which dons, Fellows, professors, headed cliques like hostesses, and claques like prima donnas, stuck poisoned pens between one another's shoulder-blades, and vied with one another conversationally in epigrammatic farts and counterfarts'[24] Burn recited in his book how Burgess had mentioned 'the celebrated creative queers as the word then was' and other military and classical male partnerships, but Burn told me that Burgess had never mentioned Housman in that context. Burgess was not recognising Housman as one of his own kind.

It is easy to see how Housman's lecture caused such a stir. The printed version of his lecture[25] began with a somewhat convoluted but challenging quotation from Coleridge's *Anima Poetae.* It boiled down to three questions: Can you be a critic of poetry if you are not a poet? Are your talents as a critic and as a poet commensurate? And what if you are a bad poet? This teasing challenge, these unanswerable questions, were reminding his audience that he was a poet talking about poetry and therefore something of a challenge for literary critics who were not themselves poets. He did not push his point too far. He might have gone as far as Ben Jonson's pithy 'to judge of poets is only the faculty of poets; and not of all poets, but the best'. He did not wish to set himself up as a target.

He opened with an 'on the one hand and on the other', graciously thanking those who had done him the honour of appointing him, but characteristically putting them in their place: 'I condemn their judgement and deplore their choice'. He was not setting himself up as a literary critic. He challenged 'someone in this home of mathematics to tell me what are the chances of one appearing among that small number of people who are called classical scholars ... all I know is that I am not he'. Referring to the twenty years that had passed since his Inaugural:

> I have not so much improved as to become a literary critic, nor so much deteriorated as to fancy that I have become one. Therefore you are not about to be addressed in that tone of authority which is appropriate to those who are, and is assumed by some of those who conceive themselves to be literary critics.

Housman, emerging now as a born subversive, was laughing in church: 'All my life long the best literature of several languages has been my favourite recreation', which, he said, must have done him some good, quickened his perception, sharpened his discrimination and mellowed the rawness of his personal opinions. 'But personal opinions they remain, not truths to be imparted as such with the sureness of superior insight and knowledge.' Nor was he going to wrap them up in ingratiating false modesty. 'When hereafter I may say that things are thus and thus, you will not insist on my saying instead that I humbly venture to conceive them so or that I diffidently offer the suggestion to your better judgement.'

This was the vintage Housman of his classical papers. He was a man used to telling others what was what. He settled down to enjoy his version of 'the Emperor has no clothes'; implicit in all he said was 'I am no expert but I know what I like.'

And in true Housman style, he expressed his personal opinions. He dealt summarily with his particular *bêtes noires*. He condemned The Age of Wit: 'Poetry, as a label for this particular commodity, is not appropriate.' He swept away the sham poetry produced between Milton's *Samson Agonistes* in 1671 and the *Lyrical Ballads* of 1798. The eighteenth century, he said, had been dominated by the intelligence, involving as he put it 'some repressing and silencing of poetry', and involving 'some touches of frost to the imaginative life of the soul'. He dismissed Wordsworth enthusiasts, attracted by the poet's philosophies and views of nature, but deaf 'to that thrilling utterance which pierces the heart and brings tears to the eyes of thousands who care nothing for his opinions and beliefs'. Everything, he said, is capable of being said in prose but some prose had a powerful effect, for example the forty-ninth psalm in the Book of Common Prayer: '"But no man may deliver his brother, nor make agreement unto God for him" that is to me poetry so moving that I can hardly keep my voice steady in reading it.' Thus, 'poetry is not the thing said but a way of saying it.'

And so he challenged his audience: 'Is there such a thing as pure unmingled poetry, poetry independent of meaning?' He answered his own question with a quotation from Coleridge: 'Poetry gives most pleasure when only generally and not perfectly understood.' This he buttressed with an assertion of his own: 'Meaning is of the intellect, poetry is not.' He identified four poets of the eighteenth century in whom he could hear and recognise the true poetic accent emerging clearly from the contemporary dialect, Collins, Christopher Smart, Cowper and Blake. He asked what other characteristic they had in common and answered outright 'They were mad.' He added, 'Collins and Cowper, though they saw the inside of madhouses, are not supposed to have written any of their poetry there; and Blake was never mad enough to be locked up. But elements of their nature were more or less insurgent against the centralised tyranny of the intellect.'

This was his prologue to exalting Blake, 'For me the most poetical of all poets is Blake. I find his lyrical note as beautiful as Shakespeare's and more beautiful than anyone else's', because 'Blake's meaning is often unimportant or virtually non-existent, so that we can listen with all our hearing to his celestial tune.' Likewise Shakespeare, 'who had so much to say would sometimes pour out his loveliest poetry in saying nothing.' For Housman, Shakespeare's 'Take O take those lips away' was 'nonsense but it is ravishing poetry.'

For Housman it was 'Blake again and again, as Shakespeare now and then, gives us poetry neat, or adulterated with so little meaning that nothing except poetic emotion is perceived and matters.' He quoted eight stanzas from Blake beginning 'My Spectre around me night and day / Like a wild beast guards my way;' and expressed his own emotional reaction to them:

> I am not equal to framing definite ideas which would match that magnificent versification and correspond to the strong tremor of unreasonable excitement which those words set up in some region deeper than the mind.

Housman next began to talk of the physical effects which poetry had on him. 'My skin bristles ... a shiver down the spine ... constriction of the throat ... precipitation of water to the eyes; and there is a third which I can only describe by borrowing a phrase from one of Keats's last letters where he says, speaking of Fanny Brawne, "everything that reminds me of her goes through me like a spear". The seat of this sensation is the pit of the stomach.' In this he was expressing the common reactions of many people to poetry, music and even the graphic arts. He was not hesitating in being open about his own feelings and sensibilities.

Lastly he turned to his own poetry, 'I know how this stuff came into existence.' He quoted Wordsworth's 'spontaneous overflow of powerful feelings', and Robert Burns' 'I have two or three times in my life composed from the wish rather than the impulse, but I never succeeded to any purpose.' Speaking for himself:

> the production of poetry, in its first stage, is less an active than a passive and involuntary process; and if I were obliged, not

to define poetry, but to name the class of things to which it belongs, I should call it a secretion; whether a natural secretion like turpentine in the fir, or a morbid secretion, like the pearl in the oyster. I think that in my own case, though I may not deal with the material so cleverly as the oyster does, is the latter; because I have seldom written poetry unless I was rather out of health and the experience, though pleasurable, was generally agitating and exhausting. If only that you may know what to avoid I will give some account of the process. Having drunk a pint of beer at luncheon – beer is a sedative to the brain, and my afternoons are the least intellectual portion of my life – I would go out for a walk of two or three hours. As I went along, thinking of nothing in particular, only looking at things around me, there would flow into my mind, with sudden and unaccountable emotion, sometimes a line or, sometimes a whole stanza at once, accompanied, not preceded, by a vague notion of the poem which they were destined to form part of. Then there would usually be a lull of an hour or so, then perhaps the spring would bubble up again. I say bubble up, because, so far as I could make out, the source of the suggestions thus proffered to the brain was an abyss which I have already had occasion to mention, the pit of the stomach. When I got home I wrote them down, leaving gaps, and hoping that further inspiration might be forthcoming another day. Sometimes it was, if I took my walks in a receptive and expectant frame of mind; but sometimes the poem had to be taken in hand and completed by the brain, which was apt to be a matter of trouble and anxiety, involving trial and disappointment, and sometimes ending in failure. I happen to remember distinctly the genesis of the piece which stands last in my first volume [LXIII *I hoed and trenched and weeded*]. Two of the stanzas, I do not say which, came into my head, just as they are printed, while I was crossing the corner of Hampstead Heath between the Spaniard's Inn and the footpath to Temple Fortune. A third stanza came with a little coaxing after tea. One more was needed, but it did not come: I had to turn to and compose it myself, and that was a laborious business. I wrote it thirteen times, and it was more than a twelvemonth before I got it right.

That was it. Time only for a self-mocking:

> By this time you must be sated with anatomy, pathology and autobiography, and willing to let me retire from my incursion into the foreign territory of literary criticism. Farewell forever. I will not say with Coleridge that I recentre my immortal mind in the deep Sabbath of meek self-content; but I shall go back with relief and thankfulness to my proper job.

Housman sat down after revealing more of himself at one sitting than he had ever done in the rest of his life put together.

His subjective and deeply emotional response to poetry, his modest but undoubtedly accurate account of his own poetic process, took his listeners far beyond the persona and reputation of the Kennedy Professor of Latin and creator of *A Shropshire Lad*. His delight in the world of un-literal things, his almost mystic response to incantations and to the feeling tones of poetry without literal meaning, his undisguised emotional response to poetry were things the audience would have least expected from this slight, prim and normally very reticent figure.

He had notably not done an academic job. He had not turned to the definitions of poetry coined by other poets. Although he referred to Wordsworth's 'spontaneous overflow of powerful feelings', there was no mention of Wordsworth's 'emotion recollected in tranquility', nor were there *ex cathedra* views of the poet's mission, such as Wordsworth's 'Poems to which any value can be attached were never produced on any variety of subjects but by a man who being possessed of more than usual organic sensibility had also thought long and deeply ... to create a taste, if necessary, where none before existed.' Nothing could have been further from Housman's mind. There were no allusions to Coleridge's 'willing suspension of disbelief', no doffing his cap to Pope's 'What oft was thought but ne'r so well express'd', nor to Keats' 'negative capability', even though his personal description of how poetry came to him exemplified Keats' insight. There was no reference to Shelley's *A Defence of Poetry*, none to Sidney's *Apology for Poetry*. Apart from wheeling in Plato to support his claim that the best poets were mad, there was no mention of Aristotle's *Art of Poetry* or any other ancient authority or poet. Nor did he mention any contemporary scholar or poet by name. He referred neither to fashionable academics nor poets. There were no references to F.R. Leavis, Cambridge lecturer and co-founder of *Scrutiny*, who had the previous year produced *New Bearings in English Poetry* which concentrated on the poetry of T.S. Eliot, W.B. Yeats, Gerard Manley Hopkins, Ezra Pound, William Empson and Ronald Bottrall but not that of Housman. There was no mention of T.S. Eliot's Clark Lectures of 1926 which we know Housman attended. William Empson, the English poet and critic who had produced his famous *Seven Types of Ambiguity* in 1930 exploring the potential variety of meanings in poetry, had not been mentioned, nor had I.A. Richards who had produced *Principles of Literary Criticism* in 1924 and concentrated on detailed attention to the text and the problems surrounding verbal communication. Housman was seemingly detached from all of that stuff.

Housman with his characteristic self-direction and tunnel vision was more interested in solving the problem for himself, saying how the name and nature of poetry struck him. He was not interested in how it had struck others, nor the relationship of his own propositions to theirs. He had resisted the historical survey. Those were issues in which he was simply not interested. He had chosen the simplest way forward. His posture: I am a poet. You are asking me this question. I shall tell you how it is for me. Thus his lecture, lacking academic foundations, was built entirely on subjective foundations. His three references to Coleridge and his use of the *Lyrical Ballads* as a transition point suggest that he identified with the Romantic poets and saw himself as one of them. His lecture had uncovered his sense of the mysterious unconscious origins of his poetic expression.

The day after the lecture the congratulatory letters began to arrive. But from the very beginning Housman expressed himself as entirely dissatisfied with the lecture, a position from which he never retreated, whoever praised it; he invariably refused to sign copies of it. To Harold Butler, his successor as Professor of Latin at University College, he wrote 'I am not proud of my lecture, which I wrote unwillingly; but I am rather afraid that Platt, as you say, would have liked it.'[26] Housman recognised Platt as a kindred spirit and could imagine the enjoyment he would have taken in his teasing ironies. To Sydney Cockerell, Housman related how Mackail had come up to him afterwards to say that 'in his opinion "Take O take those lips away" was Fletcher's'. Mackail was wrong; in fact, the song quoted by Housman was from Shakespeare's *Measure for Measure*. Housman's reaction suggested the relaxed amusement of a man who knew he was right.[27]

Max Beerbohm wrote to say he had been amused by the lecture, music to Housman's ears for he greatly enjoyed Beerbohm's cartoons.

His congratulation provided an opportunity for Housman to send Beerbohm 'the idea of a pair of cartoons which I have cherished many years'. He enclosed descriptions of *Gladstone & Disraeli in heaven* and *Disraeli & Gladstone in hell*. Housman also sought to amuse Beerbohm with his 'vision of grandpapa and great-grandpapa reading the works of Mr Aldous Huxley, with the legend:

Is T.H. Huxley Esq., P.C.,
this how Leonard bred his brat?
The Rev. T. Arnold, D.D.
Good gracious! even worse than Matt.'

Housman added a rather barbed 'Rothenstein was here the other day and told me that with advancing years you have grown too benevolent to do caricatures.'[28] Housman's talent for amusement was still flourishing, even when he was feeling less than pleased with his lecture.

On 20 May he sent Laurence a copy: 'I am not proud of this which I wrote against my will and am not sending copies outside the family.' He commented ironically 'its success here has taken me aback. The leader of our doctrinaire teachers of youth is reported to say that it will take more than twelve years to undo the harm I have done in an hour.'[29] Housman was probably referring to I.A. Richards and F.R. Leavis. Richards, a fellow of Magdalene College, Cambridge, author of *Practical Criticism* (1929), *The Meaning of Meaning* (1923), *Principles of Literary Criticism* (1925), and *Science and Poetry* (1926), had been invited to teach for the new English Tripos in 1929. Leavis, also currently lecturing at Cambridge, had just produced his *New Bearings in English Poetry* (1932) and could also be counted as part of the opposition. None of their writings was mentioned by Housman; all were antithetical to his simple views. He sent Kate a copy of his lecture, 'which you are not obliged to read. The Senate House was packed, and I am being paid compliments which the lecture itself does not deserve, so I suppose I must have delivered it well.'[30] He sent godson Gerald Jackson a copy: 'Here is the lecture. I am not going to catechize you on it, so you are not obliged to read it.'[31] He and Gerald knew that in the early 1900s Housman had sent Gerald a poem, 'Towards answering the first question of the Catechism, What is your Name?'. His was Gerald Christopher Arden Jackson.

Those who speak in public know all about the doubtful value of congratulations and Housman was not to be taken in by them. But as a performer he had no doubt about his capacity to hold an audience.

Later in May he returned at more length to the subject with Laurence. 'The painful episode is closed.' He quoted a sentence he had omitted from his final speaking text: 'Not only is it difficult to know the truth, but to tell the truth when one finds it, to find words which will not obscure it or pervert it, is in my experience an exhausting effort.' Laurence had approved of his brother's 'separation of poetry from sense', but observed that his brother's own poetry was written 'without producing a single line that did not mean something – and mean it in phrases chosen with almost judicial correctness'. Housman's riposte was defensive. 'I did not say that poetry was the better for having no meaning, only that it can best be detected so.'[32] But the fervour with which he had quoted lines of Blake and Shakespeare had indicated that there was for him a 'pure self-existent poetry', quintessential poetry that lay beyond meaning and sense. There had been an uncharacteristic failure on Housman's part to think through the implications of what he was going to say and a failure to express and link his themes convincingly. He had quoted Coleridge on three occasions but in praying him in aid of meaningless poetry he had not understood Coleridge's position. For Coleridge, poetry had to be both intelligible and mysterious, what was intellectually visible and defined by words and what remained invisible and evocative.

Housman had made no claims for his own poetry nor said anything about where he placed his own work on the poetic ladder. His lecture had led Laurence to say that his brother's poetry was not of the most poetical kind by his own standards, and belied his own theory about meaning in poetry.

Housman had had his arm twisted to give the lecture. He had been seduced into making general statements about poetry. Why on sober reflection had he been willing to go on with such a rainbow-chasing task? In the event, neither his heart nor his mind had been fully engaged. Yet all he said about his personal reactions to poetry, his personal judgements about poetry, his sensations in encountering what he thought of as the greatest poetry, the ways in which he composed his poetry and how his poetry came to him bore the hallmarks of truth and integrity. But he had not managed to say and demonstrate the obvious: that the best poetry is a miraculous fusion of form and meaning. He had done scant justice to the wonderful scope and variety of the best poetry; he had not quite avoided stereotyping some schools of poetry. So there was some deficiency in his analysis, as there was bound to be. But there was another element. His time at University College had shown him to be a wonderfully witty and effective speaker, a great performer on his feet. He had once again demonstrated that decisive yet seductive style; that instinct for making an impact that would be remembered. This was certainly what he achieved. In retrospect he may have feared that his anti-intellectualism had gone too far, that hanging the whole of his judgement of poetry on his own subjective reactions and his personal physical sensations was too much generalising from personal experience. Maybe he reflected on the possibility that he had rather devalued his life's work. Having spent his whole life pondering on meanings, his lecture sounded like that of a man who has had his fill of meaning. These may all have been the sources of some continuing inner distress about his lecture. But whatever the causes, he had at least not sacrificed integrity to a personal self-aggrandizing agenda. And he had certainly made an impact destined to have a long afterlife.

PART XV

Last flights to France

Whatever Housman thought, the Leslie Stephen Lecture had heightened his public profile and enhanced his public reputation.

Reviews and comment were almost wholly congratulatory, although he was used by some to support their personal agendas. For its September 1933 issue, *Scrutiny* had asked one Gorley Putt to review *The Name & Nature of Poetry* with two other books under the ironic caption 'Go to the Professors'. He wrote:

> Many who enjoyed the charm of Professor Housman when he delivered his Leslie Stephen lecture will be sorry to see its appearance in cold print. He elected to pour Johnsonian scorn on the metaphysicals, and with Arnold to dismiss the eighteenth century. But his valuable discrimination between the normal 'solidity of excellence' of Dryden and Pope, and their occasional lapses in mistaking 'impure verbiage for correct and splendid diction,' has been overlooked by those who prefer to intone with the professor poetry which, 'does but entangle the reader in a net of thoughtless delight.[1]

Housman would be used as a stick to beat the moderns and as an object of scorn by the defenders of the moderns, even though his lecture had made no specific attack on the quality of any contemporary poet.

T.S. Eliot speaks

In great contrast was T.S. Eliot's review in *The Criterion*,[2] an influential literary magazine founded in 1922. With his background in foreign exchange and his business experience as a director of the publishing

Figure 43 T.S. Eliot with Lady Ottoline
Morrell, 1920. © National Portrait
Gallery, London.

house Faber and Faber, his review displayed a worldly, fair-minded and analytical assessment of Housman's lecture. He was prepared to make his points quietly and diplomatically. He had understood perfectly where Housman was coming from and seems to have appreciated how Housman had cleverly positioned himself on the unassailable ground of personal opinion.

He opened with a compliment. Housman was a master of prose because of what Eliot identified as 'a certain emotional intensity' – which would please Housman. He cleverly positioned Housman both as a romantic poet and an eighteenth-century wit – which would also please Housman. He acknowledged the inherent limitations of the public lecture which calls for selection and not 'connected profundity', thereby outlawing blame for what Housman had not said. Eliot's headlines for the content of the lecture were the Essence of Poetry Theory, the Pure Poetry Theory, and the Physiological Theory. His conclusion: 'None of these theories can be flatly denied without equal error: I do not believe that Mr Housman maintains any of them to a vicious [unsound] degree'. So he reduced Housman's lecture to a matter of opinion which was exactly the position Housman had put himself in. He then took Housman's lecture apart with even-tempered, fair-minded precision.

> There are a great many things worth saying about one kind of poetry or another; and a good many might not have been said if their authors had not been under the impression that they were talking about all poetry, when they were only talking about the kind of poetry they liked. Those who indulge in the Essence of Poetry fantasy are given to using touchstones, or test lines which are almost always true poetry, and usually very great poetry. What none of them gives us, yet we are apt to delude ourselves into believing they give us, is an absolute dividing line between Poetry and not-Poetry ... Whichever assertion you make will depend upon some definition of Poetry, explicit or implicit, which you cannot compel anyone else to accept. I feel a certain sympathy with Mr Housman's acid comments on the poetry of the seventeenth and eighteenth century... But when he suggests that the 'poetry' and the 'wit' in the metaphysicals can be separated as the sound and rotten parts of an apple or banana with a knife, I am more than doubtful.

In this Eliot appeared wiser than Housman. He was even wiser seeking to respond to Housman's question. 'Am I capable of recognizing poetry if I come across it?' He himself would unhesitatingly reply in the affirmative.

> But there is more to it than that. You cannot divide human beings, in this respect, as you might separate compasses which are true from those which have more or less deviation. Mr Housman's quotations, in this lecture, show about as sensitive and refined a perception as any human being can aspire to. But, in this way is he quite fair to Dryden? And what is much more important ... is he quite fair to Blake?

He confronted Housman's assertion 'Meaning is of the intellect, poetry is not.' 'I should not like to deny this, still less to assert it.' As for the assertion, 'Poetry indeed seems to me more physical than intellectual', Eliot would not deny that but was not sure what 'physical' and 'intellectual' meant.

He wholeheartedly accepted that Housman was recounting the authentic processes of a real poet when he said 'I have seldom written poetry unless I was rather out of health.' 'I believe that I understand that sentence. If I do it is a guarantee – if any guarantee of that nature is wanted – of the quality of Mr Housman's poetry.' Eliot's was a masterly review and it did Housman justice. Whatever light years may have separated the poetry of these two poets, such a review could only encourage Housman to think well and respectfully of Eliot.

Although Housman may have thought ill of the structure or logic or quality of his lecture, the public had liked the music of it and its inner resonances and what it had told them about the essential Housman. He must have reread his emotional words and realised that with all his talk of his tears, shaking voice, unreasonable excitement and celestial music, he had opened his heart in public without any obvious ill effects. It had been a late-in-life catharsis. Its effects would become clear in the final phase of that life.

The Evelyn Nursing Home

1933 was to be something of a watershed in Housman's life and career. Early June saw him in the Evelyn Nursing Home in Trumpington Road thanking Petica Robertson for a bunch of flowers, 'although I have not had them put in my bed-room, the matron has joyfully carried them off for hers.'[3] It emerged in a letter to Percy Withers that he had been sent there because of the 'misbehaviour of my heart', which had been 'momentary, and I was unconscious of it; and it is now behaving with monotonous correctness'. What he called 'my real trouble' was

> nervous depression and causeless apprehensions, aggravated by the fact that I am going to move into new rooms next term; the necessary alterations in the new rooms, and the making of new furniture and so forth, give me perfectly unreasonable worry to look forward to; and I have been disappointed of a companion for France in August.

Housman was opening himself to Withers in a new way and was looking for any comfort he could find. He was also looking forward to taking lunch from the Withers on his way to Worcestershire, 'But do not produce port, which I am probably better without.'[4]

Meanwhile in Trinity he was being very open with the Dean, Professor Henry Hollond: 'My heart is not behaving quite properly and my nervous condition is low.'[5] He evidently felt no impulsion to behave in a macho fashion about his health, indeed he was prepared to give chapter and verse to any colleague or acquaintance he happened to be writing to. Laurence proposed he visit them in Somerset. Housman accepted, 'but I suppose I ought to warn you that I am not in rude health' and gave him the whys and wherefores of his week in the nursing home.'[6] He gave Kate, his surrogate mother, much the same account he had given to Percy Withers. Her reply had evidently shown empathy for he replied:

> I am touched and sorry to hear about your own somewhat similar troubles in the past, of which I had no suspicion; though one of the thoughts on which I dwell is that I am much better off than many of my fellow creatures. The nights are not specially difficult, unless I am lying waiting to be called in the morning.

Perhaps his nervous condition was not being helped by his continuing alienation from his lecture:

> I am sending back the lecture unsigned, because I am refusing to sign it for anybody, as I think little of it. I have thrown away a large number of press cuttings which I might have sent to you if I had thought of it, though they were great rubbish. I enclose those which I picked out of the crowd, which you can read at your leisure, though I should like them back sooner or later. Only one is hostile, but the favourable ones in many cases are not intelligent, and tend to make more fuss about it than it deserves.[7]

That year, the summer was hot and trying for him. After lunch with the Withers on his way to Worcestershire he confided in them: 'I am worse rather than better. In previous visitations of this nervous trouble I have been physically strong and able to take good long walks; but at present, though my heart appears to be all right again, I am feeble, partly no doubt because of this weather.' One of the Withers' daughters was to be married and Housman was intending to send her 'one of those cheap presents which literary men do send'. He added, 'I ought perhaps to apologise to you as a father, as I think I have told you that the person who at first was the head of the Richards Press threw *A Shropshire Lad* behind the fire as "the filthiest book he had ever read.'"[8]

Whatever his physical afflictions, Housman was not ready to give up France and had his sights on a motor tour in Anjou and Touraine. Yet he seemed unable to get his lecture out of his mind. He told Witter Bynner: 'I do not think highly of my lecture, which I wrote against the grain and almost under compulsion.'[9] When Sydney Roberts asked him for the manuscript Housman let him have it: 'I enclose the MS, which however lacks 2 pages. Probably I destroyed them as containing things too bad to be read.'[10]

Grant Richards was in financial difficulties again but this time Housman could not reply with his usual equanimity.

> It distresses me that you are again in difficulties, the more so because this time I cannot relieve them. I am finding £450 a year for the education of a godson, and this will go on for four years. I am also involved in the expense of changing my rooms, making repairs and buying furniture, and a lift which has to be put in will cost £324 ... These various worries may be partly accountable for the bad nervous condition in which I now am; and the doctor also says that my heart is out of order, for which this hot weather is not good. We are both of us in trouble.[11]

And so he refused John Masefield's invitation to join a committee to award the Gold Medal for Poetry instituted by George V. 'I am at present in a bad condition of nerves, which visits me from time to time; and if I am better at that date I shall be going abroad.'[12]

Escape to France

Housman was acting on an assumption that his bouts of nerves lasted for about three months and so organised a flight from Croyden in late August for a three weeks tour. From the beginning, the trip was ill-fated. Letters to Kate were one continuous medical bulletin. He had consultations with at least two doctors and was given medication which seemed at the time to help. His companion was turning up trumps: 'kind and as helpful as can be possibly imagined. I am still ridiculously feeble, and the mistakes in this letter are not all due to the hotel pen.'[13] He pressed on gamely to Tours and Nantes which turned out to be 'a poor place as I suspected it was.'[14] At least he was on the mend. 'My throat now gives me no pain at all.' He had recovered his voice and 'My strength improves though I can hardly in this hot weather take enough exercise to do me good.' At Les Sables d'Olonne, 'the heat here is pleasantly tempered by the sea breeze.' At Royan, he found that his own state mirrored that of the pound which was sinking from 84 francs to 79 to the pound. He was not finding Royan agreeable. 'This is a beastly place, all noise and mosquitos, and the heat continues stifling. But I managed to get a very good lunch today with the first oysters of the season and the first guns popping in the distance.'[15] He was due to drive east to Clermont Ferrand via Angouleme and Limoges and he asked Kate to write, 'if it would amuse you.' On 6 September he was reading her reply after breakfast. It had taken his letter to Exeter and her reply to Clermont Ferrand in central France only five days in total. He gave her the latest bulletin on his health. 'As my fatigue persisted without abatement I have seen a doctor here, who has given me something which makes me feel rather better, and also advice about food. He does not find anything particularly wrong with my heart.' He finished his letter with, for him, a relatively effusive, 'Love to you and Clemence.'[16]

Back in Cambridge he was feeling better. 'Whether it is the cooler weather, or whether the disease is running its natural course, I feel stronger and more comfortable. My doctor is satisfied with me, says my heart is behaving well, and thinks that my tour has probably done me good: all the same I should not like to go through it again.'[17] Later in the month he dissuaded Grant Richards from coming to Cambridge. 'You would therefore find me wretched company, and I cannot honestly recommend you to come. On the other hand if I were selfish I should be glad to see you, because your company might do me good.'[18]

In October he produced another bulletin for Kate:

> The doctor has given me a tonic which took away the horrid inward feeling of fatigue, and I am getting to walk more strongly, though very gradually and with ups and downs ... I wake up too soon and have a rather disagreeable time till I get into my bath. I find too that I cannot turn with interest to work. My lectures however give me no trouble. My appetite is quite normal.[19]

Grant Richards continued to be worried by Housman's health. Having been to Cambridge to see him in October he had offered to help him, possibly in moving to a more comfortable and convenient set of rooms. Housman, a man of habit, was clearly not looking for one because he replied 'Your talent for practical affairs is only equalled by your amiability and readiness to help; but at present at any rate I do not look forward to my changing my rooms as a likely event. If it ever occurs, I will certainly remember and take advantage of your noble offer.'[20]

In November he returned to his medical bulletins, this time to Withers with a long account of his nervous trouble, his subsequent influenza and its symptoms, his treatment by his own doctor with something known among doctors as 'honeymoon mixture ... I have now left it off without experiencing relapse; but I walk sluggishly and am low in spirits.' He was troubled by an excessive sensitiveness to noise that prevented his getting back to sleep if awakened in the early morning. He may have realised that he was becoming a bit of a bore on the subject of his health because he ended this long recital with: 'Well woe has made me eloquent, and you ought to be satisfied at least with the length of this egotistic letter.' Housman was becoming sharply aware of his own mortality; he was feeling that 'I had best stay at home.' Nevertheless 'My lectures are no trouble to me', although 'I find I cannot get up a real interest in work and study. I read chiefly novels and Lecky's history of England in the eighteenth century.'[21]

He was now taking more trouble to be empathetic and sympathetic. H.V. Morton, the travel writer, had written to him previously and now, when he again wrote, Housman could say:

> When last I heard from you, some years ago, you wrote me a desponding and not altogether clear letter ... Despondency is still to be observed in your style: but after all I often despond myself. I should be pleased to see you again (before *I* die let us say) and if you gave me enough notice I could probably be in my rooms any time before 1 or after 4, except that the morning of Wednesday and Friday are always occupied.[22]

John Drinkwater sent him a copy of *The Summer Harvest: Poems 1924–1933*, causing Housman to open up: 'Reading the first ones reminds me that I have probably never told you how much I was interested and pleased by the first volume of your autobiography.'[23] He was not tempted, however, to go to London to see a performance of Laurence's play, *Nunc Dimittis*. 'Although much better than I have been and no longer actually feeble, my spirits are rather low and the visit to London would worry me in prospect if not in act.'[24]

However, he was not feeling so much in need of friends and sympathy that he was prepared to sacrifice self-respect and integrity; in December 1933 Richards may have repeated the request for financial help he had made five months earlier. Housman replied sharply 'If I did what you ask, because it is painful to refuse, it would be cowardice, and I should be angry with myself afterwards, and ashamed; and you yourself would be obliged to think me weak.'[25]

He wrote spiritedly to Houston Martin in Philadelphia: 'You are an engaging madman, and write more agreeably than many sane persons; but if I write anything of an autobiographical nature, as I have sometimes idly thought of doing, I shall send it to the British Museum to be kept under lock and key for 50 years.'[26] Here again was that train of thought about what he might eventually reveal and what secrets he might keep for a long time.

Meanwhile John Carter had joined with John Sparrow to print Housman's Inaugural Lecture to University College. John Carter was a bibliographer and bibliophile, John Sparrow an author, bibliophile, editor and fellow of All Souls, Oxford. Housman wrote to John Carter thanking him and his 'fellow fanatic'. The first of Housman's twenty-five copies went immediately to his American bibliophile fan, Houston Martin, with his notorious remark: 'This may give you a certain amount of unwholesome pleasure. Do not ask me to autograph it, for it is rhetorical and not wholly sincere.'[27] A further copy went off to Percy Withers: 'I think that most likely you have never seen the enclosed lecture, which has just been reprinted by a couple of besotted admirers. It is no use asking me to autograph it.'[28]

To Jeannie Housman he referred to it as 'a reprint by two infatuated admirers which I probably sent to Basil, when it was in manuscript to read ... I don't autograph it, as it is not good enough.' He slipped in the information that 'the Cambridge University Press has managed to sell 12,000 copies of my Leslie Stephen lecture in England, not counting America,'[29] by any reckoning a lot of copies of something he so despised. He gave Martin Secker the publisher his standard explanation: 'I am refusing to autograph copies of this lecture, and also of a more recent one which you may have heard of, because I do not think well enough of them.'[30] This was Housman taking self-respect and integrity to ridiculous lengths.

With Seymour Adelman, he sought to put straight the early history of *A Shropshire Lad*.

> It was only one publisher who was offered *A Shropshire Lad* and declined it. The firm which published it at my expense was the joint firm of Kegan Paul, Trench, Trubner & Co. I kept Mr Grant Richards waiting until Kegan Paul & Co signified that a 2nd edition would have to be again at my own expense. It is a great exaggeration to talk of a boom in connection with the 2nd edition: such boom as there was began with the war of 1914.[31]

He was still not feeling sufficiently strong and pulled out of a projected journey to Algiers with Grant Richards: 'I do not possess the spirits and patience required for so long a journey, and cannot nerve myself for the distant absence and the return. So I shall not claim your devoted services in escorting me.'[32] Nor did he feel like standing in for the Master: 'The University has given me a holiday for this term, and I am not inclined to raise clouds of my own on the clear sky. The natural functionary to take the Master's place is the Senior Tutor; and in his present incarnation he would do very well.'[33]

Enter Ezra Pound

In January 1934 the next issue of *The Criterion* published Ezra Pound's essay, 'Mr Housman at Little Bethel'.[34] Pound, an American poet, thirty years younger than Housman, is regarded as one of the most important figures in twentieth-century literature, whose work exerted great influence on other poets including T.S. Eliot. Here was another poet talking about another poet's view of poetry. Pound was a totally different personality from T.S. Eliot, was not naturally inclined to be as respectful and diplomatic, and could match Housman in irony and in confrontation. Naturally, he admired Housman's 'dog sense' in having upset 'the clique of critics of critics', but the biter was about to be well and truly bit.

Pound questioned Housman's lofty statement on the subject of versification. Housman had declared that 'a few pages of C. Patmore and F. Myers contain all, so far as I know, or all of value which has been written on such matters; and to these I could add a few more'. Pound's put-down was almost complete: 'I could, if Mr Housman is interested, supply him with a list of works, which if not specifically catalogued as "treatises on metric", "prosody taught in ten lessons", "tiny tots' guide to the muses", would at least supply him with an idea here or there.' Yet he was also admiring of Housman's footnote on the subject:

> one of the most masterly summaries of a small section of the problems of metric that I have ever had the pleasure to come on. I doubt if anyone has done anything better in English, that is to say, listed a larger number of more important – some of them possibly fundamental – issues in so small a compass.

Pound questioned Housman's assumption that he was well read: 'I have barged into no single indication that Mr Housman was aware of the world of my contemporaries.' He chaffed Housman's use of the term 'eighteenth century': 'Housman has dragged in an "eighteenth century" which he defines as a condition and not a chronological measure.'

He scorned Housman's elevation of poets who were mad.

> On page 38 Mr Housman descends to bathos, slop, ambiguity, word-twisting and is like to finish off the respect one had been feeling for him. If the Greek word there translated means 'madness' in the sense of Smart's and Collins's and Willie Blake's being occasionally sent off to do a week-end in an asylum ... Plato was ... cutting loose from all the known facts of Greek poetry, none of whose great makers were either lunatics, moon chewers, village idiots, or general imbeciles, nor were the best Latins, nor was Dante, nor Guido, nor Villon, nor Gautier, Corbiere, Browning; and Mr Housman can pack that sentimental drool in his squiffer, and turn his skill to throwing the dart in the pub next adjacent.

He added 'Saxpence [*sic*] reward for any authenticated case of intellect having stopped a chap's writing poesy! You might as well claim that railway tracks stop the engine. No one ever claimed they would make it go.'

His final dig at Housman:

> on page 47 our author goes down, deeply down, to that jocularity expected of men holding academic honours, and feeling a need

to unbend, to meet, to mingle humanly with their audience. Rats, terriers, the 'bristling' of Mr Housman's skin under the razor, if a poetic thought darts through his memory, and last but not Keast [*sic*], Fanny Brawne!

Expressed in the vernacular with a wonderful verbal dexterity, Pound's words were not simple entertainment; he had made several palpable hits on Housman's lecture.

Intimations of mortality

It was a sunny spring in the Cambridge of 1934. Jeannie told him about a forthcoming visit by Laurence in July which he hoped to coincide with, although he had to admit 'I am still not strong nor comfortable, but I hope to go with some friends for a short stay in Cornwall, which may be good for me.' He had given up the idea of changing his rooms and was very relieved about it, 'for the noisiness of the new ones would have been too much for me at present.'[35] To Kate he was more explicit. 'It is no good pretending that I am well for I have made no progress at any rate since the beginning of the year, and am neither strong nor comfortable. However life is endurable, and my heart seems to be steady enough.' But back in Bromsgrove, there had been more omens. Bertie Millington had died and Dr George Fletcher, 'you may remember as a ginger young man sitting a few pews in front of us in church. I found him in practice at Highgate when I was there; and he was *the* old Bromsgrovian.'[36]

Yet nothing interrupted his scholarly productions. He sent four foolscap sheets of notes to Dr Frank Robbins, director of Michigan University Press, on Robbins' progress in deciphering the papyrus Housman had written about in the 1927 edition of *Classical Philology*, subsequently following up with another two pages. Housman was still publishing papers at much the same rate as previously, two in the year of his lecture and now four in 1934.

Curiosity about him and his poetry had increased, especially among Americans, and there was a regular flow of composers wishing to set his verses to their music, which he invariably allowed, as long as there was no reproduction of the words. There was a regular flow of anthologists asking for permission to include his poems in their anthologies, which he just as invariably refused in the case of *A Shropshire Lad* (except in America where there was no copyright). He tried to control the number of *Last Poems* included in anthologies. He always opposed having his poems included in school books. He refused to write verses in books of his poems but usually agreed to autograph copies if an addressed package was provided for return. A steady stream of would-be or practising poets on both sides of the Atlantic sent him volumes of their latest poetry for which he generally expressed gratitude and occasionally commented on. But he generally did not give more than a polite response to supplementary questions or requests for advice.

This, on top of his lecturing, writing papers for the learned journals and correspondence with fellow scholars, must have provided a sufficient base load to keep him fully busy by any normal standards. He used pen and ink, did not have a secretary and appears to have made little or no use of the telephone.

Most unknown correspondents were answered politely. Some with whom he had become pseudo-intimate through correspondence were treated differently. Houston Martin who put to him a series of questions about Shropshire managed to extract from Housman more details than were contained in the answer he had given to Pollet.

I am Worcestershire by birth: Shropshire was our western horizon, which made me feel romantic about it. I do not know the county well, except in parts, and some of my topographical details are wrong and imaginary. The Wrekin is wooded and Wenlock Edge along the western side, but the Clees and most of the other hills are grass or heather. In the southern half of the county, to which I have confined myself, the hills are generally long ridges running from north to south, with valleys, broad or narrow, between. The northern half is part of the great Cheshire plain. The Wrekin is isolated.[37]

Housman never mentioned either to Pollet or to Houston Martin a detail he mentioned in a letter to Laurence on 5 October 1896:

I ascertained by looking down from Wenlock Edge that Hughley Church could not have much of a steeple. But as I had already composed the poem which refers to a steeple and could not invent a name that sounded so nice, I could only deplore that the church at Hughley should follow the bad example of the Church at Brou, which persists in standing on a plain after Matthew Arnold has said that it stands among mountains. I thought of putting a note to say that Hughley was only a name, but then I thought that would merely disturb the reader. I did not apprehend that the faithful would be making pilgrimages to these holy places.[38]

In his quest for information, Houston Martin was also targeting John Sparrow and Laurence Housman, causing Housman to tell Sparrow: 'Mr Houston Martin, though I am always telling him how silly he is, cannot be repressed, and is now pestering my brother for things which he has no hope of extracting from me.'[39] He described Martin to Laurence as 'a lunatic, but not unintelligent. I have expressed so much contempt of his aims and activities that he has now let me alone for some time.'[40] But one undeniable fact about Housman was that if his correspondents were not in his own business of textual criticism, he could and would tolerate fools gladly, as long their approach to him was polite and considerate. He was prepared to tolerate Houston Martin indefinitely, because he judged him to be 'an engaging madman' who wrote 'more agreeably than many sane persons',[41] and because 'You are always kind and friendly, and your anthology of opinions ought to foster my self-esteem and smooth my descent to the grave.'[42] Later in the year Housman was able to formulate a justification for his tolerance of Martin: 'I congratulate you on your 20th birthday and your approach, I hope, to years of discretion. I did not realize how frightfully young you were: it explains and perhaps excuses much.' He ended 'I thank you for your good wishes and you have mine.'[43]

Another regular correspondent was Witter Bynner, the American poet, translator and playwright to whom Housman wrote at least thirty times.

Charles Wilson, 'the Pitman poet' from Willington, County Durham, did not achieve the same level of intimacy as Martin. After Wilson's first letter in January 1927, Housman replied more than forty times to letters bearing presents, invitations and requests for autographs and photographs. In his later years Wilson dealt in books and autographs; his motive in writing to Housman was to get his signature in return. But Housman never closed the door in his face and even produced the odd line of authentic communication: 'Although I do not altogether approve of your political activities, I am sorry that they have brought upon you a chill and consequent illness.'[44]

Housman was open to developing friendships of a kind with people he had never met. In essence this group of pen pals became a circle of surrogate friends, but essentially without real bonds. Housman initiated none of this correspondence, but like a puppet master, had total control, free to say what he felt like saying.

However, when he received a letter from Josephine Johnson about the order of composition of the stanzas in *A Shropshire Lad LXIII*, the question he himself had raised in his *Name & Nature of Poetry* lecture, he reverted to type: 'I am much obliged by the kindness of your letter. One of your four guesses is right: I do not say which, because if I allowed the truth to be known, critics would start up and say they had known it all along.' [45] And, of course, if he had revealed his own order of composition he would have invited comment from those who believed their own chosen order made better sense.

A year later he would add just a little more information in answer to another correspondent: 'I have received several guesses at the order of some or all of the stanzas… If I had to guess myself, I am sure I could not tell which was last and which was last but one; though I think I could guess which two came first.' [46] One wonders why he could not say that what he finally wrote and had printed was what mattered. Why on earth did he invest with so much significance what was in essence a childish charade and tease?

Eduard Fraenkel

Trinity had appointed as a research fellow Eduard Fraenkel, forbidden by the Nazis to continue teaching at Freiburg University because he was a Jew. Housman supported this appointment and supported his candidature in the election for Corpus Professor of Latin at Oxford. Fraenkel's reputation justified his candidature. [47] His status as a person ideologically outlawed by German society could have led Housman to identify him and his predicament as analogous to the man for whom 'hanging isn't bad enough and flaying would be fair/For the nameless and abominable colour of his hair'. There is no evidence that Housman consciously made a connection between the hate directed at Oscar Wilde in England and the hate directed at Jews, gypsies and homosexuals in Nazi Germany, but it seems very likely. When Housman sent Fraenkel a testimonial, he said of his candidature, 'if it proves successful the University ought to join in the chorus of *Heil Hitler*'. [48] And he ended this testimonial with the words 'I cannot sincerely say that I wish Dr Fraenkel to obtain the Corpus Professorship, as I would rather that he should be my successor in Cambridge.'

Less than a month later, when Fraenkel had been elected, Housman had to write to the editor of *The Sunday Times:* 'I have been asked by scholars at Oxford to answer a note by *Atticus* concerning the election of Dr Eduard Fraenkel to the Corpus Professorship of Latin.'[49] In his column, *Atticus* had made the shade of Connington, the first Corpus Professor, ask 'Is, then, Oxford so barren in Latinity that she has to choose an ex-professor from Freiburg University to fill the chair and occupy the rooms which once were mine?' *Atticus* had gone on to say,

> for Oxford to welcome the refugee – exiled under the Nazis' preposterous Aryan rule – was very right and proper. But to press upon him one of the few gilt-edged prizes in her gift, with the likelihood of his holding it for a quarter of a century, is a different proposition ... And what will be the opinion in the Oxford common rooms of this sentimental gesture of anti-Nazi internationalism.

Housman dealt head on with this thinly disguised prejudice. 'Atticus gives the answer in his next words; "Herr Fraenkel is a Latinist of European reputation." I do not know who the other candidates were, but they cannot have been Latinists of European reputation; for no Englishman who could be so described was young enough to be eligible.' Sure enough, a week later Housman received a letter from one of the candidates, a Scotsman, Alexander Souter, Professor of Humanity at Aberdeen University, whose pedigree included being editor of the Oxford Latin Dictionary and formerly Professor of New Testament Greek and Exegesis at Oxford. Housman defended himself with finesse, 'If I had known that you were a candidate or realized that you were under 65 I should not have expressed myself exactly as I did. Now I must adhere to the theory that Scotchmen are not Englishmen.' Frankly, it did not sound as though Souter was objecting to Fraenkel's election, for Housman went on:

> Fraenkel told me that you had written him a very kind letter ... In the testimonial I wrote him I gave some sketch of his writings, and this is now to some extent diffused in Oxford. He has been lecturing there with much acceptation, and the younger students at any rate approved of his election; and I do not think there will be any feeling against him.[50]

At the same time as he was giving Fraenkel such unprejudiced support he was resolutely opposed to any further recognition for himself. He was still refusing honours, this time a renewed offer of Doctor of Letters from Oxford which he had refused five years previously in May 1928.

By the end of March 1935 he had identified what he regarded as a set of new physical symptoms. He told Kate:

> About six weeks ago I had a turn of not being able to sleep lying down, and consequently four sleepless nights in succession ... I am less well than I have been since I came back from France last September, in point of strength for walking and studying, and also I have not much appetite ... I do not mind much things which properly belong to old age, but the nervous annoyance every morning, and undue sensitiveness to noises which I used not to mind, are extras, and do not show any sign of leaving off. My work is no tax on me, except that I have had to write the University's Address to the King on this so-called jubilee, which was a worry, though there is no reason why it should be.

He ends with a line which conveys more plainly than usual how much he was feeling the need for love and attention. 'No more except love from your affectionate brother.'[51]

On 12 April 1935 a letter to Jeannie about her recovery from illness showed him warm, effusive, less distanced, without ironies, simply conveying affection.

> This is great and glorious news, especially when one thinks of this time last year, and I am very grateful to you for letting me know and rejoice ... It would indeed give me great pleasure to visit you again, and the beginning of July, to include the visit of Clemence and Laurence, would probably suit me very well. I am better than I was at my last visit two years ago, but I cannot expect to get rid of what is partly old age ... Kate wrote to me very cheerfully about herself and her family, a fortnight ago, and Laurence also seems busy and happy.[52]

He was doing his best to recreate their childhood family bonds.

He sympathised and empathised with Percy Withers who was encountering problems with his builders: 'What a perfidious race they are we have learnt from our experience in repairs to the College ... One advantage of living in this charming world is that however bad one may think one's own lot is it is always easy to find someone whose lot is worse.'[53]

He was thinking again of going to France. The human spirit does not easily give up pleasures that have become a part of the very rhythm of life, his annual visits to *la belle France*. He was expecting to go there for three weeks in August. Come June he was telling Kate and Jeannie that his doctor had counselled against walks of more than a mile but he was looking forward to the family gathering later in the month.

Also in June, John Masefield had been awarded the Order of Merit and Housman wrote 'When I wrote to congratulate Bridges I was obliged to condole with him at the same time for having an unworthy companion; but Andrew Gowland Hopkins and I presume Vaughan Williams are proper recipients of the honour like yourself.'[54] Quite how he took Vaughan Williams' subsequent election as an honorary fellow of Trinity is not known; time and chance can bring strange bedfellows.

Contrary as ever, he told Laurence of his defiance of doctor's orders: 'The doctor does not want me to take walks of much more than a mile, and I myself am often inclined not to do more than twice that amount. I still go up my 44 stairs two at a time, but that is in hopes of dropping dead at the top.'[55] Subsequently Laurence produced a special attraction: he would come and stay in Cambridge in the second week in August with his car, which appealed greatly to Housman because Ely, Peterborough and 'a lot of good churches are within reach (of which I know only some).'[56] He was feeling closer to his family than he had since childhood, although Clemence never seems to be other than at the fringes. Perhaps she had her own reasons for not worshipping at her brother's shrine.

Suddenly Housman found himself back in the Evelyn Nursing Home and Withers had to be told that

> The doctor has sent me here for a fortnight or perhaps a week ... I hope the latter... In the state I have been in for the last week I could not have gone to stay in yours or any man's house. You probably know all about Cheyne-Stokes breathing, described in Arnold Bennet's Clayhanger: sleepless nights spent in recurrent paroxysms of failure of breath, which can be combated if one is

broad awake but which overwhelm one if one dozes. Last night they conquered it with morphia and I slept long and almost continuously, but to-day I have been rather sick in consequence, and the treatment is to be varied, with oxygen as a second string.[57]

By 23 June Housman was still in the nursing home and Percy Withers went to Cambridge to collect him for his next visit, much to Housman's relief. He did his best to reassure his hosts. 'My heart does not trouble me, but my breathing makes my nights unquiet and has to be countered by drugs; and there is no prospect of a real cure.'[58] Professor D'Arcy Thompson of the University of St Andrews had fruitlessly visited the nursing home during Housman's absence and Housman wrote 'I am sorry to think of your visit to the nursing home, and all in vain, but it was very kind of you. I am now passing from house to house of friends and relations, and improving more or less.'[59]

Percy Withers left a record in *A Buried Life* of the visit.[60] Housman had talked little but had brought him the recently printed copy of his comic verse. 'You won't think much of them because I don't myself.' Withers had not been surprised to see that Housman was in one of his quiet and silent moods yet that same evening, dinner with the president of Magdalene and his wife, who were also staying, was anything but silent. They had a memorable evening in which Housman's vitality, high spirits and good companionship was notable.

> How after his recent grave condition, and with a heart in the critical state it was in, how it was possible that he should show not the smallest indication of ill health, or physical disability, but on the contrary talk abundantly and well, and laugh and keep us in laughter with a flow of excellent stories, I cannot conceive ... And it proved equally incredible to the Gordons when I told them the following morning how serious Housman's condition had been and still was. They were lost in amazement.

Yet as the visit wore on, Withers was seeing Housman differently from those who saw him more frequently and he saw what must have been the truth. 'Housman had suddenly become old and broken.' That morning after the night before 'he looked ill, and sad and anguished' and was content to spend his time alone in their sitting-room, reading, dozing, thumbing through newspapers and magazines, volunteering nothing, making no comments on their new home and the trials and tribulations they had gone through in converting what had been an ancient water-mill, only exerting himself after tea to take a gentle stroll with Withers himself. Withers observed: 'The unquestioning and the silence were not as in former days. They seemed indicative of a mind remote from transitory things. He was more ill, and felt more ill than we knew, and his quiet and disinterestedness were the signs.' These were Withers' own observations and hypotheses but Housman had also told him of his physical symptoms, of the miseries of his nights. So Withers hit on the idea of taking him his morning tea much earlier, at latest by 6.30am, when he would find Housman

> always propped up in bed, reading. The whole weight of illness and dolour was on his face. I longed to arrange his pillows ... But it was an occasion for dispatch ... A word of greeting from me, a doubtful response, if any, from him, the cup deposited on the table by his side, and I was gone. I knew there was a conflict between gratitude and rebelliousness going on, and pityingly I left him alone with it.

Withers was encountering 'a sad and moving spectacle', inducing in himself 'discomfort and self-reproach'. He and his wife thought differently. 'Where I saw only neglect, desuetude and loneliness, she saw contentment and tranquility.'

The matter was settled for Withers when Housman suddenly lowered his book and seeming on the verge of tears spoke from the heart

> of the delicious quiet of the room – he had rarely experienced such stillness, such undisturbed peace, anywhere at any time – and what it had meant to him and how grateful he felt for it. I do not give the exact phrases he used. His words were few but deeply impressive, yet the look on his face told even more than they.

When Housman went on to Jeannie's, he wrote movingly to Mrs. Withers 'I was glad to hear that you said I seemed happy while with you, for indeed the fact was so, and everything conspired to give peace and enjoyment, and I make warm returns of thanks to you and your husband for your care and kindness.'[61]

It was not just the Withers who received Housman's gratitude. It was a case of thanks all round, to Jeannie for 'the happy effects of my stay with you, which has given me just what I needed; and I am most grateful to you for your kindness and for the care which you took for my ease and comfort.'[62] And to Kate: 'It was very pleasant to see you again, and I was glad that we were able to manage it, and in such pleasant circumstances ... I don't think I ever congratulated you on all the news in your last letter ... and the demand for your historical work in America.'[63] To Percy Withers himself, he chose his words with care: 'I continued in Worcestershire the tranquil laziness of Epwell and I am rested though not strong.'[64]

Once out of the nursing home Housman was more forthright with Grant Richards: 'The continuation of my life beyond May 1933 was a regrettable mistake, and the bright side of the weakening of my health since the end of February is that it encourages me to hope for an earlier termination of the affair.'[65] This naturally caused Richards to want to see him, but Housman did not think that was a good idea because of Laurence's intended visit and his own resolutely optimistic intention of going to France for three weeks in August. Richards could have been forgiven for not quite knowing what to make of the situation.

There was something else he *might* have done to cheer himself up. Geoffrey Tillotson, a lecturer in English at University College, was handling the reprinting of Housman's comic poems, *The Parallelogram, The Ampisboena* and *The Crocodile*; they were to be published in a limited edition of fifty-five copies in 1935. Housman had been offered copies and replied that six would be ample 'as no one outside my own family will be likely to want one'. Housman was evidently not tempted to re-invent himself or to find new purpose as a writer of comic verse, something for which he had undeniable facility and talent. By now he would have been able to call on a vast store of potential material derived from academic life; his verse had always been mightily enjoyed by brother Basil, and here was Tillotson reinforcing that judgement. Yet Housman was wholeheartedly negative in thanking Tillotson: 'I am much beholden to you and your associates for squandering your pains on what Martial I am afraid would call "*difficiles nugas*," [difficult trifles] adding perhaps "*stultus labor est ineptiarum*" [Foolish is the labour spent on puerilities].'[66] Alas, not only had the Muse of *A Shropshire Lad* and *Last Poems* deserted him, the muse of comic verse was flatly refusing to sing in public. It was a sign of his age and deteriorating health that ambition, such a powerful motivation in Housman, could not change direction and seemed to be withering away.

Indeed, a common predicament for people at his stage in life and at his age is to ask themselves the question, what next? Here he was at the top of the tree of scholarship and a poet likely to have a lasting reputation. There was no retirement age for professors at Cambridge; he still had his role as a university professor; he still had his regular lectures to give which he could do for as long as he was able, and could at the moment do with a 'look no hands' insouciance. There was nothing in his current situation to oblige him to seek change. He was living a fully institutionalised life which bore him along on its routines and timetables, and provided him with food and lodgings and enough spare time to follow his personal inclinations for travel, church architecture, good food and good wine. He had become accustomed to the narrow life of a scholar. He had neither wife nor partner to stimulate change or enhance his pleasure. Although he was alone for much of his time he was living in college and never obliged to feel lonely, so he never applied the word lonely to himself. He was in a pleasurable rut and although his lecture 'The Name & Nature of Poetry' had sold 12,000 copies and its publication had awakened interest in his University College Introductory Lecture, Housman was not prompted to develop any further objectives or identify new challenges for himself. Moses was long gone, Platt too; completion of Manilius told Housman that his real life of classical scholarship was over. He was decidedly uninterested in capitalising on his success by accepting honours and decorations, or by further exploitation of his poetry or poetic reputation or his talent for comic verse. Now that his life with Manilius was over his life was without a star to guide it. Instead his focus was on enjoyment, creature comforts and his health.

Housman was faced by diminution of his physical powers and a certain incapacity to tolerate noise or cope with inexplicable anxieties. This came through in a letter to Percy Withers of 24 November 1934:

> The perpetual recurrence of discomfort every morning between waking and finishing my toilet is wearisome in the extreme, apart from the feeling of physical fatigue which is frequent and is probably a natural sign of old age. My life is bearable, but I do not want it to continue, and I wish it had ended a year and a half ago. The great and real troubles of my early manhood did not render those days so permanently unsatisfactory as these.[67]

To open up to Withers like that was a measure of how close their relationship had become. He had found the advice of his retired doctor friend of little practical use: 'On your expert advice I left off alcohol for a week, with no effect except the production of gouty symptoms, or symptoms I am accustomed to regard as such. Your other recipe, a cold douche after my warm bath, is impracticable, because my bath is cold.'[68] He wrote placidly of the death of R.V. Laurence, a fellow member of The Family: 'He was ill for nearly two years, but so brave that he had arranged and intended to lecture on the day he died. He talked so much about me to his nurse that she has written to bespeak me for her next death-bed.'

Now Housman nourished the fantasy of getting away to France as a way of reigniting his purpose in life. France, with its geometrically arranged fields, neatly pruned trees and hedges, was so in tune with the exactitudes of his own approach to life; where ancient churches and cathedrals ministered to his inexhaustible thirst for knowledge of ecclesiastical architecture. There was also the likelihood of good food and wine at restaurants where he could air his command of French and add to his knowledge of matters culinary, information to take back and enhance his standing in the eyes of fellow gourmets at Trinity and enable him to critique the books published by Grant Richards. And surprising though it might seem, he enjoyed making an easy personal connection with the proprietors of French restaurants, appreciating and enjoying to the full the ceremonies of the table so inseparable from French culture – all made easy and accessible by the modern invention that had become indispensable to him, the hire car. These added up to a sense of living well, the aeroplane adding a certain frisson of exclusivity and danger, but all reminding him that he was alive and still had a capacity for enjoyment.

Last flight to France

He told Kate of his imminent flight to France in his characteristic throwaway sort of way: 'I am leaving here on Monday afternoon, sleeping at Croydon and crossing next day by the plane which starts thence at 9.30 p.m., so do not distress yourself about the fate of any other…I am going to Dauphine and Savoy.' Laurence's visit had buoyed him up: 'a pleasant 5 days, and we covered a good deal of ground and saw many churches.'[69]

However, it was not long before he suffered from an accident likely to happen to an old man. Entering a taxi in Lyons, he did not lower his head far enough, resulting in a nasty gash, necessitating stitches, an injection against tetanus and eight days of minor medical follow-up, yet his characteristic spirit prevailed: 'death or grave illness will be duly notified to you and the Head Porter of Trinity. I am going to Grenoble tomorrow.'[70]

A few days later, writing from a pretty spot and comfortable hotel at Annecy: 'My head is healing so well that it makes doctors exclaim. I ought perhaps to add that I am weaker than usual, but that may be due to eating too much.'[71] By the time he returned his wound had healed but over his partly shaven head he wore a *calotte* (skull cap) for some time.

For his three weeks away the weather had been 'almost uninterruptedly fine... the scenery very striking ... the works of man, in the engineering of roads up and over the hills, as striking as those of nature ... from several spots I had good views of Mont Blanc, and saw it turn rose-colour in the sunset.'

But notwithstanding these impressive experiences, he had come to an awful and momentous decision. For more than a quarter of a century, almost another lifetime, going to France had been a powerful thread running through his life. Now, he told Kate 'I do not expect to go abroad again. Comparing this year with last I have been conscious of the decline of vigour and capacity which is the sign of old age and not of anything specific like heart or nerves.'[72] He was now seeing clear writing on the wall. His flight home had not been without its moments of truth 'a very unpleasant journey' because of head winds, a delayed take-off and an unsteady take-off and landing.' Yet again Housman had survived.

Just before Housman left for France Witter Bynner had sent him a copy of his own *Guest Book* hoping that Housman would in return send him early nonsense verse but Housman was reluctant to help: 'I am afraid that I cannot make the inadequate return of sending the early nonsense given you by Laurence as I do not know what it was. I have written a good deal of nonsense, and the other members of my family remember more of it than I do.'[73] Questions about his humorous verse were now coming from America and he told Grant Richards of the recent printing 'in a private and very limited edition.'[74] But he still made a show of fighting off Witter Bynner. 'I shall not do anything to enable you to get hold of the nonsense verses you mention, and if they dwell in Laurence's too retentive memory I shall not authorize him to communicate them to you', yet he mentioned a nonsense piece

Laurence was about to publish in *The Unexpected Years* and gave him Laurence's address.[75]

So his penchant for ambiguity had not deserted him. Nor had his sense of humour; his mood seems to have been greatly lightened by his French trip. Hence a final quip to end a letter to Lily Frazer, 'Putting together your secrecy about your address and the post-mark S.W. I suspect that you are making a stay at Buckingham Palace,'[76] and the good-humoured top and tail of his reply to Houston Martin: 'Your questions though frivolous are not indecent, so I suppose I must humour you ... With all good wishes for your health and sanity.'[77] Lily Frazer had given him news of her husband's book sales and caused him to observe: 'But the fame to which they are a testimony must have something like the effect of a mattress to lie on, keeping one from contact with the hard cold ground.' This theme he repeated to Houston Martin, this time about himself, 'Certainly I have never regretted the publication of my poems. The reputation which they brought me, though it gives me no lively pleasure, is something like a mattress interposed between me and the hard ground.'

By comparison, the minute sales of his life's work on Manilius was more like the thin blanket the dead soldier was laid on in *Illic Jacet*. Housman's mind was constantly impelled to dwell on the public's seemingly insatiable appetite for *A Shropshire Lad* compared with a virtually non-existent demand for *Manilius I–V*. His reputation in the wider world rested unequivocally on his poems, a reputation underlined by a request from the illustrious W.B. Yeats for permission to include Housman poems in his *Oxford Book of Modern Verse 1892–1935*. Yeats had been awarded the Nobel Prize for Literature in 1923 and here for the first and only time Housman felt cornered: 'It would naturally be a pleasure to me to meet any wish of yours.' He felt obliged to give reasons for his reluctance to comply:

Some thirty years ago requests to include pieces from *A Shropshire Lad* had become so disproportionate to the meagerness of my output that I began to refuse my consent, and this practice I have ever since maintained, alleging an inflexible rule, so that I cannot now desert it without breach of faith ... As regards my later volume, which is more meagre still, I have tried to discourage anthologists, partly by that consideration, and partly on the ground there are too many anthologies in the world already, but have not laid down a rule.

He buttressed his argument with prejudice: 'I am however unwilling to countenance an anthology which by its very conception allots so much importance to Hopkins, not chiefly because I myself regard him as a moth blundering round a candle but from a craven fear of being someday made to look foolish if, for instance, posterity decides that Doughty was the epoch maker.'[78] This was neither a convincing position, nor a convincing defence of it. Subsequently he thought better of denying a request from the luminous Yeats and agreed to the inclusion of five poems from *Last Poems*: 'If you condescend to edit the collection, I suppose I must not be above contributing to it.'[79] In the event, Yeats included seven poems by Hopkins and none by Doughty.

Lily Frazer had asked him to translate her husband's essay on Renan. Housman saw that as a task beyond him:

> I have never undertaken any job unless I thought that I could perform it to my own satisfaction: and I am not skillful in translation … moreover my strength and spirits are now barely sufficient for my own proper work. My life ought to have come to an end more than two years ago: age and weakness of heart in combination cause me to spend my days in fatigue and somnolence, except for periods after meals, and I often feel as if I had no marrow in my bones.[80]

Housman sounded as though he was more than ready to turn his face to the wall. He had reached the final stage of his obsession with death, the stage in which he himself was now personally involved.

Back in the nursing home

4 October 1935 saw him back in the nursing home. He wrote to Kate:

> Since I came back I have been going downhill at a great pace, the chief blame for which is being laid upon my 44 stairs which gives my heart more work than it can manage, so that I have breathlessness, weakness, and dropsical swelling of the ankles and knees. I lecture without difficulty, but the ten minutes' walk to and fro was so exhausting that I now have a lecture-room within the walls of the College. I am to change into a ground-floor set of rooms, and one of the younger Fellows has nobly made over his set to me; but it will be a great nuisance and will raise grave and probably insoluble problems about accommodating my books.

He was temporarily staying in the nursing home while he recovered. He had been relieved of examination duties, 'the chief terror of the winter'. He could take a taxi to college twice a week for his lectures. 'People are very kind in taking trouble on my behalf … the red ink is an accident and has no lurid significance.'[81] Laurence had also offered to help with his books but Housman rightly replied:

> The boys from the college Library seem to be experienced in such matters and Andrew Gow is very kindly giving an eye to the matter. I am reduced to great weakness by sleepless and distressed nights, the sedatives having failed; so that even if I were in college I could not offer you hospitality or society. None the less I am grateful to you for offering to sacrifice so much of your time.[82]

He sent his love to Clemence, yet given that Laurence now had a motor car, it was very strange that Clemence never seems to have met him again. At the beginning of November he told Kate: 'I have had four tranquil nights in succession, partly due to champagne: the doctor, though he did not suggest it, approves of the results,'[83] a faint echo of his Housman-knows-best approach to life.

But whatever his physical condition, Housman was not inclined to let H.G. Broadbent print his words in the programme for a recital of the Wenlock Edge song cycle by Vaughan Williams, against whom he was still bearing a grudge. He did permit himself to say 'There is too, if I remember right, a particular reason why neither this composer nor I should wish to see the words in the programme.'[84] On this occasion he chose the rapier rather than the bludgeon, possibly because Vaughan Williams had been elected an honorary fellow of Trinity.

Still in the nursing home, but feeling better, he hoped to be equal to the pleasure of dinner with Sydney Roberts and his daughter to meet Lord Charnwood, the politician and man of letters. This may have been the occasion when it fell to Roberts' eldest daughter, not long out of school, to be the hostess: 'Daddy,' she said, 'I'll probably have to sit next to him. What on earth shall I have to talk about?' She need not have worried. Housman put her at her ease at once and was entirely amiable.[85]

Housman was now expecting to move into his new rooms. When he did he found the bathroom and lavatory 'the last word in luxurious and scientific plumbing'. Like a small boy with a new toy he questioned Kate: 'Did you ever hear of a thermostat? A thing which watches the thermometer and sends the temperature up when it begins to fall.' Kate, hoping to cheer him up, had told him she had been praying for him. Housman did not let her get away with that.

> I abandoned Christianity at 13 but went on believing in God till I was twenty-one, and towards the end of that time I did a good deal of praying for certain persons and for myself. I cannot help being touched that you do it for me, and feeling rather remorseful, because it must be an expenditure of energy, and I cannot believe in its efficacy.[86]

His nephew Denis Symons wrote and was treated to a full description of his new quarters on the ground floor and the teething troubles, with only modest reference to his health. 'I get to sleep with reduced doses of a bromide washed down by champagne.'[87] To Jeannie he was more expansive but 'the comforts round me make me more cheerful than I should otherwise be. I can get through all the work that is required of me, and I go out to dinner when invited. One of the medicines I am taking is champagne, which however is not a wine I am very fond of.'[88]

A voice from the past was that of Professor F.W. Oliver, sometime Qain Professor of Biology at University College. Housman and he had served together on the Council when Secretary Horsburgh was dismissed. His words prompted nostalgia in Housman: 'I cannot take to myself much credit for any of my actions in the reforming movement, for I was only a partisan and occasionally a mouthpiece, not a convinced reformer nor a statesman with any prevision of the great success which resulted.' He might have claimed to have been any or all of these things but he knew differently and was simple enough to be honest. He had been the right man in the right place at the right time, a man with the capacity to be a chairman among his colleagues, who could identify what they wished to achieve and had the personal skills to facilitate it, not, indeed, a mover and shaker but a man who could dot the Is and cross the Ts: 'Ker's successor and (I suppose) your colleague R.W. Chambers has been giving the Clark Lectures here this term and I have met him several times; and Lyde [Professor of Economic Geography at University College] has sent me a book on Pindar of all subjects in the world. Tonks I met three years ago in Scotland.'[89] Oliver, a botanist with artistic and poetic leanings, kept a warm remembrance of Housman and felt he had formed a bond with him. He wrote later of his regret that he had never joined Housman on country rambles or on trips to France. He remembered that Housman had demonstrated his knowledge of food and wine at the Professors' Dining Club, 'Housman was at his best at the dinner table.'[90] Now he had to interpret Housman's humour: 'When you were here in June I was in a nursing home. My descent to the grave has brought me down a staircase of 44 steps to the ground-floor, where I am stuck at present and my heart has less opportunity of making itself a nuisance.'

A sign of the times was that Housman was becoming increasingly careful about what he undertook and, for example, told Andrew Gow: 'I did not sleep last night, so I am afraid I had better not walk to Magdalene and back, and I will order a taxi to be at the Great Gate at 7.55.'[91]

Christmas in the nursing home

He was back in the nursing home for Christmas and writing shakily in pencil on 27 December to Kate:

> I have been nursing myself in College on soup, hot milk and brandy in great discomfort, and finally have come here where I receive great attention. I am fed on toast, chicken-broth, orange juice, champagne, breast of turkey, Brand's essence of chicken. I am very weak. The other night they gave me an injection of heroin instead of my usual soporific, and I learnt what it is to be totally deprived of intellect. My College fellows sympathize with me more than my family would, knowing more of my gluttony.[92]

A letter to his godson, written on 5 January 1936, also in pencil and not very legible, had to be addressed and sent to St Thomas' Hospital where Gerald was now pursuing his medical course:

> My dear Gerald
> I am so much better that I can answer civilly to letters like yours. Hitherto my indigestion and nausea have been too disabling. I shall try to send you a cheque for £450, which if I mistake not is the regular ammount [sic] and which I beg you to accept if so without demur, as I can quite well sustain it. My head has somehow got confused between your family and my nephews.
>
>   I have not yet dared to eat anything you sent from Fortnum & Mason but I hope it is keeping all right. Brawn is a thing I am very fond of at Xmas if it keeps properly.

Thanks for your gift

A.E. Housman

This is sent by the kind offices of Mr Andrew Gow of Trinity.[93]

On 10 January 1936 he was writing a letter to Laurence, again pencilled in feeble handwriting. He confessed that business matters and decisions were becoming too difficult for him. He was writing confusedly about his poem *Hell Gate*, asking for Laurence's help, 'I shall be grateful if you will take it upon you to say that I am not prepared to give permission about *Hell Gate*. I am not conscious of any strong objection, and perhaps I am foolish, but I am not strong enough to deciede [*sic*] affirmatively.'[94]

Nevertheless, five days later he was looking forward to joining The Family for lunch at St John's College ten days later, and was catching up on his correspondence in a purposeful and uninhibited manner. One letter from a certain Mr Moore caused Housman to flash: 'I refuse him permission to publish his illiterate alterations of my verses.'[95] Housman may have been wondering 'What will they do to my poetry when I am dead?' He may have had a King Canute-like feeling.

Back in his rooms writing to Kate he began to reveal the truth.

> I was in bed three weeks, leaving letters unanswered, and unable to write a cheque without advice and assistance in the early days of this year. My weakness is no longer bodily and mentally such a nuisance, but all my strength is needed for my actual work. I lectured yesterday with comfort to myself, except in crossing the Court to the lecture room, and the hearers could hear me all right. Almost every physical action is a labour. I sleep fairly well, with the usual aids, and, best of all, my inside is getting right.[96]

Within a month he was his usual self, lucid and coherent, and his final two letters to Gerald on 17 and 31 January 1936 revealed a Housman never seen before. In a strong and beautiful hand he wrote:

> My dear Gerald, Acquainted as you are with Fortnum and Mason and familiar with the female medical soul you are just the man to execute this job. After a stay in the Evelyn Nursing Home, where they are always extraordinarily kind and attentive, I send the nurses a present of something to eat, such as strawberries in season, or boxes of chocolates. Will you expend the enclosed cheque for

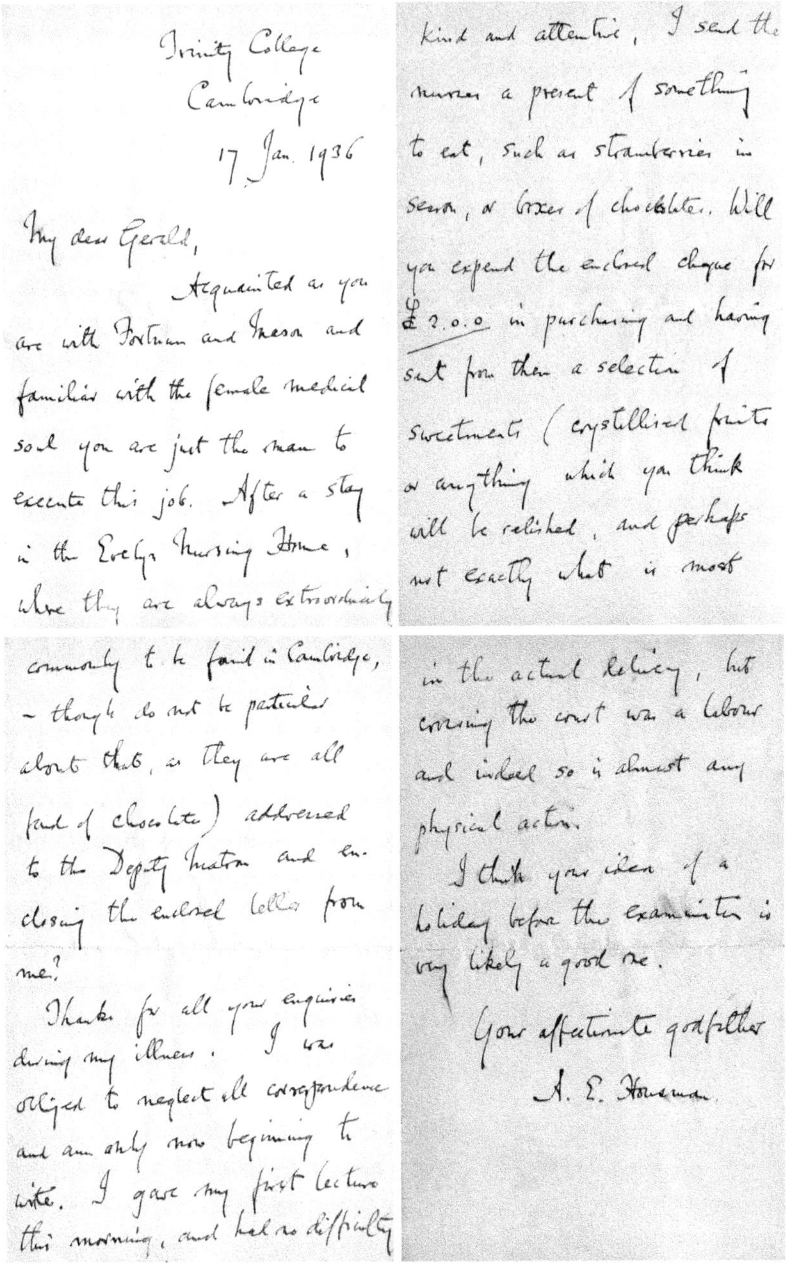

Trinity College
Cambridge
17 Jan. 1936

My dear Gerald,

Acquainted as you are with Fortnum and Mason and familiar with the female medical soul you are just the man to execute this job. After a stay in the Evelyn Nursing Home, where they are always extraordinarily commonly to be found in Cambridge, — though do not be particular about that, as they are all fond of chocolate) addressed to the Deputy Matron and enclosing the enclosed letter from me?

Thanks for all your enquiries during my illness. I was obliged to neglect all correspondence and am only now beginning to write. I gave my first lecture this morning, and had no difficulty

kind and attentive, I send the nurses a present of something to eat, such as strawberries in season, or boxes of chocolate. Will you expend the enclosed cheque for £2.0.0 in purchasing and having sent from them a selection of sweetmeats (crystallised fruits or anything which you think will be relished, and perhaps not exactly what is most in the actual delicacy, but crossing the court was a labour and indeed so is almost any physical action.

I think your idea of a holiday before the examination is very likely a good one.

Your affectionate godfather
A. E. Housman.

Figure 44 Letter from Housman to Gerald Jackson 17 January 1936. By permission of the Master and Fellows of Trinity College, Cambridge.

Trinity College 51
Cambridge
31 Jan. 1936

My dear Gerald,

I ought to have thanked you before, and this letter will hardly catch you before you start on your holi-day; but, next to walking, nothing tires me so much as writing, and I had to fight from Rupert, who seems to

shy of it. The amateur told it certainly on the sweet, and our admiration of you. Late, for I tell them that I had left the chorus to you. Harrod's proceedings in also good. The doctor told me to-day that he is not coming again for a week. I had a letter the other day from Rupert, who seems to be profiting by the retirement

of some competition. I hope that you will enjoy your holiday and that it will make you up for the examination so desired.

Your affectionate godfather
A. E. Housman

£2 0s 0d in purchasing and having sent from them a selection of sweetmeats (crystallised fruits or anything which you think will be relished, and perhaps not exactly what is most commonly to be found in Cambridge, – though do not be particular about that, as they are all fond of chocolate) addressed to the Deputy Matron and enclosing the enclosed letters from me?[97]

This detailed description of what Gerald could buy is wonderfully revealing of the marriage between Housman the exact scholar and Housman the man whose one aim in life was to please his nurses.

On 31 January he sent Gerald, then in Switzerland, news of how his efforts had been received. 'The nurses went into ecstasies over the sweets, and over admiration of your taste, for I told them that I had left the choice to you. Harrod's provender was also good.'[98] These two letters are a testament to Housman's capacity for human relationships; his care and concern for his little group of nurses reveals him at once ordinary, caring and loveable.

Now he was keeping going by sheer will power and by focusing his energies. He wrote to Grant Richards that he had 'no strength for anything beyond my actual work. I am having your books returned and I thank you for sending them but I cannot bear to look at them.' These were books Richards had sent him with a view to getting his consent to writing something about 'the country of *A Shropshire Lad*'. Housman had no more time for that particular charade: 'I am not a descriptive writer and do not know Shropshire well.'[99]

He had managed only a telegram-like communication to Percy Withers giving him a brief synopsis of the state of play: 'Internal chill, indigestion and at one time nausea.'[100] Withers' reply prompted denial in Housman: 'Your letter is so extravagantly kind and wrong-headed that I am obliged, weak as I am, to lift the pen.' He painted a much more encouraging picture of his situation. '

My misery is much less than it has been for two years and a half ... My own diagnosis ... was obstruction in what I suppose to be the upper intestine: there was a protruberance above the navel which has now vanished, and my inside is that of a new man. My nerves are not restored but are quieter than at any time since June 1933. I am surrounded by more comforts, luxury and attention than ever in my life, and take quite an interest in ordering my meals. Lecturing is far less labour than walking across the court

... A weak soporific and a glass of champagne, followed by a cup of tea at 7.30 p.m., procure me a peaceful night, except that the champagne has not a very quieting effect on the bladder. Do therefore be at peace and persuade Mrs Withers, to whom all thanks and good wishes, to imitate you.[101]

Withers felt put down by this reply and made his feelings so clear that Housman felt obliged to apologise: 'I am sorry to have written tartly: my intention was not so; and indeed the extreme and undeserved kindness and generosity of your letters move me almost to tears.' Housman felt he had to retract some of what he had said:

> On my part, perhaps the facts do not quite justify the account I gave of my surroundings, as you would think me to be pitied for being alone at nights with only a telephone for company. But, so far as I can analyse my feelings and separate bodily weariness from condition of soul, I am in better spirits than I have been for two years and a half, although particular ailments rather tend to increase.[102]

He had continued to think of visiting Jeannie in the summer but he had to admit that 'Some shadow is cast over the pleasure with which I look forward to visiting you in summer by perplexity how I am to manage your stairs. True, there are not 44 of them. But they are precipitous; and the days when I took them two at a time are not likely to return.'[103]

Having already noticed that Laurence's earnings had mounted to the super tax level, Housman saw that his play *Victoria Regina* was making his brother rich: 'I rejoice that you have made a fortune. Do not squander it as you did the proceeds of the *Englishwoman*.' He had also recovered the memory of what he had been trying to say to Laurence about *Hell Gate*: 'When you wrote to me about the setting of 'Hell Gate' I was very ill and could not make up my mind to say yes; but I now do not mind consenting. The orchestra will *drown* the words which must be pretty bad if a composer has an overwhelming admiration for them.' His letter ended with a quotation from Thomas Nashe's *In time of plague*; Laurence had asked him who wrote it.

> Brightness falls from the air;
> Queens have died young and fair;
> Dust hath closed Helen's eye.[104]

This was the last letter Laurence received from his brother.

Houston Martin, his long-standing American correspondent, now announced he was working on a biography of Housman and was brought up to date:

> I was very ill at the beginning of the year, and I am now again in a nursing home. I hope that if you can restrain your indecent ardour for a little I shall be properly dead and your proposed work will not be by its nature unbecoming...Do not send me your manuscript. Worse than the practice of writing books about living men is the conduct of living men in supervising such books. I do not forbid you to quote extracts from my letters. I think you should ask yourself whether you are literary enough for your job. You say that I may think it 'indignant and presumptious' for an American to write such a book before an English one has appeared. By *presumptious* you mean *presumptuous* and what you mean by *indignant* I have no idea.

But in spite of his tone of knockabout jocularity and the wielding of his copy-editor's pen, Housman was taking seriously the flood of questions Martin had raised: 'The best review I ever saw of my poems was by Hubert Bland, the socialist, in a weekly paper *The New Age* (1896). The American who called them (I do not know where) the best poetry since Keats is endeared to me by his amiable error.' He was also happy to put on the record yet again his personal assessment of his philosophic position: 'In philosophy I am a Cyrenaic or egoistic hedonist and regard the pleasure of the moment as the only possible motive for action. As for pessimism, I think it almost as silly, though not as wicked, as optimism. George Eliot said she was a meliorist: I am a pejorist.'[105]

Capacity to write such cogent letters encouraged him to tell Kate 'I fear I shall live to be seventy-seven'. On 2 April he wrote again to Kate:

> After the great turn for the better I took on my birthday I have not looked back. My doctor was away but his substitute managed me quite well with his opiate and the Regius Professor [of Medicine] came to see me and seemed quite satisfied. Sleep and digestion are both satisfactory and I have been reading to fill my hours.[106]

The same day he was able to tell Withers 'My term was conducted to a triumphant end, but finally I had such bad nights that I was obliged to resort to the nursing home and the 24th and 25th were very wretched, on the 26th I was wonderously renewed by morphia and am going on well.'[107]

He was now having to reassure himself that he had done what he ought to have done and consequently wrote to Sydney Roberts at Pembroke College: 'I trust that I replied to your Family invitation. I still hope to be there, though I am not so sanguine as I should like to be.'[108]

Then came signs that he was actually letting go. To Houston Martin it was a case of 'If I were well I could make a long reply to your kind but irrelevant letter.'[109] To Charles Wilson in faraway County Durham, it was a case of 'it would be a kindness if correspondents did not write to me.'[110] On 21 April 1936 he received a letter from Rolfe Scott-James, editor of the *London Mercury*, who had sought a contribution from him. Housman replied 'I am obliged by your letter, but my career and it is hoped my life are so near their close that it is to be hoped they will concern neither of us much longer.'[111]

His last written words were to Kate on a card postmarked 25 April 1936: 'Back to the Evelyn nursing home today (Saturday) A.E.H.' After his initials the word 'UGH!'[112]

Housman faces death

J.J. Thomson, Master of Trinity, saw him on the day he gave his last lecture. He was terribly ill and must have had invincible determination to lecture in such a state. He was taken to the nursing home the next day and died there on 30 April 1936.

Housman faced the end of his life with calm acceptance, albeit mercifully aided by opiates. There was nothing of Dylan Thomas' 'Old age should burn and rave at close of day.' There were no regrets, written or spoken. He was the incarnation of Shakespeare's 'Ripeness is all'. For him there would be no reunions or awakenings, no hereafter.

In his *A.E.H.* Laurence Housman recounted what his brother said to his doctor the night before he died.

> You have been a good friend to me. I know you have brought me here so that I may not commit suicide, and I know that you may not help me to it more than the law allows. But I do ask you not to let me have any more unnecessary suffering than you can help.[113]

Freud said that every man dies in his own way. In Housman's case it was a surprisingly different way from that which most people would have expected. The dying Housman held his doctor's hand for about half an hour. Few people who knew Housman would have expected him to touch another person let alone hold his hand. His reaching out for the reassurance of physical touch, perhaps imagining a mother to whom many men call for in their extremity, was unexpected.

Those who know him to be a popular English poet and the greatest classical scholar in the world might have expected his final words to have had a poetic resonance, perhaps the first line of Horace's ode *Diffugere Nives*, 'the snows are fled away', resonating to the season of the year, reflecting the transitory nature of human life; a poem which with moist eyes in the lecture hall he had once declared to be the most beautiful poem in ancient literature. Or perhaps he might have recalled one of his own elegiac first lines. Or Francois Villon's, *mais où sont les neiges d'antan* (but where are the snows of yesteryear).

Not a bit of it. His last words announced his intention to retell on the Golden Floor a risqué story his doctor had just told him.

His doctor, Reginald (Rex) Salisbury Woods, put it like this:

> No one enjoyed a good story better than he did and even to the end his whimsical sense of the ridiculous never forsook him. I was with him, knowing, as he well knew that he was about to die, for no one could fool Housman. He had started to say appreciative things in a rather affecting way, and to relieve tension before settling him down for the last time, I asked him if he would like to hear a story that had come my way. He nodded. So I told him of the divorce court judge who asked counsel to explain the expression 'platinum blonde', and advanced two alternative definitions. Lying back on his pillow and fighting for breath, Housman smiled feebly, but with obvious appreciation. Then, slowly gasping out the words, he said: 'Indeed-very-good. I shall-have to repeat-that-on the Golden Floor.' And those were his last words.[114]

It later transpired that Woods had censored his own story. He had omitted from his account the two definitions advanced by counsel: that a platinum blonde was a precious metal or a common 'ore'. His expurgated version had also omitted the vital detail that the story was about an English actor just returned from Hollywood who when asked what he did in his spare time replied 'Well I suppose you could say we spend half of our time lying on the sand looking at the stars, and the other half lying on the Stars looking at the sands!' Rex Woods had a very good sense of humour and an ear for a punch line and this sounds like the version that prompted Housman's last laugh.

30 April 1936: Housman dies

At his funeral service in Trinity College Chapel a chapter of Ecclesiastes was read and a hymn composed by Housman in 1925 was sung to a tune by Melchior Vulpius harmonised by J.S. Bach. Housman has observed amusedly in 1925 'To which the choir unless forcibly restrained will add "All glory to the Father/All glory to the Son/ All glory to the Spirit/ While endless ages run". The hymn, endorsed by Housman 'For My Funeral', was so headed by Laurence when he later published it in *More Poems*.

The hymn printed the initial letters of thou, thy, thine and thee in lower case. That was not a matter of Housman shouting at the top of his voice, more like something done to make a quiet point or to place a last blame on the printers. Housman was quietly relocating himself on the spectrum of religious belief. He had been sent forth and was now being called home. And although Housman may still have claimed to be an atheist, this is the hymn of an agnostic. Here there is pastoral sunshine and shade, a sense of content, of peace, of beneficent neutrality. This is not the cold grave of his poems. And his return to the earth, together with all created creatures, would have the assured blessing of never having to go again through the business of life.

> O THOU that from thy mansion
>   Through time and place to roam,
> Dost send abroad thy children,
>   And then dost call them home,
>
> That men and tribes and nations
>   And all thy hand hath made
> May shelter them from sunshine
>   In thine eternal shade:
>
> We now to peace and darkness
>   And earth and thee restore
> Thy creature that thou madest
>   And wilt cast forth no more.

It was fitting that Housman should have had a funeral service at Trinity, where he had spent the final twenty-six years of his life. Among the congregation were fellows of Trinity and heads of colleges. His brother Laurence represented the family with his nephews Jerry and Denis Symons. Also present was Gerald Jackson, who had visited his godfather several times during his last illness.

Housman's ashes were buried in the churchyard at Ludlow in Shropshire, totally appropriate for the author of *A Shropshire Lad* but hardly relevant to the actual life of A.E. Housman. There is no record that he was offered a service in Westminster Abbey, which his merit as a great scholar and poet could have earned him. He had been insufficiently ambitious, insufficiently interested in honours, insufficiently interested in networking and self-promotion; in death he harvested the inevitable consequence, neglect. To some extent this would be remedied in his centenary year when a window in Westminster Abbey's Poet's Corner was dedicated to him.

Posthumous publications published by Laurence Housman
More Poems and Additional Poems
and De Amicitia

Housman was dead and buried but he was to have an immediate afterlife as a poet. He had appointed his brother Laurence as his literary executor:

> I direct my said brother Laurence Housman to destroy all my prose manuscript writing in whatever language and I permit him but do not enjoin him to select from my verse manuscript writing and to publish any poems which appear to him to be completed and to be not inferior in quality to the average of my published poems and I DIRECT him to destroy all other poems and fragments of verse.[1]

Laurence both obeyed and disobeyed his elder brother. He took his brother's words as a green light to publish what he wished.

Before the year was out, Laurence published *More Poems*, a collection of forty-nine poems. Most existed in manuscript and four had been published before. However, Laurence cobbled together five verses from one of his brother's notebooks and three verses from another notebook, to make a single poem. He also combined three separate and seemingly unrelated quatrains to make another poem. Laurence seems broadly to have done his duty but could not resist the temptation to add his own creative touches.

A year later, in 1937, Laurence published his *A.E.H.*, containing twenty-three additional poems. Of these, all but four were backed by manuscripts, yet again Laurence could not resist his own creative impulse, using two separate fragments from the notebooks to create a single poem, and publishing seven poems of only four lines each.

Laurence further disobeyed his instructions by not destroying the four notebooks; instead he tore them apart, discarded some sheets, cut up the remainder and pasted down the pieces on larger sheets. This is not the place to elaborate on that process or its results. Suffice to say the final resting place of the mutilated notebooks was mainly in the United States Library of Congress where '165 folio sheets arranged in 7 groupings ... 266 manuscript pieces ... glued to 149 of the sheets' provided a textual mishmash for scholars and literary archaeologists to puzzle over.[2] Laurence had created just the sort of textual mess Housman had worked all his life to avoid.

Laurence had more to say. In July 1942, six years after Housman's death, in the words of John Carter, bibliographer and bibliophile, Laurence 'presented a small packet of papers to the Trustees of the British Museum with the stipulation that it was to remain unopened for twenty-five years. Thereafter it was "to be made accessible to the Council of the Society of Authors for publication".[3] The package, still in the British Library, contained a twenty-page article in Laurence Housman's handwriting titled *A.E. Housman's De Amicitia* together with Housman's pocket diary for 1888 and fourteen leaves from those for 1889 to 1891.

In October 1967 John Carter was enabled to publish Laurence's article with annotations in the magazine *Encounter*. This important document gave Laurence's account of the relationship between Housman and Moses Jackson, and of the temporary and unexplained interruption of the friendship between the two men. Laurence's article made other biographical statements. Laurence asserted that his brother had a craving to be liked which he interpreted also as a craving to be understood. Housman's craving to be liked was evidenced by his annotation 'This is me' against a paragraph in *Seven Pillars of Wisdom*, but 'craving to be understood' was a figment of Laurence's imagination, never remarked on by anybody else and never evident in anything Housman ever said or did. Laurence continued 'and in order that understanding might be possible, he left these records to be found by one of whose sympathy he could be sure'. That may have been a reasonable assessment of Housman's intention, but he obviously shrank from leaving any personal statement about himself in his own hand. There was nothing to prevent him. It was Laurence's hope that though the foolish and the obdurate, and those of hard understanding may reprobate what is here disclosed, many – the more intelligent, the more charitable, the more kindly of understanding – will, I believe, think differently; and having fuller knowledge be able to have more liking also for the man, who, in his own life-time, could not let himself be better known.

Then, in a candid and passionate statement about society's attitude to homosexuality, Laurence expressed his own 'social reason' for recounting the story of Housman and Moses Jackson:

the precious balms of the righteous have broken many heads, and many hearts and ruined many lives. I have a hope that, twenty-five years hence, their day of evil power will be gone; and that society, may at long last, have acquired sufficient common-sense to treat the problem less unintelligently, less cruelly, more scientifically. And if not, it may help to that end for the world to be given knowledge that one to whom it is deeply in debt for the beauty of his poetry and the eminence of his scholarship was one of the sufferers whom it has in the past found it so foolishly easy to despise and to condemn.

In October 1967, when John Carter was reading these final words of Laurence's paper, the passage of time and changing attitudes enabled Sparrow to write: 'His hope was fulfilled almost exactly on time. These papers were unsealed on 11 July 1967; the much more liberal Sexual Offences Act (1967) went on to the Statute Book on 27 July.'[4]

Laurence's self-directed mission was to publish those poems which Housman had not allowed to appear because they were in Laurence's words 'too autobiographical and ... referred to certain persons (or to one person) still alive. But from the fact he had not destroyed them ... their publication had been left to my discretion, and ... he had no objection to their autobiographical nature being recognised after his death.'[5]

Laurence proceeded to identify the four poems in *A Shropshire Lad* which he believed to be the most autobiographical, one of which, *Others, I am not the first, / Have willed more mischief than they durst*, he described as 'the most direct expression of personal experience – and suffering'. Housman himself had inconveniently described the same poem as a 'poem contrasting the passions of youth and the unwholesome excitement of adultery with the quiet indifference of death', a gloss not entirely at odds with Laurence's statement, but only if one reads the word 'adultery' in the sense of 'forbidden love'.

Laurence judged that fourteen *More Poems* and seven *Additional Poems*, just less than one-third of the total, met his criterion as being 'the most direct expression of personal experience ... all ... have some degree of connection with the trouble which overshadowed the whole of my brother's life'. It is likely that Laurence's choice of some of these twenty-one poems may have been affected by his natural bias. Only four stand out as registering keynotes in Housman's life. Only four fit exactly Housman's circumstances and prompt the question: Why else were they written?

Two are expressions of the sharpest and most painful turning point in Housman's life, his farewell to Moses Jackson:

> SHAKE hands, we shall never be friends; give over
>   I only vex you the more I try.
> All's wrong that ever I've done or said,
> And nought to help it in this dull head:
>   Shake hands, goodnight, goodbye.
>
> But if you come to a road where danger
>   Or guilt or anguish or shame's to share,
> Be good to the lad that loves you true
> And the soul that was born to die for you,
>   And whistle and I'll be there.

This poem dating back to 1893 fits the scenario of their temporary parting. Its revelation of steadfast commitment is of a piece with his words in that last letter to Moses Jackson, 'I would much rather have followed you round the world and blacked your boots', and his subsequent words to Arthur Pollard 'Now I can die myself: I could not have borne to leave him behind me in a world where anything might happen to him', and his confession to Gerald in 1931, 'If you could have any idea of what my feeling for your father was and still is you would not grudge me the pleasure'. It is all seamless.

A companion piece which Laurence printed alongside also dated from 1893:

BECAUSE I liked you better
　　Than suits a man to say,
It irked you, and I promised
　　To throw the thought away.

To put the world between us
　　We parted stiff and dry:
"Farewell," said you, "forget me."
　　"Fare well, I will," said I.

If e're, where clover whitens
　　The dead man's knoll, you pass,
And no tall flower to meet you
　　Starts in the trefoiled grass,

Halt by the headstone shading
　　The heart you have not stirred,
And say the lad that loved you
　　Was one that kept his word.

Laurence also printed in *Additional Poems* four lines dating from 1900 with their reprise of the goodbye handshake:

He would not stay for me; and who can wonder?
　　He would not stay for me to stand and gaze.
I shook his hand and tore my heart in sunder
　　And went with half my life about my ways

Also left for Laurence to reveal at last in *Additional Poems* was the poem of 1895 that went to the root cause of everything that Housman suffered, the primal curse of intolerance;

Oh who is that young sinner with the handcuffs on his wrists?

And what has he been after that they groan and shake their fists?

We have seen that in *Last Poems* Housman had dared to voice his open and passionate rejection of the social and religious laws to which he had been expected to conform:

THE laws of God, the laws of man,
He may keep that will and can;
Not I: let God and man decree
Laws for themselves and not for me;

Among the many poems Laurence would have us believe are direct expressions of personal feeling or experience was *Far known to sea and shore*, written in 1922, but not published in *Last Poems*. It was ostensibly a poem about the Campanile in Venice which collapsed in 1902 and was subsequently rebuilt. Andrea the gondolier featured in the final stanza of this poem

It looks to north and south,
    It looks to east and west;
It guides to Lido mouth
    The steersman of Triest.

Andrea, fare you well;
    Venice, farewell to thee.
The tower that stood and fell
    Is not rebuilt in me.

Laurence was interpreting its imagery 'guides to Lido mouth' and 'The tower that stood and fell / Is not rebuilt in me' as frankly phallic. Housman did not himself select the poem for *Last Poems*. A banal ceremonial piece, it was clearly inferior to the average of Housman's published work. Laurence was not justified in resurrecting it. Laurence's judgement was being coloured by reading into it knowledge of his own homosexual experiences.

Notwithstanding Laurence's uncertain memory on dates and details and his tendency to embroidery, these poems witness the truth of his assertion

my brother's love for Jackson ... was deep and lasting and it caused him great unhappiness. Even in memory the emotion of it remained. Only two years before his death I had proof of it. In Alfred's rooms at Trinity College Cambridge, two portraits hung near together over the fireplace – the one a portrait taken in youth, the other in late middle age. The youthful one, I learned later, was of Adalbert (the A.J.J. of poems [*sic*] XLII in *Last Poems*). I asked

Alfred, when I was staying with him two years before his death, whose was the other. In a strangely moved voice he answered, 'That was my friend, the man who had more influence on my life than anyone else.'[6]

This was a central truth of Housman's life whether we choose to regard the attachment of Housman for Moses Jackson as 'love', 'friendship', 'idealisation' or even as an expression of Housman's constant longing for love.

Epilogue

The two products of Housman's life have had very different fates. His great work of textual scholarship like many traditional crafts has become less relevant to life today. Like other scientific research, classical scholarship is prone to being overtaken by new discoveries and re-evaluations. In a book on Propertius published by a Fellow of St Anne's College Oxford in 2001 the name Housman appeared in only six places, and in one note Housman was put firmly in his place, by a woman too. The scholarship, at which he laboured so long and devotedly, was a self-directed vocational impulse. It produced a great contribution to Latin scholarship but was in essence a surrogate life.

Housman's poetry still maintains its position among the most quoted and most remembered poetry in the language. In Yeats' phrase, it is poetry that has gone 'into the general memory' because of its instant accessibility and memorability. Although published in 1896 *A Shropshire Lad* speaks to the problems of today, speaks eloquently of the painful mutability of human relationships, and speaks in a confronting yet comforting way about the inevitability of death, a subject contemporary man seeks generally to avoid. When he voices his outrage at the laws of God and Man which deny him the freedom to be as he was made, he speaks to one of today's most threatening problems – the still lethal effects of intolerance. Housman's poetry is susceptible and responsive to changes in society and changes in its readers so that in a more tolerant society some of Housman's poems, classified in anthologies as love poems, can be read as they were intended, from man to man.

What of the man and his journey through life, what has that left us? Not wishing to join the herd, unafraid of silence, he is in stark contrast to those who always place themselves centre stage, the extroverts, the energetic communicators, the mere talkers. His brother Laurence remembered him as 'a shy, proud and reticent character; even to his intimates he was provokingly reserved.' But Laurence also confessed 'I myself knew very little of his life in its day-to-day activities.' Housman's letters have opened our minds to additional dimensions of the man, how his relationships with others were formed and the part he played in helping them to grow, his generosity and kindness of spirit, his seemingly inexhaustible fund of wit and irony, his constant instinct to see the funny side of things, his small but real circle of friends, a workaholic who nevertheless kept space in his life for travel and for the companionable pleasures of the table, all coupled with constant reticence on personal matters, self-effacement and an integrity which shone at its brightest in his famous lecture *The Name & Nature of Poetry.*

The nature of Housman's profound attachment to Moses Jackson remains an enigma, most convincingly defined as an idealisation, rooted in deep feeling but not dependent on reciprocation. However we define Housman's 'love', one thing is certain. It was sufficiently powerful to endure a lifetime so that he was able to make to Gerald Jackson a direct confession of his continuing feelings for his father Moses, and besides supporting him in his studies left him £300 in his will. In all this Housman so conducted himself that Rosa Jackson and her sons all came to recognise Housman as their friend.

As a human spirit he was an epitome of faithfulness, an exemplar of Keats's words, 'the holiness of the heart's affections.' In the successful conduct of his life, and in the manner of his dying, he was an undoubted embodiment of Man's unconquerable mind and the hero of his own hidden life.

References

Abbreviations

A.E.H.   Alfred Edward Housman
Burnett   The Letters of A.E. Housman, 2 vols, Oxford, 2007
HSJ   *Housman Society Journal*

Part I Childhood

1 L. Housman, *The Unexpected Years*, p. 57.
2 K.E. Symons, *Alfred Edward Housman*, p. 10.
3 J. Pugh, *Bromsgrove and the Housmans*, Appendix C, p. xxxix.
4 L. Housman, *A.E.H.*, p. 24.
5 L. Housman, *The Unexpected Years*, p. 97.
6 Ibid. p. 58.
7 Ibid. pp. 37–38.
8 Ibid. p. 62.
9 R.P. Graves, *A.E. Housman*, p. 21.
10 K.E. Symons, quoted by R.P. Graves, *A.E. Housman*, p. 21.
11 L. Housman, *The Unexpected Years*, p. 71.
12 Ibid. p. 76.
13 Ibid. p. 77.
14 Ibid. p. 19.
15 K.E. Symons, *Alfred Edward Housman*, p. 9.
16 L Housman, *The Unexpected Years*, p. 19.
17 K.E. Symons, *Alfred Edward Housman*, p. 12.
18 L. Housman, *The Unexpected Years*, p. 22.
19 Ibid. p. 96.
20 K.E. Symons, *Alfred Edward Housman*, p. 8.
21 C. Jenkins, '"Uncle Joe": the Revd Joseph Brettell Housman. Part II,' *HSJ*, Vol. 31 (2005), p. 107.

22 Ibid. p. 108.
23 L. Housman, *The Unexpected Years*, p. 94.
24 Ibid. p. 86.
25 K.E. Symons, *Alfred Edward Housman*, p. 25.
26 L. Housman, *The Unexpected Years*, p. 85.
27 Ibid. p. 44.
28 Ibid. p. 87.
29 J. Pugh, *Bromsgrove and the Housmans*, pp. 46–101.

Part II Oxford

1 A.E.H. to Lucy Housman, 21 Oct. 1877, in Burnett, I, p. 19.
2 A.E.H. to Lucy Housman, 29 Oct. 1877, Burnett I, p.21.
3 A.E.H. to Edward Housman, 12 Feb. 1878, Burnett I, p. 23.
4 A.E.H. to Elizabeth Wise, 17 Feb. 1878, Burnett I, p. 29.
5 A.W. Pollard, 'Some Reminiscences', in K.E. Symons, *Alfred Edward Housman*, p. 30.
6 N. Page, *A.E. Housman*, p. 35.
7 C. Stray, 'Attractive and Nonsensical Classics, Oxford, Cambridge and Elsewhere', CUDC Bulletin 27, 1998.
8 A.W. Pollard, 'Some Reminiscences', in K.E. Symons, *Alfred Edward Housman*, p. 30.
9 P.G. Naiditch, *Problems in the Life and Writings of A.E. Housman*, pp. 134–135.
10 F.L. Lucas, *The Greatest Problem and Other Essays*, p. 185.
11 D. McKie, 'Jacksoniana', *HSJ*, Vol. 37 (2011), p. 138.
12 A.E.H. to K.E. Symons, 4 April 1881, Burnett I, p. 52.
13 D. McKie, 'Jacksoniana', *HSJ*, Vol. 37 (2011), p. 138.

Part III The Patent Office

1 A.W. Pollard, 'Some Reminiscences' in K.E. Symons, *Alfred Edward Housman*, p. 31.
2 P.G. Naiditch, *A.E. Housman at University College, London*, p. 202.
3 A.S.F. Gow, *A.E. Housman*, p. 6.
4 G. Richards, *Housman 1897–1936*, p. xv.
5 Ibid. p. xiv.
6 Ibid. p. xiv.
7 J. Diggle and F.R.D. Goodyear, *The Classical Papers of A.E. Housman*, Vol I, p. 7.
8 P.G. Naiditch, *Additional Problems in the Life and Writings of A.E. Housman*, p. 9.
9 P.G. Naiditch, 'Further Information on A.E. Housman and the Civil Service Examinations of 1882', *HSJ*, Vol 33 (2007), p. 87.
10 D.E. Moggridge, *Maynard Keynes*, p. 107.
11 Ibid.
12 A.W. Pollard, 'Some Reminiscences' in K.E. Symons, *Alfred Edward Housman*, p. 32.

13   P.G. Naiditch, *A.E. Housman at University College, London*, p. 241.
14   M. Pattison, *Isaac Casaubon*, p. 437.
15   Ibid. p. 204.
16   Housman quoted in C.O. Brink, *English Classical Scholarship*, p. 132.
17   L. Housman, 'A.E. Housman's "De Amicitia"', *Encounter*, Oct. 1967, p. 35.
18   Ibid. p. 41.
19   Ibid. p. 41.
20   Ibid. p. 41.
21   Ibid. p. 39.
22   T.E. Lawrence, *Seven Pillars of Wisdom*, p. 563.
23   St John's College, Oxford, Library, Housman Cabinet, I, row b, shelf 6.
24   J. Diggle and F.R.D. Goodyear, *The Classical Papers of A.E. Housman*, Vol. 1, p. 29.
25   Ibid. p. 40.
26   Ibid. p. 55.
27   Ibid. p. 62.
28   Ibid. p. 108.
29   Ibid. p. 65.
30   Ibid. p. 91.
31   Ibid. p. 120.
32   Ibid. p. 129.

Part IV Re-entry to the academic life

1   P.G. Naiditch, *A.E. Housman at University College, London*, p. 8.
2   Ibid. p. 7.
3   A.E.H. to The Council of University College London, 19 Apr. 1892, Burnett I, p. 72.
4   P.G. Naiditch, *A.E. Housman at University College, London*, p. 42.
5   H.E.D. Blakiston, 'Ellis, Robinson', *Oxford Dictionary of National Biography*.
6   P.G. Naiditch, *A.E. Housman at University College, London*, pp. 9-12.
7   Ibid. pp. 21-22.
8   Ibid. pp. 9-12.
9   J. Maycock to A.E. Housman, 15 June, 1892, S. Adelman, *The Name & Nature of A.E. Housman*, p. 30.
10   P.G. Naiditch, *Additional Problems in the Life and Writings of A.E. Housman*, p. 9.
11   Introductory Lecture, Delivered Before the Faculties of Arts and Laws and of Science in University College, London, October 3, 1892, by A.E. Housman, M.A., Professor of Latin, Cambridge 1937.
12   A.E.H. to UCL Fellowship Committee, Nov/Dec 1893, Burnett I, p. 75.
13   A.W. Pollard, 'Some Reminiscences' in K.E. Symons, *Alfred Edward Housman*, p. 3.
14   R. Holmes, *Coleridge: Darker Reflections*, p. 7.
15   A.E.H. to M. Pollet, 5 Feb. 1933, Burnett II, p. 327.
16   A.E.H. to Seymour Adelman, 21 Jun. 1928, Burnett II, p. 77.

17   L. Housman, *Echo de Paris*, p. 14.
18   Sydney Cockerell to *The Times Literary Supplement*, 10 Nov. 1936.
19   A.E.H. to L. Housman, 14 Dec. 1894, Burnett I, pp. 78-79.
20   L. Housman, *The Unexpected Years*, p. 163.
21   P. Withers, *A Buried Life*, p. 21.
22   E. Mendelson, *Later Auden*, p. xiv.
23   J. Nicolson, *The Perfect Summer*, p. 234.
24   A.E.H. to M. Pollet, 5 Feb. 1933, Burnett II, p. 329.
25   J. Bayley, *Housman's Poems*, p. 27.
26   P. Withers, *A Buried Life*, p. 84.
27   A.E.H. is thought to have made this statement during his Oxford days.
28   *Empedocles on Etna* included in C. Dyment, *Matthew Arnold*, pp. 9-44.
29   A.E.H. to M. Pollet, 5 Feb. 1933, Burnett II, p. 328.
30   L. Housman, *A.E.H.*, p. 14.
31   Reviews collected in P. Gardner, *A.E. Housman: The Critical Heritage*.
32   A.E.H. to L. Housman, 20 Mar. 1896, Burnett I, p. 85.
33   A.E.H. to L. Housman, 27 Apr. 1896, Burnett I, p. 86.
34   A.E.H. to P.L.G. Webb, 17 Jun. 1896, Burnett I, p. 87.
35   A.E.H. to L. Housman, 26 Sep. 1896, Burnett I, p. 88.
36   A.E.H. to L. Housman, 5 Oct. 1896, Burnett I, p. 90.
37   A.E.H. to L. Housman, 4 Dec. 1896, Burnett I, p. 91.
38   A.E.H. to L. Housman, 24 Dec. 1896, Burnett I, p. 92.
39   A.E.H. to L. Housman, 1 May 1897, Burnett I, p. 94.
40   A.E.H. to L. Housman, 12 May 1897, Burnett I, p. 94.
41   A.E.H. to Lucy Housman, 25 Jun. 1897, Burnett I, p. 96.

Part V Pastures new

1   A.E.H. to Lucy Housman, 22 Sep. 1897, Burnett I, p. 97.
2   A.E.H. to Lucy Housman, Oct. 1897, Burnett I, p. 100.
3   A.E.H. to Elizabeth Wise, 11 Jan. 1898, Burnett I, p. 105.
4   P.G. Naiditch, *A.E. Housman at University College, London*, p. 117.
5   R.W. Chambers, *Man's Unconquerable Mind*, p. 737.
6   G. Richards, *Housman 1897–1936*, Appendix V, p. 439.
7   T. Pakenham, *The Boer War*, p. 536.
8   J. Pugh, *Bromsgrove and the Housmans*, Appendix E, p. lxvii.
9   R.P. Graves, 'A Letter from G. Herbert Housman', *HSJ*, Vol. 3 (1977), p. 12.
10   R.P. Graves, 'A Letter from L/C G. Herbert Housman', *HSJ*, Vol. 6 (1980), p. 6.
11   J. Wilde, 'A Loosening of Silk Ribbons – Laurence Housman, John Murray and the publishing sensation of 1900', *The Times Literary Supplement*, 2 Nov. 2012, p. 14.
12   L. Housman, *The Unexpected Years*, p. 164.
13   J. Wilde, 'A Loosening of Silk Ribbons', p. 14.
14   Ibid. p. 15.
15   L. Housman, *The Unexpected Years*, p. 164.
16   J. Wilde, 'A Loosening of Silk Ribbons', p. 15.

17 A. Sutro, *Celebrities And Simple Souls*, p. 132.
18 P.G. Naiditch, *A.E. Housman at University College, London*, p. 129.
19 Ibid. p. 131.
20 Ibid. p. 134.
21 Ibid. p.136.
22 Ibid. p. 139.
23 R. Aldington, *A.E. Housman & W.B. Yeats*, p. 6.
24 G. Richards, *Housman 1897–1936*, Appendix I, p. 395.
25 Ibid. p. 439.
26 P.G. Naiditch, *Problems in the Life and Writings of A.E. Housman*, p. 23.
27 R.W. Chambers, *Man's Unconquerable Mind*, p. 371.
28 Ibid. p. 372.
29 Ibid. p. 152.
30 P.G. Naiditch, *Problems in the Life and Writings of A.E. Housman*, p. 152.
31 R.W. Chambers, *Man's Unconquerable Mind*, p. 377.
32 P.G. Naiditch, *Additional Problems in the Life and Writings of A.E. Housman*, p. 45.
33 A.E.H. to Grant Richards, 11 Aug. 1903, Burnett I, p. 154.
34 *The Classical Review*, Vol. 18, No 1, Feb. 1904, p. 63.
35 J. Diggle and F.R.D. Goodyear, *The Classical Papers of A.E. Housman*, Vol. I, p. 377.
36 J. Diggle and F.R.D. Goodyear, *The Classical Papers of A.E. Housman*, Vol. II, p. 534.
37 Ibid. p. 539.
38 Ibid. p. 563.
39 Ibid. p. 635.
40 J. Diggle and F.R.D. Goodyear, *The Classical Papers of A.E. Housman*, Vol. III, p. 903.
41 Ibid. p. 964.
42 P.G. Naiditch, *Additional Problems in the Life and Writings of A.E. Housman*, pp. 65–66.

Part VI Who am I?

1 P.G. Naiditch, 'Three Notes on the Library of A.E. Housman', *HSJ*, Vol. 11 (1985), p. 35; see also his 'The Extant Portion of the Library of A.E. Housman: IV. Non-Classical Materials', *HSJ*, Vol. 31 (2005), pp. 155-158.
2 G. Robb, *Strangers*, p. 82.
3 Ibid. p. 82.
4 Ibid. p. 186.
5 Ibid. p. 37.
6 D.E. Moggridge, *Maynard Keynes*, p. 379.
7 M. Egremont, *Siegfried Sassoon*, p. 464.
8 N. Nicolson, *Portrait of a Marriage*, p. xiii.
9 S. Rowbotham, *Edward Carpenter*, p. 334.
10 L. Housman, *The Unexpected Years*, p. 120.

11   T.E. Lawrence, *Seven Pillars of Wisdom*, p. 563.
12   G. Richards, *Housman 1897–1936*, p, 369.
13   T.E. Lawrence, *Seven Pillars of Wisdom*, p. 562.
14   T.E. Lawrence, *ibid*, p. 563.
15   J.E. Mack, *A Prince of our Disorder*, p. 420.
16   Ibid. p. 423.
17   Ibid. p. 427.
18   A.E.H. to Lucy Housman, 15 Oct. 1900, Burnett I, p. 127.
19   B. Shultz, *Henry Sidgwick*, p. 407.
20   Ibid. p. 385.
21   A.E.H. to Horatio Brown, 6 Sep. 1901, Burnett I, p. 132.
22   A.E.H. to Walter Ashburner, 13 Sep. 1901, Burnett I, p. 133.
23   A.E.H. to Walter Ashburner, 8 Jul. 1902, Burnett I, p. 135.
24   A.E.H. to Walter Ashburner, 27 Aug. 1908, Burnett I, p. 225.
25   A.E.H. to Kate Symons, 26 Nov. 1908, Burnett I, p. 230.
26   A.E.H. to G. Richards, 15 Feb. 1910, Burnett I, p. 246.
27   A.E.H. to Walter Ashburner, 1 Jun. 1926, Burnett I, p. 617.
28   A.E.H. to Kate Symons, 23 Jun. 1926, Burnett I, p. 620.
29   A.E.H. to Kate Symons, 23 Jun. 1926, Burnett I, p. 620.
30   A.E.H. to P. Withers, 7 Jul. 1926, Burnett I, p. 622.
31   A.E.H. to Kate Symons, 11 Dec. 1930, Burnett II, p. 221.
32   P. Withers, *A Buried Life*, p. 79.
33   G. Richards, *Memories of a Misspent Youth*, p. 252.
34   Ibid. pp. 258-259.
35   AEH to G. Richards, 21 Feb. 1898, Burnett I, p. 105.
36   A.E.H. to G. Richards, 22 Jul. 1898, Burnett I, p. 109.
37   A.E.H. to John Lane, 2 Aug. 1898, Burnett I, p. 110.
38   A.E.H. to G. Richards, 24 Jul. 1898, Burnett I, p. 109.
39   G. Richards, *Author Hunting*, p. xiii-xix.
40   Ibid. p. xvii.
41   W. Rothenstein, *Men and Memories 1872–1900*, p. 61.
42   Ibid. pp. 62-63.
43   Ibid. pp. 64-65.
44   Ibid. p. 281.
45   Ibid. p. 308.
46   Ibid. p. 316.
47   W. Rothenstein, *Men and Memories, 1900–1922*, p. 39.
48   Ibid.
49   A.E.H. to W. Rothenstein, 23 Jan. 1907, Burnett I, p. 202.
50   A.E.H. to A. Rothenstein, 26 Jan. 1907, Burnett I, p. 203.
51   A.E.H. to W. Rothenstein, 23 Apr. 1907, Burnett I, p. 205.
52   A.E.H. to W. Rothenstein, 22 Mar. 1910, Burnett I, p. 249.
53   W. Rothenstein, *Men and Memories, 1900–1922*, p. 343.

Part VII Paradoxical Housman

1   A.E.H. to Lucy Housman, Sep. 1904, Burnett I, p. 162.
2   M. Sturgis, *Passionate Attitudes*, p. 101.

3   Ibid. p. 100.
4   A.E.H. to Walter Ashburner, 13 Sep. 1901, Burnett I, p. 133.
5   A.E.H. to Gilbert Murray, 22 Sep. 1903, Burnett I, p. 156.
6   A.E.H. to Gilbert Murray, 25 Oct. 1904, Burnett I, p. 166.
7   A.E.H. to W. Rothenstein, 14 Jan. 1907, Burnett I, p. 202.
8   M. Pattison, *Isaac Casaubon*, p. 358.
9   A.E.H. to W. Stewart, 17 Feb. 1905, Burnett I, p. 171.
10 A.E.H. to L. Housman, 9 Aug. 1903, Burnett I, p. 153.
11 G. Richards, *Housman 1897–1936*, p. 7.
12 A.E.H. to J.L. Garvin, 11 Oct. 1905, Burnett I, p. 183.
13 A.E.H. to L. Housman, 30 Apr. 1907, Burnett I, p. 206.
14 A.E.H. to Editor, *Country Life*, 7 Nov. 1907, Burnett I, p. 213.
15 A.E.H. to Mr Thompson, 16 Mar. 1909, Burnett I, p. 235.
16 A.E.H. to G. Richards, 24 Nov. 1904, Burnett I, p. 169.
17 G. Richards, *Housman 1897–1936*, p. 62.
18 A.E.H. to G. Richards, 8 Jun. 1905, Burnett I, p. 177.
19 A.E.H. to G. Richards, 13 Jun. 1905, Burnett I, p. 177.
20 A.E.H. to G. Richards, 27 Jun. 1905, Burnett I, p. 178.
21 A.E.H. to G. Richards, 6 Jul. 1905, Burnett I, p. 179.
22 T.B. Haber, *Thirty Housman Letters to Witter Bynner*, p. viii.
23 A.E.H. to W. Bynner, 3 Jun. 1903, Burnett I, p. 146.
24 A.E.H. to W. Bynner, 13 Oct. 1903, Burnett I, p. 157.
25 A.E.H. to W. Bynner, 14 Dec. 1903, Burnett I, p. 158.
26 A.E.H. to W. Bynner, 20 Mar. 1905, Burnett I, p. 158.
27 A.E.H. to G. Richards, 15 Nov. 1905, Burnett I, p. 185.
28 See Burnett I, note p. 197.
29 A.E.H. to G. Richards, 26 Jun. 1906, Burnett I, p. 196.
30 A.E.H. to G. Richards, 24 Jan. 1906, Burnett I, p.189.
31 A.E.H. to G. Richards, 17 Aug. 1906, Burnett I, p. 199.
32 A.E.H. to G. Richards, 17Aug. 1906, Burnett I, p. 199.
33 A.E.H. to G. Richards, 7 Nov. 1909, Burnett I, p. 242.
34 A.E.H. to G. Richards, 11 Nov. 1909, Burnett I, p. 243.
35 A.E.H. to G. Richards, 20 Dec. 1920, Burnett I, p. 458.
36 G. Richards, *Housman 1897–1936*, p. 221.
37 A.E.H. to H. Jackson, 29 Apr. 1906, Burnett I, p. 194.
38 A.E.H. to H. Jackson, 26 Jun. 1908, Burnett I, p. 222.
39 A.E.H. to G. Murray, 17 Oct. 1908, Burnett I, p. 226.
40 A.E.H. to G. Richards, 27 Jun. 1908, Burnett I, p. 223.
41 L. Housman, *The Unexpected Years*, p. 237.
42 A.E.H. to L. Housman, 7 Feb. 1908, Burnett I, p. 203.
43 A.E.H. to L. Housman, 17 Feb. 1908, Burnett I, p. 215.
44 L. Housman, *The Unexpected Years*, p. 340.
45 A.E.H. to L. Housman, 1 Mar. 1908, Burnett I, p. 218.
46 A.E.H. to L. Housman, 27 Jun. 1908, Burnett I, p. 222.
47 A.E.H. to L. Housman, 16 Dec. 1908, Burnett I, p. 231.
48 A.E.H. to L. Thicknesse, 11 Aug. 1909, Burnett I, p. 238.
49 A.E.H. to L. Housman, 9 Jun. 1910, Burnett I, p. 251.
50 A.E.H. to G. Richards, 29 Jun. 1907, Burnett II, p. 211.
51 A.E.H. to G. Richards, 2 Jul. 1907, Burnett I, p. 211.

52   A.E.H. to G. Richards, 4 Jul. 1908, Burnett I, p. 224.
53   A.E.H. to A. Rothenstein, 28 May 1909, Burnett I, p. 236.
54   A.E.H. to G. Richards, 23 Jan. 1909, Burnett I, p. 234.
55   A.E.H. to An Unknown Correspondent, 24 Oct. 1910, Burnett I, pp. 255–256.

Part VIII Cambridge – The glittering prize

1   There is no mention or record of Housman having submitted his name.
2   Cambridge University Archive.
3   R. St John Parry, *Henry Jackson, O.M.*, pp. 32–33.
4   A.E.H. to H. McLeod Innes, 21 Jan. 1911, Burnett I, p. 260.
5   A. Jackson, *A Fine View of The Show*, p. 11.
6   Ibid. p. 12.
7   Ibid. p. 15.
8   A.E.H. to Rosa Jackson, 17 Dec. 1908, Burnett I, p. 232.
9   A. Jackson, *A Fine View of the Show*, p. 19.
10   Ibid. p. 20.
11   A.E.H. to E. Wise, 11 Jul. 1911, Burnett I, p. 270.
12   E. Griffin, *The Selected Letters of Bertrand Russell*, Vol. 1, p. 367.
13   P. Lubbock, *The Diary of Arthur Christopher Benson*, p. 214.
14   N. Annan, *The Dons*, pp. 7-9.
15   R.W. Chambers, *Man's Unconquerable Mind*, p. 381.
16   P.G. Naiditch, *A.E. Housman at University College, London*, p. 156.
17   R.W. Chambers, *Man's Unconquerable Mind*, p. 380.
18   A.E.H. to A. Rothenstein, 22 Jan. 1911, Burnett I, p. 261.
19   A.E.H. to M. Platt, 19 Jan. 1911, Burnett I, p. 258.
20   A.E.H. to Margaret, Lady Ramsay, 26 Jan. 1911, Burnett I, p. 262.
21   A.E.H. to E. Gosse, 19 Jan. 1911, Burnett I, p. 259.
22   A.E.H. to L. Housman, 30 Jan. 1911, Burnett I, p. 262.
23   A.E.H. to W. Ashburner, 30 Jan. 1911, Burnett I, p. 263.
24   A.E.H. to L. Housman, 11 Jun. 1911, Burnett I, p. 268.
25   A.E. Housman, *The Confines of Criticism*, ed. J. Carter.
26   R. St John Parry, *Henry Jackson, O.M.*, p. 164.
27   A.E. Housman, *The Confines of Criticism*, ed. J. Carter, p. 8.
28   Ibid.
29   S. Cockerell, Diary for 9 May 1911.
30   A.W. Pollard, 'Some Reminiscences' in K.E. Symons, *Alfred Edward Housman*, p. 33.
31   A.E.H. to F.M. Cornford, 17 May 1911, Burnett I, p. 267.
32   A.E.H. to W. Bynner, 17 May 1911, Burnett I, p. 267.
33   A.E.H. to Professor Israel Gollancz, 9 Jun. 1911, Burnett I, p. 268.
34   A.E.H. to P.W. Ames, 13 May 1913, Burnett I, p. 306.
35   A.E.H. to A.C. Benson, 16 May 1913, Burnett I, p. 306.
36   G. Farmelo, *The Strangest Man*, p. 89.
37   A.E.H. to G. Richards, 28 Aug. 1911, Burnett I, p. 272.
38   A.E.H. to G. Richards, 30 Aug. 1911, Burnett I, p. 274.
39   A.E.H. to W.H. Garrod, 24 Oct. 1911, Burnett I, p. 277.
40   A.E.H. to Kate Symons, 30 Dec. 1911, Burnett I, p. 281.

41   A. Burnett, *The Letters of A.E. Housman*, Vol. I, note p. 279.
42   W.S. Blunt, *My Diaries*, part 2, p. 387.
43   G. Richards, *Housman 1897–1936*, p. 386.
44   A.E.H. to H. Foxwell, 29 Nov. 1911, unpublished.
45   R. Freeman, Private note on Foxwell for the author.
46   A.E.H. to Edward Marsh, 1 Oct. 1912, Burnett I, p. 297.
47   A.E.H. to G. Richards, 31 Dec. 1911, Burnett I, p. 283.
48   A.E.H. to G. Richards, 4 Jan. 1912, Burnett I, p. 284.
49   A.E.H. to G. Richards, 1 May 1912, Burnett I, p. 289.
50   A.E.H. to J. Mackail, 22 May 1912, Burnett I, pp. 291-293.
51   A.E.H. to G. Richards, 2 Jul. 1912, Burnett I, p. 293.
52   A.E.H. to G. Richards, 7 Sep. 1912, Burnett I, p. 296.
53   A.E.H. to M. Platt, 26 Dec. 1912, Burnett I, p. 301.
54   A.E.H. to A. Rothenstein, 14 Feb. 1913, Burnett I, p. 304.
55   A.E.H. to T. Hardy, 28 Nov. 1912, Burnett I, p. 299.
56   A.E.H. to L. Thicknesse, 8 Mar. 1913, Burnett I, p. 304.
57   A.E.H. to G. Richards, 17 Jan. 1913, Burnett I, p. 302.
58   A.E.H. to J.G Frazer, 21 May 1913, Burnett I, p. 307.
59   A.E.H. to Wilfred Meynell, 10 Jun. 1913, Burnett I, p. 309.
60   A.E.H. to G. Richards, 23 Sep. 1913, Burnett I, p. 312.
61   A.E.H. to G. Richards, 24 Sep. 1913, Burnett I, p. 313.
62   A.E.H. to W. Rothenstein, 8 Oct. 1913, Burnett I, p. 314.
63   A.E.H. to L. Housman, 10 Oct. 1913, Burnett I, p. 314.
64   A.E.H. to W. Bynner, 12 Oct. 1913, Burnett I, p. 315.
65   A.E.H. to E. Gosse, 11 Dec. 1913, Burnett I, p. 317.
66   A.E.H. to An Unknown Correspondent, 15 Jan. 1915, Burnett I, p. 318.
67   A.E.H. to G. Richards, 9 May 1914, Burnett I, p. 324.
68   A.E.H. to G. Richards, 31 May 1914, Burnett I, p.325.

Part IX *The Great War 1914–1918*

1   A.E.H. to G. Murray, 14 Oct. 1914, Burnett I, p. 330.
2   D. Hibberd and J. Onion, *The Winter of the World*, No. 45, p. 53.
3   Ibid. No. 106, 'Before Action', p. 116.
4   L. Housman, *A.E.H.*, p. 106.
5   A.E.H. to L. Thickness, 24 Nov. 1914, Burnett I, p. 331.
6   A.E.H. to E. Gosse, 27 Jan. 1915, Burnett I, p. 333.
7   A.E.H. to G. Richards, 14 Feb. 1915, Burnett I, p. 335.
8   A.E.H. to Sir James Frazer, 7 Mar. 1915, Burnett I, p. 337.
9   A.E.H. to L. Thicknesse, 7 Mar. 1915, Burnett I, p. 338.
10   G. Richards, *Housman 1897–1936*, p. 131.
11   Ibid. p. 132.
12   Ibid. p. 136.
13   A.E.H. to G. Richards, 7 Apr. 1915, Burnett I, p. 339.
14   A.E.H. to G. Richards, 14 Apr. 1915, Burnett I, p. 340.
15   A.E.H. to G. Richards, 3 Oct. 1915, Burnett I, p. 345.
16   A.E.H. to Kate Symons, 5 Oct. 1915, Burnett I, p. 356.
17   A.E.H. to G. Richards, 15 Jul. 1915, Burnett I, p. 343.

18   A.E.H. to G. Richards, 3 Feb. 1915, Burnett I, p. 353.
19   A.E.H. to G. Richards, 10 Feb. 1916, Burnett I, p. 253.
20   A.E.H. to G. Richards, 29 Mar. 1916, Burnett I, p. 258.
21   A.E.H. to G. Richards, 6 Apr. 1916, Burnett I, p. 359.
22   A.E.H. to G. Richards, 15 Apr. 1916, Burnett I, p. 360.
23   A.E.H. to G. Richards, 26 Jun. 1916, Burnett I, p. 363.
24   A.E.H. to W. Rothenstein, 29 Jun./2 Jul. 1916, Burnett I, pp. 363–364.
25   A.E.H. to A. Rothenstein, 10 Jul. 1916, Burnett I, p. 364.
26   G. Richards, *Housman 1897–1936*, p. 157.
27   Ibid. p. 153.
28   Ibid. p. 153.
29   A.E.H. to G. Richards, 4 Oct. 1916, Burnett I, p. 367.
30   A.E.H. to G. Richards, 5 Dec. 1916, Burnett I, p. 370.
31   A.E.H. to G. Richards, 14 Oct. 1917, Burnett I, p. 381.
32   P. Withers, *A Buried Life*, p. 10.
33   A.E.H. to G. Richards, 14 Oct. 1917, Burnett I, p. 381.
34   A.E.H. to G. Richards, 22 Aug. 1917, Burnett I, p. 380.
35   A.E.H. to W. Cross, 18 Nov. 1917, Burnett I, p. 383.
36   A. Jackson, *A Fine View of the Show*, p. 107.
37   Ibid. p. 153.
38   Ibid. p. 170.
39   Ibid. p. 171.
40   Ibid. p. 174.
41   P. Withers, *A Buried Life*, pp. 16–17.
42   A.E.H. to P. Withers, 18 Jan. 1918, Burnett I, p. 385.
43   A.E.H. to M. Withers, 10 Mar. 1918, Burnett I, p. 387.
44   A.E.H. to A. Rothenstein, 6 Jul. 1918, Burnett I, p. 390.
45   A.E.H. to J. Drinkwater, 10 May 1918, Burnett I, p. 389.
46   A.E.H. to G. Richards, 14 Jun. 1918, Burnett I, p. 390.
47   A.E.H. to A. Rothenstein, 22 Aug. 1918, Burnett I, p. 391.
48   A.E.H. to G. Richards, 11 Oct. 1918, Burnett I, p. 393.
49   A.E.H. to M. Richards, 14 Nov. 1918, Burnett I, p. 394.
50   A.E.H. to G. Richards, 25 Nov. 1918, Burnett I, p. 394.
51   R. Monk, 'Russell, Bertrand Arthur William, third Earl Russell (1872–1970)', *Oxford Dictionary of National Biography*, p. 11.
52   Ibid. p. 13.
53   A.E.H. to H.A. Hollond, Jan. 1919, Burnett I, p. 398.
54   R. Monk, *Ludwig Wittgenstein*, p. 41.
55   Ibid. p. 271.
56   Ibid. p. 585.
57   Ibid. p. 428.
58   G. Richards, *Housman 1897–1936*, pp. 446–447.
59   R. Monk, *Ludwig Wittgenstein*, p. 262.
60   A.E.H. to E. Gosse, 9 Apr. 1917, Burnett I, p. 375.
61   A.E.H. to E. Gosse, 13 Apr. 1917, Burnett I, p. 377.
62   A.E.H. to E. Gosse, 20 Jan. 1919, Burnett I, pp. 399–401.
63   Footnote, Burnett I, p. 401.
64   A.E.H. to G. Richards, 15 May 1919, Burnett I, p. 407 (footnote refers to Blunt's Index).

65 A.E.H. to M. Richards, 15 Jul. 1919, Burnett I, p. 411.
66 A.E.H. to Siegfried Sassoon, 23 May 1919, Burnett I, p. 408.
67 Burnett note, Burnett I, p. 408.
68 M. Egremont, *Siegfried Sassoon*, p. 134.
69 A.E.H. to J.W. Mackail, 23 May 1919, Burnett I, p. 408.
70 A.E.H. to H. Jackson, 14 Jul. 1919, Burnett I, p. 409.
71 A.E.H. to Reginald St John Parry, 3 Jan. 1920, Burnett I, p. 426.

Part X After the war

1   A.E.H. to G. Richards, 21 Jul. 1919, Burnett I, p. 411.
2   A.E.H. to G. Richards, 29 Aug. 1919, Burnett I, p. 414.
3   A.E.H. to G. Richards, 17 Sep. 1919, Burnett I, p. 416.
4   A.E.H. to J.C. Squire, 20 Aug. 1919, Burnett I, p. 412.
5   A.E.H. to J. Trotter, 27 Sep. 1919, Burnett I, p. 417.
6   A.E.H. to G. Richards, 9 Oct. 1919, Burnett I, p. 418.
7   A.E.H. to T. Hardy, 17 Oct. 1919, Burnett I, p. 418.
8   A.E.H. to M.R. James, 22 Oct. 1919, and footnote on Haldane, Burnett I, p. 419.
9   A.E.H. to E. Oppenheim, 8 Oct. 1919, Burnett I, p. 417.
10 A.E.H. to J.S. Phillimore, 30 Nov. 1919, Burnett I, p. 422.
11 A.E.H. to G. Richards, 30 Nov. 1919, Burnett I, p. 421.
12 A.E.H. to G. Richards, 30 Nov. 1919, Burnett I, p. 421.
13 A.E.H. to G. Richards, 2 Dec. 1919, Burnett I, p. 423.
14 A.E.H. to G. Richards, 10 Dec. 1919, Burnett I, p. 424.
15 A.E.H. to G. Richards, 16 Dec. 1919, Burnett I, p. 425.
16 A.E.H. to M. Richards, 21 Dec. 1919, Burnett I, p. 425.
17 A.E.H. to L. Housman, 4 Dec. 1919, Burnett I, p. 423.
18 A.E.H. to P. Withers, 18 Jan. 1920, Burnett I, p. 428.
19 A.E.H. to A. Rothenstein, 21 Feb. 1920, Burnett I, p. 431.
20 A.E.H. to W. Rothenstein, 13 Apr. 1920, Burnett I, p. 435.
21 A.E.H. to Kate Symons, 27 Apr. 1920, Burnett I, p. 437.
22 A.E.H. to F.M. Cornford, 3 May 1920, Burnett I, p. 439.
23 J. Carter, *A.E. Housman: Selected Prose*, p. 163.
24 A.E.H. to P. Withers, 4 May 1920, Burnett I, p. 439.
25 A.E.H. to G. Richards, 24 May 1920, Burnett I, p. 441.
26 A.E.H. to G. Richards, 1 Jul. 1920, Burnett I, p. 442.
27 A.E.H. to Kate Symons, 26 Jul. 1920, Burnett I, p. 444.
28 A.E.H. to G. Richards, 12 Aug. 1920, Burnett I, p. 445.
29 A.E.H. to G. Richards, 21 Aug., Burnett I, p. 447.
30 A.E.H. to G. Richards, 5 Sep. 1920, Burnett I, p. 449.
31 G. Richards, *Author Hunting*, p. 213.
32 A.E.H. to G. Richards, 16 Sep. 1920, Burnett I, p. 451.
33 A.E.H. to L. Housman, 21 Sep. 1920, Burnett I, p. 451.
34 A.E.H. to Kate Symons, 30 Oct. 1920, Burnett I, p. 453.
35 A.E.H. to F.M. Cornford, 14 Oct. 1920, Burnett I, p. 455.
36 A.E.H. to G.C. Williamson, 24 Oct. 1920, Burnett I, p. 255.
37 A.E.H. to G. Richards, 12 Dec. 1920, Burnett I, p. 458.

38   A.E.H. to G. Richards, 20 Dec. 1920, Burnett I, p. 458.
39   A.E.H. to M. Platt, 23 Dec. 1920, Burnett I, p. 460.
40   A.E.H. to W. Rothenstein, 28 Dec. 1920, Burnett I, p. 461.
41   A.E.H. to P. Withers, 28 Dec. 1920, Burnett I, p. 461.
42   A.E.H. to G. Richards, 5 Jan. 1921, Burnett I, p. 463.
43   A.E.H. to P. Withers, 1 Jun. 1921, Burnett I, p. 406.
44   A.E.H. to G. Richards, 14 Jul. 1921, Burnett I, p. 469.
45   A.E.H. to G. Richards, 21 Jul. 1921, Burnett I, p. 469.
46   A.E.H. to G. Richards, 1 Sep. 1921, Burnett I, p. 471.
47   A.E.H. to G. Richards, 27 Sep. 1921, Burnett I, p. 472.
48   A.E.H. to G. Richards, 20 Oct. 1921, Burnett I, p. 473.
49   A.E.H. to G. Richards, 27 Oct. 1921, Burnett I, p. 474.
50   A.E.H. to P. Withers, 30 Oct. 1921, Burnett, I p. 475.
51   A.E.H. to A.C. Pearson, 16 Nov. 1921, Burnett I, p. 477.
52   A.E.H. to Sir Herbert Warren, 6 Dec. 1921, Burnett I, p. 478.
53   A.E.H. to P. Withers, 30 Oct. 1921, Burnett I, p. 475.
54   A.E.H. to S. Cockerell, 16 Dec. 1921, Burnett I, p. 480.
55   G. Richards, *Housman 1897–1932*, p. 190.
56   A.E.H. to P. Withers, 3 Mar. 1922, Burnett I, p. 484.

Part XI Last Poems A Requiem for Moses Jackson

1   A.E.H. to G. Richards, 3 Apr. 1922, Burnett I, p. 487.
2   A.E.H. to G. Richards, 9 Apr. 1922, Burnett, I p. 488.
3   A.E.H. to G. Richards, 22 Apr. 1922, Burnett I, p. 489.
4   A.E.H. to G. Richards, 22 Apr. 1922, Burnett I, p. 489.
5   A.E.H. to G. Richards, 19 Jun. 1922, Burnett I, p. 499.
6   A.E.H. to J.B. Priestley, 15 Apr. 1922, Burnett I, p. 489.
7   A.E.H. to P. Withers, 22 Apr. 1922, Burnett I, p. 490.
8   A.E.H. to J. Drinkwater, 26 Apr. 1922, Burnett I, p. 491.
9   A.E.H. to M. Withers, 17 May 1922, Burnett I, p. 494.
10   A.E.H. to P. Withers, 23 May 1922, Burnett I, p. 495.
11   A.E.H. to Lady Anderson, 3 Jun. 1922, Burnett I, p. 494.
12   G. Richards, *Author Hunting*, p. 215.
13   A.E.H. to G. Richards, 15 Jun. 1922, Burnett I, p. 498.
14   A.E.H. to J.W. Mackail, 26 Jun. 1922, Burnett I, p. 501.
15   A.E.H. to J.W. Mackail, 18 Jul. 1922, Burnett I, p. 503.
16   A.E.H. to J.W. Mackail, 25 Jul. 1922, Burnett I, p. 505.
17   A.E.H. to G. Richards, 26 Jul. 1922, Burnett I, p. 501.
18   A.E.H. to G. Richards, 24 Aug. 1922, Burnett I, p. 509.
19   A.E.H. to G. Richards, 24 Aug. 1922, Burnett I, p. 509.
20   A. Jackson, *A Fine View of the Show*, p. 242. Also Burnett I, p. 516.
21   Ibid. p. 243. See also A. Jackson, 'A Pivotal Friendship', *HSJ*, Vol. 36 (2010).
22   A. Jackson, 'A Pivotal Friendship', *HSJ*, Vol. 36 (2010), p. 34.
23   A.E.H. to A.W. Pollard, 17 Jan. 1923, Burnett I, p. 533.
24   A.E.H. to T. Hardy, 27 Nov. 1914, Burnett I, p. 332.
25   G. Richards, *Housman 1897–1936*, p. 200.

26 A.E.H. to G. Richards, 12 Oct. 1922, Burnett I, p. 515.

27 A.E.H. to G. Richards, 8 Nov. 1922, Burnett I, p. 524.

28 G. Richards, *Housman 1897–1936*, p. 204.

29 A.E.H. to G. Richards, 26 Oct. 1922, Burnett I, p. 519.

30 A.E.H. to F.C. Owlett, 18 Mar. 1924, Burnett I, p. 561.

31 A.E.H. to P.V. Love, 14 Feb. 1927, Burnett II, p. 10.

32 L.W. Dodd, *Literary Review*, 23 Dec. 1922.

33 A.E.H. to An Unknown Correspondent, 6 Apr. 1926, Burnett I, p. 614.

34 W.R. Benet, *The Bookman* (N.Y.).

35 E. Gosse, *The Sunday Times*, 22 Oct. 1922.

36 D.C.T, *Cambridge Review*, 22 Oct. 1922.

37 J.C. Squire, *The London Mercury*, Nov. 1922.

38 J.B. Priestley, *The London Mercury*, Dec. 1922.

39 Unsigned review in *Outlook*, Dec. 1922.

40 J. Freeman, *The Bookman* (London), Dec. 1922.

41 Clement Wood, *The Nation* (N.Y.), 21 Feb. 1923.

42 F.L. Lucas, *New Statesman & Nation*, 20 Oct. 1923.

43 J.F. Macdonald, *Queen's Quarterly*, Fall 1923.

44 A.E.H. to J. Drinkwater, 22 Oct. 1922, Burnett I, p. 518.

45 A.E.H. to E. Gosse, 25 Oct. 1922, Burnett I, p. 519.

46 Barrie to A.E.H., Burnett I, footnote p. 529.

47 E.M. Forster to A.E.H., 22 Feb. 1923, Burnett I, footnote p. 537.

48 A.E.H. to E.M. Forster, 25 Feb. 1923, Burnett I, p. 537.

49 E.M. Forster to A.E.H., 28 Mar. 1928, Burnett I, footnote p. 538.

50 J.M. Heath, ed., *The Creator as Critic And Other Writings by E. M. Forster*, pp. 124–130.

51 A.E.H. to W. Bynner, 6 Feb. 1923, Burnett I, p. 537.

52 A.E.H. to P. Withers, 22 Dec. 1922, Burnett I, p. 529.

53 A.E.H. to G. Richards, 3 Oct. 1922, Burnett I, p. 513.

54 A.E.H. to G. Richards, 12 Oct. 1922, Burnett I, p. 515.

55 A.E.H. to G. Richards, 14 Oct. 1922, Burnett I, p. 515.

56 A.E.H. to L. Housman, 5 Dec. 1922, Burnett I, p. 527.

57 A.E.H. to L. Housman, 11 Dec. 1922, Burnett I, p. 527.

58 *The Times*, 21 Dec. 1922.

59 A.E.H. to G. Richards, 4 May 1923, Burnett I. p. 541.

60 A.E.H. to R. Bridges, 2 Jul. 1923, Burnett I, p. 544.

61 A.E.H. to G. Richards, 24 Jul. 1923, Burnett I, p. 545.

62 A.E.H. to Kate Symons, 18 Aug. 1923, Burnett I, p. 546.

63 A.E.H. to G. Richards, 23 Sep. 1923, Burnett I, p. 548.

64 A.E.H. to H.W. Garrod, 2 Nov. 1923, Burnett I, p. 552.

65 A.E.H. to E.V. Lucas, 3 Nov. 1923, Burnett I, p. 553.

66 J.J. Thomson, *Recollections and Reflections*, p. 316.

67 S.C. Roberts, *Adventures with Authors*, p. 127.

68 N. Page, *A.E. Housman*, p. 104.

69 A.E.H. to G. Richards, 12 Jan. 1924, Burnett I, p. 558.

70 A.E.H. to I. Gurney, 22 Jul. 1924, Burnett I, p. 566.

71 A.E.H. to C.A. Alington, 24 Jul. 1924, Burnett I, p. 567.

72 A.E.H. to R. Bridges, 27 Aug. 1924, Burnett I, p. 569.

73 A.E.H. to A. Rothenstein, 2 Sep. 1924, Burnett I, p. 569.

74   A.E.H. to J.B. Priestley, 18 Sep. 1924, Burnett I, p. 570.

75   A.E.H. to R. Bridges, 25 Sep. 1924, Burnett I, p. 572.

76   A.E.H. to G. Richards, 1 Oct. 1924, Burnett I, p. 572.

77   A.E.H. to G. Richards, 3 Nov. 1924, Burnett I, p. 575.

78   A.E.H. to Macmillan, 16 Nov. 1924, Burnett I, p. 576.

79   A.E.H. to P. Higgins, 28 Dec. 1924, Burnett I, p. 577.

80   A.E.H. to P. Withers, 31 Dec. 1924, Burnett I, p. 578.

81   A.E.H. to Sir James Frazer, 1 Jan. 1925, Burnett I, p. 579.

82   A.E.H. to Sir Ernest Rutherford, 1 Jan. 1925, Burnett I, p. 579.

83   A.E.H. to F.W. Hall, 3 Feb. 1925, Burnett I, p. 583.

84   A.E.H. to Sir Joseph J. Thomson, 22 Feb. 1925, Burnett I, p. 585.

85   A.E.H. to University College Appointments Committee, 15 Mar. 1925, Burnett I, p. 587.

86   A.E.H. to A.S. Gow, 26 Mar. 1925, Burnett I, p. 588.

87   A.E.H. to W. Bynner, 15 Apr. 1925, Burnett I, p. 589.

88   A.E.H. to P. Withers, 20 May 1925, Burnett I, p. 590.

89   A.E.H. to R. Torrence, 1 Jun. 1925, Burnett I, p. 591.

90   A.E.H. to A.S. Gow, 27 Jun. 1925, Burnett I, p. 592.

91   A.E.H. to Kate Symons, 5 Jul. 1925, Burnett I, p. 593.

92   A.E.H. to Kate Symons, 22 Dec. 1925, Burnett I, p. 604.

93   A.E.H. to Kate Symons, 9 Apr. 1927, Burnett II, p 19.

94   A.E.H. to G. Richards, 7 Aug. 1925, Burnett I, p. 594.

95   A.E.H. to L. Housman, 18 Aug. 1925, Burnett I, p. 595.

96   A.E.H. to J.D. Duff, 26 Aug. 1925, Burnett I, p. 596.

97   A.E.H. to L. Housman, 19 Sep. 1925, Burnett I, p. 597.

98   A.E.H. to L. Housman, 8 Dec. 1925, Burnett I, p. 603.

99   A.E.H. to A.F.S. Gow, 4 Jun. 1926, Burnett I, p. 597.

100 A.E.H. to G. Richards, 6 Oct. 1925, Burnett I, p. 597.

101 A.E.H. to P. Withers, 25 Dec. 1925, Burnett I, p. 605.

102 A.E.H. to L. Housman, 29 Dec. 1925, Burnett I, p. 606.

103 A.E.H. to R. St John Parry, 17 Jan. 1926, Burnett I, p. 607.

104 J. Carter, *A.E. Housman: Selected Prose*, pp. 154-160.

105 A. Burnett, *The Poems of A.E. Housman*, p. 251.

106 A.E.H. to P. Withers, 23 Apr. 1926, Burnett I, p. 615.

107 A.E.H. to P. Withers, 7 Jul. 1926, Burnett II, p. 622.

108 A.E.H. to P. Withers, 21 Sep. 1926, Burnett II, p. 625.

109 A.E.H. to S.C. Roberts, 14 Oct. 1926, Burnett I, p. 630.

110 A.E.H. to A.C. Pearson, 14 Oct. 1926, Burnett I, p. 631.

111 A.E.H. to A.C. Pearson, 15 Oct. 1926, Burnett I, p. 631.

112 A.E.H. to G. Richards, 21 Oct. 1926, Burnett I, p. 633.

113 J.D. Tunnicliffe & M. Buncombe, 'A.E. Housman and the Failure of Grant Richards Limited in 1926', *HSJ*, Vol. 11 (1985), pp. 101–106.

114 A.E.H. to G. Richards, 21 Oct. 1926, Burnett I, p. 633.

115 A.E.H. to G. Richards, 4 Nov. 1926, Burnett I, p. 636.

116 A.E.H. to G. Richards, 14 Nov. 1926, Burnett I, p. 638.

117 A.E.H. to G. Richards, 30 Nov. 1926, Burnett I, p. 640.

118 A.E.H. to Allen & Unwin, 8 Dec. 1926, Burnett I, p. 640.

119 A.E.H. to G. Richards, 17 Dec. 1926, Burnett I, p. 641.

120 Burnett I, footnote p. 642.

121 A.E.H. to Macmillan, 27 Dec. 1926, Burnett I, p. 642.

122 A.E.H. to Kate Symons, 3 Jan. 1927, Burnett II, p. 3.

123 A.E.H. to A. Rothenstein, 16 Jan. 1927, Burnett II, p. 5.

124 A.E.H. to G. Richards, 22 Jan. 1927, Burnett II, p. 7.

125 A.E.H. to G. Richards, 1 Mar. 1927, Burnett II, p. 13.

126 A.E.H. to G. Richards, 15 Mar. 1927, Burnett II, p. 15.

127 A.E.H. to C. Clemens, 2 Feb. 1927, Burnett II, p. 8.

128 A.E.H. to J. G. Leippert, 30 Mar. 1927, Burnett II, p. 17.

129 A.E.H. to C. Wilson, 18 May 1927, Burnett II, p. 26.

130 A.E.H. to C. Wilson, 7 Aug. 1927, Burnett II, p. 31.

131 A.E.H. to Professor A.Y. Campbell, 5 Apr. 1927, Burnett II, p. 17.

132 A.E.H. to S.C. Roberts, 27 Apr. 1927, Burnett II, p. 22.

133 A.E.H. to Henry Holt and Co., 13 May 1927, Burnett II, p. 33.

134 A.E.H. to G. Richards, 22 Aug 1927, Burnett II, p. 33.

135 G. Richards, *Housman 1897–1936*, p. 42.

136 A.E.H. to G. Richards, 17 Oct. 1927, Burnett II, p. 38.

137 A.E.H. to Kate Symons, 20 Sep. 1927, Burnett II, p. 34.

138 A.E.H. to S. Cockerell, 14 Oct. 1927, Burnett II, p. 37.

139 Takeshi Obata, 'How A.E. Housman's Poetry was Accepted in Japan before the World War', *HSJ*, Vol. 8 (1932), pp. 29–35.

140 A.E.H. to Sir James G. Frazer, 22 Oct. 1927, Burnett II, p. 39.

141 A.E.H. to W. Ashburner, 4 Nov. 1927, Burnett II, p. 41.

142 A.E.H. to G.B. Saul, 8 Nov. 1927, Burnett II, p. 42.

143 A.E.H. to Pauline Hemmerde, 8 Dec. 1927, Burnett II, p. 44.

144 G. Richards, *Housman 1897–1936*, p. 239.

145 A.E.H. to G. Richards, 13 Dec. 1927, Burnett II, p. 45.

146 Burnett II, footnote p. 45.

147 A.E.H. to G. Richards, 19 Jan. 1928, Burnett II, p. 53.

148 G. Richards, *Housman 1897–1936*, footnote p. 241.

149 A.E.H. to G. Richards, 24 Apr. 1928, Burnett II, p. 67.

150 A.E.H. to Kate Symons, 28 Dec. 1927, Burnett II, p. 46.

151 A.E.H. to B. Housman, 29 Dec. 1927, Burnett II, p. 47.

152 A.E.H. to R. Bridges, 31 Dec. 1927, Burnett II, p. 48.

153 A.E.H. to G. Richards, 17 Jan. 1928, Burnett II, p. 51.

154 A.E.H. to G. Richards, 14 May 1928, Burnett II, p. 72.

155 G. Richards, *Housman 1897–1936*, p. 247.

156 A.E.H. to Lady Gosse, 17 May 1928, Burnett II, p. 72.

157 A.E.H. to E. Blunden, 18 Feb. 1928, Burnett II, p. 59.

158 A.E.H. to G. Richards, 19 Jan. 1928, Burnett II, p. 53.

159 A.E.H.to W. Rothenstein, 24 Jan. 1928, Burnett II, p. 55.

160 A.E.H. to G. Richards, 30 Jan. 1928, Burnett II, p. 57.

161 A.E.H. to W.E. Leonard, 9 Feb. 1928, Burnett II, p. 58.

162 A.E.H. to Margot, Lady Howard de Walden, 16 Feb. 1928, Burnett II, p. 59.

163 A.E.H. to E. Wrench, 22 Feb. 1928, Burnett II, p. 61.

164 A.E.H. to W. Rothenstein, 17 Feb. 1928, Burnett II, p. 59.

165 A.E.H. to Sir James Barrie, 20 Feb. 1928, Burnett II, p. 61.

166 A.E.H. to W. Rothenstein, 25 Feb. 1928, Burnett II, p. 61.

167 A.E.H. to G. Richards, 28 Feb. 1928, Burnett II, p. 62.

168   A.E.H. to T.S. Eliot, 12 Mar. 1928, Burnett II, p. 63.
169   A.E.H. to Mr Finkelstein, 15 Apr. 1928, Burnett II, p. 64.
170   A.E.H. to P. Withers, 23 Apr. 1928, Burnett II, p. 66.
171   A.E.H. to S. Adelman, 6 May 1928, Burnett II, p. 68.
172   A.E.H. to H.A. De Rue, 12 May 1928, Burnett II, p. 71.
173   A.E.H. to Registrar to the University of Oxford, 10 May 1928, Burnett II, p. 70.
174   G. Richards, *Housman 1897–1936*, p. 242.
175   A.E.H. to G. Richards, 4 Jun. 1928, Burnett II, p. 76.
176   G. Richards, *Housman 1897–1936*, p. 243.
177   A.E.H. to G. Richards, 31 May 1928, Burnett II, p. 76.
178   G. Richards, *Housman 1897–1936*, p. 243.
179   A.E.H. to S. Adelman, 21 Jun. 1928, Burnett II, p. 77 and footnote 1.
180   A.E.H. to G. Richards, 22 Jun. 1928, Burnett II, p. 79.
181   A.E.H. to G. Richards, 25 Jun. 1928, Burnett II, p. 81.
182   A.E.H. to The Richards Press, 1 Jul. 1928, Burnett II, p. 82.
183   A.E.H. to The Richards Press, 3 Jul. 1928, Burnett II, p. 83.
184   A.E.H. to G. Richards, 14 Jul. 1928, Burnett II, p. 86.
185   A.E.H. to S.C. Roberts, 3 Jul. 1928, Burnett II, p. 83.
186   A.E.H. to G. Richards, 9 Oct. 1928, Burnett II, p. 93.
187   G. Richards, *Housman 1897–1936*, p. 245.
188   A.E.H. to H.W. Garrod, 17 Dec. 1928, Burnett II, p. 99.
189   A.E.H. to Kate Symons, 19 Dec. 1928, Burnett II, p. 100.

Part XII Last things

1   A.E.H. to R. Bridges, 28 Dec. 1928, Burnett II, p. 101.
2   A.E.H. to P. Withers, 28 Dec. 1928, Burnett II, p. 102.
3   A.E.H. to A.C. Pearson, 30 Dec. 1928, Burnett II, p. 103.
4   A.E.H. to G. Richards, 10 Jan. 1929, Burnett II, p. 104.
5   A.E.H. to R.P. Finberg, 1 Feb. 1929, Burnett II, p. 109.
6   A.E.H. to Lord Stamfordham, 22 Feb. 1929, Burnett II, p. 113.
7   G. Richards, *Housman 1897–1936*, p. 253.
8   Ibid. Appendix VII, p. 446.
9   J. Scott, 'Housman's Continental Life', *HSJ*, Vol. 40 (2014), p. 80.
10   A.E.H. to L. Housman, 2 May 1930, Burnett II, p. 186.
11   G. Richards, *Housman 1896–1936*, p. 252.
12   A.E.H. to L. Housman, 16 Feb. 1929, Burnett II, p. 111.
13   A.E.H. to P. Withers, 29 Mar. 1929, Burnett II, p. 119.
14   A.E.H. to Sir Joseph J. Thomson, 27 Mar. 1929, Burnett II, p. 119.
15   A.E.H. to H. Foxwell, 16 Jun. 1929, unpublished, Kwansei University Japan.
16   A.E.H. to M.A. Jackson, 25 May 1929, Burnett II, p. 129.
17   A.E.H. to Kate Symons, 1 Jul. 1929, Burnett II, p. 134.
18   A.E.H. to G. Richards, 19 Aug. 1929, Burnett II, p. 140.
19   A.E.H. to G. Richards, 14 Sep. 1929, Burnett II, p. 141.
20   A.E.H. to Kate Symons, 26 Sep. 1929, Burnett II, p. 144.
21   A.E.H. to A. Rubin, 17 Nov. 1929, Burnett II, p. 153.

22 A.E.H. to G. Richards, 30 Dec. 1929, Burnett II, p. 161.

23 A.E.H. to J. Housman, 30 Dec. 1929, Burnett II, p. 162.

24 A.E.H. to M. Platt, 31 Dec. 1929, Burnett II, p. 163.

25 A.E.H. to M. Platt, 4 Feb. 1930, Burnett II, p. 169.

26 A.E.H. to G. Richards, 5 Feb. 1930, Burnett II, p. 170.

27 A.E.H. to G. Richards, 29 Mar. 1930, Burnett II, p. 178.

28 A.E.H. to G. Richards, 9 Apr. 1930, Burnett II, p. 179.

29 A.E.H. to A.E. Scholfield, 6 Mar. 1930, Burnett II, p. 174.

30 C. Williams, 'Poetry at Present', in *Critical Heritage*, pp. 226-233.

31 A.E.H. to C. Williams, 8 Mar. 1930, Burnett II, p.174.

32 A.E.H. to M. Bridges, 22 Apr. 1930, Burnett II, p. 181.

33 A.E.H. to Kate Symons, 30 May 1930, Burnett II, p. 188.

34 R.W.B. Lewis and N. Lewis, *The Letters of Edith Wharton*, pp. 458-459.

35 Ibid. p. 599.

36 A.E.H. to Edith Wharton, 1 Jul. 1930, Burnett II, p. 192.

37 A.E.H. to H. Foxwell, 29 Apr. 1930, unpublished, Kwansei University Japan.

38 A.E.H. to C. Clemens, 2 Feb. 1927, Burnett II, p. 8.

39 C. Clemens, *An Evening with A.E. Housman*, p. 8.

40 A.E.H. to C. Clemens, 8 Aug. 1930, Burnett II, p. 198.

41 A.E.H. to W. Ashburner, 27 Dec. 1930, Burnett II, p. 227.

42 N. Nicolson, *Harold Nicolson Diaries & Letters 1930–39*, p. 90.

43 A.E.H. to G. Richards, 22 Oct. 1930, Burnett II, p. 211.

44 A.E.H. to Kate Symons, 29 Dec. 1930, Burnett II, p. 229.

45 A.E.H.to J. Housman, 26 Dec. 1930, Burnett II, p. 226.

46 A.E.H. to P. Withers, 26 Dec. 1930, Burnett II, p. 227.

47 A.E.H. to Grant Richards, 3 Feb. 1931, Burnett II, p. 232.

48 A.E.H. to P. Robertson, 8 Feb. 1931, p. 223.

49 A.E.H. to R.W. Chambers, 26 Feb. 1931, Burnett II, p. 236.

50 A.E.H. to A. Rothenstein, 1 Jan. 1931, Burnett II, p. 231.

51 A.E.H. to G. Richards, 19 Feb. 1931, Burnett II, p. 234.

52 A.E.H. to W. Makin, 26 Feb. 1931, Burnett II, p. 236.

53 A.E.H. to L.W. Payne, 1 Mar. 1931, Burnett II, p. 237.

54 A.E.H. to Prof. C. Maccole, 15 Dec. 1930, Burnett II, p. 224.

55 A.E.H. to A. Rubin, 1 Mar. 1931, Burnett II, p. 237.

56 A.E.H. to H.S. Jones, 28 Dec. 1930, Burnett II, p. 228.

57 A.E.H. to R. Hackforth, 12 Mar. 1931, Burnett II, p. 239.

58 A.E.H. to D.S. Robertson, 13 Mar. 1931, Burnett II, p. 239.

59 J. Diggle and F.R.D. Goodyear, *The Classical Papers of A.E. Housman*, Vol. III, p. 1007.

60 Ibid. p. 1012.

61 Ibid. p. 1047.

62 Ibid. p. 1090.

63 Ibid. pp. 1058-1069.

64 A.E. Housman, *M. Manilii Astronomicon*, Vol. I, p. xix.

65 Ibid. p. xliii

66 A.E. Housman, *M. Manilii Astronomicon*, Vol. V, 2nd ed., p. v.

67 Ibid. p. xxiii.

68 Ibid. p. xxvi.

69   H.W. Garrod, *The Profession of Poetry and Other Lectures*, p. 224.

70   A.E. Housman, *M. Manilii Astronomicon*, Vol. V, p. xxxv.

71   Ibid. p. xxxvi.

72   Ibid. p. xxxvii.

73   S. Adelman, *The Name and Nature of A.E. Housman*, p. 51.

74   P.G. Naiditch, *Additional Problems in the Life and Writings of A.E. Housman*, p. 69.

75   L. Housman, *John O'London's Weekly*, Vol. 36 (16 Oct. 1936), p. 108.

76   G.L. Watson, *A.E. Housman*, p. 185.

77   P. Withers, *A Buried Life*, p. 15.

78   Ibid. p. 14.

79   L. Housman, *A.E.H.*, pp. 24–25.

80   P. Withers, *New Statesman & Nation*, May 1936.

81   A.E.H. to Elizabeth Wise, 30 Jul. 1890, Burnett I, p. 64.

82   G. Richards, *Housman 1897–1936*, p. 159.

83   A.E.H. to W. Ashburner, 21 Jun. 1903, Burnett I, p. 148.

84   J. Bourne, *Housman and Heine*, pp. 104–117.

85   A.E.H. to Lascelles Abercrombie, 20 Jul. 1931, Burnett II, p. 251.

86   A.E.H. to L. Morgan, 23 Jul. 1931, Burnett II, p. 252.

87   N. Goodison, 'A Poet's Argyllshire Holiday', *Country Life*, 25 Oct. 1973, p. 1275.

88   A.E.H. to H. Stewart, 26 Nov. 1931, Burnett II, p. 267.

89   A.E.H. to P. Withers, 20 Dec. 1931, Burnett II, p. 270.

90   A.E.H. to Kate Symons, 1 Mar. 1929, Burnett II, p. 115.

91   A.E.H. to C. Wilson, 4 Jun. 1931, Burnett II, p. 247.

92   A.E.H. to J. Housman, 31 Dec. 1931, Burnett II, p. 271 and footnote 2.

93   M. Egremont, *Siegfried Sassoon*, p. 291.

Part XIII Paris 1932

1   A.E.H. to S.C. Roberts, 16 Jan. 1932, Burnett II, p. 274.

2   A.E.H. to S.C. Roberts, 6 Feb. 1932, Burnett II, p. 276.

3   A.E.H. to G. Richards, 16 Jan. 1932, Burnett II. p. 273.

4   A.E.H. to Kate Symons, 29 Jan. 1932, Burnett II, p. 275.

5   A.E.H. to D.B. Harden, 2 Feb. 1932, Burnett II, p. 276.

6   A.E.H. to S.C. Roberts, 15 Feb. 1932, Burnett II, p. 278.

7   A.E.H. to J.C. Squire, 18 Feb. 1932, Burnett II, p. 279.

8   A.E.H. to Mr Dooher, 18 Feb. 1932, Burnett II, p. 280.

9   A.E.H. to G. Richards, 23 Feb. 1932, Burnett II, p. 281.

10   A.E.H. to L. Housman, 1 Mar. 1932, Burnett II, p. 283.

11   A.E.H. to C. Clemens, 4 Mar. 1932, Burnett II, p. 284.

12   A.E.H. to S. Meech, 17 Mar. 1932, Burnett II, p. 286.

13   A.E.H. to P. Withers, 29 Apr. 1932, Burnett II, p. 291.

14   A.E.H. to W. Rothenstein, 4 May 1932, Burnett II, p. 292 and Burnett footnote.

15   A.E.H. to G. Richards, 18 May 1932, Burnett II, p. 293.

16   A.E.H. to P. Withers, 10 Aug. 1933, Burnett II, p. 369.

17   A.E.H. to Kate Symons, 18 Aug. 1933, Burnett II, p. 371.

18   A.E.H. to Kate Symons, 24 Aug. 1933, Burnett II, p. 372.

19   A.E.H. to L. Frazer, 26 Sep. 1935, Burnett II, p. 494.

20   A.E.H. to G. Richards, 26 Aug. 1921, Burnett I, p. 471.

21   A.E.H. To W. Bynner, 17 Aug. 1935, Burnett II, p. 488.

22   D. McKie, 'Housman Abroad', *HSJ*, Vol. 39 (2013), p. 37.

23   A.E.H. to G. Richards, 22 May 1922, Burnett II, p. 494.

24   G. Robb, *Strangers*, p. 158.

25   G. Brassai, *The Secret Paris of the 30's*, unpaginated.

26   Ibid.

27   A.E.H. to G. Richards, 31 May 1932, Burnett II, p. 296.

28   A.E.H. to G. Richards, 3 Jun. 1932, Burnett II, p. 296.

29   A.E.H. to G. Richards, 12 Jun. 1932, Burnett II, p. 298.

30   A.E.H. to G. Richards, 16 Jun. 1932, Burnett II, p. 300.

31   G. Richards, *Housman 1897–1936*, p. 266.

32   T. Jones, *A Diary with Letters 1931–1950*, p. 93.

33   L. Housman, 'A.E. Housman's "De Amicitia"', *Encounter*, Oct. 1967, p. 39.

34   P.G. Naiditch, *Problems in the Life and Writings of A.E. Housman*, 'Housman in Paris', p. 56.

35   J. Diggle and F.R.D. Goodyear, *The Classical Papers of A.E. Housman*, 'The Application of Thought to Textual Criticism', Vol. III, p. 1060.

36   A.E. Housman, *M. Manilii Astronomicon*, Vol I, p. xliii.

37   J.E. Mack, *A Prince of Our Disorder*, p. 228.

38   A.E.H. to V. Rice, 15 Oct. 1932, Burnett II, p. 311.

39   L. Housman, *Echo de Paris*, p. 56.

40   J.M. Heath, *The Creator as Critic and Other Writings by E.M. Forster*, p. 492.

41   A.E.H. to Kate Symons, 15 Jun. 1932, Burnett II, p. 299.

42   A.E.H. to F.W. Fobes, 24 Jun. 1932, Burnett II, p. 302.

43   A.E.H. to A. Rubin, 24 Nov. 1932, Burnett II, p. 315.

44   A.E.H. to H. Martin, 25 Nov. 1932, Burnett II, p. 317.

45   A.E.H. to G. Richards, 30 Jun. 1932, Burnett II, p. 302.

46   G. Richards, *Housman 1897–1936*, p. 265.

47   A.E.H. to A.F. Scholfield, 3 Oct. 1932, Burnett II, p. 308.

48   A.E.H. to Kate Symons, 13 Oct. 1932, Burnett II, p. 310.

49   A.E.H. to P. Withers, 4 Nov. 1932, Burnett II, p. 318.

50   A.E.H. to Kate Symons, 22 Dec. 1932, Burnett II, p. 320.

51   G. Richards, *Housman 1897–1936*, pp. 265–266.

52   A.E.H. to G. Richards, 29 Jan. 1933, Burnett II, p. 325.

53   G. Richards, *Housman 1897–1936*, p. 266.

54   A. Jackson, *A Fine View of the Show*, p. 250.

55   A.E.H. to G. Richards, 7 Jul. 1933, Burnett II, p. 359.

56   A.E.H. to G. Jackson, 9 Nov. 1925, catalogue, Sotheby's New York sale, 18 Jun. 2010.

57   A.E.H. to G. Jackson, 19 May 1927, Trinity Add. Ms a.551.

58   A.E.H. to G. Jackson, 19 May 1927, Trinity Add. Ms a. 551.

59   A.E.H. to G. Jackson, 14 Feb. 1928, Trinity Add. Ms a. 551.

60   A.E.H. to G. Jackson, 4 Aug. 1928, Trinity Add. Ms a. 551.

61   A.E.H. to G. Jackson, 2 May 1929, Trinity Add Ms a. 551.

62 A.E.H. to G. Jackson, 6 Apr. 1932, Trinity Add Ms a. 551.
63 A.E.H. to G. Jackson, 15 Jul. 1930, Trinity Add Ms a. 551.
64 A.E.H. to G. Jackson, 15 Oct. 1930, Trinity Add Ms a. 551.
65 A.E.H. to G. Jackson, 7 Nov. 1930, Trinity Add Ms a. 551.
66 A.E.H. to G. Jackson, 6 Jan. 1931, Jackson family archive.

Part XIV Academic apotheosis and swansong

1   G. Richards, *Housman 1897–1936*, p. 267.
2   A.E.H. to G. Richards, 5 Feb. 1933, Burnett II, p. 330. Burnett footnote on questionnaire, pp. 327–330.
3   A.E.H. to M. Pollet, 5 Feb. 1933, Burnett II, p. 327.
4   Ibid. p. 328.
5   Ibid. p. 328.
6   Ibid. p 328.
7   Ibid. p. 327.
8   Ibid. p. 329.
9   Ibid. p. 329.
10 Ibid. p. 329.
11 Ibid. p. 329.
12 Ibid. p. 329.
13 Ibid. pp. 329–330.
14 B. Pascal, *Pensées*, p. xxi.
15 G. Leopardi, *Canti*, p. 178.
16 D. Karlin, *Rubaiyaat of Omar Khayyam*, p. xxv.
17 A.E.H. to G. Richards, 28 Sep. 1933, Burnett II, p. 380.
18 A.E.H. to H. Martin, 28 Mar. 1933, Burnett II, p. 337.
19 A.E.H. to G. Bullett, 22 Apr. 1933, Burnett II, p. 340.
20 A.E.H. to Kate Symons, 17 Mar. 1937, Burnett II, p. 334.
21 A.E.H. to G. Richards, 28 Mar. 1933, Burnett II, p. 338.
22 A.E.H. to S.C. Roberts, 20 Apr. 1933, Burnett II, p. 339.
23 E. Pound, 'Mr Housman at Little Bethel', *The Criterion*, Jan. 1934.
24 M. Burn, *Turned Towards the Sun*, p. 62.
25 A.E. Housman, *The Name & Nature of Poetry*.
26 A.E.H. to H.E. Butler, 15 May 1933, Burnett II, p. 344.
27 A.E.H. to S.C. Cockerell, 16 May 1933, Burnett II, p. 345.
28 A.E.H. to M. Beerbohm, 16 May 1933, Burnett II, p. 345.
29 A.E.H. to L. Housman, 20 May 1933, Burnett II, p. 347.
30 A.E.H. to Kate Symons, 20 May 1933, Burnett II, p. 348.
31 A.E.H. to Dr G.C.A. Jackson, 20 May 1933, Burnett II, p. 348.
32 A.E.H. to L. Housman, 24 May 1933, Burnett II, p. 349 .

Part XV Last flights to France

1   G. Putt, 'Go to The Professors', *Scrutiny*, Oct./Sep. 1933, pp. 206-208.
2   T.S. Eliot, *The Criterion*, Oct. 1933, pp. 151-4.
3   A.E.H. to P. Robertson, 5 Jun. 1933, Burnett II, p. 352.
4   A.E.H. to P. Withers, 7 Jun. 1933, Burnett II, p. 352.

5   A.E.H. to Professor H. Hollond, 16 Jun. 1933, Burnett II, p. 354.

6   A.E.H. to L. Housman, 15 Jun. 1933, Burnett II, p. 354.

7   A.E.H. to Kate Symons, 24 Jul. 1933, Burnett II, p. 366.

8   A.E.H. to P. Withers, 10 Aug. 1933, Burnett II, p. 369.

9   A.E.H. to W. Bynner, 4 Aug. 1933, Burnett II, p. 369.

10 A.E.H. to S.C. Roberts, 3 Jul. 1933, Burnett II, p. 358.

11 A.E.H. to G. Richards, 7 Jul. 1933, Burnett II, p. 359.

12 A.E.H. to John Masefield, 19 Jul. 1933, Burnett II, p. 364.

13 A.E.H. to Kate Symons, 24 Aug. 1933, Burnett II, p. 372.

14 A.E.H. to Kate Symons, 29 Aug. 1933, Burnett II, p. 374.

15 A.E.H. to Kate Symons, 1 Sep. 1933, Burnett II, p. 375.

16 A.E.H. to Kate Symons, 6 Sep. 1933, Burnett II, p. 376.

17 A.E.H. to Kate Symons, 13 Sep. 1933, Burnett II, p. 378.

18 A.E.H. to G. Richards, 28 Sep. 1933, Burnett II, p. 380.

19 A.E.H. to Kate Symons, 25 Oct. 1933, Burnett II, p. 382.

20 A.E.H. to G. Richards, 1 Nov. 1933, Burnett II, p. 384.

21 A.E.H. to P. Withers, 10 Nov. 1933, Burnett II, p. 385.

22 A.E.H. to H.V. Morton, 13 Nov. 1933, Burnett II, p. 386.

23 A.E.H. to J. Drinkwater, 14 Nov. 1933, Burnett II, p. 387.

24 A.E.H. to L. Housman, 30 Nov. 1933, Burnett II, p. 391.

25 A.E.H. to G. Richards, 6 Dec. 1933, Burnett II, p. 392.

26 A.E.H. to H. Martin, 14 Dec. 1933, Burnett II, p. 395.

27 A.E.H. to H. Martin, 20 Dec. 1933, Burnett II, p. 396.

28 A.E.H. to P. Withers, 20 Dec. 1933, Burnett II, p. 396.

29 A.E.H. to J. Housman, 20 Dec. 1933, Burnett II, p. 397.

30 A.E.H. to M. Secker, 25 Dec. 1933, Burnett II, p. 398.

31 A.E.H. to S. Adelman, 30 Dec. 1933, Burnett II, p. 399.

32 A.E.H. to G. Richards, 7 Jan. 1934, Burnett II, p. 402.

33 A.E.H. to J.R.M. Butler, 15 Jan. 1934, Burnett II, p. 403.

34 E. Pound, 'Mr Housman at Little Bethel', *The Criterion*, Jan. 1934.

35 A.E.H. to J. Housman, 7 Mar. 1934, Burnett II, p. 407.

36 A.E.H. to Kate Symons, 18 Mar. 1934, Burnett II, p. 409.

37 A.E.H. to H. Martin, 14 Apr. 1934, Burnett II, p. 415.

38 A.E.H. to L. Housman, 5 Oct. 1896, Burnett I, p. 431.

39 A.E.H. to J. Sparrow, 19 Jun. 1934, Burnett II, p. 431.

40 A.E.H. to L. Housman, 20 Jun. 1934, Burnett II, p. 431.

41 A.E.H. to H. Martin, 14 Dec. 1933, Burnett II, p. 395.

42 A.E.H. to H. Martin, 23 Mar. 1934, Burnett II, p. 413.

43 A.E.H. to H. Martin, 26 Sep. 1934, Burnett II, p. 442.

44 A.E.H. to C. Wilson, 14 Feb. 1935, Burnett II, p. 461.

45 A.E.H. to J. Johnson, 23 Mar. 1934, Burnett II, p. 412.

46 A.E.H. to An Unknown Correspondent, 12 Apr. 1935, Burnett II, p. 467.

47 A.E.H. to The Electors of the Corpus Professor of Latin, 17 Nov. 1934, Burnett, p. 448.

48 A.E.H. to Dr Eduard Fraenkel, 12 Nov. 1934, Burnett II, p. 447.

49 A.E.H. to The Editor of *The Sunday Times*, 18 Dec. 1934, Burnett II, p. 456.

50 A.E.H. to Professor A. Souter, 25 Dec. 1934, Burnett II, p. 457.

51   A.E.H. to Kate Symons, 31 Mar. 1935, Burnett II, p. 465.
52   A.E.H. to J. Housman, 12 Apr. 1935, Burnett II, p. 467.
53   A.E.H. to P. Withers, 4 May 1935, Burnett II, p. 469.
54   A.E.H. to J. Masefield, 3 Jun. 1935, Burnett II, p. 474.
55   A.E.H. to L. Housman, 9 Jun. 1935, Burnett II, p. 476.
56   A.E.H. to L. Housman, 15 Jun. 1935, Burnett II, p. 477.
57   A.E.H. to P. Withers, 18 Jun. 1935, Burnett II, p. 478.
58   A.E.H. to P. Withers, 23 Jun. 1935, Burnett II, p. 480.
59   A.E.H. to Professor D'Arcy Thompson, 1 Jul. 1935, Burnett II, p. 481.
60   P. Withers, *A Buried Life*, pp. 108–114.
61   A.E.H. to M. Withers, 3 Jul. 1935, Burnett II, p. 482.
62   A.E.H. to J. Housman, 17 Jul. 1935, Burnett II, p. 484.
63   A.E.H. to Kate Symons, 19 Jul. 1935, Burnett II, p. 484.
64   A.E.H. to P. Withers, 21 Jul. 1935, Burnett II, p. 485.
65   A.E.H. to G. Richards, 27 Jul. 1935, Burnett II, p. 486.
66   A.EH. to G. Tillotson, 17 Jul. 1935, Burnett II, p. 483.
67   A.E.H. to P. Withers, 24 Nov. 1934, Burnett II, p. 450.
68   A.E.H. to P. Withers, 30 Dec. 1934, Burnett II, p. 458.
69   A.E.H. to Kate Symons, 22 Aug. 1935, Burnett II, p. 489.
70   A.E.H. to Kate Symons, 28 Aug. 1935, Burnett II, p. 490.
71   A.E.H. to Kate Symons, 3 Sep. 1935, Burnett II, p. 491.
72   A.E.H. to Kate Symons, 19 Sep. 1935, Burnett II, p. 492.
73   A.E.H. to W. Bynner, 17 Aug. 1935, Burnett II, p. 497.
74   A.E.H. to G. Richards, 20 Sep. 1935, Burnett II, p. 492.
75   A.E.H. to W. Bynner, 12 Oct. 1935, Burnett II, p. 497.
76   A.E.H. to L. Frazer, 25 Sep. 1935, Burnett II, p. 494.
77   A.E.H. to H. Martin, 27 Sep. 1935, Burnett II, p. 495.
79   A.E.H. to W.B. Yeats, 25 Oct. 1935, Burnett II, p. 501.
80   A.E.H. to L. Frazer, 26 Sep. 1935, Burnett II, p. 494.
81   A.E.H. to Kate Symons, 24 Oct. 1935, Burnett II, p. 500.
82   A.E.H. to L. Housman, 28 Oct. 1935, Burnett II, p. 501.
83   A.E.H. to Kate Symons, 2 Nov. 1935, Burnett II, p. 502.
84   A.E.H. to H.G. Broadbent, 4 Nov. 1935, Burnett II, p. 502.
85   S.C. Roberts, *Adventures with Authors*, p. 128.
86   A.E.H. to Kate Symons, 10 Nov. 1935, Burnett II, p. 504.
87   A.E.H. to Denis Symons, 11 Dec. 1935, Burnett II, p. 508.
88   A.E.H. to Jeannie Housman, 11 Dec. 1935, Burnett II, p. 509.
89   A.E.H. to Professor F.W. Oliver, 14 Dec. 1935, Burnett II, p. 510.
90   G. Richards, *Housman 1897–1936*, Appendix V, p. 438.
91   A.E.H. to A.F.S Gow, 19 Dec. 1935, Burnett II, p. 511.
92   A.E.H. to Kate Symons, 27 Dec. 1935, Burnett II, p. 513.
93   A.E.H. to G. Jackson, 5 Jan. 1936, Trinity Add Ms a. 551.
94   A.E.H. to L. Housman, 10 Jan. 1936, Burnett II, p. 515.
95   A.E.H. to The Richards Press, 18 Jan. 1936, Burnett II, p. 516.
96   A.E.H. to Kate Symons, 18 Jan. 1936, Burnett II, p. 516.
97   A.E.H. to G. Jackson, 17 Jan 1936, Trinity Add Ms a. 551.
98   A.E.H. to G. Jackson, 31 Jan. 1936, Trinity Add Ms a. 551.
99   A.E.H. to G. Richards, 20 Jan. 1936, Burnett II, p. 517.
100 A.E.H. to P. Withers, 20 Jan. 1936, Burnett II, p. 518.

101 A.E.H. to P. Withers, 23 Jan. 1936, Burnett II, p. 519.
102 A.E.H. to P. Withers, 28 Jan. 1936, Burnett II, p. 520.
103 A.E.H. to J. Housman, 31 Jan. 1936, Burnett II, p. 521.
104 A.E.H. to L. Housman, 11 Mar. 1936, Burnett II, p. 526.
105 A.E.H. to H. Martin, 22 Mar. 1936, Burnett II, p. 527.
106 A.E.H. to Kate Symons, 2 Apr. 1936, Burnett II, p. 529.
107 A.E.H. to P. Withers, 2 Apr. 1936, Burnett II, p. 530.
108 A.E.H. to S.C. Roberts, 22 Apr. 1936, Burnett II, p. 531.
109 A.E.H. to H. Martin, 21 Apr. 1936, Burnett II, p. 523.
110 A.EH. to Charles Wilson, 21 Apr. 1936, Burnett II, p. 532.
111 A.E.H. to R.A. Scott-James, 21 Apr. 1936, Burnett II, p. 532.
112 A.E.H. to Kate Symons, 25 Apr. 1936, Burnett II, p. 533.
113 L. Housman, *A.E.H.*, p. 121.
114 R.S. Woods, *Cambridge Doctor*, p. 93.

Posthumous publications published by Laurence Housman: More Poems *and* Additional Poems *and* De Amicitia

1 P.G. Naiditch, 'A.E. Housman's Last Will and Testament', *HSJ*, Vol. 36 (2010), pp. 60–63.
2 T.B. Haber, *The Manuscript Poems of A.E. Housman*, 'The Notebooks and the Library of Congress Manuscript Collection'.
3 L. Housman, 'A.E. Housman's "De Amicitia"', *Encounter*, Oct. 1967, p. 33.
4 Ibid. p. 34.
5 Ibid. p. 34.
6 Ibid. p. 39.

Bibliography

Adelman, S., *The Name and Nature of A.E. Housman*, Bryn Mawr, PN, 1986.

Aldington, R., *A.E. Housman & W.B. Yeats: Two Lectures*, Hurst, Berkshire, UK, 1955.

Annan, N., *The Dons: Mentors, Eccentrics and Geniuses*, London, 1999.

Bayley, J., *Housman's Poems*, Oxford, 1992.

Bell, A.S., *ed.*, *Fifteen Letters to Walter Ashburner*, Edinburgh, 1976.

Bennett, A., *Untold Stories*, London, 2005.

Bennett, A., *Six Poets Hardy to Larkin: An Anthology*, London, 2014.

Birch, J.R., *Unkind to Unicorns: Selected Comic Verse of A.E. Housman*, Cambridge, 1995.

Blakiston, H.E.D., 'Ellis, Robinson (1834–1913)', *Oxford Dictionary of National Biography*.

Blunt, W. S., *My Diaries: being a personal narrative of events 1888–1914*, London, 1919.

Bourne, J., ed., *Housman and Heine: A Neglected Relationship*, Bromsgrove, UK, 2011.

Bowlby, R.P.L. *The Making and Breaking of Affectional Bonds*, London, 2005.

Brassai, G., *The Secret Paris of the 30's*, London, 1976.

Bray, A., *The Friend*, Chicago, 2003.

Brink, C.O., *English Classical Scholarship: Historical reflections on Bentley, Porson and Housman*, Cambridge, 1985.

Burn, M., *Turned Towards the Sun*, London, 2003.

Burnett, A., *The Poems of A.E. Housman*, Oxford, 1997.

Burnett, A., *The Letters of A.E. Housman*, 2 vols, Oxford, 2007.

Butterfield, D. and Stray, C., eds., *A. E. Housman: Classical Scholar*, London, 2009.

Carroll, N., *Humour: A Very Short Introduction*, Oxford, 2014.

Carter, J., *A.E. Housman: Selected Prose*, Cambridge, 1962.

Carter, J., Sparrow, J.H.A. and White, W., *A.E. Housman: A Bibliography*, Godalming, UK, 1982.

Cartwright, J., 'Star-defeated sighs: Classical cosmology and astronomy in the poetry of A. E. Housman', *Housman Society Journal*, Vol. 37 (2011), pp. 47-76.

Casey, J., *Afterlives: A Guide to Heaven, Hell and Purgatory*, Oxford, 2009.

Chambers, R.W., *Man's Unconquerable Mind*, London, 1939.

Child, F.J., *English and Scottish Ballads*, Cambridge, MA, 1904.

Clemens, C., *An Evening with A.E. Housman*, Webstor Grove, MO, 1937.

Clucas, H., *Through Time and Place To Roam: Essays on A.E. Housman*, Salzburg, Austria, 1995.

David, E., *French Provincial Cooking*, London, 1960.

Davidson, J., *The Greeks & Greek Love*, London, 2007.

Davis, W., *Into the Silence: The Great War, Mallory and the Conquest of Everest*, London, 2011.

Diggle, J. and Goodyear, F.R.D., eds., *The Classical Papers of A.E. Housman*, 3 vols, London, 1972.

Dudgeon, J., *Roger Casement: The Black Diaries*, Belfast, 2002.

Duff, C., *A Handbook on Hanging*, London, 1928.

Dyment, C., *Matthew Arnold: An Introduction and a Selection*, London, 1948.

Efrati, C., *The Road of Danger, Guilt and Shame: The Lonely Way of A.E. Housman*, London, 2002.

Egremont, M., *Siegfried Sassoon: A Biography*, London, 2005.

Eliot, T.S., *The Use of Poetry and The Use of Criticism*, London, 1933.

Empson, W., *Seven Types of Ambiguity*, London, 1930.

Fairhurst-Douglas, R., *Victorian Afterlives*, Oxford, 2002.

Farmelo, G., *The Strangest Man: The Hidden Life of Paul Dirac*, London, 2009.

Fenton, J., ed., *The New Faber Book of Love Poems*, London, 2006.

Fischer, D.H., *The Great Wave, Price Revolutions and the Rhythm of History*, London, 1996.

Gardner, P., ed., *A.E. Housman: The Critical Heritage*, London and New York,1992.

Garrard, G., *A Book of Verse: The Biography of the Rubaiyat of Omar Khayyam*, Stroud, UK, 2007.

Garrod, H.W., *The Profession of Poetry and Other Lectures*, Oxford, 1929.

Goodison, N., 'A Poet's Argyllshire Holiday', *Country Life*, 25 October, 1973.

Gow, A.S.F., *A.E. Housman: A Sketch, Together with a list of his writings and Indexes to his Classical Papers*, Cambridge, 1936.

Graves, R.P., 'A Letter from G. Herbert Housman, January 7, 1892', *Housman Society Journal*, Vol. 3 (1977), pp. 12–14.

Graves, R.P., *A.E. Housman: The Scholar-Poet*, London, 1979.

Graves, R.P., 'A Letter from L/C G. Herbert Housman 6365 "E" Coy. 4th Battalion King's Royal Rifles', *Housman Society Journal*, Vol. 6 (1980), pp. 6–9.

Gray, E., *The Poetry of Indifference from the Romantics to the Rubaiyat*, Amherst, MA, 2005.

Griffin E., ed., *The Selected Letters of Bertrand Russell*, London, 1992.

Haber, T.B., *The Manuscript Poems of A.E. Housman*, Minneapolis, MN, 1955.

Haber, T.B., *Thirty Housman Letters to Witter Bynner*, New York, 1957.

Haber, T.B., *The Making of A Shropshire Lad: A Manuscript Variorum*, Seattle, WA, 1966.

Hamilton, R., *Housman the Poet*, Exeter, UK, 1953.

Hawkins, M.M., *A.E. Housman: Man Behind a Mask*, Chicago, IL, 1958.

Haynes, G., 'The Importance of Housman's Lad', *Housman Society Journal*, Vol. 37 (2011), pp. 110-120.

Heath, J.M., ed., *The Creator as Critic and Other Writings by E.M. Forster*, Toronto, 2008.

Hibberd, D. and Onions J., *The Winter of the World: Poems of the Great War*, London, 2007.

Holden, A.W. and Birch, J.R., eds, *A.E. Housman: A reassessment*, New York, 2000.

Holmes, R., *Coleridge: Early Visions*, London, 1990.

Holmes, R., *Coleridge: Darker Reflections*, London, 1998.

Homer, *The Iliad*, translated by Robert Fagles, Introduction and Notes by Bernard Knox, London, 2001.

Hopkinson, N., 'The Book of Moses: Housman, Manilius and M.J. Jackson', *Housman Society Journal*, Vol. 37 (2011), pp. 88-103.

Horwood, F.C., *A.E. Housman, Poetry & Prose: A Selection*, London, 1971.

Housman, A.E., *M. Manilii Astronomicon*, 5 vols, London, 1903–1930.

Housman, A.E., *The Name & Nature of Poetry*, Cambridge, 1933.

Housman, A.E., *The Confines of Criticism: The Cambridge Inaugural, 1911*, ed. J. Carter, Cambridge, 1969.

Housman, L., *All-Fellows: Seven Legends of Lower Redemption*, London, 1896.

Housman, L., *All-Fellows, and The Cloak of Friendship*, London, 1923.

Housman, L., *Echo de Paris: A Study from Life*, London, 1923.

Housman, L., *A.E.H. Some Poems, Some Letters and a Personal Memoir by his Brother*, London, 1937.

Housman, L., *The Unexpected Years*, London, 1937.

Housman, L., "A.E. Housman's "De Amicitia"", *Encounter*, October, 1967, pp. 33–41, annotated by J. Carter.

Hussey, A., *Paris: The Secret History*, London, 2006.

Jackson, A., *A Fine View of the Show: Letters from the Western Front*, www. lulu.com, 2009.

Jackson, A., 'A Pivotal Friendship', *Housman Society Journal*, Vol. 36 (2010), pp. 45–53.

Jackson, A., 'Moses Jackson's Family', *Housman Society Journal*, Vol. 38 (2012), pp. 79-88.

Jebb, K,. *A.E. Housman*, Melksham, UK, 1992.

Jeffery, B., *Michel Houellebecq and Depressive Realism*, 2011, Alresford, UK, 2011.

Jenkins, C., '"Uncle Joe": the Revd Joseph Brettell Housman. Part II,' *Housman Society Journal*, Vol. 31 (2005), pp. 106–126.

Jenkins, C., '"My father's family was Lancashire" The Housmans of Lune Bank in the Nineteenth Century', *Housman Society Journal*, Vol 36 (2010), pp. 77-101.

Jones, H.S., *Intellect & Character in Victorian England*, Cambridge, 2007.

Jones, T., *A Diary with Letters, 1931–1950*, London, 1954.

Karlin, D., ed., *Rubaiyat of Omar Khayyam*, Oxford, 2009.

Kellner, B., *Carl Van Vechten and the Irreverent Decades*, Norman, OK,1968.

Kuhn, W., *The Politics of Pleasure: A Portrait of Benjamin Disraeli*, London, 2006.

Lawrence T.E., *Seven Pillars of Wisdom*, London, 1926.

Leopardi, G., *Canti*, translated and annotated by J. Galassi, London, 2010.

Lewis, R.W.B. and Lewis, N., *The Letters of Edith Wharton*, London, 1988.

Lubbock, P., ed., *The Diary of Arthur Christopher Benson*, London, 1926.

Lucas, F.L., *Authors Dead and Living*, London, 1926.

Lucas, F.L., *The Greatest Problem and Other Essays*, London, 1960.

Maas, H., ed., *The Letters of A.E. Housman*, Cambridge, MA, 1971.

Maas, H., *Ernest Dowson: Poetry and Love in the 1890s*, London, 2009.

Maas, H., *A.E. Housman: Spoken and Unspoken Love*, London, 2012.

Mack, J.E., *A Prince of our Disorder: The Life of T.E. Lawrence*, Abingdon, UK, 1976.

McKenna, N., *The Secret Life of Oscar Wilde*, London, 2004.

McKie, D., 'Jacksoniana', *Housman Society Journal*, Vol. 37 (2011), pp. 129-163.

McKie D., 'Housman Abroad', *Housman Society Journal*, Vol. 39 (2013), pp. 21-78.

Marlow, N., *A.E. Housman: Scholar and Poet*, London, 1958.

Mendelson, E., *Later Auden*, New York,1999.

Moffat, W., *E.M. Forster: A New Life*, London, 2010.

Moggridge, D.E., *Maynard Keynes: An Economist's Biography*, London, 1992.

Monk, J.H., *The Life of Richard Bentley, D.D.*, 2nd edition, 2 vols, London and Cambridge, 1833.

Monk, R., *Ludwig Wittgenstein: The Duty of Genius*, London, 1990.

Monk, R., 'Russell, Bertrand Arthur William, third Earl Russell (1872–1970)', *Oxford Dictionary of National Biography*.

Naiditch, P.G., 'Three Notes on the Library of A.E.Housman', *Housman Society Journal*, Vol. 11 (1985), pp. 87–90

Naiditch, P.G., *A.E. Housman At University College, London: The Election of 1892*, Leiden, The Netherlands, 1988.

Naiditch, P.G., *Problems in The Life and Writings of A.E. Housman*, Beverley Hills, CA, 1995.

Naiditch, P.G., *Additional Problems in The Life and Writings of A.E. Housman*, Los Angeles, CA, 2005.

Naiditch, P.G., 'The Extant Portion of the Library of A.E. Housman: IV. Non-Classical Materials', *Housman Society Journal*, Vol. 31 (2005), pp. 155-158.

Naiditch, P.G., 'Further Information on A.E. Housman and the Civil Service Examinations of 1882', *Housman Society Journal*, Vol. 33 (2007), pp. 87–90.

Naiditch, P.G., 'A.E. Housman's Last Will and Testament', *Housman Society Journal*, Vol. 36 (2010), pp. 60–63

Nicolson, J., *The Perfect Summer*, London, 2006.

Nicolson, N., *Harold Nicolson: Diaries & Letters 1930–39*, London, 1971.

Nicolson, N., *Portrait of a Marriage*, London, 1973

Nuttall, A.D., *Dead from the Waist Down: Scholars and Scholarship in Literature and the Popular Imagination*, New Haven, CT, and London, 2003.

Oakley, E., *Inseparable Siblings: A Portrait of Clemence & Laurence Housman*, Studley, UK, 2009.

Obata, T., 'How A.E. Housman's Poetry was Accepted in Japan before the World War', *Housman Society Journal*, Vol. 8 (1982), pp. 29-35.

Origo, I., *Leopardi: A Study in Solitude*, London, 1953.

Padel, R., 'The Housman Lecture, The Name and Nature of Poetry', *Housman Society Journal*, Vol. 37 (2011), pp. 7-20.

Page, N., *A.E. Housman: A Critical Biography*, London, 1983.

Pakenham,T., *The Boer War*, London, 1979.

Parry, R. St J., *Henry Jackson, O.M., Vice-Master of Trinity College & Regius Professor of Greek in the University of Cambridge: A Memoir*, Cambridge, 1926.

Pascal, B., *Pensées*, Translation and Introduction by A.J. Krailsheimer, London, 1995.

Pattison, M., *Isaac Casaubon*, 2nd edition, Oxford, 1892.

Pound, E., 'Mr Housman at Little Bethel', *The Criterion*, January, 1934.

Pugh, J., *Bromsgrove and the Housmans*, Housman Society, Bromsgrove, 1974.

Putt, G., 'Go to The Professors', *Scrutiny*, October/September, 1933.

Richards, G., *Memories of A Misspent Youth, 1872–1896*, London, 1932.

Richards, G., *Author Hunting by an Old Literary Sports Man*, New York, 1934.

Richards, G., *Housman 1897–1936*, Oxford, 1941.

Ricks, C., ed., *A.E. Housman: A Collection of Critical Essays*, Englewood Cliffs, NJ, 1968.

Ricks, C., ed., *A.E. Housman: Collected Poems & Selected Prose*, London, 1988.

Robb, G. *Strangers: Homosexual Love in the Nineteenth Century*, London, 2003.

Roberts, S.C., *Adventures with Authors*, Cambridge, 1966.

Robinson, O., *Angry Dust: The poetry of A.E. Housman*, Boston, MA, 1950.

Robertson, S.L., *The Shropshire Racket*, London, 1937.

Rothenstein, W., *Men and Memories, Recollections of William Rotherstein, 1872–1900*, London, 1931.

Rothenstein, W., *Men and Memories, Recollections of William Rotherstein, 1900–1922*, London, 1932.

Rowbotham, S., *Edward Carpenter: A Life of Liberty and Love*, London, 2008.

Sager, P., *Oxford & Cambridge: An Uncommon History*, London, 2005.

Schultz, B., *Henry Sidgwick: Eye of the Universe., An Intellectual Biography*, Cambridge, 2004.

Scott, J., 'Housman's Continental Life', *Housman Society Journal*, Vol. 40 (2014), pp. 79–85.

Scott-Kilvert, I., *A.E. Housman*, London, 1955.

Shaw, R., *Housman's Places*, Bromsgrove, 1995.

Skutsch, O., *Alfred Edward Housman, 1859–1936*, London, 1960.

Spender, S., *The Making of a Poem*, London, 1955.

Steiner, G., *Lessons of the Masters*, London, 2003.

Stray, C., 'Attractive and Nonsensical Classics, Oxford, Cambridge and Elsewhere', *Council of University Classical Departments Bulletin*, Vol. 27 (1998).

Stray, C., ed., *Gilbert Murray Reassessed: Hellenism, Theatre, & International Politics*, Oxford, 2007.

Sturgis, M., *Passionate Attitudes: The English Decadence of the 1890s*, London, 2011.

Sutro, A., *Celebrities and Simple Souls*, London, 1933.

Symington, N., *Narcissism: A New Theory*, London, 1993.

Symons, K.E., *Alfred Edward Housman: Recollections by Kate E. Symons, A.W. Pollard, L. Housman, R.W. Chambers, A. Ker, A.S.F. Gow, J. Sparrow*, Bromsgrove, UK, 1936.

Takeuchi, Y., *The Exhaustive Concordance to the Poems of A.E. Housman*, Tokyo, 1971.

Thomson, J.J., *Recollections and Reflections*, London, 1936.

Timpanaro, S., *The Genesis of Lachmann's Method*, ed. and trans. by G.W. Most, Chicago, 2005.

Tunnicliffe, J.D. and Buncombe, M., 'A.E. Housman and The Failure of Grant Richards Limited in 1926', *Housman Society Journal*, Vol. 11 (1985), pp. 101-106.

Vernon, M., *The Philosophy of Friendship*, Basingstoke, UK, 2005.

Watson, G.L., *A.E. Housman, A Divided Life*, London, 1957.

Weeks, J., *Coming out: Homosexual Politics in Britain from the Nineteenth Century to the Present*, London, 1977.

Weeks, J., *Sex, Politics and Society: The Regulation of Sexuality since 1800*, London, 1981

Wellesley, D., *Letters on Poetry from W.B. Yeats to Dorothy Wellesley*, Oxford, 1964.

White, W., *A.E. Housman A Bibliography*, Godalming, UK, 1982.

Wilde, J., 'A Loosening of Silk Ribbons – Laurence Housman, John Murray and the publishing sensation of 1900', *The Times Literary Supplement*, 2 November, 2012, pp. 14–15.

Wilson, A.N., *The Victorians*, London, 2002.

Winn, J. A., *The Poetry of War*, Cambridge, 2008.

Withers, P., *A Buried Life: Personal Recollections of A.E. Housman*, London, 1940.

Woods, R.S., *Cambridge Doctor*, London, 1962.

Woudhuysen, H.R., *A.E.H. – A.W.P.: A Classical Friendship*, Tunbridge Wells, UK, 2006.

Index

NOTE: Works by Housman (AEH), including individual poems, appear directly under title (or first line); works by others under author's name